Like Letters in Running Water

A Mythopoetics of Curriculum

STUDIES IN CURRICULUM THEORY

William F. Pinar, Series Editor

jagodzinski • Postmodern Dilemmas: Outrageous Essays in Art&Art Education

jagodzinski • Pun(k) Deconstruction: Experifigural Writings in Art&Art Education

Huebner • The Lure of the Transcendent: Collected Essays by Dwayne E. Huebner. Edited by Vikki Hillis. Collected and Introduced by William F. Pinar

Pinar (Ed.) • Queer Theory in Education

Reid • Curriculum as Institution and Practice: Essays in the Deliberative Tradition

Westbury/Hopmn/Riquarts (Eds.) • Teaching as a Reflective Practice: The German Didaktic Tradition

Joseph/Bravmann/Windschitl/Mikel/Green • Cultures of Curriculum

Doll • Like Letters in Running Water: A Mythopoetics of Curriculum

Like Letters in Running Water

A Mythopoetics of Curriculum

Mary Aswell Doll

 LAWRENCE ERLBAUM ASSOCIATES, PUBLISHERS

2000   Mahwah, New Jersey   London

Lawrence Erlbaum Associates, Inc., Publishers
10 Industrial Avenue
Mahwah, New Jersey 07430-2262

Cover design by Kathryn Houghtaling Lacey

Cover art by Carol Scott

Library of Congress Cataloging-in-Publication Data

Doll, Mary Aswell.
    Like letters in running water : a mythopoetics of curriculum / by Mary Aswell Doll.
        p. cm.— (Studies in curriculum theory)
    Includes bibliographical references and index.
    ISBN 0-8058-2984-9 (cloth : alk. paper)
    ISBN 0-8058-2985-7 (pbk. : alk. paper)
    1. Literature—Study and teaching. 2. Myth in literature.
    3. Education—Curriculum—Philosophy. I. Title. II. Series.
LB1575.D64 2000
807.1—dc21   99-087406
                                                                         CIP

Books published by Lawrence Erlbaum Associates are printed on acid-free paper, and their bindings are chosen for strength and durability.

Printed in the United States of America
10 9 8 7 6 5 4 3 2 1

Contents

Preface

Yin and Yang

Highest good is like water. Because water excels in benefitting the myriad creatures without contending with them and settles where none would like to be, it comes close to the way.

—Lao Tzu (551–479 B.C.E./1975, p. 64)

It was while visiting Bill Pinar in Japan that I came across the format I knew I would use for this book. It was December. I had just unpacked my suitcase and was trying to find an extra space for my belongings. I opened the nightstand drawer and there, instead of a Bible, lay *The Teaching of Buddha* (1990) with a description of three ways of being in the world. One way is like letters carved in rock, another like letters written in sand. The third is like letters written in running water. Three ways, each described with simile. Being and likeness, similes of being. And yet, how different is the Japanese way. Two years later I am again in Japan, again in winter, this time as a television viewer of the Nagano games of the Olympics. They say the monks must have prayed very well, for snow in this southernmost site for the games is abundant, even causing postponement of several Alpine events. The Olympics hold a comfortable familiarity for me; I understand the challenge of competition, grace beneath the clock. But the background seeps into the foreground, even in television land, and I am aware that although I have viewed winter games before, this viewing is different because of that place. It is like nothing I have ever known or remembered.

A Western writer helps make sense to me of the Eastern reality called Japan. "And always the water, the sound, the plash and drip of it, as if here were a people making constant oblation to water as some peoples do to what they call their luck" (Faulkner, 1956, p. 184). William Faulkner writes of being a Westerner in Nagano, of what strikes the Western ear. While terribly important competitions play out against famously efficient scoreboards, perhaps it is merely the sound of water that reminds us of our insignificance, our dependence on the elements.

This book is about elementary things, like water. And it is about the necessity of being in foreign places. It is about trying to make a place in the head for imagining foreignness. From the elementary grades on, school has been the place for learning rationally, thinking critically, and for homogenizing. It has championed knowing knowns, welcoming neither foreignness nor commutation. It has thus, tragically, ignored the basics. The base of basics, Madeleine Grumet (1995) reminds, is a springboard into fantasy, memory, time, relation, feeling, aggression. If aesthetic experience lives on the other side of the boundary from the cookie cutter and if artists and athletes regularly pass between the known and the unknown, then, Grumet continues (1988), we can, all of us, be commuters. The foreign place inside our own heads wants such visitation.

But how to obtain the passport? I turn to those on the edge of curriculum theory to help chart the way. Bill Pinar (1988, 1991) talks about the place of place in curriculum, about how knowing where we come from before we can teach, have relationships, make money is autobiography's lesson plan. Those who reconceptualize curriculum—their work is cited throughout the book—take travel ventures, insisting with Maxine Greene (1971) that learning is reorienting and that place is metaphor. Similarly, but differently, revisionists of depth psychology enjoin a journey backward into an older, pagan territory. Myth, story, and poetries of imagination celebrate complexity and humor, fantasy and personification. A mingling of "pagan feelings" (Hillman, 1996a) makes it impossible to dogmatize. Imagine! The very stone of institution's architecture—dogma—crumbles in the wake of story's flow! But, isn't that the Buddha's lesson of the three ways? That, in any case, is what I think and why I chose to write this book.

ACKNOWLEDGMENTS

For helping me in my journey through these pages I am indebted to Father Thomas Chambers and Dean Judith Miranti for granting me a sabbatical and to my colleagues Tom Ellerman, Raymond Gitz, Diana Schaubhut, Wanda Wagner, and Nathalie Williams; and, of course, to my students. I also thank Alan Block, Ann Dean, Susan Edgerton, Marla Morrris, Paul Salvio, and Delese Wear for sharpening my ideas. To Celeste Schroeder and Mary Beth Cancienne I thank for creating and performing, with me, a dance-narration of chapter 12. I am grateful to Naomi Silverman, for believing in my project and encouraging me all along, as well as to Nadine Simms for answering all my thousand questions so promptly—both with Lawrence Erlbaum Associates. Josh Steinert deserves my gratitude for his computer assistance. And last but not least, I wish to thank Bill Pinar, not only for giving me the opportunity to appear in his cutting-edge series, but also for providing incisive comments about my work. So many thanks, Bill, for introducing me to a circle of curricularists whom I am honored to call my friends and whose influences can be felt in this book.

—Mary Aswell Doll

Introduction

Fiction as Food

The goal of teaching is to be clear, that of literature … to reveal clarity as a pipe dream.

—Keller (1997, p. 70)

I'm afraid I find literature more useful than the … psychological-recipe books.

—Lessing (1995, p. 217)

Curriculum theorists have long called for what writers do best: create fictions. An other world, illuminated experience, a poetics of experience, poetries of imagination, living in imaginary gardens—these metaphorical ways of expressing the life of the mind have occupied the theories of curricularists for half a decade (Bruner, 1986; Connelly & Clandinin, 1991; Dewey, 1934; Gotz, 1987; Greene, 1965, 1995; Grumet, 1989; Gunn, 1982; Haggerson, 1986; Heath, 1983; Krall, 1979; Leonard, 1983; Macdonald, 1995; Macdonald & Leeper, 1966; Rugg, 1963; Steinbergh, 1991). For these theorists the teaching-learning act is not a static enterprise of simples, any more than the student or teacher is a unity of singles. There is no such thing as single self, simple truth, straight label. What exchanges occur between beings in the classroom are complicated conversations

(Pinar, 1995), called *curriculum*, the root of which is *flux*. And the way into the flux involves imagination, what writers concern themselves with best.

Strange. The students I teach in literature classes frequently comment, "While it was only a story, I learned a tremendous amount." Of course they learned; sadly, of course, they discounted that learning. In a culture that considers the humanities as the stepsister in the academy—an enterprise that will not fatten the pocketbook—my students are like so many other nonreaders whose only experience with books is with the textbook. (Textbook: that which is difficult to hold in the hand; that which offers its columned pages to the magic marker; that from which one memorizes facts to pass true-false questions.) Something in our culture persuades students that reading and discussing and writing about reading are, somehow, "mere" exercises. But, together with curriculum theorists, I insist that the engagement with fiction (prose, drama, poetry, myth, fairy tale, dream) can be a learning experience of the first order—not because students hunt down symbols or identify themes, not because they check boxes on multiple choice tests, and not because they echo the professor's beliefs: safe activities all. None of these. Rather, out of the very chimney corner from which the humanities huddle, fiction disturbs the status quo. Feelings thought to be central get routed. Peripheral imaginings begin to take root. One can, indeed, "learn a tremendous amount" from fiction. One learns about one's self. One learns about living. But the learning is subtle. Fiction, Virginia Woolf (1929/1957) writes, is "like a spider's web, attached ever so lightly perhaps, but still attached to life at all four corners" (p. 43). The webbed connections fiction weaves go to the root of one's being—if one will just let the spider spin.

Like Letters in Running Water: A Mythopoetics of Curriculum explores ways in which fiction yields transformative insights for educational theory and practice. Metaphors and similes used by writers offer new ways of thinking about and relating with such educational concepts as race, Whiteness, class, gender, identity, place, body, being, authority, and so forth; and such pedagogical frames as qualitative research, Marxian analysis, action research, postmodernism, and so forth. The basic premise of the book is that reading literary fictions is not an "only" experience. On the contrary, fiction—more than fact—teaches wisdoms about the human condition precisely because fiction connects readers with what courses within themselves. To connect with this coursing is to attend to social, outer issues addressed by traditional pedagogies with greater, deeper awareness.

Writers of literary fictions revivify the imagination. It is the purpose of curriculum, I argue, to engage the imagination, such that it is possible to think more metaphorically, less literalistically, about one's world and one's presuppositions about that world. When stories are told, one sees ideas differently; when images are heard, one hears differently, more introspectively. But, to engage the imagination, different teaching strategies need to be employed. An ineffective way to teach literature privileges symbol hunting and theme grasping: a multiple choice approach to reading that considers reading to be some Thing to be mastered on some Test. Such a reductive method of teaching literature reduces reading to a fact-finding mission, having little to do with inner turmoil. Teaching the imagination, on the other hand, requires readers to tap into their inner turmoil, their coursings, as they read. That which "moils" is the coursing of inner images which, once shaped or expressed, give distance to one's deepest feelings, prejudices, and fears. Literature has a potential power, thus, to transform a world—not necessarily to change the world, but to grasp more coherently the world within as well as without. By discussing, selecting, and writing about the metaphors, symbols, and images found in sufficiently difficult fictions, I hope to suggest new ways for student readers to recover their own curriculum material.

I see three distinctive features of my book. One, I offer an etymology of the word *curriculum,* to my knowledge not previously discussed in pedagogical writings. The root of curriculum, as William Pinar and Madeleine Grumet (1976) unearthed, is *currere*: the "running" of a course. Like the one who studies it, curriculum is a moving form, running with experience as it is lived by both researcher and student. "This conscious and explicit participation in an aesthetic experience—it becomes like an archeology—illustrates the reciprocity of objectivity and subjectivity in the student's and teacher's experience of the curriculum" (Pinar, in Pinar, Reynolds, Slattery, & Taubman, 1995, p. 415). Curriculum is also, according to Webster (1981), a coursing, as in an electric current. The work of the curriculum theorist should tap this intense current within, that which courses through the inner person, that which electrifies or gives life to a person's energy source. This coursing is what Ted Aoki calls "the flow from who one is" (in Pinar et al., 1995, p. 428). The task of the teacher, accordingly, is to select shocking material. Only that which shocks can spark a coursing connection between reader and text, reader and world. The teacher is not a psychoanalyst, because analysis of the inner contents of the psyche is not the primary purpose of pedagogy, nor is it the pedagogue's expertise. Rather, the teacher serves the function of introducing difficult cultural material with the intent of sparking student imagination and initiating the energy flow from within. Such a process should result in learning that has, as its root trace, an authenticity not discoverable by traditional teaching pedagogies.

Two, I insist that literature is not "mere." It is time for the humanities to light their own fires. My book argues that fiction is not only necessary for pedagogy, fiction is the lie that pedagogy needs in order to uncover the truths that make us human. My discussion will not refer to literature as a prop to theory—a quote here, a line there. Rather, I will consider the literary texts fully, similar to the work I have already published on Samuel Beckett, Tom Stoppard, Margaret Atwood, and others. In such a way I intend to forefront fiction's metaphors as ways of seeing educational ideas.

The third distinctive feature of my book is identifying literalism as the problem of our culture. Nothing, it seems, matters to our collective sensibilities anymore because all is laid out for us to see. To paraphrase Virginia Woolf, there is no room for one's unknown. It is as if the surfaces of our lives are so glassy bright that the undersurfaces are lost in the glare. One day's headlines on page one read "I am angry," "Middle-class household hid horror of starvation," "Elder abuse is a rising trend," "Men head to Washington to claim roll [sic] in social ills" (The Times-Picayune, 1997, p. A1). The events of May 1999 will be remembered as the season of student killings and bomb threats. Although events of homicide, suicide, fratricide, sorocide, infanticide are the daily stuff of pulp fiction, and although soaps and talk shows recount misconduct cases, none of these story lines are really stories. What is numbing in all the public anger is the lack of truly shocking material. The stories are modern myths without the metaphors.

Consequently, I argue that the problem in our culture is not illiteracy, but the literalisms that make us ill. Texts are everywhere being literalized: copied, imitated, mimicked. These "readings" are pitiful attempts at creating meaning when the only meanings one seeks to find are those outside the self. Only when connections are made to that which courses within can learners approach the outer problems of race, gender, and identity. What are the ways of listening to the inner ear and tapping the inner currents? This question is of urgent importance in an age of a growing, dangerous literalism.

My work seeks to continue the important distinction Pinar and Grumet make (1976) between "curriculum" and "currere." Currere has proposed an ontological context that has been discussed by a distinguished group of curriculum theorists and literary critics. Significant titles in this curriculum theorist group include Maxine Greene's (1973) Teacher as Stranger, (1978) Landscapes of Learning, and (1988) The Dialectic of Freedom; Dennis Sumara's (1996) Private Readings in Public; and Alan Block's (1995) Occupied Reading. Greene's existential approach to teaching argues for "wide awakeness" as a way to spur imagination. Sumara's use of Michael Ondaatje's (1992) The English Patient as trope for classroom practice argues for readers to be like nomads, seeking to find common dwelling places while searching for meanings. Block's notion of "occupation" propounds the idea that the field of reading itself has made colonists of readers, who cannot own, or truly live in, what they read. Jerome Bruner's (1986) Acts of Meaning argues for the narrative mode, as opposed to the paradigmatic mode, and places emphasis on the subjunctive—condition contrary to fact—as key to reaching that mode. My work differs from these by its breadth as well as depth-discussions of significant writers and classroom practices.

Certainly, numerous other curriculum theorists seek to distinguish curriculum as a "running" rather than a course. Their articles and chapters have discussed important words that insist on curriculum's connection to lived experience. Mikio Fujita's (1985) "Modes of Waiting," Harold Rugg's (1963) Imagination, Theodore Roszak's (1970) "Educating Contra Naturam," Max van

Manan's (1991) *The Tact of Teaching*, James Macdonald's (1995) interest in the mythopoetic, John Leonard's (1983) idea of illumination and mystery, David Smith's (1991) hermeneutical inquiries and David Jardine's (1992) explorations of ambiguity—all are part of the *currere* discussion. Too, insights drawn from such writings as William Pinar's (1988) "Time, Place, and Voice" and his (1994) *Autobiography, Politics and Sexuality* bring new phenomenological subject matters into the curriculum field; as does William Schubert and George Willis's (1991) *Reflections from the Heart of Educational Inquiry*. My work combines the interdisciplinary use of spiritual, psychological, and autobiographical material—as do the previously mentioned books—with focus always on the poetical aspects of these fields.

In the field of literary criticism my project is sympathetic with the fact-fiction distinctions offered by Walter Ong's (1982) *Orality*, which privileges hearing and storytelling as tribal experiences; Roland Barthes's (1974) *S/Z*, which proposes "writerly" texts as those that engage readers in indeterminacy, not didactics; Wolfgang Iser's (1989) *Prospecting*, which continues his 1978 interest in gaps, games, and "dyadic interactions." Certainly important too are Louise Rosenblatt's classic (1938) *Literature as Exploration*, which argues for reading as working out ways of living and Jacques Derrida's (1992) *Acts of Literature*, which insists on the not-said as rupturing cause for "remarking."

This brief survey of some of the major influences in reading and curriculum is meant to indicate two directions. I find similarities with all of these ideas, because all of them answer my students' impatience with reading as a "mere" exercise. This impatience derives from a cultural disparagement of the humanities in general and of reading print in particular. But I also find differences between what I propose to do and what the classics and recent writings on reading and curriculum have done. Namely, I take a backward, vertical path in a discussion that has tended to be horizontal. In other words, my interests in mythopoetics is an interest shared by depth psychology and women visionaries. With this backward, downward move I attempt to provide *currere* with a sense of that which "courses" through time, through memory, through dream, through culture—images, moments, symbols found in "writerly" texts. My vertical excavations attempt to connect readers "back" and "down" into their own depths, such that the key curricular concepts with which I work—imagination and authenticity—take on an older, more primal understanding, even as we begin a new millennium.

As an interdisciplinary scholar, I draw on my background in aesthetics, religion, and psychology as well as my more than thirty years of teaching English and world literature. My work is informed by the neo-Jungian approach of James Hillman's (1996b) *The Soul's Code* as well as his earlier, groundbreaking (1975b) *Re-Visioning Psychology*; Toni Morrison's work to expose the "deep trouble of the Western fable" (in Tate, 1983, p. 125); Samuel Beckett's explorations into the zero point; numerous playwrights and fiction writers; and erotic feminist writings. This sampling of my sources is meant to indicate the direction of my *currere* discussion as a "coursing" of passion and suffering—both necessary to reignite the fires of imagination and recharge world views. Language, as James Joyce (1939) might pun, is not just the letter but the litter—the leftover echo that lingers somewhere in another mindplace, and beckons.

And so it is fiction in all its manifold manifestations that I believe is the place for curricular work. I call attention to four characteristics of fiction that may allow teachers and students to live in language differently, more poetically, less literally. First is the material itself. Fiction's world is unfamiliar. Not only do we read of other locales, we read of different characters facing obstacles unlike ours, in language that we cannot imitate. To de-literalize deadened imaginations the teacher would do well to introduce such foreignness. The assumption here is that bad habits and boredom account for poor reading and blockheadedness. Students can be like tourists dependent on their teachers to be tour guides through the maze. Resist the impulse to clarify, I urge. Allow the material to loom "inexplicable in the light of ignorance—then and then only may it be a source of enchantment" (Beckett, 1931, p. 11). Attending closely to the style of the writer is attending to the writer's mind at work, different from any generalities one might wish to utter about the writer (Brown, 1997). This attending means noting word selection, in the reverent belief that words contain angels; they are emissaries with etymologies. Attending to writers' words helps prevent us from uttering "things made up in our subjective minds" (Hillman, 1975b, p. 9). Fiction's difference should thus be a destabilizing experience. The shock of confrontation with that which is utterly Other helps push dogma off its stone. Biddy Martin (1997) encourages teachers to reread texts with students so as to feel "the selvedges of language" (p. 9)—"selvedge" composed of "self" and "edge" and suggesting danger but also excitement. By studying short textual passages, students can experience the two-edged characteristic of fiction's unfamiliarity: its wonder, its risk.

Second, is a teaching method for fiction probably not favored in survey courses: slowness. There are ways of "surveying" without the lateral approach. Reading aloud slows; attending to punctuation slows. Time is a matter of attention, of attending, which is where all the varieties of instants grow. Giving students time to linger over a passage, to dwell inside it, is a gift teachers can afford to offer. Slowing the pace, even stopping the talk to allow for silence, dramatically alters classroom dynamics. It was said of Beckett that *Waiting for Godot* (1954) was a play where nothing happens—twice. I sometimes think that Beckett wanted to bore his audience out of their minds. If bored out of one's mind, does one go to another mind?

A third characteristic of fiction is its fluidity. Fiction has a way of seeping, especially when it is shared in schools. Sumara (1996) calls this "schooling the literary imagination," a phrase meant to suggest the wonderful opportunity teachers have in a place called school to develop relatedness through shared readings. Clearly, this is unlike the experience in French class, say, where the dominant purpose of being in the room is to master grammar. I recall how we used to hide behind our books, a gesture as futile as sweeping peas under a knife, in the belief that Mrs. Wash would not see us, not call on us. We dared not show our ignorance (which meant "incorrect answer"). That classroom behavior might also occur in history class, where we were to memorize facts and explain the reasons men start wars. Talking points. But my memory of laboratory science classes was of its attaining a seeping quality: We experimented, things exploded, we marveled at what we could *not* do. We moved around and laughed among ourselves and with the teacher. Something here was like our combustible reactions to fiction, where "correct" was no more meaningful than "incorrect."

Fiction's fluidity creates a different classroom atmosphere, akin to opera, where many voices and sounds mingle; akin to performance. There are many ways to perform fiction, some of which could include taking parts in dialogue, rewriting texts, or recording critiques into tape recorders or video cams. Regardless, performing fiction is necessarily dialogical and improvisational, taking authority away from text or teacher. The fifty-minute class becomes a stage, like life itself, all of us actors trying to remember our lines. How many classes, after all, prepare us for the truly dramatic moments in life: sustaining relationships, parenting, loving, dying? Fiction's fluidity allows for the seeping in of life outside the text, including the audience, as well as the seeping out from the text. What is emphasized in performance is less text, more context. It is performance that transforms because of the active involvement of the actors (Denzin, 1997).

"Anarchy!" the skeptic might shout. Where anything is possible, there is indeed an uncertain proscenium. The wall between stage and audience, text and reader, teacher and student disappears. In its place are living bonds. But consider this: In Polynesian mythology, the creation of the world was said to come about by the octopus. Seeing the octopus imaginally, we see tentacles spiraling from the center, languid in liquid, allowing for life in the middle. The tentacles express a way of understanding that does not proceed by walls of separation but by bonds that define relations (Comandini, 1988).

Fourth, fiction is food. Fiction feeds the soul's hunger; words are like food for starved souls. Recall Richard Wright's words about reading fiction in his autobiography (1937/1966) originally titled *American Hunger*: "I grew silent, wondering about the life around me. It would have been impossible for me to have told anyone what I derived from the novels, for it was nothing less than a sense of life itself" (p. 295). We hunger for that which has to do with a basic structure in the depths of consciousness—memory, story (Estess, 1974). One could say that a key consequence of literalism is an appalling lack of intimacy—not just intimacy with another, but an intimacy—a knowing—with who lives within. We forget where we come from. Perhaps we can learn to say, "Yes, I remember. What an addition to company that would be" (Beckett, 1980, p. 16). My classes are after breakfast and before lunch, and after lunch and before dinner, and after dinner. It is my job as English professor to feed the company. Think of it! Our symposia could become a banquet, a matter of caring for the soul. "Culturally," Thomas Moore (1992) writes, "we have a plastic esophagus, suited perhaps to fast food and fast living, but not conducive to soul, which thrives only when life is taken in in a long, slow process of digestion and absorption" (p. 206). One way to slow down, reflect, and feed the inner self is through engagement with fiction. Perhaps our hunger will help us find our own words to express our own selves and our own stories.

I asked my students to write one of their family stories. It took a while for them to hear what I meant. Didn't they grow up with stories their mother told them about her mother? Didn't they have stories about Inez and Charlie at the Thanksgiving table? I prodded. Glimmers began to appear. "Oh, you mean *stories*," they said. They did not understand that their stories were real, as real as bread. One student was absent for several subsequent classes while we were working on the assignment, then finally appeared shaking her head. "I have no stories," she said.

To have no stories, to lack memory, to have a mouth but no words is to keep oneself in a constant state of hunger. When people say they are sex starved I think they really have a famine of feeling. They are the nonerotic ones who feed on porn. When people say they are frustrated I think they lack art. What this book hopes to do is call for a new literacy of the imagination that will introduce strangeness, encourage slowness, express fluidity, and feed the other mind: the soul. We can't all hope to be artists or poets, but we can value words not merely as communication but as holding "something urgent and important beyond just information" (Faulkner, 1956, p. 178).

And so, this book takes fiction seriously, using writerly imagination as the means whereby to make the journey into individual and collective consciousness. How do writers yield understandings about social forms, consciousness, modes of action? Consider what Frederick Douglass says of his journey from slavery:

> I would at times feel that learning to read had been a curse rather than a blessing. It had given me a view of my wretched condition, without the remedy.... The silver trump of freedom had roused my soul to eternal wakefulness. Freedom now appeared to disappear no more forever. (1841/1994, p. 62)

Can that which is not fact (fiction, poesis) provide insight into facts that stare us in the face? Facts like racial hatred, gender discrimination, classed separation, social constructions of identity? Facts that inevitably provide the rationale for ethnic cleansing, surgical strikes, and hate Web sites—the abominations of 20th-century technologies? My hope in this book is that literature can undo literalism by showing literalism's dreadful fallout. As Toni Morrison (1998a) said, "oppressive language does more than represent violence. It is violence." This is literalism's horror.

Mythmaker poets and cinematographers, along with writers, have helped us to imagine the horrors of our time differently—to see it for what it is in all its shock but to take us beyond the literalism. I think here of the movie *Bent* (1997), based on the Holocaust play by the same title. The true history of queers in concentration camps is largely untold. The movie story is riveting, not because of the literal horror, but because of the creative power of the prisoners' words that act imaginatively on another stage of being, another dimension altogether. Two homosexual prisoners are ordered to move rocks from place to place in a torture reminiscent of Sisyphus in Hades. They are ordered not to touch one another. The audience watches their back and forth, back and forth; then listens as the power of words transfuses the situation. They make love verbally, words being all they have. They fall in love. Words create eros. Words are food for the famished soul.

Samuel Beckett's work is applicable in this context. His drama consists of stylized, ritualized, performance acts that often portray situations of abandonment. Characters are left adrift in a universe that is utterly mute to their dilemma. Because his plots lack external action, Beckett focuses attention on dialogue. *Waiting for Godot* , although not a political play, can nevertheless be seen as the dilemma facing political prisoners or those subject to the cruel whim of sadistic masters, such as that seen in *Bent* (1997). Two tramps are isolated in unfamiliar territory; they must wait for instruction; they have no guideposts, nothing but themselves. What do they "have" to do during the duration? How do they endure? Unlike those of us used to cell phone props or quick fix solutions, the tramps have only their words to "do." They pass time by playing with the only reality they have: words. It is not that silence does not speak or that waiting does not move or that the human spirit cannot survive. Words "do."

Literary texts, at the very least, complicate thinking, keeping questions about meaning, agency, and value open for discovery, not in any particular literary strategy or any one text's formal dimensions, but in reflections uttered aloud about what guides the interpretation. Once uttered, interpretations can be discussed, debated, and exchanged rather than dogmatized. My belief is that theory needs the wisdom of writers; therefore, it is to the writers I turn who are, I believe, the closest our culture can come to wisdom figures, able not only to help us see the damage of our dogmas but to find our way out of the bramble.

My book is divided in sections offering a reinterpretation of the Buddha's three types of people. People who are like letters carved in rock, the first section, are those who easily give way to anger and retain their anger for a long time. This is the mode of rock-solid hatred on a personal level and institutional absolutism on a collective level. Ideals written in stone become dogma, and dogmatic ideals require absolute obedience. The way of the rock cannot be moved. I use William Faulkner, Toni Morrison, Richard Wright, and the modernist writers Virginia Woolf, D. H. Lawrence, and James Joyce in this section as among those who clearly demonstrate the intransigence of a culture molded from the stones of a too solid belief in founding principles.

People who are like letters written in sand, the Buddha says, are those who give way to anger but whose angry thoughts quickly pass away. The sand mode can be considered the opposite of the rock mode because alternatives are glimpsed. There is a crack in the foundation such that what once was ideal may not appear so firmly pedestaled. This mode is characterized by a tension between the opposites. Here, I discuss oppositional tensions of gender issues as expressed in myth and fairy tale and literature, notably in the works of Kate Chopin, Gustave Flaubert, Anne Sexton, and Tennessee Williams.

People who are like letters written in running water are those who do not retain their passing thoughts and whose minds are always clear. The Buddha's model of the fluid self provides an alternative mode to the other two, akin to post-structuralist conceptions of self. This is the mode of mindfulness and focused attention (Hanh, 1987), of simple coming and going. It is the mode of what Bakhtin (1981) calls "linguistic homelessness" (p. 366). No one ideal is grasped—not love, not home, certainly not purity—because to grasp is to begin a hardening process. I choose writers who embrace difficulty in their work, like Jamaica Kincaid, Toni Morrison, William Faulkner (again), and Eudora Welty, but in that embrace are able to let go the entangling arms of hate. I call on Native-American writing here also, particulary that of Leslie Marmon Silko, to suggest that older, nonEuropean cultures have eluded the trap of oppositionalism. Other more primal cultures have valued sound rather than sense; that is, speakings that communicate through voice's timbre, language's rhythm, embodied gesture, and the melodies of conversation. Too, texts once were found in bird sightings, leaf turnings, and the force and slant of wind. There are many ways to read letters written in running water.

Finally, this book is intended for classroom readings. To that end I have selected texts most commonly used in literature and writing courses—with a few esoteric exceptions. I have also included more lengthy extracts from student writings than from scholarly writings with the intention of foregrounding the learning voice. By listening to the voices we teach, I hope to keep open my own mind as teacher and author, not in the romantic belief that all wisdom is in the student, but in Buddhism's belief that there is no belief (Batchelor, 1997), no authority: Authority is a washed-out concept. Wisdom's teachings come from many sources—written and spoken—as well as from archaic sources found in depths. Reading with the third eye, listening with the inner ear, we can, perhaps, at last, come to regard wisdom, not knowledge, as education's only real concern.

Like Letters Carved in Rock

BLOCKHEADEDNESS

A book is an ax for the frozen sea within.

—Kafka (in Weaver, 1994, p. 137)

With your milk, mother, I swallowed ice.
And here I am now, my insides frozen.

—Irigaray (1981, p. 61)

We are … what we do not know.

—Pinar (1995, p. 23)

An image runs throughout the writings of authors who depict either themselves or others as prisoners. It is the image of the closed door. On one side of the door is a prisoner, locked in, lacking the key for exit. On the other side lies freedom, escape, entrance. Doors can be literal barricades, such as that experienced by the wife in Charlotte Perkins Gilman's (1892/1985) *The Yellow Wallpaper* or the first wife of Edward Rochester in Charlotte Brontë's (1847/1985) *Jane Eyre*. These two women are prisoners for different "reasons." Gilman's character is being "protected" by her doctor-husband, who only wants what is best for his sick darling and hates to have her write a word. And so she is put in an attic room with yellow wallpaper, which has a sub-pattern of a woman stooping and creeping about behind bars. Here, in isolation, the prisoner-wife identifies with the creeping woman and comes to sense in those ghostly slitherings a true picture of her attic debasement. Edward Rochester's Jamaican Creole wife is also locked in an attic apartment, also demented, imprisoned behind doors. In *Jane*

1

Eyre the reader knows this woman only by her hideous laugh and her night rage of setting fires.

The doors in these two 19th-century works serve as metaphors for blocks against consciousness. To keep doors closed, for those on the outside, is to keep otherness at bay; and for those on the inside, closed doors ensure the "Philadelphia treatment." Gilman's story retells her own bouts with breakdown, according to which she was instructed by her doctor to "have but two hours' intellectual life a day. And never touch pen, brush or pencil as long as you live" (in Jacobus, 1986, p. 230). In her edited, groundbreaking collection of fictional accounts of breakdown, my mother (Aswell, M. L., 1947) wrote, "If the wing of madness hovers over us, we must make use of the writer's perception and of his social perspective to understand those who have been felled by it" (p. ix). It was the preferred treatment of my mother's day (my mother was from Philadelphia) to administer shock therapy when isolation did not "cure" maddened souls. Or, more drastically—as in the case of the mother of a friend of mine—when irrational behaviors exploded beyond the threshold of social acceptance, lobotomies were performed. Such stone age "treatments" were "necessary," the medical men reasoned, blaming others for what but for the grace of God could befall them. In Charlotte Brontë's novel, one wonders if Edward Rochester were more upset by his first wife's madness or her Creoleness. After all, he was an aristocratic land holder, the master blue blood of his county, whose dalliance with a woman of color would have brought social scorn on his house if progeny ensued. Doors provided convenient barricades against which patriarchal social selves could be bolstered. With Robert Frost (1914/1993) we might ask what the door was walling in or walling out.

Bolstering keeps sides apart. To turn one's attention away from that which terrifies or disturbs a nice little life can be, in the course of things, dangerous. I am reminded of this fact by my proximity to the Mississippi River. No matter how many levees they erect, the waters will rise when they must and my house could be swept away. I know people who live in gated communities, not so much to protect themselves from the mighty river, but from Them—dark skinned Others. One Tom McDermott was quoted recently as saying, "It would be nice for them not to even come in. Dubuque's been pretty much a white town, and it's been a nice little town. They're going to bring them in and there's going to be all sorts of problems" (1991, p. A18). Harold Rugg (1963) calls such turning away a conscious decision of "utter concentration" that not only shuts out external stimuli but shuts up imagination, keeps imagination silenced, blocked.

Such utter concentration—call it stonewalling—was, and is, the result of a system built on the stones of carefully rationalized beliefs, which the belief-holders call "facts." Women went mad, it was thought, because they were hysterical, weak, inferior. White men would taint their bloodlines, it was thought, by marrying "inferior" Black women. And racial superiority could be guaranteed, it was thought, by eliminating Jews, gypsies, and queers. In addressing the phenomenon of rationalized hate, indicated in varying degrees by the preceding examples, James Hillman (1996b) describes what blocks the imagination, hardening its flow, preventing access to the ghosts. Each life, he writes, is formed by a particular image. In the case of the evildoer, like a Hitler, the particular image becomes demonic in its "single track obsession, its monotheistic literalism that follows one prospect only" giving rise to "serial reenactments of the same act" (p. 246). In an earlier work, Hillman (1979a) suggests that imaginary travel into metaphorical underworlds could open doors to the unconscious, where invisibles hold sway. Those who do evil, however, cannot deviate from their singleminded purpose because their minds are set, like ice, on the one mission they feel compelled to serve. Hitler reportedly was said to have remarked, "my heart remains ice-cold"; and when warned of impending doom, said, "but don't you see, I cannot change" (Hillman, 1996b, p. 217).

My poem describes what I see in the Hitler phenomenon, relevant even today. Written like a singsong nursery rhyme, the poem is meant to suggest not only the lullaby (naïve) comfort one feels when holding on to belief, but also the phenomenon of childish violence; that is, violence committed by children:

Looney Tunes

I have a firm conviction as firm as firm can be,
I don't know what to do with it; guess I'll hang it on a tree.
That way my friends can see it and watch it wag and wave;
That way we'll all salute it as we shout and rant and rave.

Or else I'll put it in my trumpet and blast it in the air
So when I sound out loud and clear the folks can stop and stare.
They'll listen to the cadence; they'll goose step to the beat.
They'll love my firm conviction as they march right down the street.

A conviction that is strong and firm, that sounds the clarion call,
Can thus be shown to flourish, even pave the way to war.

Hillman (1996b) identifies belief, "the habit of belief," he calls it (p. 268), as descriptive of the American character of mediocrity. We achieve comfort and security from the walls we put around our houses or our beliefs, until belief is no longer "couched," but "set." "I believe in one God, the Father Almighty." How on high are those capitals uttered every Sunday in the Catholic church, how preventing of gaps! Frost's stone wall demonstrates that it wants down by the "elvish" mischief of spilled boulders. Walls want gaps. If two can pass inside the gap, the wall no longer separates the one from the other. Teachers can think of their work as elvish when they allow spaces for students to pass through. "I never really thought about life in such depth until I started reading in this class,"

Jennifer wrote. "To me, life was either this or that, no questions asked." The either-or life of our students, conditioned by their parents' beliefs, needs rigorous spade work by poets and teachers. Not to allow for gaps, for absences into which another reality can be made present, is to wall out the other, utterly. The point, as Bill Pinar (1993) puts it, is that "our otherness is our cultural unconscious" (p. 60). "If what we know about ourselves—our history, our culture, our identity—is deformed by absences, denials, and incompleteness, then our identity—both as individuals and as Americans—is fragmented" (p. 61).

Indeed, the Eurocentric culture is a chronically hard-boiled, belief-ridden tradition, which, the nursery rhyme knows, is nevertheless as flimsy as Humpty Dumpty. Mythically, hardboiled, hardheaded, coldheartedness is personified as the god Cronus. It is useful to flesh out this abstraction of the icy heart and hard head if for no other reason than that it gives form to idea and helps to see an idea more clearly. And so, who is this Cronus? Aesthetically, he is Rodin's "Thinker," chin on hand, straining at the bowels. Educationally, he is driven by chronologies and synchronies, making sure the time line is straight and all points of view are the same. Psychologically, he is egoism rigidified by excessive rationalism. Metaphorically, he has a stone in his belly—myth's image for the compulsion to swallow fantasy and childish imagination. Mythically, he is the sky god who thought he could abort the prophecy that his children would overthrow him by swallowing them. Cronus thought by using his head he could thwart fate, so one after the other he gulped down Hestia, Demeter, Poseidon, Hera, and Hades. But with his last son, Zeus, his wife tricked him and fed him a stone wrapped in swaddling clothes. Zeus grew to manhood and challenged the father's reign. The rest is history, according to Freud and Faulkner.

That Cronus is so old and humorless is important. He must have everything just so because he fears he has nothing. He is at the end of all life, the end of time, a mile marker etched in marble at the end of the millennium. He is the schoolmaster's watchdog. He is why I wrote this poem:

My Old Man

My old man has a hard head.
He fills it with clocks and bottles.
He turns it slowly in the morning
to look down his window at us.

My old man is never late.
He watches time from the corner of his eye.
He can gauge when it is ten till.
You could say he has an obsession.

My old man, of course, is me.
I throw him a bone now and then.

He needs a friend, poor fellow,
because I never talk to him,
pretending he is someone else.

In one of his innumerable blockhead characters, Samuel Beckett (1958b) gives us the sense of what this end-of-century Cronus figure is like. He is Unnamable, our old, old progenitor from whom we have learned to live only in our heads, telling our same old tales in monologue:

I have always been sitting here, at this selfsame spot, my hands on my knees, gaz ing before me like a great horn-owl in an aviary. The tears stream down my cheeks from my unblinking eyes. What makes me weep so? From time to time. There is nothing saddening here. Perhaps it is liquefied brain. (p. 293)

This figure is the patriarch (God? Hamm? Descartes? Kant? Freud? Thomas Jefferson?) whose philosophical ramblings from the brain reduce his words to babble. In Beckett's (1958a) *Endgame*, Hamm feels these ramblings as same old questions, same old answers, which are draining out of him: "Something drip-ping in my head, ever since the fontanelles.... Splash, splash, always on the same spot" (p. 50). Beckett portrays rationalizing as a very tired, very worn out habit that the die-hard ego is so terribly reluctant to relinquish. The situation of always finding answers to the same questions, or of always devising systems with which to analyze the same problems is the way of the West. It is a way that seeks ever-new "facts" with which to rationalize away old fears. It is a way that causes great sadness.

Each book in the section that follows is an "ax" to crack the frozen seas of imagination. That the characters in this section do not release their imagina-tions but rather hold on to their blocks of belief until they harden to become "facts" is why they were selected. My purpose is not to judge their intransigence; my purpose is to look at the social conditions built into the foundational struc-tures of society that enable blockheadedness. As James Hillman (1996b) wrote, "The capacity to deny, to remain innocent, to use belief as a protection against sophistication of every sort—intellectual, aesthetic, moral, psychologi-cal—keeps the American character from awakening" (p. 268). With Faulkner, the image of the closed front door becomes the obsessive symbol that fires Thomas Sutpen's rage in *Absalom, Absalom!* (1936/1987) and becomes, as well, the cold hate that drives Abner Snopes to arson, in *Barn Burning* (1970). For these White men, the door that is shut against their entrance becomes their metanarrative, that which carves the plot line of their being into stone.

I pair Toni Morrison with William Faulkner for several reasons not the least of which is that Morrison wrote her Master's thesis on Faulkner and has clear Faulknerian undertones in her work. But more significantly, I think, is the pair-ing of two writers who see race and economics as key issues facing post-Civil War America. Faulkner shows how the unequal distribution of wealth and power negatively effects poor Whites and women, not to mention all Blacks. He shows how the American myth of Southern aristocracy has been falsely constructed in order to preserve patriarchal systems of control. Morrison shows how separatism, for African-Americans, is not the paradise they assume. She employs the symbol of the Oven as a sort of metal Constitution or Bible, on which is carved the founding belief of the African-American community: "Beware the Furrow of His Brow." Morrison's terrifying novel *Paradise* (1998b) is perhaps the strongest fictional account I have read of the real dangers of literalism. Letters carved in stone (like, she implies, literalistic readings of the Bible or the Constitution) are missives of intolerance. To read Morrison is to see pieces of American history come alive before our eyes. It is to feel story's power for helping us to see how wrongheaded it is to "solve" our country's race problem either by a social utopia or a political paradise. To turn to extremism is to play into the hands of what Cornell West (1994) calls a "paralyzing pessimism" (p. 158). It is, however, precisely because Faulkner and Morrison avoid pessimism in their accounts of hardhearted hatred that I both begin and end my book with them. For although they write narratives around the social, political, psychological, and economic issues of race, they do not write diatribes. They tell all the truth but they tell it slant, as Emily Dickinson would say.

In this first section, I include Richard Wright's autobiographical account *Black Boy* (1937/1966) partly because my father was Wright's editor. Wright rages against the Jim Crow South, which closed all doors of opportunity for African-Americans. But it is the teachings of the fundamentalist African-American church, which demanded a code of obedience to Whites, that Wright particularly indicts. Richard was called a hardhearted ingrate by his own family for his refusal to act in a docile manner and for his insistence on reading and writing his way out of oppression. Wright's rage is directed against belief and innocence, qualities so many middle class Americans hold as endearing, but which Wright sees as the very qualities that perpetuate evil.

My inclusion of Southern writers and Southern issues in this section is deliberate. My reasons are threefold. First, I live in the South now and have come to re-cognize my Southern roots from my Tennessee-born father who, like so many Southerners, fled the South. I used to think the North, where I grew up and was educated, was enlightened because we weren't the South with its drawl and plantations. As Faulkner's (1936/1987) Shreve sarcastically says to Quentin, "The South. It's better than the theater, isn't it. It's better than Ben Hur, isn't it" (p. 271). "Better" because it is more violent and haunted. But it is a mistake to think, as Shreve does, that the North is exempt from its own violence and racial hatred. The South, at least, knows it is haunted. And that is the second reason I choose Southern writers: They are the ones to acknowledge the ghosts in the attic and by so doing, they refuse to remain culturally unconscious about racism. Faulkner's mythic Yoknapatawpha County is, certainly, his way of deconstructing the Myth of the South. The White lady in her gossamer gowns and the big white house of the Southern plantation are neither pure nor clean. Behind the facade of gentility lie dirty family secrets. The most socially prominent members of the upper class—judges, lawyers, ministers—had secret slaves in the family. As Edward Ball (1998) detailed in his genealogical research, 4,000 Black people were enslaved by his forebears, and their descendants number between 75,000 and 100,000 living Americans. And in my morning paper, the descendants of Thomas Jefferson voted not to include in their Monticello Association the relatives of his slave and alleged mistress, Sally Hemings. "We're not racist," one descendant said. "We're snobs" (Reed, 1999, p. A3). In talking and writing about this "attic" history of Southern families, that which ghosts our shared historical past can be—at the very least—faced.

A third reason I emphasize Southern writers is related to the second reason. It is in the South that Whites have developed a fantasy about aristocracy and landed privilege. The fantasy is based on false histories, yet it persists in codes of privilege that are given respectability and visibility. Worse, these codes give permission for the spread of White supremacy fictions that can easily be found on Web sites known as "hate zones." In a recent election in Louisiana for the United States Senate, the former Ku Klux Klan Grand Wizard, David Duke, came in a frightening third, after running ads about his book, which is modeled on Hitler's *Mein Kampf*. For curriculum theorists, literary fictions about the South provide an effective avenue for exposing social fictions.

Finally, I end this section on blockheadedness with three high modernists, Virginia Woolf, D. H. Lawrence, and James Joyce to suggest that class and belief issues are also what block imagination. Woolf and Lawrence reveal the evils that privilege brings to the upper class. In Woolf's case, women's bodies were the privilege men could invade. Writing in cotton wool prose, Woolf's style uses words to obfuscate the hidden text of her time. Beneath the pleasant summer surfaces of daily living lay an ugly fact to which even the women felt they had to comply: All doors were open to their bodies. In Lawrence's case, it was civilization's very "civilized" code that shut the door to erotic desire. Writing against upper class "niceness," Lawrence broke through the social code of gentility to reveal that the cost of sexual repression is deadly, emotional rage. With both American and British works, I hope to demonstrate that the way to crack through blockheadedness is by understanding how literalisms kill.

1

The Character
of Wood or Brick

Every tradition grows ever more venerable—the more remote it is from its origin, the more confused that origin is.

—Nietzsche (1878/1996, p. 96)

Their heads are so hard that almost nothing else (except violence) will do the work.

—O'Connor (1969, p. 291)

"Mr. Compson raised his feet once more to the railing, the letter in his hand and the hand looking almost as dark as a negro's against his linen lap" (p. 110). Reading that sentence from Faulkner's (1936/1987) *Absalom, Absalom!* one gets the sense of the oxymoron that lies at the very structure of an idea termed "the Old South." Mr. Compson, we assume, is White. Did Faulkner write "negro" intentionally, or was that just a figure of speech? Did the hand look shadowed, dark, against the leg of Mr. Compson? Or could it be that the White father had Black blood? Faulkner doesn't tell. Later, another scene echoes this one in the memory of Mr. Compson's son, now in another setting. "He (Quentin) could see it (a letter) plainly as he saw the one open upon the open text book on the table before him, white in his father's dark hand against his linen leg" (p. 259). There the reference to Mr. Compson's dark hand occurs again, like an obsession. But here "the one open upon the open text book" is a different letter, and the scene is different—even though the image is similar. The whole novel is like that: different similars. Circles, echoes, and repetitions of key images reverberate as they might in nightmare, acquiring a ghostly quality. These repetitions serve the function of ritual (which long ago prepared initiates to enter a realm of sacred mysteries). But not quite. For here, ritual repetitions are ossified, preventing access to sacred space. Just so, the novel never reveals the inner secrets about family life in the South. All that the reader knows is what can be gleaned by bits and pieces of memory relayed by unreliable narrators. All Faulkner leaves us with is interpretation. All we know is that we cannot know.

Faulkner is as good a White source as I am familiar with to inquire into the contradictions of the past and, more particularly, into the constructed fictions of tradition. With its legendary myth of hospitality, sweeping oaks, and large pillared plantations, fleshed out by the image of gentlemen in linen suits, the South would like to live as a frozen tableau of elegance in the White imagination. But, Faulkner refuses the reader the luxury of that belief. Instead, his work is deliberately tangled, convoluted, and contradictory. My brother called Faulkner's style a "game" played with (against?) the reader, Faulkner even going so far as to tack on a genealogy filled with intended inconsistencies (Aswell, 1984). To believe that truth can be determined if it comes straight from the horse's mouth is to take mere sayings literally. For the reader, the challenge Faulkner poses is extreme: Faulkner questions not only who we are as readers, but who we have been taught to think we are as members of a race, a class, a gender. Teaching Faulkner, however, offers the opportunity for opening discussion into the basic fictions of history, like "tradition," "Southern gentility," or "American Dream."

Traditioning, as L. E. Donaldson (1987) calls it, seeks to make permanent the lies of the past; forgetting, ignoring, or repressing, for example, the American history of slavery. Joe Kincheloe (1993) writes that when Black history is excluded from Southern history, the lie of traditioning is kept alive. Traditioning is by nature uncritical, unquestioning, inauthentic, and exclusive. It seeks to preserve a pure past by building a very large mausoleum for the housing of its myth. The South, then, becomes not a place at all, but a trope, "an idea in narrative form" (Humphries, 1996, p. 120). In a brilliant move to expose the lie of the South, Faulkner uses the very methods of traditioning to subvert it. As well, he forces us to accept the fact that tradition is always, always, selected (McGee, 1993).

Faulkner shows that traditions are "selected" in at least four ways. They can be literalized around single metaphors; they can be narrated by word of (unreliable) mouth; they can be relayed by a conspiratorial "we"; they can be memorialized by monuments to false icons. In *Absalom, Absalom!* the narrative is told by three different people to Quentin Compson, a 20th-century college student trying to understand his Southern identity. The reader looks over the shoulder of Quentin and becomes, like him, mired in the mystery of place. It is not just the miasma of the 19th-century swamp that perplexes and draws us in. Questions about race, gender, sexuality and identity simmer beneath a story of the big house. At the heart of this darkness (resonances with Conrad's work are deliberate) lies the figure of Thomas Sutpen, whose fall from great wealth is the result of a tragic flaw of Attic proportion. But this is not a Greek myth; it is the American myth of the deep South. The tragedy is not just the hubris of one man's lust to own a white house and father a White son; it is, more fundamentally, the sin of ownership, otherwise known as slavery.

Whiteness is the issue that underscores the fantasy of Southern gentility. Whiteness, seen as the absence of Black blood, is the myth. That one of the narrators is Mr. Compson, who, in the scene cited, is described with a hand "almost as dark as a negro's" is the hint that gives slip to the lie. It is Faulkner's way of inserting innuendo into the American South's quest for an unsullied tradition. What is at stake is Quentin's questions about this Southern past of his, shrouded in mystery: its assumed Whiteness. How does his personal past connect with his regional past? How implicated is he in the sins of his father? What about the reader's questions about place? Reading this novel begins a journey into an understanding that place is pedagogy demanding interrogation.

I bring the reader into these comments because I read this novel with Quentin. Like him, I look at scraps of paper and letters as he looks at them, trying to make sense not only of them but of my history. Images proliferate, texts overlap. I am intertwined just as the American character is intertwined with the history of Black blood, the legacy of the South. I adopt my own point of view and enter into the stories about Thomas Sutpen's design, becoming another figure in the carpet. My viewpoint is like Wallace Stevens's (1923/1993) thirteen ways of looking at a blackbird (Watkins, 1967/1984). Each critic's reading of the text is a "fourteenth way" (Teachers: Beware your presumed interpretive authority; Students: Beware the Cliff Notes). Then, inside the text, three characters tell Sutpen's story, each telling situated in a particular perspective arising from a particular moment in that narrator's life. Each story thus evolves out of "one constant and perpetual instant" (Faulkner, 1936/1987, p. 177), which—like Sutpen's design—is literal because limited. The traditions of the South, Faulkner indicates, are founded on such autobiographical tellings from narrators who cannot get past their "one constant and perpetual instant." In James Olney's terms, narrators like these lack critical awareness because their stories are formed from "the single metaphor" (1972, p. 43). Whereas Robert Parker (1990) reads Faulkner's novel as about the artifice of storytelling, I read it with Richard Poirier (1971) as a novel about the artifice of history, when "history" is nothing but tradition reauthored, recreated, and selected.

The single metaphor that sits at the center of Thomas Sutpen's imagination (and at the heart of the novel), freezing it, turning it to stone, is that of the closed door. From it, ripple out the stories of the other narrators. Recall the moment. Sutpen as a poor White boy is bid by his father to deliver a message to the plantation owner for whom his father is a White planter. The time is pre-Civil War. Young Sutpen goes to the front door, only to be told by a Black slave butler that he must use the back door. Slam. In that instant, young Sutpen falls from innocence. He gains knowledge of class and of race. This means four things: He is worth less than a Black house slave; he becomes conscious of his skin; he has no background; he has no past. Faulkner recounts this fall from innocence into knowledge as a totally skewed way of seeing things, a seeing of such (selected) intensity that what before was only "felt" antagonisms, silences, and insults become afterwards "known" grounds for utter and complete hatred.

Young Sutpen's instantaneous understanding of his worthless marketable status is what drives his life. It is the acorn of his character (Hillman, 1996b). Faulkner identifies Sutpen's drive to become rich (own a white house, father a White son) with the image of a Black man and horse, sometimes the two together, as in a roan horse. Black imagery with White imagery is suggestive of the entanglement of the two colors, the two races, the impossibility of imagining one without the other. Sutpen, for instance, recalls another insult in his youth when he and his sister are made to get out of the middle of the road by a fast-driving carriage driven by a Black coachman. Thrown to the side of the road, he recalls this image: "then it was all dust and rearing horses and glinting harness buckles and wheel spokes" (p. 288). From there, Sutpen is described by Faulkner as a fast rider on a roan horse raising dust (pp. 35, 51, 56), an image repeated, ominously, by his two sons—one Black, one White—riding fast and in tandem (pp. 130, 165). These sons—because they are together, because they are homosexually linked, because they threaten Sutpen's drive to construct a past for himself, because the Black son is only one drop Black—will bring Sutpen's quest for revenge against classism to ruin. But not before Sutpen, ever intent on perpetuating his line with pure White sons, once again is associated with a horse when he stands with a horse whip over his mistress Milly, who had just given birth to a girl in his stable. It is the horse, not the woman, who fulfills Sutpen's passions. It is the passion of the horse that drives Sutpen to seek a mare for White sons—not daughters. Sutpen on his roan horse, riding fast and raising dust, becomes a recreation of the horse god (Tuso, 1968), destined to be destroyed by his own rituals.

Of the unreliable narrators in the novel, Rosa Coldfield seems to me the most fascinating. In Faulkner's world, it was the White, upper and middle class women on whom the selected stories of tradition rested. They honored a code everyone knew but no one uttered. And so they were complicit in the patriarchy, knowing that their duty was to keep house, plan meals, count the laundry, listen behind doors, and lock the skeletons in the closet. Above all, they were to marry. The White women and the White men all knew this. Before the War, women were made into ladies. After the War, they turned into ghosts. Rosa Coldfield is such a ghost, living as she does in "dead time" (p. 21) and being not quite a person, because she did not marry. Her narrative to Quentin ushers from one specific time in the past when she suffered an insult to her womanhood from Thomas Sutpen. Her grim voice and bitter words relay forty-three years of hatred, which was like a drug's "very poppy's root" (p. 465) to her being. What she relays to Quentin, then, is necessarily skewed by her paralysis of memory (Parker, 1990). Primo Levi makes a similar point about memory, calling it "fallacious" when it is too rigid (in Horowitz, 1994, p. 52). How can Quentin understand his past?—how can I?—when first person narratives about the past are so selectively produced?

What happened to Rosa was that Sutpen had had the classless audacity to make clear the condition under which he would marry her when his first wife, her sister, died. The one thing Rosa needed in the system in which she lived was the respectability of marriage. The one thing Sutpen needed in that same system was the respectability of sons. Both were victims of a system both despised. But in Rosa's view, Sutpen's insult was to make plain, with words, that her worth was only as good as that of a breeding mare. By calling attention to her sexual function, Sutpen broke the code of genteel silence about the only real purpose of White women. Rosa recalls: "He had not even waited to tether his horse; he stood with the reins over his arm (and no hand on my head now) and spoke the bald outrageous words exactly as if he were consulting with Jones or with some other man about a bitch dog or a cow or mare" (p. 210). Resonances of the scene in the stable with Milly resound.

Hatred, then, is the reason Rosa summoned Quentin before he left for college, to accompany her to Sutpen's Hundred so that she could punish Sutpen's only living White male heir (her nephew). Like her father, she is driven to nurture an "immaculate morality," to protect her class with its code of silence. Unlike her father, she must live under the patriarchy's stipulations. Although Faulkner's White women all are marginalized by gender, the unmarried White, classed women are the most marginalized because they have broken the patriarchal code. Her words to Quentin come out of a "cold alert fury" to demonize the man who put into words her female worthlessness. She calls Sutpen a devil, not because he spoke bluntly, but because he did not honor unspokenness. He did not speak obliquely, as any classed man would. "He wasn't a gentleman. He wasn't even a gentleman. He came here with a horse and two pistols and a name which nobody ever heard before" (p. 13).

Rosa's portrait emerges as if she is a very old child, arrested at a crucial stage of development. She sits in a chair too tall for her, so her legs hang straight down unable to touch the floor, "like children's feet" (p. 4). Faulkner's women, except for Black women, are generally pictured as infants in a grownup world. Their men are their fathers. Rosa and her sister Ellen Coldfield are both like that: made foolish and impotent by the dehumanizing demands of gender and class. Ellen Coldfield, we learn from Rosa, carried on like a schoolgirl when planning her daughter's wedding. There was, in all the fuss over the trousseau, a furious unreality that forced women to put their butterfly lives on display. When acting the role of the successful matriarch, women like Ellen become "foolish unreal voluble preserved," speaking "bright set meaningless phrases" for the benefit of "a soilless and uncompelled peasantry" (p. 83).

Those words come from Rosa Coldfield. The critique she offers of her sister would be funny if it were not smart. Rosa understands the full condition of White women's enslavement inside the patriarchal family. "As Engles reminds us in *The Origin of the Family, Private Property, and the State*," writes Mary Jacobus (1986), "the word 'family' derives from 'famulus' or household slave" (p. 238). Women like the Coldfield sisters share a slave's fate—bound not by chains but by psychic arrest. Their development as humans must, according to the code of their tradition, be stalled lest they come to see how limited they really are. Although they enjoy certain economic privileges, such as riding in carriages and fingering expensive merchandise, the White women of the South are tethered like breed mares by their gender. Bill Pinar makes this point succinctly: "The passive aggression of slave holders toward their wives and daughters, as they mystified them into objects of hyperfemininity and social uselessness, needs to be theorized and taught" (1993, p. 67).

Minnie Cooper, in Faulkner's (1970) "A Dry September," is another manifestation of the White woman archetype (as I will call this) whose stories are unreliable. In this instance, the unreliability causes murder. The story concerns the alleged rape of a middle-aged spinster, Minnie, by a Black man, Will Mayes. I interpret "dry" in the title to refer to the sin of Minnie's frigidity, for which a Black man must be sacrificed so as to relieve the town of its curse of the aging maiden. The rape is a hoax and Will Mayes is the scapegoat. Even the men are sexually frustrated, "dry," as we see in Faulkner's description of McLendon, the leader of the lynch mob. He is the epitome of the disenfranchised White man similar to Thomas Sutpen. I interpret McLendon's "furious, rigid face" (p. 65) and clock-like motions as manifestations of his sexually repressed lust for Black flesh. His repressed sexuality is further suggested by the metaphor of his living in a "bird cage," which cages his energies only until the next kill. The lynching satisfies a secret lust; but Mayes's death offers no atonement, because the sacrifice was meaningless and yields no fruit.

After the men rush to form a posse and lynch Will, the focus returns to Minnie. The rush to judgment is what I identify as a haste motif in Faulkner whereby fury is revealed by speed. In other works, fast-driven horses raise dust; here, cars are "hurled up," (p. 70), brakes slam, headlights glare, screen doors crash open, and McLendon "whirls" (p. 65), rips, and flings. That is the male way of showing the fires of hatred. The female way is more studied. From the outset the reader sees how feckless Minnie is. Having nothing to do, she spends mornings swinging on the porch in her lace cap; after a nap, her afternoons are spent in the stores with the other ladies "where they would handle the goods and haggle over the prices in cold, immediate voices" (p. 67). She is Ellen Coldfield all over again: playing meangirl games on lower class merchants. A key scene occurs at the end of the story, when Minnie (having kept her reputation intact, having proven that she is desirable as a woman—all a lie) goes to the picture show:

> It was like a miniature fairyland with its lighted lobby and colored lithographs of life caught in its terrible and beautiful mutations ... the lights flickered away; the

screen glowed silver, and soon life began to unfold, beautiful and passionate and sad, … while beyond them the silver dream accumulated, inevitably on and on. (p. 75)

Commenting on this passage, my student Tonia wrote:

> I feel that this particular passage is a metaphor for Minnie Cooper's life. She is actually being a voyeur of how she would like herself to be. The lights flickering away represents how she used to be—beautiful, popular, happy, young, and marriageable—but all that has passed away. Now she is a screen on display for the entire town as they look at her and talk about her and laugh at her being an old maid.

The story of rape that Minnie Cooper tells the town is perhaps the most extreme example of the unreliable narrator that I have been discussing in terms of decoding tradition. Teaching mostly young women in a Southern college, I see my students distancing themselves from the plight of the traditional Southern White woman, because many of them feel advanced or liberated: "We're over that!" In many cases, they rush into pleased protests against "White woman" behaviors like those of Minnie and the Coldfield sisters. Occasionally, however, I get a student like Tonia (a Black woman) who recognizes the similarity between the fairy tale and the reality and understands the possibility that the fairy tale still exists. Then, discussion can begin by questioning a system of values White girls have been taught from mothers who have been taught by mothers who have been taught by mothers—all in the interest of keeping the thing going.

Besides literal metaphors and unreliable narrations, another way traditioning occurs is by the conspiratorial "we." Of the several methods in Faulkner's work used to subvert the patterns of traditioning, this one is my favorite, for it catches me unaware as I am reading Faulkner. All of a sudden I am drawn into the circle of "we," made to look through their eyes, almost made to think as they do. The strategy is disconcertingly humorous. This is not the royal "we" of a queen, as in "We welcome you to our court"; nor is it the "we" of Carson McCullers's (1940/1988) Mick, in *The Heart is a Lonely Hunter*, who wants to find a "we" for company. Rather, Faulkner's "we" is the watchers, the spectators: those characters who speak for an entire county as if all its various members were one body speaking with one voice, in monotone. The function of "we" is to keep time static. "We" gives the sense of the claustrophobic small town that has never grown up and doesn't want to. "We" could either be the snobs who peer out at the world behind curtains, whispering and snickering like third graders. Or "we" could indeed be a child "we." In either case "we" represents an early stage in the evolvement of human consciousness. If it is like "we the people," there is something basically disempowering in "our" consensus (the majority rule of democracy), as Liz Ellsworth (1989) asserts. The conspiratorial "we" is Faulkner's way of showing how reductive and how dangerous small town unison watching is, returning everything observed to a single cause, a single effect.

It is what Cameron McCarthy and Warren Crichlow (1993) argue is the evil of essentialism:

> The world is a vast Lacanian mirror in which theorists of racial purity and racial essence see themselves standing in front of their ancestors. It is the perfect image, the snapshot history collected in the nuclear family photo album. It is the story of the singular origin, the singular essence, the one, true primary cause. (p. xiv)

Constructions of the past around the repetition of "our" belief are indicated by Faulkner's opening, in *Absalom, Absalom!* Let me set the scene. Quentin sits in Miss Rosa Coldfield's office before going North to college. The "dry vivid dusty sound" of sparrows can be heard (remember "Dry September"?). Rosa keeps the blinds closed because when she was a girl "someone had believed" that closing blinds keeps the dark cooler and that light carries heat. Rosa reenacts the "belief" of "someone" like herself. She is a "we" shutting herself off from a "them." She sits in the darkness of White privilege. Of course, the "them" that intrudes is Thomas Sutpen, the White upstart without a past on a black horse. Sutpen is the threat of "them" to the entire classed code of her town. So the town itself begins to take on the "we" in ensuing chapters. It looks and listens, becoming the personification of "our" prejudices and fears. "The stranger's name went back and forth among the places of business and of idleness and among the residences in steady strophe and antistrophe: *Sutpen. Sutpen. Sutpen. Sutpen*"(1936/1987, p. 35). The town, like a Greek chorus, speaks as "we" might, until it becomes "we": a being in its own right, a fleshed character capable of spying and registering belief. As it watches the movements of this Sutpen stranger beginning transactions to acquire one hundred acres of land, the town feeds on rumor and hearsay, "the gullet of public opinion" (p. 61). But the town knows only as much as it sees behind its blinded windows ("The town now believed that it knew him," p. 48), as if knowledge can be verified by belief.

Spectator knowledge, based on speculation, is that which seeks to be verified by spectacles, that which makes a spectacle. "*Spectator*: one that looks on or beholds, especially one witnessing an exhibition (as a sports event). *Spectacle*: (a) something exhibited to view: an impressive display esp. for entertainment, (b) an object of curiosity or contempt (more at SPY). *Spy*: to watch in a furtive manner for the purpose of secretly obtaining information for usu. hostile purposes" (Webster, 1981). Faulkner's spectators think that seeing is believing and that believing is knowing; therefore, a White man on a black horse riding fast out of nowhere can build respectability brick by brick by erecting a spectacle in front of "our" eyes, "the largest edifice in the county, not excepting the courthouse itself" (p. 45). And by virtue of that spectacle, the house bigger than the courthouse itself, "we" give respectability to that man. "*Respectability*: worthy of note; having claims to consideration; of consequence" (Webster, 1981). Traditions are built from just such spectacles. To make a spectacle is to put on a show. To build a tradition is to house spectres, who live unreal, weightless lives.

Sutpen has two spectacles for the town to gawk at. One is his daytime parade, mimicking the way "we" parade our "stainless wives and unimpeachable lineage" in finery. Knowing how the town believes that class is revealed by clothes, Sutpen has his own parade. He costumes his coachman ridiculously in a linen duster and top hat, "looking exactly like a performing tiger" (p. 24). The architect he hires apes Parisian fashion, dressed in a stovepipe hat. Circus antics are Sutpen's mockery of a classed code of clothing that he had learned from his past. That was when he had made a spectacle of himself, dressed clownishly in his father's patched, too big, worn out pants—thinking nothing of the way he looked. In front of the white door he had stood barefoot, when a Black butler in a tuxedo, "monkey dressed " (p. 288), refused his entry. Sutpen was insulted again by a horse-drawn carriage driven by a "nigger coachman in a plug hat" (p. 288). The same scene in a different story repeats the same insult of clothes. This time, it is Abner Snopes, in "Barn Burning" (1970), dressed in hat and black frock coat so as not to be dwarfed by anything, so as to minimize the hugeness of the white door that will not grant him entry. And like Sutpen, Snopes's refused entry is enforced by an old Black man dressed up in a fancy linen jacket. For the Southern, White male under class, insults received by Black house servants caused their hatred not against Blacks but against an upper class, White system from which they were shut out. It is a system they see as a circus, although "we" remain unaware of its hoops. It is like the poster Abner's son admires: "the scarlet horses, the incredible poisings and convolutions of tulle and tights and the painted leers of comedians" (1970, p. 21).

At night, Sutpen orchestrates another spectacle. "We" ride out to the biggest house in the county, bigger than the courthouse, to view an entertainment that gives the lie to "our" airs. In reality it is a ghastly spectacle, worse than a cock fight. In his stable at night, Sutpen pits his Black slaves against one another, the winner to fight the master. The spectacle is Sutpen's argument for White supremacy, a show he insists be watched by his son and daughter and the gentlemen of Jefferson, as proof of bloodright. More, the voyeurism such a spectacle encourages is the result of latent homoeroticism and inverted desire on the part of plantation owners for Black flesh—an exoticism forbidden by the decorum of their class (Haymes, 1995; Pinar, 1991).

Faulkner demonstrates that the "honorable tradition" for which the South fought in the Civil War was utterly without foundation. It was propped up by no more than one spectacle propped up by another spectacle—what Rosa calls "a raree show" (1936/1987, p. 17). Even Ellen Coldfield plays the role of a duchess, a part she created for herself. But at base the tradition of nobility was "as primitive as the land they settled" (Pinar, 1993, p. 65). The reader feels these primitive conditions as so many pages are spent describing Sutpen's plantation being built plank by plank out of the swampy "spirit-ridden forest" (p. 115). But "we" need to believe in the charade of *noblesse oblige* and Sutpen, "playing the scene to the audience" (p. 87), needs to be stage manager, although he is worse than a "troglodyte" (p. 115). Sutpen's ringmaster entertainments indicate not only that he knew he could fool the town but that, in so doing, he could, at last, wrest respectability for himself.

Part of Sutpen's wresting had to do with his literal wrestling matches with his slaves. His intimate identity with Blacks, particularly in the fighting scenes at night in his stable, reveal how Blacks provided his White invisibility with substance, something he lacked as a poor White boy. Through the physical wrestling matches with Blacks, Sutpen could transcend his invisibility—the curse that had made him poor and "soilless" (p. 83).

Day and night, Black and White intermix and commingle throughout Faulkner's work. By day "we" behave one way according to the constraints of a White superego; by night "our" Black id cavorts. Such psychosexual relationships in the South have been observed by Faulkner critics and curriculum theorists alike, several of them of Freudian persuasion (Haymes, 1995; hooks, 1990; Jenkins, 1981; Pinar, 1991, 1993; Poirier, 1971; Taylor, 1991; West, 1989). Skulking about at night, "we" blind ourselves by day. Faulkner captures the effect such repression has on women in "Dry September" when Minnie Cooper, at the fairyland cinema scene, laughs hysterically. Why does Minnie laugh?, I ask my students. The question prompts discussion, the students sometimes sharper in their understanding of psychosexual nuance than Minnie's audience—"we" who watch. Because "we" have only spectated, "we" don't understand a thing: "Poor girl! Poor Minnie!" is all "we" can say.

The day-night, Black-White fusion occurs in another Faulkner story, "That Evening Sun" (1970), the title a reference to a song with the line "I hate to see that evening sun go down." The "I" of the song could be Nancy, a Black washer-woman whose night fear becomes one of the foci of the story. Nancy literally washes the dirty linen of her White masters. She has every reason to hate to see the sun go down, for in darkness she is the Other, the Them of no count, whose body provides pleasure not only for her Black husband but for the powerful White men of Jefferson, such as the deacon of the church and Mr. Compson. This is the same Mr. Compson of both *The Sound and the Fury* (1929) and *Absalom, Absalom!* By telling the story of the South through various stages in the life of the Compson family, Faulkner circles around and around the father's duplicity and the son's "innocence." One sees the father always through the son (Kazin, 1998). But, because the son does not become his father, he breaks the cycle of generational blindness.

The other focus of "That Evening Sun" is on the narrator-"we," Quentin Compson, a young boy around the age of reason (nine). He is the same Quentin who, in *Absalom, Absalom!*, has the opened letter of his father on his desk, only partially read; and who, in *Sound and the Fury*, has finished reading the letter and commits suicide. The tragedy of Quentin Compson is that it takes him so long to come into reason, to be able to see the full truth of his father's duplicity with black women and to deduce from his father's behavior his own complicity in

Southern racism. That Quentin in the later novels does take on the sin of the father by killing himself is his unfortunate way of atoning for the guilt of being "we" too long.

The two worlds—Black and White—in "That Evening Sun" are separated symbolically by a ditch. Quentin and his younger brother and sister summon Nancy to their house, to do the chores, by "chunking" stones at her door: "We would stop at the ditch, because father told us to not have anything to do with Jesus—he was a short black man, with a razor scar down his face—and we would throw rocks at Nancy's house" (p. 79). Quentin thinks it is perfectly natural for a child to throw stones and to order a woman to "come this minute" because of father's bidding. And, of course, the irony of Jesus's name escapes the children; for, although Nancy's husband's name is Jesus, how true it is that the Son of God would have nothing to do with a family that treated its help like a possession. But young Quentin is the privileged "we," cursedly innocent. He is incapable, because of the privilege, of understanding what is really going on down the backstairs of his house, although his hearing might have told him: "We fixed a pallet in the kitchen for Nancy. One night we waked up, hearing the sound. It was not singing and it was not crying, coming up the dark stairs. There was a light in mother's room and we heard father going down the hall, down the back stairs" (p. 85).

The insidiousness of the conspiratorial "we" is also seen in this story by the assumption of Quentin's five-year-old brother. Jason is afraid of going down the lane to Nancy's house on the other side of the ditch, but he puts up a brave front. The trip is something of an adventure for him. For Nancy, however, the lane at night is a fearsome place: Her husband, she intuits, is waiting to kill her because she is carrying a White man's child. Her terror and self-disgust are reflected in her often-repeated remonstrance: "I aint nothing but a nigger." Jason, hearing her, understands immediately that he is different from her. "I aint a nigger," he says. And later, "Jesus is a nigger."

How do I understand Jason's use of that word? The word frequently occurs in Southern writing, and I find I have to address its use with my students in my Southern Literature course. One Black older woman told the class she refused to read Faulkner because he was racist. Discussion that followed her remark was angry and difficult. But I think Jason's term "nigger" (Caddy, age seven, uses it also) allows for insight, not into Faulkner's racism (I argue otherwise), but into the insidious way attitudes are adopted as truths. The child echoes Nancy's use of the word as well as its use by his parents. But even more, Jason indicates, by distinguishing himself so clearly from both Nancy and her husband ("I aint a nigger"), that he—a five-year-old—knows dysconsciously (King, 1991) that he is "we" and Blacks are "them." According to Joyce E. King "dysconsciousness is not the absence of consciousness … but an impaired consciousness" (p. 135). In other words, the child imitates the uncritical habit of mind of his parents. The tiniest indications clue him into thinking that Black servants are his reward for being White. Early, an entitlement process sets in where clearly exploitative be-haviors are accepted as normal. The norm, because it is invisible, is insensitive to unacceptable words and insulting attitudes.

As such, Jason wants Nancy to sleep on a pallet in his room, like a toy or a pet. His mother says, "I cant have Negroes sleeping in bedrooms," to which Jason cries; he wants his toy. He bargains with his mother that he will stop crying if Dilsey the cook makes a chocolate cake. He "knows" these Black women are there to please him, and by his mother's words he also "knows" they aren't good enough to sleep with. (Jason's father knows otherwise.) This "knowing" is fur-ther corroborated when Nancy calls the child "Mister Jason," a title of defer-ence usually offered by children to adults. Dsyconscious "knowing" of "we" entitlement is further indicated when the children can hear their father talking to Nancy as if she were a bad child: "There's nothing for you to be afraid of now. And if you'd just let white men alone." And later, "If you'd behave yourself, you'd have kept out of this" (pp. 84, 85).

The "we" conspiracy, this story shows, is subtly acquired early in life. If unac-knowledged, it can destroy one's soul—as in Quentin's suicide years later. The privilege of the White "we" is, therefore, personally as well as communally, dam-aging. "That Evening Sun" is one of the shorter stories in the Faulkner collection I study with my class, but it is in many ways the most provocative, particularly for Whites who think they are nonracist but still talk about Blacks as "them." Frances V. Rains (1996) calls this type of White thinking the invisibility factor, which is the corollary to racism. There is another aspect to this little story: the name Jesus. Just as I think the word "sun" in the title is a pun, drawing attention to how male children acquire their father's racist, sexist, and patriarchal habits of belief, so do I think the name Jesus refers to the Son of God as well as to Nancy's husband. For young Jason to say "Jesus is a nigger," then, might be Faulkner's way of discrediting the Eurocentric image of Jesus as White; Jesus could as well be considered Black, a dark-skinned Middle-Easterner. And for Mr. Compson to tell Jesus to stay away from his house might imply that this father is beyond the love and forgiveness of His son.

In this chapter, I have suggested that Faulkner deconstructs the agrarian South of the slavery and Reconstruction days. His work shows that the Southern "tradi-tion" has been handed down by narrators whose stories are unreliable because they emanate from a literal metaphor and involve a conspiratorial "we." Those who benefited the most from tradition were the landed gentry; among the least were poor White men who saw themselves as inferior even to house slaves. Yet, women were also marginalized in a system of ownership when not only land but bodies were owned for profit and reproduction. The White women in Faulkner are not roman-tic figures, but pawns who know at some deep level of consciousness that they have no power or worth because of the politics of tradition.

I come now to my final point about tradition. It has to do with false icons. Su-zanne Jones (1985) observes that Faulkner's slow motion technique is a way of dramatizing the status quo. I call this technique the *frozen tableau*, which serves to monumentalize the icons of tradition—the wealthy landowners and their various possessions. Placed in figurative stone, these icons achieve a kind of historicity, respectability and permanence in viewers' and readers' eyes. Like the other methods of traditioning, this one has led to the fiction known as "The South," founded in fact on hatred, repression, and inventions of the truth.

"A Rose for Emily" (Faulkner, 1970) is case in point. Faulkner takes the symbol of the big house again to stand for class, wealth, and prestige. The house, however, is rotting at its foundation, and the only occupants are Miss Emily Grierson and her silent Black butler who rarely comes out of the house. Miss Emily is the town's last and only hope for recalling a past that never was. She is a "monument" (p. 49) to lost times and past romances. The story serves as a gripping study of what Pinar (1991) terms "presentism," the assumption that the past, which was slavery, can be forgotten in the present, replaced in its stead by legend. Having repressed history, the townsfolk cling to Miss Emily's legend, embellishing it along the way. As in other Faulkner stories, the townsfolk form a unified perspective from which to view events; they are the "we" in need of an icon. "We" have nothing, "we" are nothing, without the lore of the Griersons. The mighty Griersons allow "us" to deny the horrors of the past. That "we" romanticize Miss Emily is suggested by the "rose" in the title. But as with any romance, there is a dark side to idol worship and that is the question of what prompts its need. Reading this story aids in an understanding of the many absences, denials, and exclusions that ghost the South (Pinar, 1991).

Differences between the romance of the past and its reality are, as always in a Faulkner story, complex and intertwined. "We" only see the bloom of Miss Emily's rosy past that gives luster to "our" memory. "We" also, however, need to vilify her, because she has rights and wealth "we" do not have; but "we" can afford to pity her because, after all, Miss Emily never married. The reader sees both the hypocrisy of idol worship and the irony of the idol. Such psychodynamics in Faulkner's work demand that the reader question the South's persistent need to erect monuments to a past that persists in "presentism."

That Miss Emily is lionized by the town is made clear. Words such as "monument," "pillar," "tradition," "idol" "carven torso" and "tableau" all give the impression of her as a superhuman figure who defies the passing of time, like a statue. Two frozen tableaux etch her in permanence. One is a moment captured in "our memory" of Emily standing in a lighted doorway with her father:

> We had long thought of them as a tableau, Miss Emily a slender figure in white in the background, her father a spraddled silhouette in the foreground, his back to her and clutching a horsewhip, the two of them framed by the back-flung front door. So when she got to be thirty and was still single, we were not pleased exactly. (pp. 53–54)

I give this passage to my students to analyze, in the hope they uncover hidden possibilities that the "people in our town" do not. It is a remarkable passage, withholding as much as it reveals. It is like the South itself. I spend sometimes an entire class period on the first sentence. What does the picture of Emily as slender in white and placed in the background tell about the memory of the townsfolk? About the position of daughters in a household? It dawns on students that the word "spraddled" suggests anger, which goes along with father's "clutched" horsewhip—a gesture of hostility and menace and rage. Why horsewhip? Why the anger? Is the anger addressed toward Emily or toward someone else? The phrase "back-flung front door" occupies many minutes of discussion. What story lies there? The exercise in reconstructing the history of this memory serves several functions. It serves to contrast the romantic tableau of a "long thought" memory as over against the other descriptions of Emily in the text; it serves to prod inquiry into incest; it serves as an explanation for Emily's subsequent revenge against the town and her father; it serves to highlight the convolutions of the gender code. Then the second sentence also contains much material to be mined by students. What business is it of the town's to be either pleased or not pleased as to Emily's marital status? Why is the word "pleased" significant in understanding how they view Emily? How does the reader know Emily knows the town's attitude toward her?

A second tableau of Miss Emily occurs when she is older. Although it focuses on Emily, I find it more telling about the character of the townspeople, those ever-spectating "we" folk:

> Now and then we would see her in one of the downstairs windows—she had evidently shut up the top floor of the house—like the carven torso of an idol in a niche, looking or not looking at us, we could never tell which. Thus she passed from generation to generation—dear, inescapable, impervious, tranquil, and perverse. (p. 59)

Here the "we" is clearly represented as peeping toms, noticing even Emily's whereabouts inside her own house, although "we" are oblivious of "our" intrusive snooping. What does it suggest about the townsfolk, I ask my students, that they spend so many generations—not just years—thinking about one person? Would they think so long and hard about a man? How does the phrase "carven torso of an idol in a niche" turn that person into an idea, an idea into a monument? What function do monuments serve in a community's life? What is it about the townsfolk that makes them need to monumentalize a person? What is it about Emily that they idolize? This passage offers opportunity to discuss the problem of "presentism," with its impulse to freeze the present against the realities of the past.

The story is famous, of course, as a ghost story. On one level, students love reading about a woman who killed her lover, kept his corpse, and slept with it for years. The scene at the top of the stairs in the boarded-off bedroom provides a spectacle that draws gasps (of laughing disbelief). But then I ask the students to consider Emily Grierson's motives for the kill and the necromancy. Who was this lover that she couldn't let go? Faulkner's insight into the trauma of the Southern woman is shown once again by the White woman archetype: Emily is Minnie Cooper is Rosa Coldfield (unmarried women, all). But she is also Ellen Coldfield, down to similar physical conditions like the eyes: "two small pieces of coal pressed into a lump of dough" (p. 51)—words similar to the ones describing Ellen (Faulkner, 1936/1987, p. 78). Emily Grierson, this once-slender girl of the town's remembrance, has become a "small, fat woman in black" (p. 51), not unlike Rosa Coldfield. What happens to Southern women? It is my reading that Emily Grierson's only way of avenging her father's control over her younger years was to flaunt a relationship with the least desirable beau in town. He happened to be a Yankee homosexual. What sweet revenge on a town ready to censure her every move if she could not be their idol! What sweet revenge on her father who controlled her by his horsewhip! And Faulkner's telling detail of Emily's iron-gray hair, left as the clue of her necrophilia on the pillow next to the corpse, is just one other way Faulkner has of indicating how hatred has turned her to stone. Why, I ask my students, is Emily so filled with hate? Why was Sutpen? Why Abner Snopes? Why McLendon? "Well then," my students ask, "how can Faulkner have won the Nobel Prize for literature if so many of his characters are so hateful?"

If I can push beyond the naiveté of the question, I can supply some answers toward which this chapter has been heading. Tonia, my student, can be helpful here, in her observation that the watchers are the most hateful, not the actors. Watchers are jealous of wealth and position, "hell bent on causing destruction," she remarked in an exam. I add that the actors (dispossessed White men and all White women) come to know the script, for it is the discourse into which they are enslaved. Yet, because they read their lines from the wings, the actors (those for whom the spectators live, those to whom the spectators build monuments) play the audience for fools. This tactic of undermining one's audience had been learned from slaves and was the slaves' response to the slave holders' authority (Pinar, 1991). Faulkner thus turns the table. Emily, Rosa, Minnie, and Ellen—along with Thomas, Abner, McLendon and Quentin—are the White slaves and Faulkner's conspiratorial "we" are the slave holders. By their single vision, their monuments, and their stunted stories, "we" attempt to authorize, literally, a better history for ourselves. Faulkner won the prize for literature, I tell my students, because he saw into the heart of Whiteness and knew "we" had to change.

2

Cold Eyes, Steel Bits, and Metal Ovens: Havens of Hate

And the Lord God brought forth of the ground all manner of trees, fair to behold, and pleasant to eat of: the tree of life also in the midst of paradise: and the tree of knowledge of good and evil.

—Genesis, 2: 9—New American Catholic Edition

The founding fathers … by modern standards were stone racists.

—Tilove, 1998, p. A14

… who wrote the code? Who's forcing us to use it?

—Dunmore, 1996, p. 196

"Quiet as it's kept … " begins Toni Morrison's first novel *The Bluest Eye* (1985), "there were no marigolds in the fall of 1941" (p. 2,069). This opener, like all of Morrison's openers, tells a secret that lies at the throbbing heart of the novel. The narrator knows the secret; the reader can only guess—something about Pecola's baby, magic, and seeds. The mystery is far more subtle and hidden, a truth behind a lie, than anything most readers could imagine.

Morrison, like Faulkner, uses fiction to unpack the fictions of tradition, particularly the selected tradition of the South, particularly the fiction of the pleasant, easygoing plantation. Like Faulkner, on whom she wrote a Master's thesis, Morrison tells stories that contain ghosts as well as people the reader may not wish to meet. The going inside the plots, for both writers, does not make for easy reading, because more—much more—than plot is at stake. The reading-demands these writers make on an audience are such that readers are forced to

24

complicate their assumptions not only about people but about history and memory, knowledge and innocence, good and evil; about themselves. For these two Nobel Laureates, fiction exposes the fictions of the American character, pressing readers to shatter their illusions, to read less straight, possibly even to think the unthought (Britzman, 1998a).

Morrison, more of an iconoclast than Faulkner, is therefore more difficult to read and to teach. It is my intention to address the difficulties I have had grappling with her material and to argue for the necessity of teaching her work. The question, she implies, should not be "What knowledge is of most worth?" but "What ignorance has caused most harm?" "Ignore" and "ignorant" share the same bed. To be ignorant is to lack knowledge or to know little or nothing about a subject. To ignore is more deliberate; it is to refrain, overlook, slight, disregard, or neglect (Webster, 1993). Morrison (1992) has carved out the territory of ignorance as her new frontier of narrative inquiry. The canon of American literature, she insists, has ignored the language and soul of African-Americans, thereby rendering centuries of American readers ignorant of Black truth. Rather, African presence in the canon has been constructed oppositionally to Euro-American presence and written with the master's metaphors inside the master's language. In no way, she shows, does the master's White canon reflect the life and soul of Black experience. Morrison's project is to tell what has been "kept quiet" so as to redress the willful ignorance of American letters. Clearly, such a project makes fiction not only worthy of being taught and studied but, as Bill Pinar (1998) urges, of being understood on the grounds of its own presentation—especially because the South's history has been composed of fantasies.

And so, this chapter is an attempt to pick up where Faulkner left off in the deconstruction of the American South. Faulkner shares with Morrison the use of myth and metaphor in telling the South's story. But Faulkner is a modernist in his use of the monomyth of the father; his interest is in revealing the psychodynamics of patriarchal possession and lust as these have enslaved White women, Black men and women), and unlanded, poor White men. His work does much to raise questions about what goes on behind the big front door of the big white house. Still, interest in such themes as sin and redemption and the impossibility of escape from guilt by the father gives Faulkner's work the stamp of Freudian modernism.

A very different approach is taken by Toni Morrison. Her interest in making visible the lives of Black people is, as well, the impulse for a different kind of writing altogether, one that she says calls for "non polite criticism" (Morrison, 1992). Hers is not a dialogic imagination (Bakhtin, 1981). She does not measure her work as the polar opposite of, nor in dialogue with, White work. Polarities, even dialogic ones, come out of what she calls (1992) the "slaveholders' ideology," which she describes as the "tree" upon which hangs "such fruit (as) a black population forced to serve as freedom's polar opposite" (p. 64). Accordingly, bipolar opposites operate to make all "difference" merely oppositional in nature (Maher & Tetreault, 1997). Rather, for Morrison, "difference" is a language responsibility: Language releases ontology. She writes to "unhobble" (1992, p. 13) Blacks from the demands of a racially inflected language, one consequence of which has been to rob African-Americans of their original names. The names of her characters are not Dick, Jane, or Sally; but Shadrack, Soaphead Church, or Dearly Beloved (shortened to Beloved because there was not enough rutting time to carve Dearly on the tombstone). These names had so much meaning that Pilate, in *Song of Solomon* (1987a), put hers in a little box in her ear. "When you know your name, you should hang on to it, for unless it is noted down and remembered, it will die when you do," realizes Milkman (p. 329). In that book, *Song of Solomon*, the epitaph reads "The fathers may soar/And the children may know their names" (p. 1). No, Morrison's way of putting together words and phrases and sounds uttered by the throat and tongue—her incredible, magical prose—makes Black presence (that which has not been named in the American canon) audible. In its own terms.

"Quiet as it's kept." The words puzzle. To keep "it" quiet is not the same as keeping quiet; the latter is all still, the former hovers—a secret that waits in the wings. There is something going on below the surface that lies between, within, beside, or about two opposites. I have observed that while Morrison structures her stories around two places or two houses, two genders, two types, or two races attention is drawn to this "something"—a hovering absence that is its own, completely different, third, "quiet" thing—neither entirely benign nor entirely malignant. Its presence is prepositional, a matter of prepositions like "about" or "between," which positions her intention. Her fiction refuses constructions of the easy category called *White Identity* as opposite from the label *Black Identity* because of the inferences of inferiority and the ranking of differences (Morrison, 1992). The third thing I refer to is my understanding of the suppressed, Black identity Morrison urges up from the depths of oppositionalism, long kept as servant inside the master discourse. To apprehend this new identity demands from us a reading that brings up from the depths of language itself a new understanding for White readers, as well as for Black. Morrison requires us to read in a new key, based partly on her statement in an interview that she seeks to "fret the cliché" (in Taylor-Guthrie, 1994, p. 122), which I take to mean that she upsets the lazy reader's easy reach for oppositional thinking, with such labels as "inferior" and such categories as "good versus evil." Patricia Storace (1998) in a review of Morrison's *Paradise*, makes a similar point:

> The new relationship Morrison is attempting to create with the reader is an invitation, too, to search for a new kind of critical language, one capable of describing the way a reader reads a book while simultaneously reading herself. (p. 69)

Dare I take the plunge? Dare I read myself?

One way I dare is to offer the instances of Morrison's metaphor of the hovering absence, quietly kept beneath the surface story. Derrida (1973) equates absence with difference or alterity, a definition I find fitting for what I am exploring here. I first noticed this device when teaching *Song of Solomon*, excerpted in our American literature text. Frankly, I did not know what to make of the scene of an insurance agent about to jump off a roof while referring to his jump as a flight on his own wings. What stood out to me was the multiples of negatives in the prose description of the scene: There was Not Doctor Street, No Mercy Hospital, Dead Letter Office; phrases like "not on its steps," "not the fact"; images of red velvet rose petals that would be rejected, a poorly dressed singer, and an old quilt used for a winter coat. The litany of negatives seemed to set a tone appropriate for a man about to commit suicide. And yet, the scene was festive. There were blue wings on the man, red velvet rose petals on the snow, a singer, a song, and a crowd. Indeed, the man, Mr. Robert Smith, did jump and did die, but that was not the point of the scene. The point seemed to lie within the litany of negatives, which canceled out the trauma of suicide to make space for celebration. But what was to celebrate, I wondered?

I save Morrison's celebrations for a later chapter.

This chapter concerns a rock-solid foundation of racial hatred with its prohibition against new knowledge. This chapter concerns that which simmers beneath the calm surface of the American story, a racial subtext that assumes that the American character is White; that the Black presence must be politely, quietly (sometimes violently) repressed (sometimes lynched); that there is no substance to Black presence. This subtext is a cauldron that Morrison figures as a throbbing center, a heartbeat that will not be stopped, that has the capacity for danger or grace or both. It is a subtext that recurs as I write today, in nice, quiet towns like Jasper, Texas, where a Black man was dragged to death by three Klanners. As the newspaper article put it, "three suspected White supremacists reveal a sinister undercurrent beneath the harmonious surface" (Graczyk, 1998, p. A-26).

Morrison's recurring metaphor of a hovering absence seems to serve the function of what Carl Jung called *the collective unconscious*, the contents of which, he warned, could and would erupt if not properly attended (i.e., if repressed). Of this phenomenon, Walter Brenneman (1978) wrote:

> The unconscious is the cosmic ocean ... which contains all psychological possibilities.... In the depths of the unconscious lies the collective realm. Its quality is like the underwater world of the sea. (p. 15)

Morrison's startling use of the hovering absence metaphor with its sinister undercurrent can be found, for another instance, in *Sula* (1987b), when two girls, Nell and Sula, are enjoying an afternoon of mindless, bored play by the lake. Sula invites the child Chicken Little to join them and grasps the arms of the child, swinging him out and out. Suddenly, the grip is loosened, and the child is flung, astonishingly, into the center of the lake: "The water darkened and closed quickly over the place where Chicken Little sank.... The water was so peaceful now. There was nothing but the baking sun and something newly missing" (p. 61). When, years later, Sula (who represents an adventuring type) returns to the community to visit Nell (who represents a staying type), the earlier water moment is recalled: "The closed place in the water spread before them" (p. 101). Between two opposite women a hovering absent-presence of a ghost appears. I read this as Morrison's metaphor of the enduring Black contents of the American unconscious that, like a fresh heart, beats in our midst.

But hearing the heartbeat of the Black self is impossible when the master discourse is White. That is one of Morrison's points. Her prose awakens the tin ear. Because so much of her writing depends on sounds, she seeks to strike chords that even a deafened ear cannot ignore. Although readers may refuse to listen to the racial nuances in the master discourse, we cannot ignore the linguistic rhythms of a people whose histories and memories have been molded by slavery. This chapter discusses how Morrison deconstructs the construction "race" in three prominent American discourses: the discourse of the White textbook in *The Bluest Eye*, the discourse of slavery in *Beloved* (1988), and finally, the discourse of Black officialdom in *Paradise* (1998b). In all of these ideologies, Morrison explores the unsaid of the subtexts.

The Bluest Eye is included in its entirety in the first edition of *The Norton Anthology of Literature by Women* (1985), a text used in hundreds of classrooms. I have taught this first Morrison novel in my Women and Literature class, each teaching bringing me new insights and different strategies. Much class discussion revolves around the frame text of the novel, the Dick and Jane primer. How well I remember as a child reading in the 1940s (the time period of the novel) that very primer, with its static depiction of the idealized, perfect, happy, clean, White, American family. I recall stirrings of envy: My family wasn't happy (my mother was in Bloomingdale's, a mental hospital). But my house was clean, thanks to my father's Black live-in maids who, I cringe to recall, wore white uniforms. It didn't matter to me that Jane had blue eyes and blond hair; I knew my black curls were pretty and I was the favorite child of my father. Anyway, Wonder Woman, with her flowing dark hair, provided me with my beauty model. Like the primer, I had a bow-wow and a meow-meow, a brother who played with me, friends, and good games. My only real memory of the text's impression on me was that I was in the Brownie (or mediocre) reading group, while my best friend Linda sat in her reading circle (superior to and separated from, mine—the name of which I seem to have forgotten). In other words, the Dick and Jane text mirrored my life adequately enough and I learned to read. What I did not learn to read was the falseness of that primer's constructions. So many students then and now have had their imaginations fed by similar textbook pablum. Textbook "writing" only serves to keep imagination thin.

Morrison's choice of that primer is a starting point for many class questions: What do textbooks really teach? What do we remember about those textbooks? What is the difference between a textbook and a story or novel? What differences might there be in simple aesthetics like page quality, size of book, size of print? What is the function of a textbook as opposed to a novel or story? And what is the difference in Morrison's novel between the story she is telling and the primer frame text? These considerations lead the class discussion into various pedagogical issues, not the least of which is the questioning of a culture brought up on textbooks. Who writes these texts and for what reason?, we ask. Every fall, it seems another school district publishes a list of banned books, we note. Although my students profess sublime disgust with the conservative views of school board censorship listings, I harbor suspicion that many would wish to nominate Morrison's work to the list. I tell my students this, knowing that they are secretly disgusted by what is "quiet as it's kept" (not just the rape of Pecola by her father). Why, indeed, read disgusting events? Is that what we are reading, only that? I ask.

These rhetorical questions invite response. Morrison is a novelist, not a textbook writer, as one can determine by four distinguishing qualities. First, she refuses to allow readers to be tourists in textbook land. Were that the case, her work would indulge the thin imagination by allowing easy identification with character and scene. She would be allowing a reader to become what Samuel Beckett (1931) called "a creature of habit" who "turns aside from the object that cannot be made to correspond with one or another of his intellectual prejudices" (p. 11). Beckett described habit as "the ballast that chains the dog to his vomit" (p. 9). Following this line of description, textbooks are vomit and students are regurgitators. What, I ask, does this make teachers?

Second, precisely because Morrison's work is not a textbook, its function is not to guide but to shock, not to explain but to question, not—as Morrison (1984) herself put it—to offer recipes but to ask questions. The function of storytelling is as radically different from textbook learning as verticals are to horizontals. The story, if it is a real story, takes us into a vertical dimension of ourselves where perhaps we have not journeyed before. It is alien, often terrifying; different, often embarrassing; strange, often unbelievable. Story provides a place to react violently or sublimely, for it touches another world. To journey to another storied world necessarily involves letting preformed ego habits die a bit in the head. Indeed, Morrison takes us where we might not wish to go; when we leave our safe shores, she rocks our boat. The venture—like good teaching—is dangerous.

Third, Morrison's fiction is a work of art, not a textbook, because it is visionary. Carl Jung (1930/1950) distinguished between two types of artists, the psychological artist who works with reality and the visionary artist who writes from the hinterland, "the night-side of life" (p. 95). For Morrison, however, her vision is not without social psychology; clearly, her work addresses real issues through the insertions of historical, sometimes little-known facts of America's raced past. She captures the best of what Ivor Goodson (1998) insists is essential to narrative: storytelling the self from a political and social perspective. Her "magical realism" is a not witchery, but a trait of writing that is as profound and abstruse as the self she urges up from the words she writes. Metaphors of the hovering absence, reading-shocks of encounter, the presence of speaking ghosts, the poetries of prose: All create spaces for a new vision, "the art of seeing outside ourselves, or seeing the "absence" in our work" (Hwu, 1998, p. 24). This manifold quality of Morrison's writing that rends the veil of mere reality opens the text to new visionary possibilities.

Fourth, Morrison does what the textbook does not: theory work. If, as Wen-Song Hwu asserts, pedagogy's function is to invent the conditions for invention, Morrison is as much a pedagogue as she is a Nobel Laureate. Her fiction helps us see and envision not only possibilities for more authentic selves but actualities of social practices that make us cruel (Rorty, 1989). Her work responds to Frederic Jameson's (1981) dictum to "always historicize." In interviews, articles, speeches, and essays, she articulates the function of fiction as a means of confronting the absence of the Black presence in American literature. She writes, "There seems to be a more or less tacit agreement among literary scholars that, because American literature has been clearly the preserve of White male views, genius, and power, those views, genius, and power are without relationship to and removed from the overwhelming presence of Black people in the United States" (1992, p. 5). Quiet as it's kept. The subtitle of her essay, "Whiteness and the Literary Imagination," speaks to my Whiteness and the ways in which this privilege of my skin has made me willfully innocent of racial injustice. As Valerian, the White colonist in *Tar Baby* (1987c) reflects: "And all he could say was that he did not know. He was guilty, therefore, of innocence. Was there anything so loathsome as a willfully innocent man?" (Morrison, p. 243).

In theorizing about the absence of Blackness, Morrison not only responds to the canon's "master" romance—White themes like The Fall From Innocence or The New Adam in the New World—but she situates Black stereotypes as part of the "master" plot. This plot, she insists, has been unacknowledged: quiet as it's kept. Her fiction not only recovers Blackness in the literary imagination (her word for this is "rememory") but critiques attitudes, Black or White, that perpetuate racism by hiding "class conflict, rage, and impotence in figurations of race" (1992, p. 64). At the end of the 20th century, one and a half centuries after slavery, racism is as alive as ever. My morning paper's headline reads: "President's adviser on race urges aggressive U.S. action" (Ross, 1998, June 13, p. A-1). What is sought, the article explains, is a visionary effort to correct the "poverty and disadvantage" that still "holds minorities back." How pleasantly phrased is that ill. How hardly bothersome. Such a "visionary effort" would do well to read Toni Morrison.

And so, Morrison writes against the Black-White opposition while yet bringing forth from an absence a third thing. Her imagination is what I will call *intersubtextual*. *The Bluest Eye* begins her project. The story is narrated by a very wise child, Claudia, whose wisdom reminds me of Camus's (1955) Sisyphus in hell. Sisyphus, recall, is condemned forever to roll a stone up a hill. A moment of absolute clarity is reached, Camus imagines, when Sisyphus at the summit sees the boulder roll down before him. Just then, he knows the full circle of his torment. This knowledge makes Sisyphus happy in an absurd sense. He lives with no delusions because he knows the limits of his existence. He achieves definition. Claudia makes such a recognition: "Being a minority in both caste and class, we moved about anyway on the hem of life" (1985, p. 2,075). The little word "anyway" suggests Claudia's knowledge of her peripheral existence, a knowledge that enables her to live "anyway"—in spite of being inside a closed universe. She will not be beaten down. Like a Camus existential hero, Claudia lives "without appeal" (Camus, 1955, p. 39).

The aridity of Claudia's world, birthing no marigolds in spring, is, nevertheless, a sort of desert paradise for her. Unlike Pecola, obsessed with the desire for blue eyes, Claudia feels rage at the dominant culture's intersubtextual concept of beauty. It is this concept that makes Shirley Temple an icon—but not for Claudia, child iconoclast. Being given a Shirley Temple doll at Christmas, she furiously rips it apart, smashing it to see "what it was that all the world said was lovable. Break off the tiny fingers, bend the flat feet, loosen the hair, twist the head around, and the thing made one sound—a sound ... like the bleat of a dying lamb.... Remove the cold and stupid eyeball, it would bleat still" (p. 2,077). At the center of this beauty icon, Claudia discovers "the secret of the sound. A mere metal roundness" (p. 2,077). So, too, does the reader see into the secret of such "beauty": Without real sound—resonance, voice—there is no real beauty. Visible externals like blond hair, blue eyes, and pink skin are but the sheerest cover for the gauze, starch, and rust within. Claudia here is like the African-American theorist Beverly Gordon (1993), who insists on turning inside out the notion of "voice" so as to "other" the dominant culture's set of ideals.

Morrison shows that such a perniciously dominant notion of beauty makes sad Black children like Pecola invisible not only to others but, more tragically, to themselves. Pecola and her family are the polar opposite of Claudia and her family. Between these poles lies the quiet that is kept: Pecola's invisibility, over which is layered multiple texts of the dominant discourse. Pecola is so buried beneath these texts that she cannot see herself in the Dick and Jane primer any more than she can see herself in the movies. She does not live life, she lives an imitation of life, the title of the 1934 movie Morrison mentions (p. 2,103). Perhaps the key scene in which the reader sees Pecola's invisibility is Morrison's literal rewriting of a Eudora Welty text, only with a sad Black child instead of a happy White child. These intersubtexts are, I believe, Morrison's way of demonstrating the devastating effect on selfhood such white-outs of Blackness can be.

Welty's (1979b) story "The Little Store" gives an epical sense of the lyrical life of its heroine. The unnamed White child loves to go to the neighborhood store because every step of her journey is adventure. The sidewalk has "islands" of shade; she "serpentines" her princess bike in and out of the sun; and finally she arrives at her destination, which seems like "total obscurity inside," with its mysterious barrels, sacks, and smells. Welty structures her descriptions to give the impression that, in leaving home, this happy White child is venturing into the realm of the unknown, even though she knows the sidewalk to the store "as well as I knew my own skin." That her skin is White makes all the difference to the owner, who treats her gingerly, like a princess. When her errand is completed, the story ends with a ritual weighing on the standing scales: "Mr. Sessions, whose hands were gentle and smelled of carbolic, would lift you up and set your feet on the platform, hold your loaf of bread for you, and taking his time while you stood still for him, he would make certain of what you weighed the last time, so you could subtract and announce how much you'd gained" (p. 331). Even the shift in perspective from "I" to "you" universalizes the child's experience, as if all readers are as secure as the narrator.

I teach this story, one text next to another, when I get to the companion scene in *The Bluest Eye* of Pecola at her neighborhood store. The difference is all. With the Welty story, we note how the child delights in her journey but also learns of her own "weight" or worth by completing her task. The strange smells and obscure darkness of the store world offer her the opportunity to get lost among the shelves, to select a treat with the nickel left over, and to be singled out with affection by the store owner. Her experience is even educational, precisely because not only is she validated in personhood but she is able to get lost, briefly. Lostness, Alan Block (1998) tells us, provides opportunity to learn possibility and to depart perpetually. Especially when the world is kind. Especially when the home one returns to is loving.

Pecola's experience at Mr. Yacobowski's store is a world apart. This experience hardens her already-formed perception of herself as Black and ugly. At every step of her journey there and back she is made to intuit her lack of physical beauty, what Morrison calls the "most pernicious and destructive idea in the Western world" (in Otten, 1989). She walks (does not serpentine), feeling the "painful press of the coins against her foot" (p. 2,092). The images that she sees are her "possessions" (p. 2,093) because they are other people's discards—weeds, dandelions. The walkway is cracked and uneven and makes her stumble; nevertheless, she justifies the condition of the sidewalk as better for skating than new sidewalks—although she has no skates. She is the possessor of her world made delapidated by racism: "She owned the crack that made her stumble; she owned the clumps of dandelions" (p. 2,093).

Inside the store, ready to make a candy purchase, Pecola eyes the owner. Morrison's description makes him seem like a warden of the Panopticon, whose all-seeing distaste at the child's Black presence "promotes incarceration by visibility" (Block, 1998, p. 327). To his blue eyes she is nothing: "Somewhere between retina and object, between vision and view, his eyes draw back, hesitate, and hover. At some fixed point in time and space he senses that he need not waste the effort of a glance. He does not see her, because for him there is nothing to see" (p. 2,093). The rest of the encounter describes in heartbreaking detail the shame the little Black girl is made to feel—not anger, just shame. Were she to be insulted, angry, or enraged, she could acquire Claudia's sense of being. But all this child can do to change her entrapment by his blue eyes is to wish for her own pair of blue eyes—those of the Mary Jane blue eyes on the picture of her candy wrapper. The wrapper is text for the child, teaching her that blue is beauty, is ownership, is acceptance, is worthy of being seen. Pecola eats the candy and, Morrison writes, has nine orgasms.

I teach the Welty and Morrison store scenes together for several reasons. First, it is further evidence of what I refer to as Morrison's intersubtextuality, whereby the subtext of a child's invisibility or absence hovers between the texts of the dominant discourse. Everywhere Pecola turns, she sees what she does not have, what she believes will make her real: the sky-blue eyes of the master race. Even her tormenter, the store owner, has these eyes, which make her feel all the more ugly—a Sartrean object to the Other's subjective look (Samuels & Hudson-Weems, 1990). Second, text-on-text teaching offers opportunity for pointing out the emotional quality of difference. The reader feels the happiness of the Welty White child, the despair of the Morrison Black child. And all because of skin color. There is real pathos here. The images are fraught with what Morrison describes as a "nimbus of emotion" (1995, p. 98). Analysis of this nimbus can offer what Paula Salvio (1998) calls "empathetic identification," in this case with Pecola's "whited out" emotional life. Third, because the store scene is one students might remember and relate to from their own childhoods, we can discuss the tangible, concrete manifestations of White privilege, on the one hand, and racism, on the other. By itemizing the various texts and symbols of the two worlds, Black and White, we can begin analysis of the cultural, social, and ethnic identities of those worlds.

As we see from the conclusion of *The Bluest Eye*, Pecola not only is disappeared from the American canon, she disappears from herself. Thinking she has blue eyes—the bluest eyes, prettier-than-the-sky eyes, storybook eyes—Pecola's self at the end of the novel is absorbed into the texts that have forged her imagination. I think Morrison's point, made in subsequent novels with equally wrenching effect, is that when the dominant culture conspires to ignore one's presence, one loses one's self. This is a literal matter of literacies: cultural objects, artifacts, texts, and subtexts.

If *The Bluest Eye* is about one invisible African-American child, *Beloved* is about "sixty million and more" (Morrison, 1988, n.p.), whose histories during slavery and Reconstruction have been remembered wrongly in the dominant discourse. "About" is the functional word. "About" is that which circles around these life histories, something at the center "quiet as it's kept": a secret that Morrison exposes. As she said in an interview, "My job becomes how to rip that veil drawn over proceedings too terrible to relate" (1995, p. 91). She rips the veil by turning facts into truths: "I consider that my single gravest responsibility ... is not to lie" (1995, p. 93). Traditionally, history has selected its facts by repressing memory texts; history has lied; history has not told the whole story. Even classic narratives of slaves, written in the master's language, are lies because they repress the psychic truths, the deep stories that only the mother tongue can speak (Mobley, 1993). Although history and memory have usually been considered separate categories—memory being the lesser of the two because not "objective"—Morrison disrupts these nice distinctions. The claim that "fact" is "truth" and "truth" is "objectivity" is history's narrow way of proceeding, for there are other truths, like memories (Morris, in press). Calling her project the work of rememory (a renaming of Zora Neale Hurston's phrase "memories within"), Morrison digs her narrative down into the subsoil, the under structure, the buried contents of the African-American psyche.

I found myself reading *Beloved* in disbelief, even anger. Anger, mind you, at Morrison for telling me things I could not believe, in metaphors I could not understand. Morrison's usual startling, opening sentence was the beginning of a rocky journey for me. That sentence reads: "124 was spiteful" (p. 3). It is followed by another startle: "Full of baby's venom." Then a third: "The women in the house knew it and so did the children." From the beginning I was an outsider looking in. I felt resentment toward the author for keeping me at bay. Reading a bit further, I then went back to the beginning, trying to understand how a house could be spiteful. My resistance hardened the more I read. Although I found sentences of lyricism and took delight in the concrete details of the lives I was reading, I was not used to haunted house stories being told the way Morrison was telling. It seemed everyone in the novel understood the power of ancestors as the foundation of a house (of the self), but me. As I read further, my disbelief and unease turned into denial, then anger. Morrison must be fabricating bits of history. Impossible, I said to myself, reading along; impossible that even freed slaves were treated so. No. Not.

I share this experience because I think I was reading Morrison the way she wants to be read. As she said, "My beginnings as a novelist were very much focused on creating this discomfort and unease in order to insist that the reader rely on another body of knowledge" (1984, p. 387). The other body, of course, is the Black body of knowledge that has always been here, but buried: the story within the story. My annoyance was suspended somewhat as I became caught up inside the narrative; I found myself reading with my ear. I began to listen, as one of the characters put it, "for the holes" (p. 92). The text was looping around and about two sites, Sweet Home Farm in Kentucky, and 124 Bluestone Road in Delaware, circa 1874. Between these two, in the loophole, lay things unsaid in mainstream historical texts: unspeakable thoughts, unnamed acts, unmentioned horrors, unspoken memories. The looping (present time going back, past time coming forward) formed a desolate center into which what had been whispered out of existence by White histories now was being told, history heard as a new, double-voiced text (Davies, 1994).

Indeed, Morrison questions all assumptions of Whiteness, with all privileges and norms securely fastened (McIntosh, 1992). By looping the text around and about the secret center of slavery, Morrison forces the White reader not just to shift gears emotionally but to undergo a sort of intellectual death. The process, for me, was similar to Kübler-Ross's (1969) five stages of coping with physical death, moving from denial and anger through bargaining and grieving to acceptance. The writing of this chapter is the result of that movement, the result both of my intellectual acceptance of a new harsh truth and of the emotional impact of Morrison's understated language. As she said, "I really want this emotional response, and I also want an intellectual response to the complex ideas there. My job is to do both at the same time, that's what a real story is" (in Taylor-Guthrie, 1994, p. 97).

It is at the Sweet Home site in the novel that the stories of slave life are revealed. How ironic that my Bounty paper towel is imprinted with a replica of homey Americana such as one might find in cross stitch designs: In the center is a flower basket, on either side a heart; underneath is the phrase "Home Sweet Home." Bordering the center is a garland of flowers, cascading down either side. Another set of Bounty towels has the same motif phrased differently: "Home is Where the Heart is." This is the sort of kitsch that Morrison might have had in mind, as she "frets the cliché" of Sweet Home. With her, I fret "bounty" as a double-barreled term, as in "bounty hunter," meaning "one who hunts criminals, wild animals, etc. for the reward or bounty offered for capturing or killing them" (Webster, 1993). However, the narrators of life at Sweet Home, a slave farm, are matter of fact—the way actual slave narratives often were. A striking exception is Harriet Jacobs's (1861/1997) *Incidents in the Life of a Slave Girl*, whose psychologically complex narrative observes, "The degradation, the wrongs, the vices, that grow out of slavery, are more than I can describe. They are greater than you would willingly believe" (p. 51). But at Sweet Home, the slaves hardly notice the racism at first, because the masters seem kindly and the slaves seem grateful. Sethe, for instance, talks of her mistress as "that lady," a Mrs. Garner who, for all her benevolence, nevertheless understands that Black flesh is capital with which to pay off debts and acquire human property. Mr. Garner, too, is benevolent, in his own racist way: "Now at Sweet Home, my niggers is men every one of em. Bought em thataway, raised em thataway. Men every one" (p. 10). Morrison's portrait of these Kentucky Home crackers caricatures the kind of "dysconsciousness" (King, 1991) that I hear from some of my students, when they say things like "Some of my best friends are Black," or, "I have no problem with mixed marriages," or "I don't see color," or "I don't care, so long as they _____." The egregiousness of these attitudes that so unquestionably assume White supremacy-Black invisibility is seen by Mrs. Garner's astonishment at Sethe's desire to have a wedding ceremony. In Mrs. Garner's eyes, slaves don't marry; they couple. They breed in fields. So when Sethe said she wanted a ceremony, not just "me bringing my night bucket into his cabin" (p. 59), Mrs. Garner said no.

White supremacy on Sweet Home farm changes when Schoolmaster arrives. This is the man brought in to keep order when Mr. Garner died. Schoolmaster requires me to listen with a pedagogical ear to his instructions on the slave farm. His role is to teach lessons, as in the ominous phrase "I'm going to teach you a lesson." Educators, beware of the lesson plan. How many times that cliché of "teaching a lesson" is synonymous with punishment! I am reminded of the ploy schoolmasters, even today, use to exercise "discipline" in students by having them write a line a hundred times or write an essay. Writing becomes associated with pain, English classes with torture. Teachers of writing, too, often have a schoolmasterish approach to their "discipline." The female equivalent is the schoolmarm, like a former colleague of mine who actually had rules of etiquette for the classroom written up and distributed to her charges; rules of Do Nots, like do not eat in class, do not chew gum in class, drink only from closed containers, and do not fall asleep in class. Masters and Mistresses of the old school hold the odd belief that learning proceeds with enforcement, that teaching must be authoritarian, and that the learners are to teachers as criminals are to wardens or slaves are to masters.

When Schoolmaster was brought in to Sweet Home, the pace of life changed for Sethe, Paul D., and the others:

> The information they offered he called back talk and developed a variety of corrections (which he recorded in his notebook) to reeducate them.... For years, Paul D. believed schoolteacher broke into children what Garner had raised into men. And it was that that made them run off. Now ... he wondered how much difference there really was between before schoolteacher and after. (p. 220)

The big difference the reader sees between the two White slave masters is the cruelty. When the slaves devised a plan to escape, their capture was costly. Paul D.'s bounty, $900, was only some of the sum Schoolmaster had to pay out to retrieve the others. The cost made him cruel. I couldn't believe, and indeed fought against, what I was reading. The White men under Schoolmaster's orders put on Paul D. a three-spoke collar so he couldn't lie down, and they chained his ankles together. In his mouth they placed a bit. One hundred pages earlier, Morrison had made reference to the bit when Paul D. remembers "the taste of iron" (p. 113); but although the reference at first reading seemed ominous, it was only later at the capture scenes that the full atrocity of punishment registered. Then Paul D., his hands crossed behind him, his neck connected to the axle, is hitched to a buckboard where he is placed eye-to-eye with a rooster named Mister. If story, as James Hillman (1975a) asserts, is a place for images, a reader's imagination is placed on overload in these capture scenes. For I see there an irrational world, a world turned upside down from anything I could dredge up on my own. Paul D., facing the rooster called Mister that could "whup everything in the yard" (p. 72), thinks less about "licking iron" than about the rooster looking at him, seeming to smirk. "Mister was allowed to be and stay what he was. But I wasn't allowed to be and stay what I was … Schoolteacher changed me. I was … less than a chicken sitting in the sun on a tub" (p. 72). Paul D. realizes in that moment that he would never be a Mister (Samuels & Hudson-Weems, 1990).

I need to isolate these images, remove them from their narrative sequence, so as to find their place in life, in history, in myself. I think of my student, a Black man only six years younger than me who spent ten years in Louisiana's Angola prison for a crime he did not commit. I think of the many poems he has written, the many wrenching lines, like these:

> Wretched non-person that I am,
> creator of my own world,
> where pain and shame, those non-speaking things,
> are like old friends to me;
> they keep their counsel and leave me to mine.…
> (Randolph, 1997, p. 45)

or these:

> My cries go unheard, and my tears go unfelt;
> yet I am human if only to myself.
> I plead the bitter hour to pass that clings to me like some great coat.
> I am hurled into a sea where nothing goes right for me.
> (Randolph, 1998, p. 31)

When Decker reads his work aloud, I cannot understand his great sadness, the tears that stop his reading. I watch in dismay and nonunderstanding. Morrison's work helps to nudge understanding along into a deep place where character can develop despite the depersonalizing effects of racism (Harding & Martin, 1994).

But I am not through with the images. Morrison does not let us off easy. We have to travel to Alfred, Georgia, where the fugitive slaves, once again escaped, are once again captured and forced onto a chain gang. Where prisoners are put in boxes underground, like coffins five feet deep, five feet wide. Where Paul D.'s hands are so atrophied from the bracelets "they quit taking directions" (p. 107), not even to hold his penis to urinate, not even to scoop beans into his mouth. Where forty-six Black men wake to rifle shots fired by three White men. Where breakfast could be foreskin. Where they sing "love songs to Mr. Death" and want to kill "the flirt whom folks called Life for leading them on" (p. 109). And when night comes or the rain comes, the forty-six Black men wait in mud and slime and cottonmouths. Until they escape.

Morrison's accounts of these events circle back on Sethe's attempted escape from Sweet Home and her punishment that the men called "sport" when she was captured. She was pregnant with Beloved when they caught her and took her milk. As in other works, Morrison turns the Mammy image topsy-turvey, showing how the all-nurturing breast (hooks, 1996) is the Black female's only claim to abundance. The milk that pregnant slaves fed other women's children as well as their own—the nurturing, female source of life—is stolen by White men knowing that to steal mother's milk is to take the only worth a Black woman had. In *Song of Solomon* Morrison's character Milkman acquired his nickname by the bizarre ritual his mother Ruth practiced when he was beyond weaning. "He was too young to be dazzled by her nipple, but he was old enough to be bored by the flat taste of mother's milk" (1987a, p. 13). For Ruth, the breast is power, its milk coin: "a cauldron issuing spinning gold" (p. 13). To feed this growing boy from her breast was, like Rumpelstiltskin, to "see golden thread stream from her very own shuttle" (p. 14); it was to give him wealth.

Disgusting? Intolerable? Too much for White eyes to see, for White ears to hear? Morrison overdoes it? Is it all beyond belief? My answer is yes, if belief is what dulls the mind, if the intolerable is unfamiliar, if what disgusts does not appeal to the gustatory sense. Blockheads who refuse to allow unthinkable images or impossible thoughts to seep into the brain pan will have difficulty. I find myself protesting, "But I can't teach this! It is too strong!" Too strong for what, I wonder? For change of heart? For milk sops? I need to rethink what goes on for learning, as opposed to what should be going on inside America's classrooms; teachings, I would hope, not by Schoolmasters. I need to remind myself of the function of the intolerable image, as Niel Micklem (1979) so brilliantly explains. Speaking from an archetypal perspective, which is to say from the underneath of things, Micklem writes on the healing function of that which bends back reflection: "Reflection in these distant regions of psyche is a vital activity of psychic life that immediately concerns the role of imagination" (p. 9). He goes on to say that when the psyche, or image-making function, is removed from the direct gaze of literal representation, when it is bent back or repelled, there is a turn toward a desert wasteland of hidden images. That which is hidden, that from which the "normal" gaze recoils, nevertheless contains its own vitality. The journey away from literal representation, he concludes, is a journey into an energy space that activates imagination.

It seems to me that Morrison's intention is to take us on such a downward journey. She calls her work "literary archeology" (1995): "On the basis of some information and a little bit of guesswork," she explains, "you journey to a site to see what remains were left behind and to reconstruct the world that these remains imply" (p. 92). Indeed, *Beloved* takes us to two sites that situate the slavery past of America and that require an obligatory return if a collective rebirth of any sort is to be envisioned.

The second site is 124 Bluestone Road, Delaware, a house haunted by the ghost of a sacrifice. Lest we forget. The ghost of Beloved returns to her mother Sethe lest the bad dream of the past be forgotten; for Beloved is not just a dead child returned: She is that which links past with present, providing continuity and validation. Beloved is "memory, always situated within the context of rememory" (Rushdy, 1997, p. 140). That this ghost, buried within the other story of Sweet Home farm, appears in the flesh, as it were, suggests Morrison's theme of the past: It must be made to live again, in its re-membered state, lest it be consigned to memory (Harding & Martin, 1994).

What, then, does Beloved want of her mother? Of us? Like many a baby, she throws tantrums, makes unusual demands, clamors for a kiss, upsets the narrative flow. She has, after all, a score to settle: Her mother killed her rather than allow Schoolmaster to capture them again; her mother saved her from a fate worse than death. Her mother did what she did out of true love. But death is not the end, and out of sight is not out of mind. The baby returns as a child to show her scar. The mark is the trace. Although "remembering seemed unwise" (p. 274), the child's mark will not let forgetting live. Beloved's scar of her mother's ax blow to her throat, the killing scar, "a little curved shadow of a smile in the kootchy-kootchy-coo place under her chin" (p. 239), is the mark of an act her mother wants dead. But, part of Beloved's mission in her ghostly return is to not allow forgetting.

The Black over-mark, Morrison shows, is a factor of cultural complexity. Sethe's mother, for example, had been marked by her oppressors as cattle are branded, "a circle and a cross burnt right in the skin" (p. 61). By the mark she would be known by them. But she turned the mark of the White man into the sign of the mother, "the signifier into a fully realized signification" (Harding & Martin, 1994, p. 23). When Sethe's mother was killed beyond recognition it was the mark that revealed her identity to Sethe. Beloved's mark is a similar construction, although hers registers double defiance: Sethe's defiance against the controlling word of Schoolmaster, come to demand her return into slavery; and Beloved's defiance against her mother's repressed memory.

The reappropriation of the mark is the rema(r)king of Black identity. It is that into which memory must flow again (rememory) so as not to forget, so as not to repeat. It is the mark of difference. The ghost and the mark of the ghost are what haunt 124 Bluestone Road. In a chilling scene, Sethe is with her two daughters, sitting on a rock that her mother-in-law had sat on when she was alive. Sethe's mind fills with memories of her mother-in-law. As she sits, the touch of her mother-in-law's fingers at the back of her neck seem almost palpable, almost soothing, until the fingers start choking her so that she cannot breathe. This strange scene is Sethe's unconscious reenactment of guilt at the killing of Beloved. Responding to Sethe's exclamations, Beloved seems to emerge from beyond the looking glass as she soothes her mother's throat, "gathering color darker than Sethe's dark throat, and her fingers were mighty cool" (p. 97). Beloved's touch is like the touches from the other side of memory. The scene forms a kind of Pietà, the mother seated, "yielding up her throat to the kind hands of one of the two kneeling before her" (p. 97). It is after that moment at the throat that Beloved lays claim to her mother and tries, psychically, to eat her up. The reader sees the baby's ravenous hunger is for that which she had been denied by her infanticide: mother's milk.

How can a ghost be hungry? Why such hunger? Why a book with a ghost as a living, breathing presence? As David Miller (1989) observes in *Hells and Holy Ghosts*, a ghost's function in theology has traditionally been holy, as in the spirit that moves between the Father and the Son. Miller, thinking in part of Morrison's work, remarks that to give up the ghost, forget its presence, would cost "peril to society and the individual soul" (p. 181). Surely, Beloved's hunger to be seen, to be heard, to be fed and petted and "paid" attention to is her way (Morrison's way) of demanding the past be valued. For if all trace be gone, all relics lost, all stories forgotten, all ghosts buried, there might just be all hell to pay.

In an essay published shortly after the publication of *Beloved*, Morrison (1989) commented on the peculiar quality of Black language—its ghostliness, if you will. Black language, she said, is "fraught." It has holes, spaces, and gaps for the reader or listener to enter into the act of communication. As such, Black language holds no authority by itself, but only in the web it creates with the reader-listener. Agreeing with what Henry Louis Gates, Jr. (1988) called "signification," Morrison saw that the soul-saving function of Black language is to obscure apparent meaning, that which is found to exist within the larger White discourse. The toxic effect of the master discourse can thus be laughed away by communal parody, the African-American practice of exchanging words of slander, vexation, and insult. Tricking, such as that found in orality or jazz, allows Black language to partake freely of paradox, contradiction, and multiple perspectives. It can be seditious, rebellious, outrageous, nonsensical, disruptive; it can be anything *but* literal. "The worst of all possible things that could happen," Morrison said in an interview, "would be to lose [black] language" (in Gates & Appiah, 1993, p. 373).

Morrison's point in *Paradise*, I believe, is that the focal community there is a hell on earth precisely because the citizens of Ruby pay no attention to the spirit of the ancestors, located in Black language. *Paradise* is based on an obscure chapter of 19th-century American history, in which former slaves emigrated west from the South, lured by such ads as "Come Prepared or Not at all" (Gray, 1998). The way the settlers of this novel came "prepared" was to etch a slogan onto the side of a metal oven (capitalized as the Oven) placed in the center of town: Beware the Furrow of His Brow. The community, thus, governed itself by the Word: part Bible, part Constitution, the anchor of belief and power. Because the founding fathers of this Black microcosm root out their mother tongue, they forge a community of officialdom that merely imitates the dominant culture from which they seek refuge. Ironically, the Black founders enslave the soul of Black folk who live there.

Paradise, then, is about the worst of all possible things. The literalism that lies at the center of this community is Morrison's commentary on what ideology does to imagination and behavior. Patricia Storace (1998) observed that the novel can be read as an allegory about the founding of a nation (the 8-Rock pilgrims parallel the Plymouth Rock pilgrims) with such noble values as hard work, morality, law, and order. Perhaps the novel is Morrison's warning about constrictions to the American national character, Black and White, when institutions (church, family, school, state) carve a single ordering vision for people. And it is language, she shows, that becomes the worst of all possible things when it is used to sanction ignorance, preserve privilege, and lose ambiguity.

There are, as in her other works, two sites where the action takes place: the town Ruby and, on the outskirts, a convent. The two are opposite in every way: Ruby is patriarchal, the convent is matriarchal; Ruby is law-based; the convent is emotion-based; Ruby invents documentation from the Bible to justify its existence, the convent is sacrilegious; Ruby is intolerant of difference, the convent is a haven for the oppressed. And so on. Ruby is politically right, the convent is politically left. I believe it is Morrison's intention to show these two sites as alternative lifestyles: one way destined to kill life and repeat the errors of history; the other opening the life force out to its fluid connection with humanity (but destined to be killed because it is powerless and female). That one way is steeped in Western patriarchal values and the other is not is no accident either. This latest work by Morrison challenges Western-Eurocentric culture to complexify its discourses and critique its means of validation.

The way Morrison issues her challenge is inside her writing style itself. It is not so much what she writes as how she writes that the reader hears the point. When at the site of the patriarchy, she employs White writing; when at the convent, the sentences are like the Morrison sentences we are used to from her other works—sentences that are as fluid as speaking or dreaming: Black language. She implies in these two very different discourses that no matter if the patriarchy be Black or White, its domination and exclusiveness are matters of language.

For example, the style Morrison employs when describing the doings at Ruby is folksy in the manner of Thornton Wilder's (1985) *Our Town*. One feels the smug comfort of earlier American times when town life was uncomplicated by ethnic or racial difference—pure. The innocence of the inhabitants makes their imaginations thin. All is all it is; nothing hovers: There is no "playing in the dark" because of the categorical nature of belief. In other words, the subtext of Black Ruby is White:

> As Deek drove north on Central, it and the side streets seemed to him as satisfactory as ever. Quiet white and yellow houses full of industry; and in them were elegant black women at useful tasks; orderly cupboards minus surfeit or miserliness; linen laundered and ironed to perfection; good meat seasoned and ready for roasting. It was a view he would be damned if K.D. or the idleness of the young would disturb. (p. 111)

The character Deek is fully satisfied. The insults of his people's enslaved past have been completely rubbed out of his mind. He is in absolute possession of himself and his town. He is the new Adam in his newfound paradise. For these reasons, Deek is dangerous.

Another White subtext that I hear Morrison echo is Shirley Jackson's (1948/1988) "The Lottery." Jackson's point, like Morrison's, is that when rituals lose their archetypal significance, when their actions become rote instead of rite, then rituals revert to violence. Rituals, like myths, cannot be deliberately forged; the objects that endow rituals with meaning cannot be sanitized or flattened. As Morrison (1974) said, "To deliberately create a myth is a contradiction in terms" (p. 88). In "The Lottery" Jackson shows how a ritual of necessary sacrifice, once suffered to restore cosmic balance and harmony, becomes an excuse for bloodletting when the "box" is desacrilized:

> There was a story that the present box had been made with some pieces of the box that had preceded it, the one that had been constructed when the first people settled down to make a village here. Every year, after the lottery, Mr. Summers began talking again about a new box, but every year the subject was allowed to fade off without anything's being done. The black box grew shabbier each year; by now it was no longer completely black but splintered badly along one side to show the original wood color, and in some places faded or stained. (p. 464)

This story, a favorite in American classrooms, is a study of juxtapositions. On the one hand is the smalltown atmosphere filled with Norman Rockwell-types. The names are of English stock: Adams, Anderson, Bentham, Graves, Hutchinson, Summers. The womenfolk gossip and do the cooking; the menfolk run the businesses and are civic minded. The country is young, the season is young, and the ritual of a stoning sacrifice, although old, has been modernized. It, too, is young. Jackson shows how easily a community can slip into scapegoating.

The parallel to Jackson's box is Morrison's Oven. Like the box, the Oven is the object once endowed with purpose and significance. It once represented the founding of Ruby, the story of the town's history. However, because the story of the past is not storied but turned into an icon, it becomes a static symbol. Because it does not connect with Black ancestry, it does not speak the mother tongue. Morrison draws particular attention to this point in the first descriptions of the Oven as having an "iron" lip (p. 6). With overtones of slavery—"iron" in the mouth—one would think the Oven would "speak" against enslavement. Instead, the mouth of the Oven, with its iron lip, speaks a controlling story, with its narrow path of Biblical, White-man righteousness:

> And they have never forgotten the message or the specifics of any story, especially the controlling one told to them by their grandfather—the man who put the words in the Oven's black mouth. A story that explained why neither the founder of Haven nor their descendants could tolerate anybody but themselves. (p. 13)

The controlling story in the Oven's mouth is a threat, a selected piece of history. As such, the Oven represents the worst of history when memory is forgotten—in this case the memory of the real past of slavery. Whereas once the Oven was like a hearth around which stories were told and meals cooked, eventually its power deadens when its symbolism decays. It no longer speaks for the community; it speaks only for some in the community, the 8-rock men and their male descendants who insist on the "uncorruptible worthiness" (p. 194) of purity.

As in the Jackson story, a failure of communal spirit parallels the failure of the community symbol to be a vessel of value.

> The Oven that had witnessed the baptized entering sanctified life was now reduced to watching the lazy young.... The oven whose every brick had heard live chords praising His name was now subject to radio music, record music—music already dead when it filtered through a black wire trailing from Anna's store to the Oven like a snake. (p. 111)

Eventually, a clenched fist painted on the side of the Oven indicates the degree to which the young of the town had become disenchanted. No one confessed to the "ugly-up," so the situation worsened when the slogan "Beware the Furrow of His Brow" became "Be the Furrow of His Brow," a phrase "that drove them crazy" (p. 217).

Both Jackson's story and Morrison's novel indicate that when the supporting myths and rituals of a culture are denigrated or forgotten, scapegoating occurs. In "The Lottery," an ancient, meaningful blood sacrifice is turned into a stoning. In *Paradise* a group of men that thinks itself righteous turns against its neighbor, killing a group of women, believing that the convent is really a coven. These acts are crazy. I think Morrison is saying four things here. First, she is making a feminist point about female symbols. In both shape and function, an oven is female symbolically. Its roundness, like a womb, is a container for precious, life-giving contents. Its function, to cook or bake, is nurturing and sustaining. When, she implies, that which traditionally symbolizes the female is usurped by males, a basic order is disturbed. Second, she is making an aesthetic point about language. When words become hardened and values become institutions, they become dangerous. Whoever controls the accepted notion of God presides over what is socially acceptable. As the philosopher Serres (1982) said, "interpretation kills." As Morrison said, "peasant stories don't pass judgments" (in Gates & Appiah, 1993, p. 132). Third, Black separatism is a wrong response to White supremacy. And fourth, unconventional people give life and energy to communities. Morrison insists on this last point. "The most respectable person is that woman who is healer and understands plants and stones and yet they live in the world" (in Gates & Appiah, 1993, p. 82). "I am enchanted, personally, with people who are extraordinary" (in Gates & Appiah, 1993, p. 374).

Ultimately, as Denise Heinz (1993) observes, Morrison implies that "community" is a state of mind. To boast that one lives in a gated community tells me something about that one. It tells me of the fear and hatred one has been taught to have for the Other. The psychosocial dimension of community requires an understanding of the inextricability of White and Black cultures (Edgerton, 1996). It requires a letting-in of the ghosts, those who spectre both personal as well as historical pasts. It requires a skeptical reading of master discourses, especially those that do not offend. But it also requires a letting in of the ghosts inside writing. By this I mean not only the implications hovering around single words but also those that hover subtextually inside and between texts. This is a matter of reading with the ear.

This chapter has attempted to give voice to some of the subtexts I have heard within Morrison's works. I have argued that Morrison writes intersubtextually so as to write over the Whiteness that colors the American literary imagination. With sleight of hand she actually buries the White texts so as to feature what has been silenced: the Black child, the repressed memory, the Black language. Coming up through these burials, or hovering absences, as I have called them, is the third thing, another kind of speaking, one that voices the Black soul. This voicing is not exclusively the province of the Black race; rather, it is a different way of using language, such as that which poets understand and use, such as Beckett (1965) writes when he imagines primal speakings: "I wandered in my mind, slowly, noting every detail of the labyrinth, its paths as familiar as those of my garden and yet ever new, as empty as the heart could wish or alive with strange encounters" (p. 106). I see it now as my challenge, as a teacher of literature, to continue to place text on text, the better to hear borrowings and burials, the better to encounter strangeness. Forbidden knowledges, then, might break through the walls of the master discourse (de Castell & Bryson, 1998). Then our task could be to introduce ourselves to ourselves (Gilliam, 1974). Then the classroom might be a community. The third thing.

3

Bluebeard's Cellar:
A Native Son's Underworld

… we do not recognize the full reality of anima … until invisible forces of the unconscious underworld overpower and make captive our normalcy.

—Hillman, 1975, p. 208

I go to encounter for the millionth time the reality of experience and forge in the smithy of my soul the uncreated conscience of my race.

—Joyce, 1966, pp. 252–253

Even before reason there is inward movement which reaches out towards its own.

Plotinus, 205 270, 111. 4. 6

Early in the pages of his autobiography *Black Boy* (1945/1993a), Richard Wright tells us his encounter with "Once upon a time." Those magical four words ushered the young boy into an undiscovered realm of his imagination. Never before had he experienced such a world as that portrayed in the fairy tale of Bluebeard and his wives. "My imagination blazed," he writes of the story (p. 45). Before that, he had lived, a hungry and hungering child, in the isolation of a misery born of deprivation so profound that not even his mother could salve him. Indeed, even his mother tormented him. In those Jim Crow days, Richard Wright's mother and grandmother tried to teach Richard to be subservient to the White man's cruel and unjust laws. They beat him physically, believing that the stings from a wet towel or a hard stick could subdue his rebellious spirit. But those physical torments, hard as they were, did nothing to deter the young boy from his interest in "the forbidden and enchanting land" (p. 47) of words.

It was not just any fairy tale that fired Richard's imagination. Fortunately for posterity, the story of "Bluebeard" was the spark that kindled Richard Wright's sensations to such a degree that they would emblazen his entire writing purpose. And what a tale it is! "Bluebeard" is the story of a man despised because of his physical difference and his strange past. Not only does he grow a blue beard but he also harbors a secret, having murdered all seven of his wives. Their bloody bones lie in the cellar of his castle, buried behind a locked door of the back stairs. Ranged against the wall are all seven corpses, hanging by their hair. The eighth wife uncovers the mystery when, curious, she disobeys her husband and uses the forbidden key to unlock the forbidden door. The ghoulish images in Bluebeard's cellar are such stuff as nightmares are made on.

Wright recalls the impression the tale made as its unfolding was whispered to him by a boarder in his grandmother's house:

> As her words fell upon my new ears, I endowed them with a reality that welled up from somewhere within me.... The tale made the world around me be, throb, live. As she spoke, reality changed, the look of things altered, and the world became peopled with magical presences. My sense of life deepened and the feel of things was different, somehow. (p.45)

Violence, murder, blood, and deception form the basics of Bluebeard's story. The pages of Richard Wright's fiction are filled with similar pathological images. Bodies in his fiction are decapitated, thrust into furnaces, hacked, thrown out of windows. Murders are committed to cover up previous murders. Characters assume false names and new identities in thriller-like attempts to elude discovery by the White man. And always there is a fire scene, as if the volcano of Wright's soul is in constant eruption.

I have Richard Wright follow Toni Morrison for several reasons. Morrison's work is charted in political, historical, and social situations. Wright's work is also. Morrison's fiction draws attention to words. Wright's work does also. And Morrison, I have argued, structures twoness into her work—two communities, two houses, two characters—within which, or between or around which (intertextually) a Black presence hovers. That which is absent from the master dialectical discourse, for Morrison, is Black reality—a third thing—which she brings to light consciously and deliberately. Morrison makes visible and audible the third thing of Black identity so that its invisibility is seen anew, heard anew. Wright is different in that for him there is no appeal to a third thing. Rather, for him there is what Blake calls the "two-fold always" (in Miller, 1995) that removes illusions. For Wright, the project that drives his writing is "something": It cannot be named or placed, but it is that which fuels the fire of his rage and emanates from the embers of his soul. "Some experience will ignite somewhere deep down in me the smoldering embers of new fires and I'll be off again to write yet another novel" (1938–1945/1991, pp. 880–881). This "something" is more primal and archeytpal than Morrison's third thing precisely because it comes from the depths of unconsciousness. It is that which drives his commitment, as James Joyce put it, to "forge" the conscience of his race in the "smithy" of his soul. He writes fiction in Joycean fashion to express the "character-destiny" of his race (1938–1945/1991, p. 878). And the "something" that urges expression, I will argue, is a deeply buried (and thereby largely unconscious) element of Wright's psyche that the patriarchy tries to subdue.

If male and female are the poles of every psychic being, for Richard, growing up, one psychic pole was missing. He tells us of his father's desertion from the family, placing the young Richard inside the rigid confines of a cruel matriarchy. His literal environment, curiously, was thus governed by the patriarchy in three guises: his absent father, the White man, and the negative mother figures of his mother and grandmother. What was missing was the expression of his true Blackness, which was forbidden from expression. It was as if two worlds existed: one world for them—the people White and Black around him—and another world that he could only intuit—the world of the Black race, about whom no one seemed to care or miss. "America had kept us locked in the dark underworld of American life for three hundred years," he writes (1993a, p. 370), in images that recall Bluebeard's cellar where female bones lie. I see this very male, Black writer—Richard Wright—identifying with female invisibility, seeing an analogy between the female corpses of Bluebeard's wives and the buried lives of all American Blacks. Christopher Bollas (1987), a neo-Freudian, captures the idea of intuition's intention in his intriguing phrase "the unthought known." That which has not yet entered consciousness is nevertheless known because it emanates from an early experience with the mother, before differentiation happens. To put it archetypally, I see Richard Wright's imagination as emanating from the psychic basement of Black anima energy, which, having been enslaved for 300 years, is fiercely if defensively activated. To that end, I take up the challenge issued by a recent critic: "Perhaps it is time now for Wright's readers to pursue the 'invisible woman' in Wright's best work and thus become more aware of a critically important, but often neglected, dimension of his vision" (Butler, 1995, p. 180).

However, Wright's invisible woman is no angelic Beatrice awaiting the traveler in Dante's hell. Wright's anima figure, rather, inspires action of a demonic nature. I take my clue from the symbolic names Wright gives his characters. Bigger Thomas, in Native Son (1938–1945/1991), is no Uncle Tom. His function, as Wright himself tells us in "How 'Bigger' Was Born" (1938–1945/1991), was to "bring out more clearly the shadowy outlines of the negative that lay in the back of my mind" (p. 864). The negative is the place no one had imagined, "a life beyond this world" (p. 864), a symbolic no man's land that Wright himself would create with words, "a world that existed on the plane of animal sensation alone" (p. 866). Such a world Wright envisioned would be dangerous and exciting, primal and rebellious, dreadful and ecstatic because, by virtue of an animating animal passion, it would be a world for which all oppressed people yearned.

Bigger, thus, becomes for Wright a kind of orgiastic demon-god connecting not just Blacks but all people back to their primal selves.

Wright associates his vision of Bigger with "the springs of religion" and also with "the origins of rebellion" (p. 872). His characters are mythic and archetypal, rather than stereotypical and biographical. They are bigger. That Wright was excoriated by such Black intellectuals as W. E. B. Du Bois, Franz Fanon, and James Baldwin may be explained, I think, by their mistaking Wright's symbolism for literalism. And the famous dispute between Wright and Zora Neale Hurston may be explained by the differing viewpoint each had toward Black folk life. For Hurston, Wright fails to touch Black sympathy and understanding, preferring instead to stereotype males as savage and to ignore the experience of women altogether (in Butler, 1995, p. xxix). For Wright, Hurston is entirely too sentimental. Although I agree with Saunder Redding and Lorraine Hansberry that *The Outsider* (1953/1993b) is a less engaging novel than *Native Son*, I cannot agree with Ben Burns that Wright's vision is "without solidarity with the Negro people" (in Butler, 1995), because it is not just for Blacks that Wright writes. Wright seeks to create, phoenixlike, a new solidarity for all humanity, birthed from the fires of a destroyed patriarchy.

Such a new vision for all of humanity is fearful, fascinating, troubling, and awful. These descriptors are similar to the words Rudolf Otto (1958) uses to describe numinous experience as "something inherently or wholly other ... before which we therefore recoil in a wonder that strikes us chill and numb" (p. 28). A tension between the forces of creativity and destruction is seen by Wright's most symbolically named character, Cross Damon—the kind of symbolically "bigger" character Wright was trying to express in his earlier works. As an archetypal outsider, Cross Damon does what many of us might wish: He escapes an unbearable past by manufacturing a new identity for himself. A subway wreck provides him with the opportunity he unwittingly seeks to leave his troubles behind; so with the forged name Lionel, Cross Damon births himself anew. He births himself from the underground—analogy of Bluebeard's cellar—and names himself after a train. Character, in other words, is forged from steel. Character is a cross between demon and daimon. The daimon is the cross this character must bear. And, to further play with Wright's symbolic name, Lionel acts in such a way as to propel himself on a driving, fast forward train track that is all movement and all action. He is fierce, forceful, and forged; he is outside the mainstream; he is psychopath; he is devil; he is god. He is that which inspires "dread or awe or the fear of ghosts" (Otto, 1958, p. 28).

I will consider three of Wright's characters (himself in *Black Boy* and *American Hunger*, Bigger Thomas in *Native Son*, and Lionel Cross Damon in *The Outsider*) as expressions of character-destiny wrought from Wright's daimon. But first I must remark on the relevance of the daimon—a theory as old as Plato and as new as Hillman. In his *The Soul's Code: In Search of Character and Calling* (1996b), James Hillman offers the fascinating thesis that each life is formed by a particular image, an image that is the essence of that life and that calls it to its destiny. Corollaries with Wright are evident here, remembering Wright's Bluebeard obsession and his phrase "character-destiny." For Hillman, as for Plato, the soul is guarded by a daimon whose demands for the expression of the image may cause good or ill. The daimon is character's genius, neither nature nor nurture, but 'something else.' "The introduction of 'something else' violates our mode of thought and convenience of its habitual operations," Hillman writes. He continues, "a 'something else' disturbs minds that mistake comfortable thinking with clarity of thought" (p. 129). This wording is unmistakenly like Wright's, in that Wright never named the precise urging that led him into his writing, as if naming would do harm to its numinous content. In commenting on Joe Louis's dynamite style, Wright said: "Here's that *something*, that pent-up folk consciousness. Here's a fleeting glimpse of the heart of the Negro, the heart that beats and suffers and hopes—for freedom. Here's the fluid something that's like iron" (in Miller, E. E., 1990, p. 143). The form of daimonic expression depends on paradox: something firm that is fluid.

On another occasion Wright comments, "I had to fall back upon my own feelings as a guide.... There seems to hover somewhere in that dark part of all our lives, in some more than others, an objectless, timeless, spaceless element of primal fear and dread ... which exercises an impelling influence upon our lives all out of proportion to its obscurity" (1938–1945/1991, p. 871). What Wright speaks of here is a rewording of what Hillman describes. Because of the potency of the daimon, Hillman says it can express itself as horror (demon) or glory (genius or daimon); reading its expression requires seeing the daimon's intentions in the demon "so as to recover a fuller image of glory" (Hillman, p. 246). Again, there is a similarity between Hillman's words and Wright's, for Wright originally titled a portion of his two-part autobiography *The Horror and the Glory*, a part that was not published, however, in Wright's lifetime. As a final twist of coincidence and overlap, I find myself writing on Wright's restored text so as to complete what my father edited. For, you see, my father was Wright's first editor. It was my father who suggested that Wright end his life story *Black Boy* with his flight from the South, cutting the manuscript's length in half and excluding *The Horror and the Glory*. This was a change to which Wright agreed.

My discussion of Wright's three characters will incorporate what I understand as his three metaphors for the Black man's daimon: words, animals, and fire. Each of these metaphors expresses a sense of urgent agency. The reader should see that for Wright human freedom depends not on philosophy but on psychology and not on a theory of existence but on a theory of essence. I take my cue partly from the close association Wright had with the Freudian psychiatrist Frederic Wertham, who wrote the preface to my mother's edited collection of stories, entitled *The World Within: Fiction Illuminating Neuroses of Our Time* (Aswell, M. L., 1947). In yet another coincidence, I find in my mother's book these words from Wertham: "The dream process runs through the creative process. In collaboration with a living writer, Richard Wright, I was able to prove this for his novel *Native Son*.... the emotional experiences related to the key scene of the novel had been completely forgotten by him for eighteen years and were not available to his consciousness at the time he wrote the novel" (in Aswell, M. L., p. xxi). Wertham is saying that the unconscious has a rationalization of its own that is not always available to the conscious ego, and that the unconscious has the potential to heal that which ails. Whether one interprets Wright's psychology from a Freudian perspective (in which case, Wright writes out of an Oedipal rage to kill the father-superworld and merge with the mother-folkworld) or from a Jungian perspective (in which case, Wright's anima struggles to be equal with society's animus), psychology offers a better method, in my view, for unpacking the complexities of Richard Wright's intention. My method, consequently, will involve an attempt to descend into Wright's underworld, where one finds the unsettling images that shape his genius. Such a psychological method might be called unconsciousness raising.

The task begins inside Wright's grandmother's house with his hearing the story of Bluebeard. It is not insignificant that his grandmother was "as nearly white as a Negro can get without being white, which means that she was white" (1993a, p. 46). Even so, she subscribed to a belief in the perceived inferiority of Blacks. This belief depends on ignorance. As slave masters knew so well, the best way to keep the system of slavery going was to deny Blacks access to books, so when Granny discovered Richard learning to read she responded with punishment. For a child with a rebellious temperament, what is forbidden is alluring; this was especially so in the tale that captured Richard's imagination, for its story was his story. Richard, like the eighth wife, was forbidden access to the secret chamber. Bluebeard, a demon god, held the key that would unlock the door to life's mystery. Why would his grandmother prevent him access to knowledge, that which would make him free? What lurked in the chamber below that was so dangerous, so locked away from his grasp? The conflict of desires between the strong older woman and the rebellious male child set the tone for the symbolic subtext of Wright's autobiography, his engendered vision. As Jerry Ward writes in his introduction to *Black Boy*, "Wright came to understand that the power to structure gender ... seemed to be the exclusive privilege of certain white males.... The Black male is to be made a permanent child and denigrated into the posture of the stereotyped female—victim, unempowered!" (1993a, p. xviii). The psychological dimension of this early battle was made all the more compelling in that his first encounter with raced oppression came from his own kin, a woman gatekeeper who acted like Bluebeard. All the elements of psychomythic drama are here. The stage is discourse. The task is to unlock possible worlds through words. The hero must descend beneath the code of The White Man.

I asked my student, Sister Aquillina Mwithi, to comment on Richard's Bluebeard encounter. She writes:

Bluebeard. This is not usual for a person to have a blue beard. We all know that beards should be white with age or black. The tale seems to be referring to something greater than a human being, something which is in the blue sky, beyond human reach; or something in the vast waters of seas and oceans. Ella recounts that Bluebeard had loved and slain his seven wives. It seems that both love and hate carried the same weight. How does love and hate happen at the same time? Might it be that Bluebeard saw his wives suffer, caused them to suffer, out of love?

Writing as she does out of a Christian perspective, Sister Aquillina offers an amazing insight into the nature of this larger-than-life figure, Bluebeard, comparing him with God. She remarks how puzzling it is that God has his son killed by hanging, as Bluebeard has his wives killed by hanging. Suffering, dying, and loving combine. "Black boy was so much taken up by this story of Bluebeard," Sister continues. "He says that everything around him died. His body and soul were in the story. It seems that he found the answer to many of his questions of life, and that was what his granny refused him." As always, my students help point the way. As she offers her commentary, Sister Aquillina suggests that life's mystery is contained in the very being of the godhead, who embodies the opposite impulses of punishment and love. This is the same conclusion Jung reached upon reading the story of Job, a constant reference in Wright's work.

In his "Answer to Job," Jung (1952/1973) concludes that the relationship between Job and Yahweh forces the issue of God's relation to humankind, for Job insists on a personal interview with the almighty one to inquire into the cause of his suffering and to argue his case. Jung comes to the startling conclusion that Job is more knowing than God (Yahweh) because of his glimmering perception that it is not humankind who is incomplete without God but God who is incomplete without humankind. Paradoxically, Yahweh lacks wholeness because he lacks the wisdom that comes through suffering. This understanding, I suggest, may explain Wright's fascination with Bluebeard and the seven wives. Seven is a principle of wholeness and the wives represent the feminine principle; together the seven wives can make humanity whole. Perhaps Wright, like Job, had a glimmering perception that his "imprisonment" as a Black boy in a White racist society could serve a divine purpose, or might be divinely ordained, or might unlock the key to his "cellar," if he could find the words to release all people from gendered and raced persecution.

Language was agency for Wright, even at a young age. The word was the bridge to the world beyond, "the gateway to a forbidden and enchanting land" (1993a, p. 47). His phrasing "gateway" and "land," together with his frequent use of the word "world," as in superworld, underworld, and otherworld, endows language with a power denied Wright in his daily living. As Jung relates in the Job story, language can become the means by which consciousness is raised, words containing a dramatic potential of shifting awareness to another stage. Interlacing his commentary on Job are Jung's metaphors of drama: The Job writer "rings down the curtain" before the end of the story, and the characters are "protagonists" who "act out their roles" on "a brightly lit stage." Jung's metaphors suggest his underlying belief in the kind of action necessary for psychic transformation, which he also refers to as "divine drama" (1942/1973, p. 365). This is what he calls elsewhere "sacred action" (1942/1973, pp. 248–249). Unlike "human action," which moves sequentially and linearly, sacred action refuses the sense of an ending. The moment of truth in the Job story is not quite reached, leaving it up to the reader to complete the action inside the theater of consciousness. In other words, action is partly determined by the roles one assumes; but stirring beneath surface action is *something more* (Jung, 1952/1973, p. 365). Recall Wright's word "something" in this regard, with its appreciation for the unnamable in our lives. The making of higher consciousness involves, thus, a paradoxical lowering of consciousness. This is Wright's fascination with Bluebeard's cellar.

In Freud's house, the cellar is the locus of the id, where, as the poet Robert Bly (1990) put it, "the really dangerous and wild material" lies in waiting (p. 160). There is a nightmarish quality to Freud's id, as anyone reading *The Room* by Harold Pinter (1968) can feel; for the cellar in that play is occupied by a mysterious landlord one doesn't know and hasn't seen in a long, long time. "There was a door locked on the stairs, so there might have been another floor, but we didn't see anyone, and it was dark," relates the shifting Mrs. Sands (p. 107). The landlord is ominously waiting: "He just lies there. It's not good for me. He just lies there, that's all, waiting" (p. 110). In Pinter's Freudian schema, the landlord is "a blind Negro" who is the messenger of "the father." The cellar is a totally foreign territory occupied by a totally foreign "other" in cahoots with the patriarchy. We could say that the lord of the basement is like a plantation master who owns the land and all its workers. Let it be said that Pinter and Wright have little in common except for a raced understanding each has of the Black man's association with wild and dangerous material. Although for the White man Pinter, the Negro is patriarchy's messenger, Wright the Black man takes a Jungian perspective, not only of the cellar and its contents, but of the message from the cellar. For Jung, the cellar would be the world of the collective unconscious. This is a place where archetypes and primordial symbols provide social significance for the artist interested in writing against lordship. For Wright, this is a place in waiting, but not for patriarchy's message. Rather, this is the place of the dead bones of seven wives, waiting for resurrection.

In myth, the underworld is the place of invisibles. The Greeks called Hades its king; the Romans called Dis its ruler. How appropriate for Wright, the Dis-pised child, to feel immediate, psychic connection with Bluebeard's cellar. Lives live down there but are not seen by upperworld landlords. In the land of Dis, displacement, disinheritance, disappearance, disappointment all live. That which is disappeared from majority consciousness lives, nonetheless, down there. All illusions become disillusions, and to be disillusioned is to see through illusions, to open to an amazing otherness. As the editors of an entire journal on the subject of disillusionment write, "Disillusionment is one of life's most interesting experiences, possibly even its most fundamental one, at least for people who are willing to face their illusions" (*Spring* 58: 1995, n.p.). Buddhists know this well. Disillusioning is a process of dynamic unsettling that allows one to see from the perspective of the "other," to open to the "other" (Miller, D. L.., 1995). How appealing to Wright, the dislocated Black boy, to find a place for his imagination in Bluebeard's cellar!

Recognizing that such a place exists in story gave, I conjecture, Wright permission (against his granny's will) to tap its energy. And there he found, ironically, the heartbeat of his granny's Sunday singing, which had little to do with Sunday church but much to do with African rhythms and folk beliefs, unsung and unseen in the majority culture (Miller, E. E., 1990; Franklin, 1995). No wonder Granny feared Wright's fascination with Bluebeard. He might become a messenger of the obscene (not seen)! He might display who his people are and where they come from! He might write against the dominant discourse! He might disgrace the displaced ones! He might refuse to dissemble. He might discover that he was being "shut out of the secret, the thing, the reality ... somewhere beneath all the words and silences" (Wright, 1993a, p. 55). Such possibilities caused Granny to say that Richard would burn in hell for his fascination with words (Porter, 1984, pp. 61, 63). But, as Hillman reminds us, "the eye of the heart that 'sees' is also the eye of death that sees through visible presentations to an invisible core" (1996b, p. 146). Even at an early age, Richard Wright "saw" in the cellar of Bluebeard "the thing" that really mattered for his soul. Words were like talk that could "weave, roll, surge, spurt, veer, swell" and so transmit the folk tradition (1993a, p. 95). "I strove," he said, "to master words, to make them disappear, to make them important by making them new, to make them melt into a rising spiral of emotional stimuli ... that would drench the reader with a sense of a new world" (in Porter, 1984, p. 66). He wanted to be not just a messenger but a transmitter.

Wright saw in words and heard in voices their incantatory magic. Words could connect, draw out, and express. Words could be like salt in alchemy, bringing to the surface unconscious material (Salvio, 1998b). And as the agent or transmitter of another reality, Wright had what John Ernest calls a "multiply contingent identity," wherein each act, word or gesture becomes a kind of performance (1998, p. 1,111). I am struck by the different kinds of word-performances one sees, hears, and feels in a Wright text. In his autobiography, for example, he shares his lively awareness of the invisible world (called "superstition" by a less lively culture):

> If I pulled a hair from a horse's tail and sealed it in a jar in my own urine, the hair would turn overnight into a snake. If I passed a Catholic sister or mother dressed in black and smiled and allowed her to see my teeth, I would surely die. (1993, p. 83)

Other passages are purely celebratory "of the drama of human feeling which is hidden by the external drama of life" (1993a, p. 118). He writes of events "speaking" to him in a "cryptic tongue," which he catalogues in Whitmanesque lyricism:

> There was the wonder I felt when I first saw a brace of mountainlike, spotted, black-and-white horses clopping down a dusty road through clouds of powdered clay.
>
> There was the delight I caught in seeing long straight rows of red and green vegetables stretching away in the sun to the bright horizon....
>
> There was the languor I felt when I heard green leaves rustling with a rainlike sound.
>
> There was the incomprehensible secret embodied in a whitish toadstool hiding in the dark shade of a rotting log. (1993a, pp. 8–9)

Through words Wright expresses a poetic and dynamic quality of the cosmos. His sensibility is very like Jung's conception of the unconscious as compensatory to but different from dominant structures. This is a way of thinking that uses simile to articulate difference. This is a way of thinking that has a feminine cast, not literally but metaphorically, capable of expressing "the fact, image, and social reality of difference itself—what difference itself is like, what the experience of difference is like" (Samuels & Hudson-Weems, 1990, p. 300).

I use Wright's examples of cataloging as an assignment for my students to catalog the pluses and minuses of their feelings. In his piece "Raw Astonishment" J. P. Dufrechou (1998) wrote:

> There was the astonishment I felt when I first saw a doodle bug curl in defense in the palm of my hand.
>
> There was the half-surprised, half-disgusted look on my face that accompanied a long suck on a half-ripened lemon. And there is the gut-wreching anger that makes my face crimson and my alcoholic father wants nothing to do with me. (p. 39)

Language as incantation, language as action: Wright uses words not just to invoke ecstasy but to inspire terror. In the latter sense, he is transmitter of a different sort, more like a smithy. Words smite. He discovered this double-edged nature of language in an early incident with his father. Taking his father's words to "kill the cat" literally, obeying his father to the letter, Richard describes in hideous detail his murder of a kitten. The battle the boy waged against his parents can be seen in that single incident and serve to symbolize the absolute difference between their worlds and his. By twisting his father's words, Richard triumphed over his father. "I was happy because I had at last found a way to throw my criticism of him into his face. I had made him feel that, if he whipped me for killing the kitten, I would never give serious weight to his words again" (1993a, p. 13). He saw that words can be the means of exercising power and establishing authority in a symbolic sense even though he lacked both in a literal sense. On the other hand, his mother triumphed over his triumph. She made him realize what he had done by insisting he bury the animal. Then she made him pray that he would not die in the night for having committed that crime. The words in the prayer were too real for him: "I opened my mouth but no words came. My mind was frozen with horror" (p. 16). His mother demanded proper burial of the cat, knowing that the child would not be able to bury her words. The words were so real to him that he feared for his life! Words worked on his imagination like the smithy works on the anvil, forging terrible reality. His mother's words made him feel horror when only earlier he had reveled in the glorious power of his words over his father. Is it any wonder, given parents who had such a strongly negative effect on him, that Wright would seek to forge a new identity for himself?

Forge[1]: l. the special fireplace, hearth, or furnace in which metal is heated before shaping. 2. the workshop of a blacksmith; smithy 3. to form by heating and hammering; beat into shape. Forge[2] : to move ahead or progress slowly, with difficulty, or by mere momentum (Webster, 1993).

All of the preceding meanings apply to what I see happening in Richard Wright's life as a writer. I think the fact that he was a writer is all-important to his story: He wrote his way into a difficult survival; he wrote to save others from being hammered unnecessarily; he wrote so as not to continue the lie of his people, whom he felt had been beaten into shape; he wrote fact, he wrote fiction, he wrote poetry—all produced from the hot fire, the momentum, of his life events. He wrote like a hammersmith. He wrote because he was a blacksmith. His cultural analog is alchemy. His mythic analog is Hephaestos.

According to Jung's theory of transformation, the work the alchemists were doing, changing lead into gold, involved not just a physical process but a psychological process as well. The creation of newness, amazingly, could be seen, thus, as a human endeavor. It could be accomplished, to use the alchemical metaphor, in the laboratory of the soul with the pestle, fire, and forge of human suffering. It could occur through active confrontation with the opposites that make up the self (born both from the literal father and mother and from the symbolic male and female components of personhood). From a mixing and meshing, thrashing and cutting, a new self could be forged. "It is," Jung writes, "the old game of hammer and anvil: between them the patient iron is forged into an indestructible whole" (1940/1977, p. 288). Creation arises, then, out of conflict; newness cannot emerge without a conflict, which necessarily also involves suffering. And this alchemy, a matter of flame and fire—of burnishing, refining, and separating—can be understood on a symbolic level as a way of actively making one's self anew, rather than passively being begotten.

Like the exotic processes of alchemy, the Greeks told exaggerated stories. These would appeal to Wright, whose deepest consciousness was that of the exaggerated Westerner: individualist, revolutionary, willful (Kent, 1984). What better Greek figure to associate Wright with than Hephaestos. As the lame god, Hephaestos limps. He is wounded in his body and so he is a different god. His artwork, like the chains or the metal nets of Achilles's shield or the girl Pandora, is created out of the fire of an angry, wounded passion. Making art is playing with fire in all of its many manifestations: transformation, baptism, initiation, but also destruction.

Richard Wright played with fire at an early age. The fire incident is as formative in the creation of his artistic character as that of the cat killing. Like the other incident, this one arose out of a vague sense of rebellion against his parents. He was bored. There was a fire in the fireplace. The quivering coals fascinated him, so why not try a game? Touching some broom straws to the coals, he ignited the curtains, which turned the "white wisps of ghosts" into "red circles of flame," then into "a sheet of yellow" (1993a, p. 5). This was not an innocent act, any more than killing the cat was. If, as the saying goes, "The devil made me do it," then it was the demon-daimon making demands on Richard's mind. The fire was a kind of ritual parricide that could free him from the tyranny of his father's house in which his grandmother fanatically ruled (Porter, 1984). Later in his writings, Richard would tap those demands, employing fire scenes that would symbolically, rather than literally, burn down the house of the patriarchy.

I am drawn again to the coincidence of my writing on Richard Wright, my father's author. It is Thanksgiving, the first one I have spent alone, ever. My writing this chapter has filled the days for me, kept me "gathered together," like the song we used to sing this time of year. Last night, wondering where this chapter was heading, I thought to include some personal material. One was a letter I received from Julia Wright (1995, February 4). She and I had met at a literary gathering honoring her father. By chance, we stayed at the same bed and breakfast and had rooms across the hall from one another. "Time goes round and round and round," she wrote. "Mostly in spiral fashion but, if we are lucky, we are privileged to be able to close a few of the spirals and create circles at certain special moments of our lives. Meeting you last year closed our fathers' circle. It didn't have to happen, but it did." Julia goes on to comment on some student essays I had sent her on *Black Boy*. "The spirit of Richard's friendship with Ed nourished your teaching of the book," she observed, "and so their feedback is very special (notice the words 'nourished' and 'feedback' relating to hunger)."

Another personal matter concerning Richard Wright and my life is the remarkable coincidence of Wright's hatred of his father and the story of Cross Damon's fabricated death, together with the writing of my brother about his father. My brother, too, hated his father and, too, assumed a new identity in a desperate effort to rub out an unbearable past. Just now I got down the manuscript my brother wrote, hidden away in the closet—a pun I suppose. I had forgotten that *Into Thin Air*,[1] the unpublished manuscript, began with an actual Thanksgiving we shared just before my brother's breakdown and disappearance. The opening scene is at the table, where my brother's scorn of my chatter

---

[1]My brother's title "Into Thin Air" (a story of disappearance and descent) should not be confused with the nonfiction bestseller of the same title, by Jon Krakauer (a story of conquest and ascent).

and cooking is both funny and cruel. He was funny; he was cruel; he was filled with contempt and loneliness for his father. He, like Richard Wright, saw the shadow of his face in the face of his father but felt no kinship with the man he hated but later learned to pity. He, like Wright, wrote in a determined effort to construct a character-destiny, to remake the self. But he was so ironically unlike Wright, who found in my father a fellow escapee from the South, a friend, a White "brother."

My brother's unpublished manuscript of disappearance and remade existence (my brother changed his name from Aswell to Cutler) ends with a memory-image of our father. It is written in one remarkable, Faulknerian sentence that moves the memory-image back and back again into several pasts, such that the son blurs in words with the father:

> When I rock gently on the glider on my screened-in front porch, when the street lights hold the momentary profiles of ghostly passersby and I am snugged in darkness, unobserved, I see Daddy's balding head, lips curled tight around a wet Chesterfield butt whose ash glows brightly in the darkness, stubby fingers curled around a highball glass that holds rye whiskey, rocking gently on the screened-in front porch in Chappaqua on summer nights, speechless, hour after hour, night after night, eyes trained sadly on the long manicured lawn of his suburban estate where no person ever passed, where everything was in its place, as though to conjure forth from trim Bermuda sod and poplars planted too symmetrically the vivid animation of his stickball pals, the pinafored neighborhood flirts sashaying out of reach from pool of light to shadow and back to light, cicadas whirring, the heat of Nashville pressing, pressing through mimosas, through sweet gums and chinaberry, upon the boy sitting, watching, dreaming, longing for Harvard, for the North, escape, a new life. (Cutler, n.d., p. 439)

Was my brother Quentin Compson? Thomas Wolfe? (one of my father's other writers). He had never read Richard Wright, but yet his cat and mouse tale of the hours after acquiring his new name "Cutler" read like a page out of *The Outsider*:

> I took out the little red address book I had just purchased and flipped through the empty pages. Now, what? I couldn't write down the names of real people who had known Duncan Aswell. That would defeat the whole point of my adventure. But William Cutler needed some sort of context. What relatives did he have? No one very close. No siblings who could be listed as next of kin. An orphan, for sure. Both parents dead. My only close relative—you always had to list someone—what about a maiden aunt, elderly, living alone, a spinster? Aunt Rose. Yes I hadn't seen her in years. Doubt if she would recognize me. Her eyesight was going. We used to see her occasionally in the early years, when Mother was alive. Mother's sister. That was it. Mother's older sister Rose, who never married. Rose Evarts. Yes, the "Evarts" of my middle name was mother's maiden name, of course. Living—where? Has to be a place I know, the geography and all. In Cambridge. In a little dark house with velveteen settees and antimacassars. Cats? No.

They leave hairs on the upholstery. Certainly no dogs. No, take that back. One small dog. Pekingese or pug. Name of "Tiny." ... I wrote Rose Evarts' name in my address book. (p. 291)

As I type out that passage I see how fabrication and memory intertwine. My brother "forgot" that Evarts was the middle name of our father's nemesis, the famous editor Maxwell Evarts Perkins. And he "forgot" that our neighbor in Chappaqua was a spinster whom we called Aunt Rena. She lived in an oldlady way with antimacassars on her velveteen settees and she had a pug dog named Tiny. We think we make up stories, when in fact the stories are real. Our memories, as Marla Morris (1999) says, are texts, too.

And now for the strangest coincidence of all. Here I am writing on Richard Wright and reading my brother's manuscript, which I had read a few years earlier, and just now I come across a lengthy section I had completely "forgotten." It is about my brother's recollection of my father and Richard Wright. This piling on of coincidence is, as Freud would say, uncanny; or as Jung would say, synchronistic. Forgetting has a strange way of remembering. In any case, the relevant passage occurs as my brother is talking to his Black lover Edmund:

I've been thinking a lot about Daddy's relation with Richard Wright. You know, Wright was one of Daddy's authors. I don't know how much you know about Wright's life, but he was a very bitter man at one point. In the 'Thirties, he'd joined the Communist Party, and then he felt betrayed—like a lot of other people, of course. But he turned against white people instead of against the Soviet Union, just lashed out at the white race. Out of that rage came *Black Boy* and *Native Son*. Well, those books were edited by Daddy. Wright and Daddy got to know each other right at that time when Wright was so bitter. Daddy used to say—and he might have been wrong, but it's interesting he said this—that he was the only white man Wright trusted at the time. The only one. As I say, I can't vouch for that, but I know you've heard me talk about my trip to Paris when I was in college and got to meet Wright, and I can tell you this: Even though he hadn't seen Daddy in years, maybe a decade, when Wright came to my hotel, tears were in his eyes to be holding the son of Edward Aswell in his arms. He wouldn't stop talking about this marvelous man who had changed his life. I had to keep my big mouth shut, of course. I wouldn't have dreamed of telling him about the stupid old drunken bigot I knew who ruined everybody's life he touched. Wright just seemed to worship Daddy. Why? Because Daddy was the great white savior? Or because he knew, in some subterranean way, that Daddy was soul brother. (pp. 372–373)

Placing the newly rediscovered manuscript of my brother side by side with Richard Wright's work, and now my chapter, I find myself wrestling with the question of identity. Why is it that some people never get over their parents? How is it that some carry their angers with them to the grave? Do we ever recognize that the ones we hate the most are really the ones we hold deepest in our hearts? Throughout my brother's diatribe against our father (and there are pages of it—one could say he writes in order to "kill" his father), I find it striking that he refers to this hated figure as "Daddy." The sad truth is that my brother was never able to articulate his feelings to his father, although the opportunity presented itself often enough. Indeed, Wright and my brother both express rage, feel betrayed, construct new identities. My brother constructed his new identity literally by changing his name and occupation, moving to another state, and fabricating names to put in his address book. And although he came to recognize that Bill Cutler could not cut away from Duncan Aswell, and that the latter was his father's son, he could not accept that fact. From this I speculate that writing is not always the way into self-understanding. What matters, it seems, is face-to-face, both facing one's self and one's adversary, as Job dared with Yahweh. What matters is not being a No Face.

Karen Anthony, my student, discusses these issues when she chooses a Job reference in Wright's *The Outsider* for commentary. Karen noted that *Black Boy*, *Native Son*, and *The Outsider* all have epitaphs taken from the Book of Job. Then, she follows through with this observation:

> Cross, like Job before him, must struggle with a sense of being betrayed by a god seemingly indifferent to the sufferings of mankind yet determined that his creations pay him homage, no matter what their life circumstances. Cross's sense of intellectual honesty will not allow him the easy way out, the way of his mother and her religious convictions. He cannot, and will not, directly blame a god he has renounced, and yet he cannot help but feel that "loss that made life intolerable" (Wright, 1993b, p. 24). Where does this primal sense of loss come from? Who to blame for the *all*, if not oneself? But then, why the anger, the sense of betrayal, the feeling that a promise has not been kept? These are the questions posed in *The Outsider*. These are the issues Cross must bear witness to throughout the novel.

Karen's sorts of questions should be the first asked when considering the basics of education. As Madeleine Grumet suggests, what is basic is relation, face-to-face, including facing one's own face. Identity, she observes, "is lived before it is thought" (1995, p.16), and so education should be about human beings making sense of their lives. How ironic that my brother had decades and decades of education (at Harvey and Hotchkiss and Harvard and Berkeley), as well as class privilege, but little "basic" training in these prestigious classrooms. Richard Wright, on the other hand, had little formal education (he quit school after ninth grade) and neither class nor race privilege; but, possibly because he expected nothing from his parents or from his world, his rage was less personal.

Because of the impersonality of Wright's rage, it is connected to myth and archetype; it is symbolic; it is less human. Could we say it is divine? As Rudolf Otto puts it, "the image of divinity directs man away from the personal" (p. 236). The point is important, for it helps to explain Wright's critics' anger at him. James Baldwin, for one, could not agree with Wright's use of raw violence to explore his theory of "complex simplicity" (in Hakutani, 1996, p. 7). And yet Wright's influence can be felt in Baldwin's titles *Notes from a Native Son* (1955/1990) and *The Fire Next Time* (1963/1993). For Wright, "complex simplicity" invoked the strangeness and wonder of Black lives, together with the sordidness and violence. Opposites together. Such a volatile mix does not appear human and therefore does not normalize (or "tame") Black people because it expresses an independent reality of the soul.

Earlier I invoked Hephaestos as one of Wright's soul gods. This god, with his anvil, is necessary to feel in Wright's work because the anvil takes the argument away from a purely personal or even a purely racial quibble. There is disappointment here for some critics. Wright refuses to connect with the souls of Black folk as described by W. E. B. Du Bois. This refusal, however, moves the drama to another stage, where the divine work of sulfide must be forged. I think Dan McCall caught the intention of Wright's rage when he remarked that the hatred of "the native" is at the service of an idea of social consciousness that serves the Bigger Thomases Black and White (1988). And Roger Rosenblatt observes similarly that Bigger Thomas "is the god of the Old Testament as well as the New ... an all-powerful and vengeful god of a special creation" (1988, pp. 36–37). In a more truly awe-full sense, Wright's murderous intentions are holy because they transcend race and time. As Wright put it, "the springs of religion are ... also the origins of rebellion" (1991, p. 872).

To express the nonpersonal elements of his project, Wright had to find metaphors that would speak to the audience he was claiming. The audience had to be universal, as did the metaphors. As Robert Avens remarks, "In a world torn to pieces by pure intellect, the poet imagines and thus reestablishes relationships which are now expressed as metaphor. Metaphor replaces the simple, given, and experienced meaning of things by created, or shall we say, recreated meaning" (1984, p. 57). Two of Wright's metaphors are animals and fire: animals because they are expressive of the instinctual nature of life; fire because of its capacity to create and destroy. Both are in service of a project to declare, through blasphemy and insult and pure drive, a "magical trans-substantive power of poesis to make reality" (Hillman, 1997, p. 37).

One sees several instances of animals in Wright's work, not the least of which is the kitten he killed to challenge his father's authority. Right there, a personal act acquires a larger, symbolic sense. In *Lawd Today!* (1938–1945/1991) two parts of that work utilize animal images ("Squirrel Cage" and "Rats' Alley") to suggest Wright's intuition that the Black problem in America was not just Black and not just in the South but was part of a larger situation in which the spirit of a people had dried up, their instincts desiccated, numbed out by external social and economic forces. Wright deepened this insight when he moved out of the South to Chicago, described in the second part of his autobiography as *The Horror and the Glory*. In the North, the once-perceived land of freedom, he experienced anything but freedom. Even the Communist Party proved ideologically stifling. One incident, when he began work at a medical research institute, focuses the "something" that was missing in American life. There, he became all too aware that, as a Black, he occupied "an underworld position" (1945/1993a, p. 356) that would prevent him from access to superworld privilege. His job in the hospital was in a literal basement, where he had to clean dog, rat, mice, cat, and rabbit pens and feed the guinea pigs. Working with caged animals, he found a metaphor for what he was experiencing. He tells us that one of his duties was to assist in the slitting of dogs' vocal cords so that their howls would not cause disturbance. "They would lift their heads to the ceiling and gape in a soundless wail," he remembers. "The sight became lodged in my imagination as a symbol of silent suffering" (1945/1993a, p. 359).

Not just oppression, Wright saw the needless cruelty of science, "in the underworld of the great scientific institute" (1945/1993a, p. 367). In typical "cat and mouse" reporting, he goes on to relate how he and his Black underground workers deliberately miscalculated where to put which test rabbits in what cages for the "Aschleim-Zondek" experiment. The incident shows with comic clarity how double consciousness provides a lens through which to see the randomness of oppression and the baselessness of scientific efforts to prove racial superiority. For there in the laboratory were Black workers assisting White doctors in all seriousness; while yet the White calculations, based on specific caging, had been randomly assigned by the Blacks. The error of the caged animals became, for Wright, a metaphor for Blacks' being confined and defined by the myths of Whites:

> The hospital kept us four Negroes, as though we were close to kin to the animals we tended, huddled together down in the vast underworld corridors of the hospital, separated by a vast psychological distance from the significant processes of the rest of the hospital—just as America had kept us locked in the dark underworld of American life for three hundred years—and we had made our own code of ethics, values, and loyalty. (p. 370)

Rats, the "guinea pigs" for scientific experiments, become a deliberate metaphor in the opening scene of Native Son. Recall: It is a typical morning in the Thomas home. There is a chill, a sense of shame and insult, that pervades the cramped room where four people, attempting a life, wake to the day. As usual, a big, foot-long, black rat comes out of its hole in the wall. It attacks Bigger's leg. The fight is on between the man and the rat: Bigger with a skillet for a weapon, the rat with bared, long yellow fangs and a piping shrilly shriek for defense. This scene is mirrored at the end of the novel when Bigger Thomas, having committed a murder, is in jail. He is like a rat in a cage, meant to symbolize the moral of the story; namely, "the horror of Negro life in the United States" (1991, p. 880). In commenting on the rat, Wright says that he wrote the rat into a second draft of the novel when he recalled how many rats in Chicago bit Black children:

> At first I rejected the idea of Bigger battling a rat in his room. I was afraid that the
> rat would "hog" the scene. But the rat would not leave me; he presented himself
> in many attractive guises. So, cautioning myself to allow the rat scene to disclose
> *only* Bigger, his family, their little room, and their relationships, I let the rat walk
> in, and he did his stuff. (1938–1945/1991, p. 880)

The achievement of the novel, for Dan McCall, is an understanding of the virulence of one's rage at being always caged. "The only 'real' Negro is 'black crazy'" (1988, p. 21).

I would not be doing right by Wright if I left this chapter with his rage caged. Although he strikes out at the patriarchy in all its oppressive forms (including, he discovered, Marxism), he strikes in the manner of the blacksmith smiting iron. He strikes to forge. Like the alchemists, he works his "mettle" so as to create another world or consciousness. He strikes while the iron is hot so as to reshape the hardness of hate. A second of his shaping metaphors is fire.

Perhaps the most famous of the fire scenes occurs in *Native Son* just after Bigger has mistakenly murdered Mary Dalton. The reader feels the terror of his murder, not because of the murder, but because of the circumstances. A Black man in a White woman's bedroom is taboo, even in the so-called liberal North, even in a so-called liberal White family's home. Bigger is simply overrun with fear, and the problem the reader follows with him is how to dispose of the body he has just snuffed out. Bigger's predicament, however, has an element of dark comedy, for in a larger sense Bigger is completely innocent. But now this unfortunate turn of events labels him the criminal that the White "others" have assumed he is, anyway. Bigger Thomas is guilty even before the murder simply because he is a Black man. Now he must attempt to avoid punishment in the face of real crime.

Bigger's ratiocinations are like that of a Poe or Dostoevsky character who must go through extraordinary leaps of logic to out-think the foe. The reader follows Bigger's thinking, completely fascinated by the logical creativity of this absurdly illogical situation:

> He looked into the furnace; her clothes were ablaze and smoke was filling the interior so that he could scarcely see. The draft roared upward, droning in his ears. He gripped her shoulders and pushed hard, but the body would not go any farther. He tried again, but her head still remained out. Now.... Goddamn! He wanted to strike something with his fist. What could he do? (1938–1945/1991, p. 531)

What he does, of course, is whack off Mary's head, which is so stubbornly attached to the body that a knife would not do the job. Finding a hatchet, he sends the blade into her throat until the head rolls off. Then he stuffs the head into the furnace. Later, Bigger has a nightmare in which he holds a package. Curious as to what is inside, he unwraps it and sees his own bloody head, which he hurls into the faces of the White people chasing him. Later still, the nightmare becomes reality as Bigger and the investigators go down into the basement where the furnace is. The story of Bluebeard looms into view, as down there, in the cellar, the men see several pieces of white bone on the surface of the ashes. From there Bigger's flight turns into Bigger's fate when the cross of salvation cannot save him any more than it can save an innocent Black man. The cross for the Black man is the flaming one, because the Black man is deemed a fiend. And so the steel door of prison closes him in

The character-destiny of the Bigger Thomases about whom Wright writes is doomed and damned. Not democratic justice, not the Communist Party, and certainly not the Christian church can save poor, Black, uneducated souls. Wright makes this point clear: "In *Native Son*, I tried to show that a man, bereft of a culture and unanchored by property, can travel but one path if he reacts positively but unthinkingly ... and that one path is emotionally blind rebellion" (in Franklin, 1995, p. 219). How, then, to think differently? Enter another way, another paradigm, another place of thinking, which I believe drives Wright's blueprint for writing. He calls his blueprint "complex simplicity," an idea similar to Thomas Kuhn's "essential tension," Carl Jung's "composite of opposites," the fairy tale demon-god figure Bluebeard, or the figure of the double in literature and myth. Artists seem to have an intuitive appreciation for the paradox of things being so and not so at the same time, hate being love, hardness being soft, or as Wright phrased it, fluid being iron. This kind of thinking saves us from despair because it reminds us, puts us in the mind, to see twoness: the horror and the glory together. I say this to further the alchemy metaphor I associate with Richard Wright. I say this because artists invoke alchemy in explaining why they paint in black or why they work from the awful or why they use words like "kill" and "violate" in talking about creating new forms. In what could be a gloss of Wright's theory of "complex simplicity" Mark Hasselriis describes a double movement process in alchemy, a word that means "from Egypt": "The word "khem" in Egyptian means "black," the black soil of that country, the black land that brought forth all fertility. So the idea of blackness bringing forth greenness or redness and finally giving birth to the philosophers' stone is very much in keeping even with the landscape of the country itself" (1990, p. 213).

The place all Wright's hammering and hacking leads to is Africa, not just literally but symbolically as well. Seven years before his death in 1960, Wright traveled extensively in the Gold Coast, collecting material for a book on Africa, published in 1954 as *Black Power: A Record of Reactions in a Land of Pathos*. And in 1956 he founded the American Society for African Culture, having helped plan earlier that year in Paris the First Congress of Negro Artists and Writers. These activities, together with extensive travel in Europe and Asia, expanded Wright's vistas and vision, to the point that, the year before he died, he composed more than 4,000 haiku—an amazingly different sort of writing from his earlier work. This short biographical account is meant to suggest the wide direction Wright traveled and the many cultural influences on his imagination. Not the least of which is the symbolic importance of fire.

To work with red and black symbolically, as the alchemists did, and as Wright did, is to see spirit in nature and magic in the color black. Both are reference points that activate unconscious material. The basic, primal quality of the African outlook can be ferocious and horrendous, but not in any final negative sense; because, to combat social evil, a ferocious and horrendous courage is required. Hephaestos is such a courageous craftsman, as were the spiritual leaders of African tribes, called Masters of the Fire. And in African creation myths there are often two creators, the Red One and the Black One—black associated with the dead who are not nonexistent. The dead exist, but they do so outside, beyond, or beneath the living, in another, invisible place. In what could be considered an African blend of the Hephaestos and Bluebeard tales, there is the story of the god Marduk, who fashions the world from the dead body of Tiamat. He first slays her; then from her corpse creates the world. Working with the corpse is working the dead material into another body (Von Franz, 1972).

I find these ideas resonating strongly with Richard Wright's daimonic energy. The ideas might be ancient but they are also postmodern. That meaning can be found in the unknown is the postmodern problematic: What is knowing? What is meaning? That knowledge can be hidden in our basements leaves me trembling, discontented, confused. There is the possibility that instinct is alive, dynamic, and moving with an animal power. There is the sense that emotions like fear and dread, even hate and rage, are what can move me on out from a stuck place in my head. Indeed, Von Franz tells us that the original meaning of emotion is *emotio*, that which makes one move, a feeling generally symbolized by the element of fire.

And so I return to Mary's head in the furnace. The head, seat of an evil rationality that justifies systemic racism, must burn. Wright's protagonists light fires many, many times, leaving worlds of ashes behind. As a product of a dislocated society, Wright quests both literally and figuratively to locate social values elsewhere. But before he gets to his haiku with their gentler images of his new vision, Wright must hammer on the anvil and go by way of fluid iron. He must travel the path of the symbolic fire.

Even in his autobiography Wright seems to think of his personal story in larger, mythic terms, with psychosymbolic significance. In the opening fire scene, described earlier, Richard is drawn to fire and sets fire to Granny's curtains. Then, to hide from punishment, he "crept into a dark hollow of a brick chimney and balled myself into a tight knot" (1945/1993a, p. 5). That he seeks to retreat underneath the burning house of an oppressive relative is symbolic in itself. But he chooses the image of a womb (chimney) and a reference to the fetal position to imply that fire is baptism or initiation. And he is the setter of his own fires that destroy in order to create. Hiding, being invisible, creating accidents so as to rebirth himself, the Wright character-destiny is endowed with actions that do not apply to the world above ground (Miller, E. E., 1990).

That fire is a particularly significant symbol for Wright's quest can be seen in the whipping and lynch scenes throughout his writing. In "Long Black Song" (1938–1945/1991) White men set fire to a house under which Silas escapes: "Silas had killed as many as he could and had stayed on to burn, had stayed without a murmur.... the house was hidden by eager plumes of red" (p. 354). In "Fire and Cloud" the Black preacher Taylor is whipped, his back like "a bed of fire," a symbolic reference to the physical shame a man is made to feel for his being Black: "Fire seethed not only in Taylor's back, but all over, inside and out. It was the fire of shame" (1938–1945/1991, pp. 393, 395). And in "Big Boy Leaves Home," the protagonist witnesses Bobo's lynching: " ... the wind carried, like a flurry of snow, a widening spiral of white feathers into the night. The flames leaped tall as the trees.... Then he saw a writhing white mass cradled in yellow flame, and heard screams, one on top of the other, each shriller and shorter than the last. The mob was quiet now, standing still, looking up the slopes at the writhing white mass gradually growing black, growing black in a cradle of yellow flame" (1938–1945/1991, p. 271).[2] Is it any wonder that Bigger Thomas, in *Native Son*, is the fire stoker in Mary Dalton's furnace basement, seeing in the red bed of coals a symbol for his own "molten fury" (1938–1945/1991, p. 530)? Bigger's actual furnace and the figurative furnaces of rage are directed at the head, "symbolic source of intelligence and aspiration and achievement that is cut off for blacks" (Rosenblatt, 1988, p. 26).

A mythic sense of character wrought in fire is perhaps most clearly portrayed in *The Outsider*. Cross Damon is no more "likable" than Christ himself must have appeared to his judges. Wright implies a Christ-like quality to his Cross character in what I refer to as the Inquisition scene reminiscent of Christ being cross-examined by Pontius Pilate. It is near the end of a tale of constant (criminal) activity. Cross has metaphorically burned all his bridges. He is left in the examining room with Houston, the White humpback detective who shares an outsider identity with Cross. Refusing to accept kinship with his mother, wife, or sons, Cross has cut himself off even from his family. This is necessary for character in search of its destiny as for mythic questers in search of other worlds. In answer to Houston's question, "What are you hiding, Damon?" Cross responds, "I affirm or deny nothing" (1953/1993b, pp. 510–511). He will neither help nor hinder; he will not satisfy the logic of the superworld. Repeating his denials to the charges of his criminality, Cross answers only in a litany of denials: I belong to nothing, I subscribe to nothing, I have nothing to say, I affirm or deny nothing (pp. 512, 513). It is at this point that Cross Damon defines himself, through negativity, as the Absolute Outsider. Such a man, Houston intuits, lives on a

---

[2]The stories "Long Black Song," "Fire and Cloud," and "Big Boy Leaves Home" are all part of a collection entitled *Uncle Tom's Children: Four Novellas* (1938–1945/1991). New York: The Library of America. These stories were originally placed with my father, Edward C. Aswell, at Harper and Brothers, and began a long association between my editor-father and Richard Wright.

completely different plane. Could this man be "the return of ancient man, pre-Christian man?" (p. 426).

The question is right. An earlier fire scene has Cross burning down the church building that holds draft records. How can a church be the vessel for the records of war? Cross, assuming the new name Lionel, has been on a "train" hurtling toward the destruction of such skewed Christian values. His new name, thus, must be born in fire coming from the basement of Christianity: from older, more ancient sources of religion. Wright has Cross set fire to the building in images that recall a lynch mob. Cross, along with "a throng of others," watches the fire of "frantic flakes" (p. 230). It is, on one level, the fire of all those draft records going up in flames. But on another, more symbolic level, it is the lynching fire out of which will be created a new-old self, birthed phoenix-fashion from the ashes of the Christian-military complex. This will be, my student Tim Wilday wrote, the self unafraid of becoming reacquainted with his older, buried self.

In a poem he wrote toward the end of his life, Richard Wright expressed in haiku what his earlier writings had expressed in fiction. Although it is a lynch poem, its imagery holds out the possibility that the key to unlocking dead bones lies in reconstituted imaginings:

> There was a design of white bones slumbering forgottenly
> upon a cushion of ashes …
> The dry bones stirred, rattled, and lifted, melting themselves
> into my bones … (in Bontemps, 1974, p. 103).

With the poem as coda, I suggest that Wright had been writing in wait, all along, for the (w)right words to release him from Bluebeard's cellar.

4

"All Pulp Removed":
Sexual Repression's
Revenge

I tie my Hat—I crease my Shawl—
Life's little duties do—precisely—

—Dickinson (1862/1960, p. 212)

The conventional view of Emily Dickinson as Maid of Amherst—virginal, pure, and sentimental—was promoted by her playacting a public pose; she was producer, director, and actor for "Emily Dickinson." The only daguerreotype of her, taken when she was seventeen, reveals a schoolmarmish face with a discreet velvet ribbon clasped by an amulet around her neck. *That* Emily provoked many admirers to invent their own private Emily as, say, guardian of proper New England values or, say, quaint quirkiness. One critic, a poet, went so far as to write a book entitled *My Emily Dickinson* (Howe, 1985). To add to the convention (conventions born in shades and graves), "Emily Dickinson" only published ten poems in her lifetime. The other thousand-plus poems, hidden in a locked chest that contained forty hand-sewn albums, never saw the light of day. She kept her erotic life to herself. More, she kept her erotic life hidden inside locked poems that even today are not easily opened. But, far from being one who feared the pulp of living, the poems of Emily Dickinson purges convention of deadness; for not only does her language refuse dead metaphors, they shun conventionalities that "talk of Hallowed things, aloud—and embarrass my Dog" (in Benfey, 1999, p. 44).

I imagine "Emily Dickinson" has been played out in many classrooms, where teachers think it safe to teach the strange little nature poems penned by a Massachusetts maid. No wonder students hate poetry. As Dickinson herself advised, "Forget! the lady with the amulet" (1862/1960, p. 210). Rather than being odd odes to haunted chambers or fantasies about coaches kindly stopping—harmless, if morbid, pieces—the poetry of Dickinson reveals a woman who loathed narrow, conventional manners precisely because they are deadly. "We do not play on Graves" she writes, "Because there isn't Room" (p. 224). What fun she must have had, the Emily behind the "Emily," writing in code about her disdain of sentiment, her heretical views of Christ, and the buried orgasmic secrets of women loving women.

A year before Dickinson died (1886) D. H. Lawrence was born (1885). The year that Lawrence died (1930) saw the English translated publication of Sigmund Freud's *Civilization and its Discontents*. Although unconnected in chronological time, these three authors share a contempt for the constraints of civilized conventions, not the least of which is sexuality. As Freud put it, "the sexual life of civilized man (sic) is ... severely impaired" because "civilization makes it plain that it will only permit sexual relationships on the basis of a solitary, indissoluble bond between one man and one woman" (1930/1961, p. 58). If heteronormative, monogamous sexuality is the only sexuality "allowed" by civilization, Freud reasons, then the pleasure principle so desired by the id is ruled out of order by the superego. It is uncanny, perhaps, that Dickinson's two basic themes are love and death, as are Lawrence's—foreshadowing Freud's formulation of Eros and Thanatos as mutually opposing instincts.

This chapter concludes Part 1 with an exploration of the impact of repression on character. Dickinson, so ahead of her time, saw the repressed nature of conventional society of the late 1900s and chose to counter it by parodying the conventions from another side of the social mirror. Hers would seem to be what Paula Salvio refers to as a "performance" of identity (n.d.). D. H. Lawrence, Kate Chopin, Virginia Woolf, and James Joyce are also concerned with the effects of repression, but differently. Lawrence and Chopin focus on repressed sexuality, Woolf on false angels, and Joyce attacks the Catholic church for deadening the life force of a people. The concern of these modernists should be no less a concern for us at the turn of the century, especially for educators. For if we as teachers are parrots of repressive social codes, are we not encouraging the next generation to be zombies, or bullies?

In his letters, Lawrence is explicit about his problem with civilized "niceness," which causes us to live in painted prisons (in Beal, 1956, p. 91). His metaphors for the imprisoning effects of civilization revolve around artifice, artificiality, and decoration. He uses such words as "bric-a-brac," "fashion," "house decoration," "parasol" and "parade," for example, to suggest the stifling effect conventional upholstery has on the pulse of feeling. Being educated "up," a person turns into a corpse—described, with a nod to Joseph Conrad, as a "whited sepulcher" (Lawrence, 1923/1965, p. 67). A deadened body wars against that which quickens, quivers, intermingles, surges, heaves, throbs, pulsates, and shakes—all favorite, Lawrence sexual verbs. Like Conrad, Lawrence holds upper class women responsible for emasculating men, holding men prisoner to repressive social codes upheld by women. In one of his more misogynist remarks, he writes that the "proper" way to eat a fig (perform cunnilingus) is to "split it in four, holding it by the stump. And open it, so that it is a glittering, rosy, moist, honied, heavy-petalled, four-petalled flower.... But the vulgar way is just to put your mouth to the crack, and take out the flesh in one bite" (in Murfin, 1983, p. 132).

The theme of the prisoner runs throughout Lawrence's (1923/1965) novella "The Ladybird." Both major characters are prisoners caught "up" in the mores of nice, social circles. As the names Count Dionys and Lady Daphne imply, however, theirs is a pagan orientation that inclines toward the natural, lower realms. Through circumstances their wild energies have been ensnared—the Count because he is a prisoner of war, the Lady because she has been turned into a hot house flower. Daphne's mythic fate, to have her free river locked into a tree, is literalized by her marriage to a cultured Englishman who treats her like a sister.

The atrophied condition of these two characters is made clear by Lawrence's physical descriptions of them. The Count is but a shell of a man: His hair has thinned, his black eyes lack expression, his brow is sick. Even so, his illness gives forth a "flame of suffering" (p. 52), which becomes his phallic life-flame. More, Lawrence emphasizes the Count's comparison to a satyr (part man, part beast) that even illness cannot hide. Similarly, the Lady is seen as ailing and nerve-worn, caught inside her own guard. Lawrence rescues these two by bringing them together in erotic encounters where they share mystical nights and the thread of longing, which draws them both out of the world of light into Dionysian darkness.

People split off from their erotic natures by the strictures of convention is the neurosis that fires Lawrence's creativity while confounding his personal life. His battles with English social codes, his constant traveling, his vicious letters to Katherine Mansfield, his portraits of men shooting at the moon, his soft-porn description for eating a fig: All these furies can be seen as Lawrence's attempts to skirt issues about his own sexuality. In a review he wrote of the opera *Cavalleria Rusticana*, Lawrence foreshadows Freud: "One of the laws of the phenomenon called a human being is that, hurt this being mortally at its sexual root, and it will recoil ultimately into some form of killing.... Make any human being a really rational being, and you have made him a ... destructive force" (in Beal, 1956, p. 285). Freud writes that the "inhibition" of "instinctual satisfaction" produces "the inclination to aggression" (1930/1961, p. 94), causing not just unrest (anxiety) but wholesale "extermination" (p. 104). Indeed, war is the metaphor for sexual battle in Lawrence's "The Fox," wherein the repressed homosexual instinct causes both psychological and literal killing.

Like "The Ladybird," "The Fox" (1923/1965) suggests that political outbursts of war foretell psychic disturbance, and vice versa: Neurosis causes anxiety in the form of war. The main characters—March, Banford, and Henry—are each in their own way sexually disoriented, at war with themselves. As such, they are seen in half-lights because "civilization" does not allow them to be at peace with their sexuality. March and Banford share a repressed lesbian relationship. Henry, a misogynist, is a repressed homosexual, like Lawrence himself (Meyers, 1990; Spender, 1973). That none of the characters realizes full, sexual consciousness causes the deadening of the life force. Although the story does not take place on a literal battlefield, war is staged in one of Lawrence's favorite hated arenas—the nice sitting room—where all accouterments such as gilt mirrors, Birmingham tin ware and carpets stand as social safeguards against passion and desire (Beal, 1956).

There are three nice sitting room scenes, each like a covert operation in the sexual battle for dominance. It is Henry's plan to kill the unconscious lesbian relationship between Banford and March by conquering March's masculine nature and murdering Banford, his enemy. In the first scene, Lawrence establishes the animal nature of Henry by having him "yap" with laughter as he sits in his uniform emitting an odor like that of the fox that stalks the barnyard. Banford becomes birdlike in his presence, twittering inside her comfortable cage where doors and windows are closed against the outside nature. March, however, feels vulnerable in Henry's presence and hides in shadows and corners. No wonder: She is his prey.

In the second tea scene, Lawrence makes the identity between Henry and the fox stalking the barnyard overt. Henry has taunting, half-mocking eyes, glinting hair, and a cunningly shrewd (foxlike) manner. Whereas earlier Henry had only "sprawled" on Banford's couch, now, in the second scene, he escalates the battle over niceness by entering the sitting room in shirt sleeves, a breach of manners severe enough to cause Banford to hide behind her spectacles and to choke on her food. Later, Henry gives Banford's room the look of a lumber camp, with his knees wide apart and his way of eating mouth to plate (pp. 128–129, p. 135). Having invaded Banford's territory, he takes her mannered life as his spoil.

In the third scene Henry is banned from Banford's sitting room, but he has conquered March by having her commit to him in marriage. More importantly, Henry has won the battle of March's sexuality by claiming her masculine side for himself. March is now his booty. Lawrence symbolizes this conquest by March's symbolic change of attire. No longer in brown puttees and farm wear, she now wears dresses that reveal the contours of her body and disclose her legs.

Ultimately, the trio are doomed to disaster. Henry arranges an accident wherein Banford is killed; March succumbs to a disastrous marriage (having lost the real marriage partner of her soul); and Henry wins a deadened soul: "She would not be a man any more, an independent woman with a man's responsibility. Nay, even the responsibility for her own soul she would have to commit to him" (p. 179). It is a false victory for Henry. Although he has killed his enemy and his wife's masculinity, he has in the process also killed his own true masculinity. Lawrence indicates this by referring to Henry in the end as a "boy" who "must have her" (p. 175); but, because she does not give him her "life"—the soul of which is part masculine—he loses.

What do these themes of repressed sexuality, Eros and Thanatos, and loss have to do with education? Deborah Britzman (1998b) speaks to these questions. She writes:

> These are the conflicts—Eros and Thanatos, love and aggression—that education seems to place elsewhere. And then these forces seem to come back at education as interruptions, as unruly students, as irrelevant questions, and as controversial knowledge in need of containment.... How might educators begin to complicate not just the response to difficult knowledge on the outside but also the response to the difficult knowledge from within—that other war? (p. 133)

By introducing difficult sexual issues into the literary classroom, a teacher risks the possibility of the return of the repressed on the part of students and professors. Why talk about forbidden topics? The question urges answer in a culture that says, for example, to gays in the military, don't say, don't be gay, and everything will be okay. Simple responses to complex psychosexual identities are dangerous, urging hiding. I face these questions when I introduce difficult texts as required reading for all students, wondering how far I can push the river of my students' backgrounds. Loud denial and feigned incredulity are common responses to the situations of sexually conflicted characters. After all, nice Southern ladies and gentlemen do not have conflicted sexual identities. The social section of the daily paper presents only smiling faces of young teens with their esquires at debutante parties that, ironically, in my day were called coming out parties. Perhaps for us in the South our fear of the levee system is justified. For, as the flood seasons teach, not even dikes can keep back the waters of the mighty Mississippi, tired of being controlled by unnatural devices.

If unawakened eroticism is the subject of Lawrence's work, awakening to the life force is the subject of Kate Chopin's (1899/1985) tragic novel, *The Awakening*. Using the fairy tale "Sleeping Beauty in the Wood" as the frame piece for her novel, Chopin portrays Edna as a father's daughter who is acculturated for marriage by the father into the father's world. The fairy tale father world holds defined expectations for the daughter-princess: She must remain prepubescent; she must obey her fate (which is to marry); she must marry the man her father selects; she must remain unconscious. For the fairy tale world of the patriarchy, marriage is the key that secures the patriarchy, assuring that *she* will be wed locked while *he* rules the realm. Happiness in such a world depends on the sexual unconsciousness of the princess: That is the lesson of fairy tales. Chapter six illustrates with another fairy tale this same lesson and its impact on the lives of nuns and wives.

Recall the Beauty tale: When the king and queen produce a baby girl, a ceremony is proclaimed to which come all the fairies. One of these, the bad fairy, places a curse on the girl, saying that she will have her hand pricked by a needle and die of the wound. At once, the king demands the entire kingdom be rid of all spindles. When the girl is about fifteen or sixteen, she wanders around the palace and up to a room where a lone woman sits spinning. Curious, the girl touches the spindle and immediately falls into a sleep that lasts one hundred years. She awakens only when a prince, who has braved a difficult entrance though the palace door, kisses her. They exchange a few words, they marry, they live happily ever after.

Chopin challenges the patriarchal formula for female initiation into the world of the fathers by posing a feminist response. The Sleeping Beauty is Edna Pontellier, who has obeyed the formula by marrying but is unhappy. One afternoon she falls asleep in a cottage in the wood. But before her nap she unloosens her hair, rubs and admires her strong arms, bathes her face, and climbs into the fresh white linens. She is alone. The preparations for sleep, clearly ritualistic, suggest that here in the woods, away from the demands of the church or the family, she may begin anew. When she awakens, she is hungry, expressive of an ontological hunger that is a strengthening sign of Eros. Chopin describes Edna's strong white teeth tearing at the bread left her on a table covered with a white cloth; then Edna goes into the garden and plucks an orange from the tree. Here is Edna, reenacting the Christian communion while at the same time performing an Eve act. This mix of metaphors is Chopin's way of suggesting that Edna will disobey the commandments of the father; she will live as an awakened woman, a decision for which she must be punished.

In the tale, the spinster is responsible for putting Beauty to sleep. In the novel, the spinster figure is Mademoiselle Reisz, who, like her prototype, lives in an attic. Unlike such literary madwomen as Bertha Rochester in *Jane Eyre* or the wife in "The Yellow Wallpaper"—both of whom are locked in the attic by their husbands—this spinster occupies her attic space voluntarily. Indeed, the spinster is the opposite of the young maiden not only in age and beauty but in consciousness, for she alone disobeys or is unaware of the king's proclamation and so is not locked into his dictates. As such, spinsters are archetypal figures of female wisdom whose occupation of spinning connects them with the powerful Spider Woman (see chapter eleven).

I see Mlle. Reisz performing a necessary teaching function for Edna who, newly awakened to her erotic nature, must understand the dangers as well as delights of living from one's soul. "The bird that would soar above the level plain of tradition and prejudice must have strong wings," the older woman warns. "It is a sad spectacle to see the weaklings bruised, exhausted, fluttering back to earth" (1899/1985, p. 1,071). Under Mlle. Reisz's tutelage Edna unlearns the social code required of a Creole wife. She develops instead an elemental imagination: the fire, earth, air, and water that connect her with the cosmos. The delight she takes in swimming, for example, takes her back to the polymorphously perverse child she once was, believing that the meadows she waded in had no boundaries and that her opportunities were limitless. Edna's unlocking to her buried self takes the form of open rebellion against her husband, on the one hand, and newfound exploration of extramarital sex and with painting, on the other hand. Still, such discoveries are not sufficient to ward off the predicament for Edna's future in a closed society. She commits suicide by drowning. Chopin's description of this death complicates the stricture against suicide, for the words imply freedom rather than despair and new life rather than death:

> But when she was beside the sea, absolutely alone, she cast the unpleasant, pricking garments from her, and for the first time in her life she stood naked in the open air, at the mercy of the sun, the breeze that beat upon her, and the waves that invited her. How strange and awful it seemed to stand naked under the sky! how delicious! She felt like some new-born creature, opening its eyes in a familiar world that it had never known. (p. 1,102)

Surely, this novel presents a stark choice for women: Live and remain miserable; die and find release. Were it not for the presence of the foil character Adèle, Chopin might seem to be preaching an overly simplistic alternative about women's fate inside the patriarchy, as chapter five discusses. Such starkness, however, offers a teaching opportunity to interfere with students' inherited ideas about marriage as a fairy tale. Interference is, as Anna Freud insists, a "central dynamic" for education (in Britzman, 1998b, p. 9). A teacher could point out how Edna was not marriage material, being so much a free spirit and so little connected with convention or childrearing. That marriage was thrust on her was bound to cause problems. Students can discuss the question of the maternal instinct. Often, my women students cannot conceive (pun) that women might not like to be mothers and that the consequence of being a mother-woman might be disastrous for all concerned. They come to class with a "conceptual fortress" (Britzman, 1988b, p. 55) built around the notion of mothering. And the issue of Edna's choices raises the question of her selfishness, a taboo for women.

Teaching in a Catholic college, I imagine the long arm of the church occasionally reaching into my classroom, forbidding me to urge women to seek happiness (selfishness), damning me for depositing pagan (heretical) ideas into the empty receptacles of the innocent young. For, clearly, Chopin suggests that a third way is open to women who dare to be their natural selves, not the selves of which the church or convention approves. The third way is found in the fringe women characters, Madame Antoine in the forest cottage and Mademoiselle Reisz in her attic apartment. These fringe women live on the outskirts of society. As such, they are not influenced by the suffocating requirements for women. Chopin implies that a newly awakened consciousness needs matriarchal mentoring. The fringe characters—singular, different, Sibyl-like—offer this mentoring for Edna, whose soul in them found at least a temporary Attic home.

The advice to live from one's soul is dangerous advice. How much easier for women to starve themselves, silence themselves, or even suicide themselves, so as to remove their pulp. How much easier for teachers to teach nicely about nice topics, keeping the school a sanctum against a tumultuous world. But, as Virginia Woolf knew, removing the pulp produces deadness. A few days before she committed suicide, she wrote in her diary: "A curious sea side feeling in the air today. It reminds me of lodgings on a parade at Easter. Everyone leaning against the wind, nipped & silenced. All pulp removed" (in Bell, 1941/1984, p. 359).

Virginia Woolf's (1927/1955) *To the Lighthouse* can be read as a text against a text, fiction against fact, obfuscated fact buried inside obfuscating fiction. It presents a startlingly disguised, extremely abstracted portrait of Mrs. Ramsay, a.k.a. Julia Stephen, a.k.a. Woolf's mother: a woman, for all appearances, who was kind, beautiful, educated, selfless, well-intentioned: nice. Ideal. I began reading this novel as did Manley Johnson (1973), as "an elegy on the warmth of Mrs. Ramsay's character" (p. 76). I found her character difficult but challenging, along the lines of Erich Auerbach's (1971) reading of her as "an enigma" whose truth can never be known (p. 78). Not so. As Louise DeSalvo (1989) discovered, Woolf's mother played the role of "The Angel in the House," whose duty it was to keep the patriarchy going through the erection of woman as ideal, "The best half of creation's best,/ Its heart to feel, its eye to see" (Patmore, 1993, p. 1,600). The most important role for The Angel, it seems, was *not* to see household abuses. As DeSalvo relates, Woolf's personal family history was of a story of a mother's conspiracy with husband, uncles and half-brothers who were allowed, through a subterfuge of maternal, steely silence, to exercise male sexual privilege on virtually every female member of the house. In fact, DeSalvo comments, the woman on whom Mrs. Ramsay is based was "cold iron" (p. 118).

Teaching this novel, with its overlay of perfection, is incredibly important as an eye-opener for women students who live abused lives inside perfect homes. One such student spoke up during class. Joan described the subtexted sexual situation inside the Ramsay's household as typical for her experience, when the mother prizes beauty and harmony above all else and when the father is distant and self-centered. With my student as my guide, and Louise DeSalvo's book as reference, the class and I undertook to see through the web of Woolf's words into Mrs. Ramsay's nonactions and repressed desires.

Like Lawrence in the previous discussion and Joyce in the next one, Woolf uses war as a background metaphor for a psyche besieged by conventional norms and shut off from itself. Throughout the opening section of *To the Lighthouse*, snatches of lines from Tennyson's "The Charge of the Light Brigade" are heard in insistent dactylic rhythms, suggestive of horses thundering toward massacre. While Mr. Ramsay recites this Poet Laureate's poem about a terrible military error during the Crimean war—absentmindedly drumming out the phrases as he walks back and forth on the bluff—the lines waft in through the open window where Mrs. Ramsay sits with James. Woolf's juxtaposition of the phrases "stormed at with shot and shell" (p. 29) and "someone had blundered" (p. 31) are voiced in a "loud cry, as of a sleep-walker, half roused" (p. 29) but fall into Mrs. Ramsay's ear "with the utmost intensity" making her "turn apprehensively" (p. 29). What is she afraid of? Why apprehensive? What are the ghostly drums that jostle her awareness suddenly, making her feel a terror she cannot explain? It is she who has ambushed her children to be "stormed at" by her house guests. We learn that the house is in disrepair, the wall paper fading, the mat fading. Worse, there are no locks for any of the doors. "Still, if every door in the house is left perpetually open, and no lock maker in the whole of Scotland can mend a bolt, things must spoil" (p. 11). A locked door is at least a partial protection against the thin veils of civilization, the very sort of civility Mrs. Ramsay has been trained to uphold. But this one protection for her children she has neglected, allowing the house guests to ride her daughters "boldly" and "well" (p. 49). No wonder Mrs. Ramsay feels she is not good enough to tie her husband's shoelace: She is the "someone" who "had blundered."

And blunder she does. Not only does Mrs. Ramsay repress her role as guardian of her daughters' well being, but she represses her own covertly sexual desire for her youngest son James. Woolf emphasizes the number of times Mrs. Ramsay measures the brown stocking she is knitting against James's leg, implying a response by the boy when he stands "erect" against his mother's leg. Here is a Victorian mother, supposed to be the Angel of the House, admired for keeping certain civilized rituals (but even the meals are not on time), negotiating the public sphere—but completely lost inside her empty self. The empty self is a repressed self. As Bill Pinar insists: "Such a (repressed) self lacks access both to itself and to the world. Repressed, the self's capacity for intelligence, for informed action, even for simple functional competence is impaired" (1993, p. 61). Mrs. Ramsay, locked inside herself, cannot see to it that the doors to her daughters' bedrooms should be locked at night.

One scene makes the case for Mrs. Ramsay's repressed maternal consciousness. It occurs after a dinner party, described as an island "against the fluidity out there" (p. 147). For Maxine Greene (1995) the dinner party stands as a single, bright, cultivated, and civilized moment of meaning against outside chaos. "I was made to see what I had not particularly wanted to see," she comments. " ... it moved me to ... effect connections, to bring some vital order into existence" (1995, p. 98). But for Mrs. Ramsay, the civilized pretenses of order are only veils, particularly the veils that veil *her* eyes, *preventing* her from seeing what was really going on in the bedroom of her daughters. For, after the party served by a maid and featuring all the niceties of upper class living, Mrs. Ramsay goes upstairs to say good night to her eight children, none of whom can sleep because a pig's skull on the wall disturbs them: "Cam thought it was a horrid thing, branching at her all over the room" (p. 172). Woolf's persona, Cam, is the crooked one in the family, having been incested, like Woolf herself, by the gentlemen of the house. As a word, "cam" means "a cylinder having an irregular form such that its motion, usually rotary, gives to a part or parts in contact with it a specific rocking or reciprocating motion" (Webster, 1993). A cam needs a shaft, as my student Joan pointed out. But as Woolf portrays her fictional mother dealing with her fictional self, Cam's fear of being shafted is scarfed. By a swift turn of a mother's shawl, Mrs. Ramsay wraps the pig's skull around and around and around. After that, Mrs. Ramsay leaves the children's room unlocked, letting "the tongue of the door slowly lengthen in the lock" (p. 173).

That Mrs. Ramsay denies Cam's terror is just another indication of the Victorian mother's inability to deal with the chaos of ugly reality. Read crudely, the Ramsay household, like that of the house of the Fisherman's wife in the fairy tale, is a pig sty (Johnson, 1973, p. 73). Is it any wonder that Cam is not nice to Mr. Bankes, whom, as we read between the lines, is a lecher?

> Mr. Bankes was alive to things which would not have struck him had not those sandhills revealed to him the body of his friendship lying with the red on its lips laid up in peat—for instance Cam, the little girl, Ramsay's youngest daughter. She was picking Sweet Alice on the bank. She was wild and fierce. She would not 'give a flower to the gentleman' as the nursemaid told her. No! no! no! she would not! She clenched her fist. She stamped. And Mr. Bankes felt aged and saddened.... He must have dried and shrunk. (p. 36)

Cam is not the only child of the family whose actions could be read as reactions. Jasper shoots crows, Andrew dissects crabs, and James, pictured always with his pair of scissors, hates his father. Behaviors are texts, if one can read them.

I doubt I would have been able to read this text this way were it not for the eyes of my incest-survivor student. She who had lived through the lies and deceptions—what Woolf refers to as the "cotton wool of daily life" (1928/1976, p. 72)—became the clue finder for the class, as we made our way through the mine fields. Teaching in this manner requires close reading of the sort urged by Dennis Sumara (1996). The class enters on a common project, making Woolf's text a "commonplace" for collecting information about a dysfunctional household. Such mutual discovery and revelation become a method for possible readings of our own private worlds, which withhold more than they reveal. What appears on the surface in Woolf's novel is covered over by distracting, other, *incomplete* "texts"—fairy tale sections, poetic lines, half formed thoughts of this character-that character, arrangements of fruit on the table, arrangements of sand on the beach, the tap-tap of cricket balls, a scarf, a stocking, a pig's skull. It is almost as if Woolf wants to distract the reader from discovering the truth.

Learning to read each of these incompletions as commentaries on hidden actions is a way to develop a "commonplace for the self" (Sumara, 1996, p. 49). My students, however, reacted to our class work in generally hesitant terms, reflecting their discomfort with, or refusal to engage in, self-reflection. Tara wrote:

I often found myself confused yet aware that Woolf was coming from a place I have not yet been. Many times through her wordy paragraphs I wanted to get a quick interpretation. I cannot honestly say I understood all of her book or that I enjoyed reading every minute of it.

Kimberly wrote:

We were given assignments to interpret paragraphs on our own. This process allowed me to understand the novel more clearly, especially when other people read their interpretations. I found out that even though someone's interpretation of a passage was quite logical, my interpretation could be totally different and still be logical. In reading a book, however, I prefer straightforward ideas.

Perhaps Leslie expressed an undergraduate's response best:

To the Lighthouse was absolutely and without a doubt one of the most difficult novels that I've read. Her style of writing (conversations on the outside, personal thoughts on the inside in parentheses) allows the reader to see much more than what is on the level of appearances. Virginia Woolf leaves me very apprehensive about people and relationships. I can be speaking with my friend but thinking subconsciously something totally different.

As these selected comments indicate to me, what I had hoped to accomplish and what I actually did accomplish in the classroom were two different things. I had the lofty goal of attempting to encourage a wider conception toward "reading." I had hoped that students might acquire some skills in self-reflection. Apparently, the only one who became aware of the gulf between appearances and reality in life was Leslie. The other students seemed to regard the assignment as a classroom drill that was "testing" their powers of interpretation. Of particular interest, but of no surprise, is the discomfort students have when "straightforward ideas" are not forthcoming. This polite resistance to seeing the work as self-work derives from an embedded, deeply fortressed belief of students that the classroom is for learning the course, not for discovering what courses within.

Nevertheless, I trod onward, introducing work to my students that can never be fully cracked open. Increasingly, I feel it necessary to say in the class how I learn new ways of reading from student observations—not that their readings are better than mine, but that their readings remind me of reading all phenomena as "precarious, unstable, and always subject to revision" (Derrida, 1992, p. 73). In such a way I hope to stay alive to "reading" myself.

Being dead to the self is the focus of James Joyce's (1926/1954) The Dubliners, a work I see owing much to Virginia Woolf's intertextuality. Joyce, like Woolf, introduces many texts inside the text and, as such, is another excellent source for encouraging a reading between the lines of one's life. Part of the difficulty in reading Joyce, for my students, is their misidentifying with the narrative voice.

No tour guides here. No omniscient narrator telling us what is. Rather, we see through the unseeing eyes of the characters who remain in steady state inside their nonaesthetic settings. Of particular note is Eveline. I ask my students to free-associate with her name before they read the story: Eve, even line, lying, even, line, old-fashioned are common responses. Just so is Eveline, who lives unimaginatively—following the even line of convention, lying to herself about her true past, unable to break free because of the comfort evenness brings her, the comfort of living the eve of one's life, even when one is still in one's prime.

Eveline's problem is that she has developed an automatic self. This is the self that evidences a distrust for the spontaneous gesture while at the same time professing the opposite. "But she wanted to live. Why should she be unhappy?" (Joyce, 1926/1954, p. 47). Why the But? The exclamation is really a protest, a timid call of despair by a girl who cannot bear to depart her miserable life so as to live with Frank, her "fellow," and go aboard ship to Buenos Aires. This possibility of escape is an absolute peril to her automatic self. At the moment of decision when she must leap away from her even line, she retreats: "All the seas of the world tumbled about her heart. He was drawing her into them: he would drown her" (p. 48). Because Eveline prefers the embrace of her norm to the arms of her lover, she will carry herself forward as she has in the past, "on the tramways of convention" (Bollas, 1995, p. 134).

Eveline's inability to leave presents a potent case study for my parochial students, who literally live in parishes (as they are called in Louisiana) and who seldom cross the river. Clearly, the reader sees Eveline's surroundings as deadening: Her house, despite careful dusting, retains dust; the harmonium is broken (broken melodies), the only face on the wall is of an unknown priest (not her dead mother), whose photograph yellows with age. The house, though, is familiar; and, as battered women know, what is familiar is comforting, like a straight and even line. Between the lines, however, the reader sees that Eveline is a battered woman, abused by her father's violence and perverse sexuality and bound by her mother's deathbed request "to keep the home together." Accordingly, Eveline lives in the past, not able to "express" her "idiom" (Bollas, 1997, p. 44) in either the present or the future. The past, from what little of it she reveals, is a relief carved on a tombstone: permanent if not permeable. "They seemed to have been rather happy then" (Joyce, 1926/1954, p. 42), she says. And so the past is a "cemeterial concept" (Bollas, 1995, p. 134), safe as the grave into which she has buried herself.

When contemplating the pros and cons of eloping, Eveline "reasons" in such a way as to ensure that the negatives are more persuasive than the positives. Just what is it about Eveline's past that must, at all costs, be preserved? What grip does the past have that ensures against its modification? Eveline's idea of life is a dead negative rather than a live positive. As Allison, my student, observed, "Obviously, what others think of her is how she thinks of herself." Continuing that idea, Jennifer wrote, "She worries about what people will think of her. Some will be happy yet others will gossip. The worst part about the ones that will be happy is that they will be happy to be rid of her, not happy that she will finally be happy." Melissa commented, "Eveline would be happier if she did not have a choice at all." In her remarks, Terri said:

> While Eveline sits thinking, she hears music that a street organ is playing. I sense the music is more of a noise to her rather than a welcomed sound. It brings back memories of the night her mother passed away. She remembers the noise of the street organ then as she hears it now. Then the memories of the promise she made to her dying mother resurface. She had promised to "try to keep the family to-gether." Throughout this scene in the story, I think Eveline is looking for a reason not to leave with Frank.

Kaci, in commenting on the music Eveline hears, remarks, "The Italian music she hears is symbolic of a place other than her home in Dublin and her father's disapproval." And in commenting on the "decision" to stay, Nicole concludes, "she does not have the strength to brave the new adventure of her life with Frank. She dies spiritually and emotionally because she is scared to be happy."

Perhaps Eveline is what Adam Phillips (1993) describes as an agoraphobic, one who cannot bear the open spaces of life. This phobia of the open field ensures a "repression of opportunity" (Phillips, p. 16). To venture into the fields might take Eveline off line. As my students study Eveline, I wonder if they see in this good Catholic Christian girl any semblance of themselves. Is the reading just a mental responsibility or can it exercise an examination of their own decision-making skills? Eveline offers an excellent example of one who is clueless, merely going through the motions of a "sort of" life. It is as if her tiredness and indecision is, as Phillips observes, "a kind of blank condensation of psychic life," wherein she is simply "waiting to be repressed" (p. 78). The final description of Eveline is of her white face "passive, like a helpless animal" (p. 48). Joyce suggests that by speaking the dead language of the past, Eveline, like the other Dubliners, is not even human.

What haunts the Dubliners is death: promises to the dead, life lived in dead memories, lives that make living seem a mockery and death a romance. And so Joyce's last story in *Dubliners* is "The Dead," so titled because even in the midst of an Epiphany party, Greta and Gabriel run parallel lives, not touching each other's souls. That is the epiphany that comes to Gabriel later, when Greta tells him of her first love, who died for love of her. Gabriel can never compete with this hopelessly idealized tragedy. Joyce symbolizes the gulf between people that prevents real communication by his description of the party's dinner table. Convention requires polite banter, music, and food. But within the table setting itself lies the real textual situation: battle. The two ends of the table are "rival ends" between which run "parallel lines of sidedishes" described in such a way as to suggest the uniforms of soldiers. The decanters in the center stand "as sentries" and the bottles of stout, ale, and minerals wait like "three squads" (p. 252). Here are people gathered together for social communion when, in fact, it is conventional etiquette that militates against real talk.

The conventions about which the writers in this chapter rail form the rigid dictates of Victorian and Puritan cultures. Conventions, because they undergird norms, define norms until what is normative becomes carved in stone. Characters become like letters carved in rock, obliged against the flow of psychic energy to obey the code. It is no wonder that postmodernists see the need to double code, to confound, to interrupt, and to upset. When our students follow only the straight and narrow explanation, the straightforward plot, the straight conventions of the straight society, educators might do well to recall the deadness such automatic, ill chosen choices can bring. All of the characters discussed here were lesser humans for having had their pulp removed. Better, far better, our students greet the next millennium with enough wide awakeness to see, as did Dickinson, how blind, dumb obedience makes a beggar of being. Better, far better, to recall Emily's sly resistance, code within code, to push back the closed universe of convention so as to go "out upon Circumference—/Beyond the Dip of Bell" (1862/1960, p. 180).

Like Letters Written
in Sand

SPLITHEADS

I think that's why this is a very wonderful time, because more and more people are in such pain that they are open to another way, to another perspective on life.

—Osborn, in Kohno, 1998, p. 203

Just think about it. Do you really know who you are?

—Pirandello, 1924/1992, p. 1,502

Most people are other people. Their thoughts are someone else's opinions, their life is a mimicry, their passions a quotation.

—Wilde, 1994, p. 926

My left eye was cloudy … but my right eye was clear. It was like two sides of my nature.

—Williams, in Spoto, 1985, p. 81

In the first part, I presented characters who see themselves on the wrong side of the metaphorical door. For characters such as Thomas Sutpen, Cholly Breedlove, or Cross Damon, the door that prevents their entry keeps them shut out of privilege, opportunity, awareness, softening. Theirs is a hard life, an impenetrable ego, a blocked head. They are one-sided. Their way, the Buddha says, is like letters carved in rock, for they cannot see beyond the blocked entrance; they cannot move beyond the blocked ego; and so when they act, they act out, blindly and cruelly. These characters live among us today in the form of White supremacists, political terrorists, rapists, gay bashers, and other hate mongers who commit their volcanic acts like so many Mount Etnas.

As Matthew Fox (1997) reminds us, doors are much broader than we can imagine if they lead into "the various rooms of the states of darkness" (Fox & Sheldrake, p. 144). Darkness can be trusted, not feared. However, it was the Indo-European myth of Theseus and the Minatour that forged the Western world's conception of dark as fearsome and led a long parade of tellings about the necessity to kill the dark. In that myth, the male hero enters the dark labyrinth so as to slay the monster, conquer nature, and bring light and rationality to humankind. Previous to this telling, Carol Christ (1999) says, was the Minoan culture's worship of the dark in the caves of Crete rising like underground cathedrals. In the third cave below the earth, the imageless image of the goddess urged initiates to trust life and give up control. Early people saw the monster as something to befriend, not to kill, recognizing long before depth psychology that the monster is us. To go to the dark place is to abide inside the fertile womb where new life gestates.

A modernist telling about darkness is Joseph Conrad's (1902/1993) *Heart of Darkness*, a tale of Europe's entry into Africa and a reworking of male hero adventure stories. In this revisionist myth, the hero does not succeed in conquering the dark; it is the other way around. Kurtz, the ivory hunter, takes his European words and European ideas to the Congo, thinking these sufficient to do his business. He only sees the jungle as something to plunder. He does not see that the wilderness holds "an implacable force brooding over an inscrutable intention" (p. 1,783). Its force does not respond to the force of words like "science" or ideas like "the suppression of savage customs" (p. 1,795). Rather, the wilderness's dark is mysterious, impenetrable, prehistoric, immense. These words, mentioned frequently enough to be like a drumbeat on the imagination, are Conrad's mantra. The darkness, in the heart of Africa as in the human heart, is something to be feared the way early people feared the awesome qualities of divinity. This is the fear that comes from humility, the fear that recognizes that there are things in the universe that should never be tampered with because they are beyond human understanding. "If such is the form of ultimate wisdom," Marlow the narrator says, "then life is a greater riddle than some of us think it to be" (p. 1,811). Marlow, having been there and "peeped over the edge" (p. 1,811), returns to tell the tale, to bear witness. His story is not an adventure story in the Western tradition, "the whole meaning of which lies within the shell of a cracked nut" (p. 1,761). Its message is not about conquering; its boast does not employ pretty ideas and rational concepts; its meaning is not simple. Instead, Marlow, who "had the pose of a Buddha preaching in European clothes" (p. 1,762), brings an Eastern understanding to Western ears and eyes about meaning that is less a cracked nut than a "misty halo" (p. 1,762).

The characters in Part II of this book, like those in Part I, do not open the door to more awakened paths. Unlike the blockheads, however, these splitheads have glimpses or peeps into another side of themselves because they feel split. As such, they are dimly aware that they may be living according to others' expectations as opposed to living from their core. Social habits prevent psychic movement. These characters allow their social selves to take the place of their authentic selves, until the difference between the two is blurred. What is reality, what illusion; what is the true self, what the false? Such a person is playing a part in a script written by others. The ones who live like letters written in sand have not dug down beneath the sand to where the river flows, although they intuit "something."

Luigi Pirandello (1924/1992) introduces this theme of the unauthored self in *Six Characters in Search of an Author*. The play is witty, hilarious in parts, profound. Like many a profundity, the depth is sounded through humor, laughter breaking into the moment like a sharp Aha!. Teaching the play, I set the students into two rows facing each other. On one side are the Characters, who have a family drama they need to reenact. On the other side are the Actors, whose only reason for being is to playact; for them, life is a rehearsal. Issues of representation are immediately apparent—the Actors exist in the world of "make up" and "make believe." As Cornelio Pacheco, one of my students, observed: "The actors don't seem to understand that what they act on stage is actually something real that happens to other people in real life. If we think of ourselves as leading actors playing someone else's role, we forget who we really are." Forgetting who we are. To forget who we are is to sleepwalk through life, playact social roles, live as unawakened beings, not listen for the cracks.

Another of the themes of Pirandello's wonderful Theater of the Absurd is the reality of literature. Pirandello suggests that in contrast to the unreal lives many of us lead (falsely and without self-authority; acting, not being), there is the reality of literature's characters who can, if we let them, show us not only the drama to enliven living but also the theories to ignite authenticity. That, of course, is the overriding emphasis of this book. If we are to shed our illusions about reality, perhaps we might delve more deeply into the illusory world of literature to discover what is really real. Does that sound absurd?

In this part I discuss various distortions of authentic selves as manifested in fairy tale and social coding. The predicament of distortion is particularly valid for women. The distortions are often seen in twos, like Pirandello's two rows to suggest the split self; or they employ the metaphor of masks to suggest a hiding or covering; or they use the metaphor of glass to suggest seeing without penetrating.

Mirrors are like doors: ambivalent symbols. Mirrors reproduce images, contain them, absorb them. They can freeze or facilitate. They can erect a barrier or enable a seeing through to awareness (Anzaldúa, 1987). All that is needed is a hole no bigger than a pinprick for a glimpse into another, deeper world. In fact, the pupil of the eye is a hole through which light comes into the eye's darkness (Fox & Sheldrake, 1997). All humans can, thereby, attain threshold vision if they will. And so, there is a seeping, in this section, a dripping, a prickle, an opening ever so small but there, wherein the inauthentic playacting self feels the "point" of its dissonance with the way things are. At that point or pinprick, falseness is let go and imagination is entered into, if only for a brief moment. The characters are on their way, potentially. They are like letters written in sand.

Flannery O'Connor's work is apropos in this sanded connection. O'Connor writes in the conviction that the world everywhere evidences the grace of God, displayed by the multiple colors of a surreal landscape but unseen by characters who see only black or white. Her characters are not at home in the graced world because they are too filled with self-righteousness, smugness, pride, envy, greed, and bigotry. O'Connor often describes certain of these people with overly large or distorted eyes, suggestive of their potential for grace, except they are looking through the wrong end of a telescope. These are the very ones she selects to receive, without asking for it, God's grace. And when they have their tiny moment of revelation, often by way of a blow or a piercing and often just before they die, something happens to their eyes. Julian's mother, in "Everything that Rises Must Converge" (1983), prides herself, for example, on being a Godhigh, socially better than others and certainly better than those "on the other side of the fence" (Blacks and White trash). As with many an O'Connor story, the mother and son are at loggerheads, the son thinking his education has made him a better person than his ignorant mother. Despite his politically and socially correct views, however, the son is beyond grace; education, because it has nothing to do with matters of the heart, is beyond redemption. Rather, it is the uneducated mother whom O'Connor selects.

The story takes place aboard a bus, O'Connor's microcosm of a rainbow world, as evidenced by the many colors of the bus riders' shoes and hats. During the ride, the mother is mirrored by a Black woman who sits opposite her and wears a hat just like hers. At the end of the ride, inexplicably, the mother dies on the sidewalk, but not before there is a close up on her eyes: "One eye, large and staring, moved slightly to the left as if it had become unmoored. The other remained fixed on him (Julian), raked his face again, found nothing, and closed" (p. 284). The weird picture of the eye becoming "unmoored" suggests O'Connor's serious intention: At last, this woman has cast away the anchor of her ignorant views so she can see the "nothing" that is her son.

A glimpse into the falseness of the bourgeois soul is one of Franz Kafka's themes in his "Metamorphosis" (1915/1992). Kafka turns the reader's perceptions inside out as he takes us into the mind and sensitivity of Gregor, who wakes one morning to find himself changed into a beetle. From the beetle's perceptions we see how gross is the family, how mean their spirit and how pretentious their behaviors. This perception becomes clear when Gregor in his beetle state scrabbles into the living room to hear his sister play the violin. While the humans feign interest in the music and then outrightly ignore the sister's playing, Gregor becomes ever more entranced by its beauty. "Was he an animal, that music could move him so?" Kafka asks (p. 1,718). With the author's question, we are able to see the crassness of the human world from the beetle point of view. Conversely, we are able to sense the delicacy of animal feeling with its close attention to particulars. And yet, it is not simply the details that so move Gregor the beetle; it is an entire sense of being transported, moved, sent on a "voyage," as Gaston Bachelard (1971) calls the dynamics of the imagination (p. 21).

What the foregoing examples are meant to suggest is that, unlike the block-heads of the first part, splitheads experience movement, however slight, in their imaginations. This movement is necessary if a deeper self is to be felt, glimpsed, or intuited. Splitheads are not totally blocked because a crack, crevice, hole, or peep affords a glimpse or a murmur from beyond. In Samuel Beckett's work, the motif of storytelling moves a speaker to another place, the imagination, where figures and events play out their drama. The story fascinates the speaker because what is being storied is another side of the speaker's self, unacknowledged except in fantasy. In *Endgame* (1958a), for example, Hamm's body is full of holes. He has holes for eyes (he is blind and wears dark glasses); he has a hole in his heart, and a gaping hole in his head for which he requires a painkiller. "There's something dripping in my head. (Pause.) A heart, a heart in my head," he says (p. 18). It is through these holes that a stubborn ego consciousness cannot go but feeling can be felt. The "heart" of the story is a "hole" where a child needs rescue—presumably the childlike part of the narrator. The setting is a deserted hole. There is a feudal lord to whom paupers must make petition. One pauper, from a hole far away, petitions the lord for help: Would the lord take in the pauper's child? Hamm enjoys telling the story, which he embellishes with many a rhetorical flourish, but he is stalling, not daring to face the question, not able to open to its "hole." Drained by the efforts of bombast, Hamm in the midst of his own story readies to hear its question on more than one level. He indicates a shift in consciousness by employing images of an ebbing tide. "I don't know. (Pause.) I feel rather drained. (Pause.) The prolonged creative effort. (Pause.) If I could drag myself down to the sea! I'd make a pillow of sand for my head and the tide would come" (p. 61). Letting tides fill his head signals a moment in the narration when Hamm's roleplaying breaks down. Ceasing to play the tyrant, he could become a petitioner. Ceasing to be the teller, he could become the told. Hamm's holes, however, never fill and the drainage is never complete. He remains "the old stauncher" (p. 84), determined to stop all holes to awareness by whatever ego means he must employ. Opportunity is aborted.

The hole image suggests a place for birthing. Clearly, not all characters, not all people, dare to be reborn or to see things from the other side. For mystics, being in the hole gives the experience of bottoming out and becoming utterly receptive (Fox & Sheldrake, 1977, p. 145), as Part III discusses. But for the characters in this section, what is felt is a vague stirring, a slight dissolving, and at times a beginning of reborn consciousness. The characters here are potential artists, in the sense that Robert Musil (1994) intends:

An artist receives the impression that something he has avoided, some vague feeling, a sensation, a stirring of his will, is dissolving in him, and its elements, released from the connections in which habit had frozen them, suddenly acquire unexpected connections to often quite different objects, whose dissolution spontaneously resonates in the process. In this way pathways are created and connections exploded, and consciousness drills new accesses for itself. (p. 6)

This quotation helps to see the difficulty of being an artist of our own souls. So to be, we must unfreeze our habits and drill our stubborn consciousness. These are not heady acts. Too many of us live in our heads, more's the pity.

In this part, then, I introduce situations and characters who forge clearings for themselves, even when these clearings do not create creating spaces (Miller, D. L., 1990). But it is necessary, as the Buddha remarked, to see this interim type of character, the one written in sand, as an artist *in potentia*. Without the crack or the hole, there would be no access to something else. Without the cactus needle (Anzaldúa, 1987, p. 73) or the pinprick (Miller, J. L., 1990, p. 85), consciousness would remain ego hardened. Let us see and hear a trickling of the sand through the rock of habituated beliefs.

5

Good Girls/Bad Girls

Little Miss Muffet sat on her tuffet
eating some curds and whey.
Along came a spider, who sat down beside her,
and frightened Miss Muffet away.

—1765/1990, p. 31

In the Ice Age beauty fits tight as a mask of skin.
One cannot breathe, one stiffens to perfection.

—Oates, 1978, p. 43

When a woman walks, she should give the impression of waves rippling
over a sandbar.

—Golden, 1997, p. 157

In Western culture, two misguided and oppositional roles women have been trained to choose for themselves are the either/or of good girl or bad girl. The good girl is a particularly pernicious role to assume. I should know; I was one. Like so many of my generation, I was determined not to be like my mother. This determination, pervasive among my peers, suggests the extent of influence of the founding fathers of culture on Western female consciousness. It seems that "good" has been understood to mean sweet, docile, agreeable, and supportive. "Good" means to corset oneself for the sake of an idea (Perera, 1990), which is to be Little Miss Muffet, daddy's little girl, the pot of gold at the end of his rainbow. As such, lying there in golden pothood, good girls become idealized, perfected objects, pedestaled for the male gaze. Schooled in passivity—devitalized and dehumanized—the good girl is all surface; and so she seeks the reflecting

87

surface of the mirror to check her face for smoothness and, if she is White, the right amount of redness to offset her pale skin. She pats her hair and straightens her dress (always a dress) and keeps her legs crossed while sitting on her tuffet. Good girlism (Dean & Kolitch, 1998) is a copy of an idea of an ideal. If she were in the East, she would be a geisha. Being in the West, she is consumed with Venus envy (Haiken, 1997).

I resonate with this sketch and can remember how I fleshed out its existence in my own self-denying attempts to be something I was not. My coaches in this charade were my stepmother, who urged me to stay as sweet as I was; my mother, who bought me dolls with *Harper's Bazaar* fashion baskets; my father, who said I was his pot of gold, and my girl friends, with whom I rivaled for my boyfriends. Once, fearing that I would not be asked to the prom, I memorized phrases about cars so that I could make myself appealing to prospective dates. Once, I woke up feeling sick because I was twenty and not yet married. Once, I straightened my hair, which was naturally curly but too unruly.

Just there is a clue into the bathos of the good girl: hair. The texts I read growing up pictured girls with long, blond or dark, straight hair. If the hair was curly, these were flowing curls—unlike my kinks. Today, my students talk of bad hair days; I believe they are even more influenced than I was by the fact that hair is a special category in beauty pageants, such as the Vibrance Most Beautiful Hair Contest, awarded to the queen whose hair has the best shine, bounce, body and softness (Lorando, 1997). Growing up, I did not understand that everything is texted, including Jane Powell films and TV Hair Contests. These operate in what Valerie Walkerdine (1990) calls "systems of signification" (p. 89) that offer male definitions of females. Better to be a beauty than a beast, better a bimbo than a bitch.

Although Paula Gunn Allen (1990) blames mistaken notions of beauty on Aristotle's unities, Inés Hernández-Ávila (1995) targets the domesticated attitudes that accompany so-called civilized societies. She says, "'Civilized' to me means dominated, domesticated, tame, brought into order, brought into line, molded, indoctrinated in the art of appearance, the art of facade, trained to think in a 'civilized' manner [read Western-European]" (p. 404). Equally, feminist culture critics see Genesis 2-3 as the end of female autonomy by citing Eve's subordination to Adam. Indeed, feminist theologians have long sought ways to counter the reading of Eve as a lesser human being. Read against a nonEuropean tradition, Eve can be seen not as a temptress prompting God to be a "cosmic bellhop" (Allen, 1992, p. 67) but as an intellectual, exercising curiosity. Phyllis Trible (1996) offers an extensive rereading of the Genesis account, based on a study of the original Hebrew with its characteristic "ring composition whereby the two creatures are parallel. In no way," she emphasizes, "does the order (placing Adam's creation before Eve's) disparage woman" (p. 360).

But good girls do not challenge God's word, even if God did not write the Bible. Good girls accept unthinkingly, not only the necessity to maintain their youth and beauty, but also to subscribe to an underlying aesthetic that seduces girls to desire the domesticated life. The Mattel industry understands the power of this aesthetic. One of my students, Shannon Daigle, wrote glowingly about her Barbie dream house:

> It was an enormous, three story, hot pink, Victorian style, plastic house with an open elevator overlooking the ground below. The first floor included the dining area, which consisted of a small table and chair set (huge from Barbie's perspective, of course), and a television for Barbie to watch her favorite shows while eating dinner. The second level included ... the den for Barbie to relax in after a long day of play.

The plastic Barbie set, like the plastic life of so many women in the burbs, has an Alice in Wonderland appeal to this young writer, Alice being petite and precious compared with the large, nonbiologically degradable objects that surround her. How telling that for Barbie, as undoubtedly for girls playing Barbie, living is defined as passive leisure: eating, watching soaps, relaxing, playing all day long, being on the other end of the telephone in the mistaken belief that she controls her life.

This view of the infantile woman, with her shrunken aesthetic sensibility, is a split-off half of an incomplete whole. In Westernized culture, the good girl's opposite is not Spider Woman, but bad girl. Both good girls and bad girls are but two sides of the mirror of patriarchy that, because of its insistence on hierarchy, reflects women's lowly position on the human ladder. I am reminded here of a Georgia O'Keeffe painting of a ladder, listing to the right, suspended in turquoise air. Above the floating ladder is a starless evening sky with a half moon in her last quarter. Below the ladder is an horizon of desert land, one small mountain like a maiden's breast pointing up to the bottom rung. The painting is highly fanciful—charming. I used to read it as an expression of a limitless imagination—mine perhaps—reaching ever higher. But now I read it more ironically as an unanchoring of female symbols. The ladder, after all, is not grounded. Female symbols must be grounded, degradable—not in the "civilized" sense of degradation or lower rank but in a geological sense of organicism. Now I see that dangling ladder as a wistful challenge, not urging me to shoot for the moon, up, up; but to descend down, down into the breast of a vast, uninhabited mindscape. Were those eight rungs of the ladder to circle downward, would they form the image of a spider?

Some of Western-European culture's most formative texts present female characters as cast iron models for either good or bad. Fairy tales portray the drama as Cinderella versus stepsisters, Sleeping Beauty versus the old fairy, Snow White versus stepmother. The good girl is everything already noted (docile, beautiful, passive=reward=marriage). The bad girl is not a true member of the family romance (read patriarchy). She could be a truncated mother figure, who, because she is older, is seen as jealous and conspiring—mirror, mirror on the wall; or a big-footed sister, also jealous and conspiring—give me that glass slipper! Or, citing the modern day girlie model, she could simply be a bimbo with big hair who practices sex in small offices but who knows nothing of Eros. There are no real mothers or true sisters in fairy tales or Cosmo land. The Bible presents this dichotomy as good girl Mary versus bad girl Eve, offering the choice "be a virgin" (and win the hand of God) or "be a whore" and get out of the yard. In either case, the choice condemns women to an extreme place on the rung of the space ladder.

Kate Chopin (1899/1985) maintains this sense of opposition between good girl Adèle and bad girl Edna, in *The Awakening*. Chopin's work is receiving a much-deserved revival in college English classes not because Chopin approves the good-bad split but because she critiques it.

That Edna is the bad girl to Adèle's good girl is obvious by her differing understanding of family values. Adèle belongs squarely in the family, Edna does not. Adèle as a good Creole mother-woman is the central figure in the bourgeois drama of domesticity, sacrificing personal desire at the altar of the hearth (Black, 1992). Her sacrifices elevate her to an unreal stature of goodness. Edna, on the other hand, has an aesthetic sense not shared by her circle. She loves the music of Frederic Chopin (was Kate Chopin punning, I wonder?), she paints, she swims, she makes love outside the marriage. Eschewing the social values of her time—including, most shockingly, the gendered obligation to mother—Edna pursues the life of the sensualist in the naïve belief that she can find happiness for herself. Nowhere does this become more apparent in the novel than when Edna throws herself a party to celebrate her newfound identity as a love goddess.

In his essay "Mythic Images" (1992) Jason Smith, a former student of mine, identified the function of Aphrodite or Venus in the novel:

> The spot in which Edna and Robert have their most intense meeting is at a pigeon house. Pigeons and doves were once regarded as messengers of the goddess Aphrodite and, by their presence, even a humble place can be transformed into a temple of love. It is surely not coincidental that Chopin has chosen such a setting for this meeting. She makes her readers realize the importance of the scene by imbuing it with this mythic connotation. Perhaps Chopin's most striking use of mythic imagery in her novel is her description of Edna's banquet. We are shown what is in effect, despite its contemporary trappings, an almost pagan celebration of love. Edna has laid out her table as a sumptuous altar and garbed herself as its priestess. All that is needed is an idol and, of course, one is provided: Victor. As soon as Mrs. Highcamp sets the wreath of roses upon his head Victor is transformed into a "vision of Oriental beauty" (p. 1,077). She takes her scarf and drapes it over him, the better to mask his discordantly modern clothes, and the worshipers break into admiration at the vision, as if Eros himself had been summoned to their dinner party.... After the banquet is ended, the memory of it remains. Victor tells Mariequita, his girlfriend on Grand Isle, every detail of it. He tells her "Venus rising from the foam could have presented no more entrancing a spectacle than Mrs.

Pontellier, blazing with beauty and diamonds … " (p. 1,100). In this statement Edna is compared to Venus herself, … the Roman goddess of love (who) was, at one time, a goddess of the earth's fertility. She is one of the countless variations of the great mother-goddess…. (pp. 36–37)

These mythic undertones complicate what gentrified society simplifies, the potentialities of femaleness. "Potential" derives from the Latin *potentia*, meaning potency, power; expressing possibility, in the subjunctive, of power. Goddesses, after all, had power. Edna plays make-believe goddess for only one night, a few brief hours. (The fleeting quality of sensuality, granted only one hour at most, is a frequent motif in Chopin's work, as in "The Story of an Hour" (1900/1988)). The only woman in the novel who retains real power (autonomy) is Edna's older mentor, Mademoiselle Reisz. In the novel she functions as a crone goddess, part fairy tale godmother-stepmother-grandmother. Mlle. Reisz lives outside the circle. She occupies attic spaces, critiquing the norms from her superior position and offering wisdom, although she is a "spinster" viewed from below with suspicion. It is she who sees that for a woman to be an agent of action—that is, to fly above convention as she does—a woman must have strong wings. Chopin suggests that only the crone can fly in the face of custom and live the truly sensual life, true to her musical art and to herself. This is indeed Chopin's sad comment on the depotentiation of female power.

In 19th-century fiction, bad women who flaunt the social code by sexual transgression are punished by death or ridicule. Madame Pontellier, like her fictitious French sister Madame Bovary, commits suicide; Hester Prynne, bad with a capital A, is scaffolded. Today, when men commit adultery, their transgression tends to be dismissed as, for example, an endorphin rush needed to offset the rigors of their jobs. The phallacy of power politics, although an embarrassment for leaders of countries, is, nevertheless, not the issue here.

Anne Sexton and Joyce Carol Oates portray bad girls in contemporary society. Interestingly, both have been called primitive by literary critics—a term meant to disparage but which, when viewed from a darker perspective, reveals the power of a female aesthetic that Spider Woman teaches. Both writers demonstrate that cultural female symbols like the looking glass—once the exclusive province of fairy tale—must be reappropriated by modern female myth makers. Anne Sexton is case in point. Her *Transformations* (in Kumin, 1981) offer cheeky retellings of dumb bunny fairy tale girls. Snow White, for example, is "a lovely number" (p. 224), who, like a porcelain figure, rolls her "china-blue doll eyes/ open and shut./ Open to say, / Good Day Mama,/ and shut for the thrust/ of the unicorn. She is unsoiled" (p. 224). It is this "dust mouse" (p. 225) figure who threatens the stepmother, suddenly and ridiculously overcome with signs of age: "brown spots on her hand/ and four whiskers over her lip" (p. 225). And so, of course, Snow White flees the stepmother's house to assume domestic duties in the "honeymoon cottage" (p. 226) of the seven dwarfs. In this and other fairy tale versions, Sexton is wry, perhaps even slapstick—a tone she darkens in subsequent writings and performances that reveal her "radical discontent with the awful order of things" (1978).

Teaching Anne Sexton is, to say the least, a challenge for me as well as my students. Nervous laughter and rolled eyes begin our discussion of a poem like "In Celebration of My Uterus" (1969/1985). Occasionally, however, the shock of the encounter with Sexton's work releases energy that no amount of study of, say, Elizabeth Barrett Browning or Edna St. Vincent Millay, can. Beth Cantwell, my student, wrote this thoughtful response:

> Anne Sexton gives the reader her idea of the strength a woman possesses within her being in the poem "In Celebration of My Uterus." The physical part of a woman that makes being a woman so powerful is her organ for creating human life. She celebrates her uterus because of its power to bring forth life within and around her. All women who carry this "sweet weight" (line 11) seem "to be singing" (line 42) of and for their power, in a collective song of celebration that connects women the world over. No matter what else she does with her life the most important thing is 'this thing the body needs' (line 56), because with it she is the mother of all nations. This is power.... The uterus and the rest of a woman's body is a reason for delight. It is the "cup" (line 16) which holds the force to shape the world. It is not the dominance of men that carries the world, but instead it is the internal muscle of women that sustains all life.

Beth's commentary presents forcefully and very simply an understanding of gynocratic power that Native-American women have learned from the teachings of Spider Woman. When critics call Sexton primitive, I doubt they have this reference in mind; more probably, they simply assume that certain topics are not appropriate to high art, like poetry; or high arenas, like the academy. I recall giving a poetry reading with a woman who had just had a hysterectomy and not only wrote about it but read a poem about it in public. Her reading disturbed some listeners, who evidently felt that poetry readings should, like depositions, be guided by talking points. Afterward, the head of the Creative Writing Department caused a feeding frenzy when he issued a memo to the entire English faculty blasting Karen's lack of decorum.

Such an incident suits a discussion of Sexton, herself a prime example of bad taste in the academy. As Paula Salvio (n.d.) comments, Sexton pushed at the boundaries of decorum in the classroom, envisioning excess as the corrective to good girl teaching. Who determines what bodies of knowledge should be taught and how they should be taught? Whose body is the teacher's? Challenging conventional understandings of good taste, Sexton was openly autobiographical with her students, questioning the assumptions of highbrow art and canon-ruled institutions, admitting her false starts in writing, confessing her neuroses. Committed to the transformative processes in her work and life, Sexton urged students to interpret their readings from perspectives other than their own (Salvio, n.d.). In an effort to shake students away from the false comfort of fixed identities (of themselves, of teachers), she actually wanted students to dis-identify with characters. They should consider the trope of the mask as a means of probing the depths of their own hidden selves. Salvio comments, "Students may use the mask of a possessed witch, a patient awaiting the bells in bedlam, or the woman who marries houses" (Salvio, n.d., p. 35). "These masks do not fully conceal the student who wears them," Salvio continues. "These incomplete transformations leave interval spaces where students can, in the spirit of a Brechtian actor, comment on the character being portrayed in their writing … and perhaps explore their relationships to these characters" (pp. 35–35). Such assignment undoubtedly sounds weird to pedagogues climbing the rung of Bloom's taxonomies. "Put on the face of someone you are not!?" they might exclaim. But, as those familiar with Jungian analysis know, the idea of engaging the figments of imagination in an active dialogue is one means of self-discovery, the assumption being that the self is a fluid entity capable of many manifestations, many voices, which are hidden from conscious awareness. The more I ponder Sexton's dramatic personae in her poetry and pedagogy, the more I question the bland "Compare and Contrast" composition assignments doled to college freshmen. Students seeking to "relate" to fictional characters may only be solidifying their preformed bias of the monotonous, unified, simple self. The prevalence of same-same papers, well written but boring, fill my files; common thread themes are just that: common.

Sexton's poems, on the other hand, propel readers into the uncommon terrain of the unexplored psyche, which is nonhuman, perverse, grotesque, necessary (Lauter, 1979). Citing a line from Sexton's Snow White poem, Gabrielle Schwab presents a forceful argument for literature that induces otherness, in her *The Mirror and the Killer-queen* (1996). Her point is that strong fiction does not merely replicate another world; it brings readers into alien encounters. Sexton, clearly, takes the reader where she may not wish to go. She writes not only of the inner life of the female body—intestines, bowels, menstruation, labor—but, and more particularly, of the matters of the soul—madness, the longing for death. That imaging forth these demons did not save Sexton from literal suicide is a terrible irony. Although she desired union with the Mother Goddess, she was unable to transform her poetic insights into any kind of peace (Lauter, 1979). In "Jesus Raises Up the Harlot," for example, the whore lost her whoredom (her power) when saved, becoming merely Jesus's pet or daughter: "His raising her up made her feel/ like a little girl again … " (Sexton, in Kumin, 1981, p. 340). And in "When the Glass of my Body Broke" the image of multiple hands does not prefigure Spider Woman's web-making artistry, but rather the tormenting nightmare of incest: "Hands/ growing like ivy over me, / hands growing out me like hair,/yet turning into fire grass/ … the lips turning into days that would not give birth" (1981, p. 518).

Oates, another bad girl, has also been accused of being "an American primitive" (Avant, 1979, p. 36). Indeed, the intention to delve dangerously is entirely, primally consistent with Oates's aesthetic. Remarking on the peculiarities of her work, Oates (1994) commented that the writer, "a kind of priest, or a kind of magician, or even a kind of scientist," is fascinated "by the meanings that lie beneath the surface of the world" (p. 126). Her many uses of the metaphor of the hard surface are meant to suggest that contemporary female experience not only cannot get past the glass ceiling but cannot get primal enough. What Elaine Showalter (1994) calls "the fertilizing stream of a female history and a female tradition" (p. 170) has for Oates's women characters dried up, making them sterile figures or revengeful goddesses. In Oates's fiction, a surreality pervades because the other, underworld of female goddess-support has been co-opted.

My students intuitively understand this. They relate strongly to the short story "Where Are You Going, Where Have You Been?" perhaps because it captures so well their own sense of rebellion against their patriarchal mothers, in particular, and family and society in general. The family the reader meets is typically dysfunctional, with a distant father, a jealous mother, and a perfect, noncommunicating, older sister. No one communicates with anyone else, and so for intimacy Connie turns to her bored friends and to the reflection she catches of herself in mirrors. Mirrors, in fact, are key metaphors for Oates, recalling as they do a fairy tale function to induce narcissism in women. In the zombified mall of an Oates world, mirrors appear on windshields, windows, glasses, and eyes. They glint and reflect but do not admit entrance. In this vacuum, mirrors reflect mirrors in a dizzying phenomenon that bodes forth an ominous truth: Bad girls are devil's prey so long as girls settle for surface.

Like Sexton, Oates does not dodge horror in her fiction. Milan Kundera (1996) characterizes writing that is really good writing as "like a walk beneath the sky of strangeness" (p. 51) capable of taking readers to "a different planet" (p. 26). The strange planet of Oates's fiction is of a desacrilized cosmos, closed off from appeal from the depths. As Arnold Friend puts it, the place where women (mother goddesses) once came from "ain't there any more" (Oates, 1985, p. 2,290). Bad girls like Connie can be seduced because they do not know the difference between a friend and a fiend and so they fall in love with death or the devil. Bad girls, in the thrall of their own narcissistic impulses, are unable to reconnect with the deep feminine, because their own mothers provide inadequate models of female selfhood.

Oates taps a cultural problem of our time. Bad girls (the other face of the good girl) are unliberated women, split off from the goddess (Creighton, 1978/1979). In *The Goddess and Other Women* (1974), all twenty-five stories portray images of negative goddesses—either Kali, the mad mother; or Magna Mater, the devouring goddess—who are but half of a female totality. Female goddess power split off thus emanates from rage, not (as with Spider Woman) blood compassion, because the goddess is not of earth's understory. In the short story "The Goddess," from the previously mentioned collection, for example, we meet Claudia, staying at a hotel in a strange city, who thinks to herself "how good she had been, and how pretty!—if only she hadn't been so pretty, perhaps she wouldn't have been so very good!" (p. 420). Then, in the reflecting mirror of a store window Claudia glimpses a statuette of Kali with her many arms outspread. The goddess is naked, with a pot belly, long, pointed breasts, and a savage, fat-cheeked face. Most striking to Claudia is that around Kali's neck is "what looked like a necklace of skulls" (p. 408). Seeing this, Claudia felt her face flush in "a rush of quick angry blood" (p. 408). Oates implies that this encounter with a terrifying goddess figure releases the wife from the stranglehold of pretty goodness. Origins of the word "anger" come from the Greek *anchein*, meaning "to strangle" and the Old English *enge* "narrow" (Webster, 1981). When one is angry, one feels a narrowing in the throat, strangling verbal expression of what wells up. Alternative reactions, then, could range from suffocating silence to childish acting out. We see such a reaction with Claudia, who, goaded by Kali, smears the walls of her hotel with lipstick.

The good girl-bad girl is emotionally stuck, frozen into one role only, that makes her incapable of expressing emotion. Her head is not open to her heart. Rationality, Oates (1994) remarked, "is the price we pay when we do not know how the goddess is manifested" (p. 57). The Oates story "In the Region of Ice" (1975) features a mirror image of Claudia in the form of a nun. Sister Irene teaches humanities, but is so abstracted from its lessons—as she is from Christ's example of giving himself—that she cannot afford the emotional gesture of support asked of her by a suicidal student. For Weinstein, the student, ideas are real; the Shakespeare Sister Irene teaches expresses real ideas about love, not the "phony Christian love garbage" (p. 331) to which he sees she is dedicated. Sister Irene sees herself, tragically in Oates's view, as "only one person":

> She was only one person, she thought, walking down the corridor in a dream. Was she safe in this single person, or was she trapped? She had only one identity. She could make only one choice. What she had done or hadn't done was the result of that choice, and how was she guilty? If she could have felt guilt, she thought, she might at least have been able to feel something. (p. 332)

And so the good girl teacher-nun rationalizes her way out of responding to another's pain. Hers is the terrible sin of deliberative thought.

Sister Irene is one extreme; Claudia, in the goddess story, another; the young girl Connie still another. Here are three faces of the contemporary female, conditioned by social codes not to feel. Although Oates's stories show women thrilling to sexual dangers of various kinds, sex for them is nonerotic precisely because these women cannot reach what Ann Dean (in Dean & Kolitch, 1998) calls "subterranean layers of feeling," those "deeper slopes of memory" (p. 18) wherein the goddess dwells. Consequently, emotions of anger or rage are expressed in childish ways—like smearing lipstick on a hotel wall—revealing the stranglehold of thought in the expression of feeling.

How often do I find patriarchal condescension as the wall against which women wail. In graduate school I recall being incensed by my male professor's contradiction of my account of birth. I forget the discussion, only my comment. I told the class that my seventeen hours in labor were painless. I learned how to breathe, I said, from my cat. (When I told this to my uncle, he condescendingly laughed and said, "I'm sure you did!" in obvious sarcasm). My professor flat out told me I was wrong. I was so outraged that after class I snuck up to his closed office door and smeared his name plate with the word "ASSHOLE." On another occasion my ex-husband belittled my public expression of nervousness by demanding, "Do you need an ambulance?" How I sympathize with Gloria next door, constantly talked down to by her husband. "Calm down, calm down now, Gloria," Bob counsels over her slightest lip curl; or, even better because worse, "It's all right, dahling, you'll grow up." That women have been infantilized, even *wanting* to be toys for boys, is the good girl's problem. If she's not nice, she's naughty. Bad child![1]

Contemporary female poets and writers like Sexton and Oates portray this dilemma as that of women lost in a goddessless world. Their female personae represent, to paraphrase Carl Jung (1933/1971), the spiritual problem for modern women. Jung writes:

> the conscious, modern man (sic) can no longer refrain from acknowledging the might of the psyche, despite the most strenuous and dogged efforts at self-defence. This distinguishes our time from all others. We can no longer deny that the dark stirrings of the unconscious are active powers, that psychic forces exist which, for the present at least, cannot be fitted into our rational world order. (p. 463)

I insert these Jungian comments for two reasons. First, they call importance to the buried contents of the psyche or soul, which Jung and women writers, along with Romantic poets and so-called minority writers, certainly, recognize as es-

---

[1]In an amazing feat of imaginative writing, Thomas Wolfe—not known for writing from the female perspective—nevertheless achieves a breathtaking sense of woman-thought in his *Good Child's River* (1991). The protagonist, Esther, retains her connection to the earth by means of the "river" that runs through her, refreshing her with naturalistic, child-like (not good-girl-like) thoughts. Her sensuality is that of a powerful Mother Earth figure who cares not a fig for "good girlism":

> I felt the great earth move below me and swing westward in the orbits of the sun. I knew the earth, my body was the earth, I grew into the earth, and my child was stirring in me as I lay there on the earth in that green hillside. (p. 75).

This "good child" quality extends not just to mothering but to admiring other women:

> Esther had almost a lover's tenderness for Georgia's physical beauty: she liked to put her arm around the other girl, to embrace her, to nestle in to her, to stroke with a sense of affection and wonderment, the velvet and perfect texture of Georgia's skin. (1991, p. 193)

sential for full personhood. Psychic forces, necessarily of a nonrational order, wreak havoc when access to them is denied (Oates's hard surface metaphor). Second, psychic forces present themselves as intolerable images, dreadful to behold, the function of which is to stop the rational mind from the stampede of time so as to focus downward (Oates's Kali; Sexton's suicide poems). If the good girl-bad girl dichotomy is to be split asunder, the problem of the patriarchal woman might be redefined. Then what might be glimpsed are not the notions of beauty and power taught by Western-European myths, but those notions taught by goddess stories, as seen in chapter 11.

6

The Glass Coffin

When a Woman is as well seasoned in her every Joint as she, with exact and enduring Knowledge, there is nothing for it but to let her add herself up to an impossible Zero, and so come to her Death …

—Barnes (1928/1995, p. 37)

Every moment of his life he's forming you … ; and you, you of all women, listen to his voice instead of your own.

—Forster (1923/1989, p. 191)

To await the first man who awakens her and be from that moment slave to him as master is what Wotan told Brunnhilde would happen to her.

—Bolen (1992, p. 131)

And they made a coffin of glass, so that they might still look at her, and wrote her name upon it, in golden letters, and that she was a king's daughter.

—Grimm and Grimm (1823/1980, p. 235)

It's a compelling image. A beautiful young woman, in the prime of life, is buried inside a coffin made of glass and placed on view for others. "They" bury her. "They" are the patriarchy and "she" is a motherless child, having escaped a stepmother's jealousy only to live in a far away realm with seven dwarves. Her name is Snow White. Snow White is trapped. Either way she dies, either by the stepmother's nefarious designs or by the kind coffining of seven dwarves. The world of the stepmother is evil. The world of the father-dwarves is kind. This is the world that kills. Snow White dies, long live Snow White.

Long live, indeed, in deed. I have found that this tale, besides being the formative tale of my upbringing (Doll, 1995), also played a role, mostly unconsciously, in the lives of my colleagues, who grew up in the 1940s and 1950s as I did, willing ourselves into psychological burial. We were, most of us, motherless children. Our mothers were either dead or absent, either physically or mentally. We were the daughters of the patriarchy, doing its bidding. And, lo and behold!, the bidding of the patriarchy for its Snow White daughters was to obey and to "die" so as never to become real women. We were to die to our erotic natures, our deeper selves, so as to live as a perfected image. We were to remain on show, so that "they" might "look." We were the good girls—not in fiction, as seen in the previous chapter—but in real life. Our real life goodness was a Grimm tale, indeed.

Recently, I spent wonderful hours interviewing women in my kitchen, at cafés, in their living rooms, in my back yard. My purpose was to see what caused real women to make vows and to leave vows. I knew how seriously I had made my marriage vows and how traumatic it was to decide to leave after twenty-eight years inside my marriage commitment; I wanted to know about other women's experiences. What prompted us, finally, to leave? At first I ran through my set questions, ten of them, asking "At what age did you make your commitment (to marriage or the church)?" "What drew you to make your commitment (factors in your background, influential people in your life)?" "What behaviors did you exhibit while inside your commitment?" and so forth. But soon I left my prepared text in favor of dialogue. Instead of directing the conversation I found myself listening more and letting the story unfold. My interviews got better as I allowed for spontaneity. I realized that my directorial approach, the question-answer format, was something I had borrowed from too many hours of watching Good Morning America, where the format is canned: questions ticked off, no going with the unusual phrasing or the pregnant pause. So as I let women talk and as I listened better I found that, like so many other things in my life, I had been borrowing a male format of "How To Do"—in this case, "How To Do The Interview." Unlike his story, however, her story weaves back and forth. Unlike his story, women's events do not record themselves around major winnings marked by monuments of soldiers on horses. No, I was discovering that the story of the woman quest leaves a trail remarkable for its lack of marks in stone.[1] For the sake of making sense out of the rich fabric with which my interviewees provided me, I decided to divide their quest (an entering-leaving sequence) into four phases. I say "phases," not "stages," to avoid any suggestion of a logical progression toward winning (the military model), perfection (the developmental model), or health (the medical model). Women's life patterns do not work progressively and developmentally. They work in phases, which I decided to call *vision*, *arrest*, *release*, and *revision*.

---

[1] See Carol Shields (1995). *The Stone Diaries*. New York: Penguin. This remarkable novel tells the stories of women whose lives have been smothered to the extent that they disappear from their own inner lives. They are thus destined to live two lives: one visible, the other secret. The delicious irony is that their inner lives are recorded in the novel, forever readable, as if honored in stone.

VISION

and they pitied her, and said if she would keep all things in order, and cook and wash, and knit and spin for them, she might stay where she was, and they would take good care of her. (Grimm & Grimm, 1823/1980, p. 232)

We, the daughters of the patriarchy growing up in the 1940s and 1950s, were programmed from the start. We would be brides, we would do housework. Marriage or the church, these were our (basically only) two options. We would do it. It seems most of us understood what "doing it" involved, for most of us were wedded to the same vision. We would marry (we married our father substitutes) or we would become brides of Christ. This scenario was strongest in the South, where roles are more firmly fixed. But it was also strong in the part of the country I grew up in, in the 1940s and 1950s: the Northeast.

Such a scenario was indeed a vision, a haze, seen as through a veil. For some, the veil was the lure that kept us pure, allowing us to project an image of spotlessness. For others, the nun's habit was security, worn as a constant reminder of what we were about. We lived in a supposed-to-be world, pure and simple. We had undivided hearts that gladly gave our names over to another, because sacrifice was our mode and safety our mission. Faith Ann became Sister Antoinette. Rose became Sister Thomas Aquinas. Mary Aswell became Mrs. William Doll. Changing our names was a significant symbolic step in losing our birthright, although we didn't think of it like that. We were happy to change our names, for we were in love with the image that we projected. We were narcissists.

As nuns, the vision was to join a religious community that would be an extension of our homes but different, because we all would share the same husband, Christ, and we all would be together in a sisterly fashion. As wives, we would take on the names of our husbands and they would save us (from ourselves). The diminutive furnishings in Snow White's dwarf cottage suggest fairy tale's understanding of these childish ideals.

Snow White's story provided our model, our goal. In my era, besides fairy tales, we were brought up on primers that trained our female instincts into narrowly rigid patterns called social norms. We were normalized to lust after the white picket fence, the apron, the dog Spot, the cat Puff, and the half-open front door, from which Mother waved to Dick and Jane going off to school and Father going off to work. Our desires were channeled into simple, Snow White, housewifery chores like sewing, cooking, cleaning, and keeping order. Our husbands would "provide" for us and give us "everything" we would need. Sex was not a primary goal, because erotic desire was, for us at that time, culturally sublimated.

How like innocents we were to be satisfied with that sanitized arrangement! Snow White's life, nevertheless, seemed to us enchanting. Was it because her beds were teeny and her dishes teeny that housewifery seemed adorable? Was it because her duties were clearly outlined and she knew exactly what was expected? Was it that wifedom, housewifedom in particular, allowed her to be the good child forever? Was it that her countersexual image, like everything else in her world, was prepubescent? We were young and idealistic and completely absorbed by our roles. We were happy the way people in love with high ideals and false visions are happy. We were doing the right thing. We were doing Snow White.

Beverly, who left her husband after twenty-two years, saw marriage in a typically Snow White way. She did anything to "reach his expectations": Keeping a clean house and a trim body were just a few of the minor trade offs she negotiated to accomplish her major goal of security. Her role was molded around "his" expectations, and her training was "to reach" his expectations. She spent decades doing her "reaching," which included everything from learning to play tennis because he felt she should hob nob with the club set, to going back to school because he wanted her to improve her grammar. Some of us, in contrast, had to learn only a few requirements: the proper way to address an envelope was always the male name first; or we had to be reminded by our mothers-in-law about what never to talk about outside the home; or, if our husbands were convalescing, we should have dinner on the table by six. Minor stuff.

We women of the 1940s and 1950s fell into the hands of the collective principle. We were molded. The fact that Beverly was an orphan and I was reared by my father (really by women of color in white uniforms) is significant. We lacked a female role model. Those of us who had mothers, those mothers, wedded to the patriarchal vision, were what Kate Chopin termed "mother-women"—devoted exclusively to house and home—or what the Victorians named the Angel of the House. The Angel kept an orderly domestic scene so that the men of the house could pleasure themselves among the women guests or female relatives. The Angel remained silent and instructed her daughters to do likewise (DeSalvo, 1989). A conspiracy of silence surrounded upper class Victorian culture, all in the name of patriarchal privilege. A silent subterfuge trained females to be minions. Mothers trained daughters. Fathers trained daughters. Husbands trained wives. The training passed down through generations, through classes. It entered the imaginations of nuns.

Joanna became a nun in the 1960s because it was "the Catholic way to drop out, the Catholic way to be a hippie."[2] She knew she was different from her classmates in New Orleans who only wanted to marry. "The reason for going to college," she said, "was if you weren't successful in high school finding a husband, you could go to college and look. That was your goal." Knowing that was not her goal, Joanna "dropped out" into the only other acceptable goal. She be-

---

[2]I am grateful to all the women I interviewed for this chapter: Faith Ann, Rose, Joanna, Nathalie, Kathy, Wanda, Beverly, Jane, Sharon, Connie, and to Lilly, my student.

came a nun, knowing that she wanted something more than wifedom, but not knowing what "more" was.

Nathalie became a nun in the 1950s at the age of seventeen, not unusual for women in the South. She joined a religious community like many young women at the time because she admired the purity of the nun's life and wanted to do something for humanity. It was a vision. But Nathalie also had a fantasy of marriage:

> We would go, there was a place, there was an orchard, grapes, apples, peaches, and olives.... We would go up and sit in the orchard. We were totally isolated there because there was so much ground around us. In the summertime you could hear the parties because there were these large houses, stables, and pools, and all, and they would have bands, and you could hear the parties; so that was difficult at night because you thought, aw gee, this could be fun.

> Mary: This is what it is to be young and female?

> Nathalie: Yes. This is fun. They're having fun and you're not.... In the wintertime we'd go up there and sit, and you could really feel sorry for yourself. You could sit and, because the leaves were off the trees, you could see all these houses over there and people looked so warm and so cozy. You couldn't see people but you could see that, that light ... you know, people have their lights on inside? And you could see that, and it made me want, want that. They were probably in there fighting, but it looked, it looked ... it was my fantasy of what was behind that warm glow in those windows in the distance.

Nathalie's fantasy was a Great Gatsby vision of life seen as glamorous by the outsider (the one who was not living).

For other nuns, the outsider's perspective was God's will. Because it was logical to learn to love God, the logical thing to do was to become a nun, to be a social outsider. This logic led to a well regulated, totally understandable life. As Kathy put it:

> (The convent) was a very peaceful place to be ... You had no problems. Your biggest problem might be to get your studies done or to follow the rules. You were given a job ... whether it was to clean bathrooms, or the chapel, or the place where we ate.... We did it because that was expected of you.

For women, especially motherless women, what such expectations mean is that living life as defined by patriarchal institutions, like the church or marriage, is living a life that defines woman narrowly, as "good girl."

I am struck by the metaphor Karen Armstrong (1987) uses in the gripping autobiography of her life as a nun, *Through the Narrow Gate*. There is a photograph on the front cover of a gate bolstered by two unadorned stone walls taken on a bleak, leafless, late afternoon or early morning. The image is deliberately unwelcoming. Yet it is that gate, its narrowness, its difficult entry, that fascinates; for entry through its portal has beckoned so many of us seeking ... What? We entered its portals like dutiful daughters of the patriarchy. We sought challenge, some of us; specialness, some of us; the calling to a higher cause, some of us. Nuns felt called by God to go through that narrow gate and enter a life answering God's expectations. We knew (we thought) the gate was an entrance into another higher, better, more spiritual world. We did not know this other world was patriarchically defined. We never guessed that the gate's narrowness could also be a metaphor for rebirth.

In his meditations on being a monk, Thomas Moore (1994) offers a different perspective on gates:

> Monasteries are often difficult to approach physically. They may have long entrance drives, stout gates and fences, heavy doors, loud bells, a labyrinth of corridors, and notices in Latin.... we might learn this art of indirection and concealment, ultimately a means for preserving one's own spiritual integrity. (p. 39)

Moore, an ex-monk, writes rhapsodically of his years of learning "this art of indirection and concealment" won through "stout gates." He was left intact by his monastery experience after he left, having preserved his spiritual integrity. I am not sure my ex-nuns would disagree about their spiritual integrity ("once a nun always a nun," so many of them said), but I think stern aesthetics had a differing effect on women. For many, the convent meant a diminishment of authenticity. The church, like marriage, had the effect of making women feel like "pins in the hinge of power" (Proulx, 1993, p. 8).

ARREST

> And thus Snow-drop lay for a long long time, and still only looked as though she were asleep. (Grimm & Grimm, 1823/1980, p. 236)

Read psychologically, the tale of Snow White is the tale of arrested development. I call the second phase in the lives of nuns and wives the phase of *arrest*, for this is the period marked by a lack of psychic movement. We are under arrest, a loaded gun in every room (literally, in the case of Sharon). There is the sense of having one's face formed to fit the mask of the wife role or the nun role. The role *becomes* the identity until there is no true inner self, only a persona. All energy goes to fulfilling the expectations of the collective, which in the case of women define them as servile, puerile, and dependent.

Adhering to roles is especially strong during the first half of adult life, a period which Gail Sheehy (1995) describes as "the 'little death'." During this period of first adulthood the real self is costumed by a false self, which "performs" but is not "me." The real self is buried or dormant, so that it takes "a great deal of energy to keep the performance going" (Sheehy, p. 146). The effort, finally, is exhausting.

In fairy tales the glass coffin has many levels of meaning and has occurred in such other fairy tales as "The Glass Coffin," where the motif is expressed variously as a glass house or a glass mountain. As Theodor Seifert (1986), a Jungian analyst, explains:

> The glass motif always refers to two things: to 1) splitting off accessibility to, not experiencing; and to 2) clarity of vision ("everything is as behind glass"). Many see their problems clearly, and yet it no longer moves them. They tell the most horrible things from their life, speak of losses, of unfulfilled longings, of broken loves, ... but they no longer experience any feeling, no affect.... Glass isolates: We can see our feelings but are no longer moved by them. Hence the glass coffin is a perfect image of a split-off part of the soul. (p. 105)

Wanda, a nun who left the convent after thirty-five years—thirty-five years!—expresses so well, so touchingly, this phase of *arrest*:

> My spiritual life kind of went back and forth at that time. And so I think that my life then was ... there was no movement going on, Mary. There was no ... movement.... You see, I stayed fifteen years in the community after I came back from school after making the act of faith and I think that was due to the fact that my internal spiritual life, there was no movement taking place. And I didn't know exactly how to get it moving ... It's like I didn't know how to get it moving.

I hear this narrative as a mantra around the phrase "no movement," mentioned five times. The sheer act of repetition is a circling around, a caressing, of the pain. By repeating, Wanda is getting purchase on the problem, feeling it again and again in slightly different verbal constructions. Telling becomes healing. Telling and repeating become little ways of seeing into the *arrest*.

Another ex-nun, Faith Ann, who left the convent after thirty-three years (thirty-three!), gives a further insight into the *arrest*:

> What I think I see what happens is you go out and you try to project an image and you try to give people a sense of what religious life is, and you go home that day and it's not that way, no matter how honest you try to be.

Both of these ex-nuns helped me define this period in the lives of those of us caught inside our commitment, not knowing what to do or where to turn. We entered our commitment, be it community or marriage, loving the image, not the reality. We entered never having questioned our lives, because we had been kept (or we kept ourselves) in a prepubescent state. For nuns, this state could be especially severe: Do as you are told; do not have personal responsibility, sex, or freedom (Armstrong, 1987, p. 248). For wives, this state was "honor and obey." We women were used to the comfort that rules, even harsh ones, could bring. Leaving such a state, however, could be terrifying. Faith Ann articulated: "I don't want to leave sixteen years of prison. I'm frightened of freedom."

When psychic energy is arrested, silenced, or buried under false pretenses, often a second nature is developed. As Marianne in Ingmar Bergman's (1973) *Scenes From a Marriage* puts it: "I have always done what people told me to do ... my upbringing was aimed at being agreeable.... It became second nature to be deceptive, secretive. I've pretended constantly to please everybody. It was that consideration that finally killed off love" (in Long, 1994, p. 139).

Bergman's exploration of frozen inner life, as seen in such films as *Winter Light* (1961), *Persona* (1966), and *Scenes From a Marriage* (1973), demonstrates how role-playing buries lives. The more we live life for others' expectations, the less eros we are able to feel. Arrested psychic development is, as one nun said, "the feel of not to feel it" (Armstrong, 1987, p. 241). "It" is the free expression of eros in many manifestations: warmth, spontaneity, profanity, profusion, generosity, humor, perversity, joy, feeling, touching. But women have been enculturated to be ladies, wives, or nuns; serving—not seeking pleasure. Theodor Seifert explains this phenomenon of what I call Snow White's arrested development as buried eros: "It is the eros toward the other and toward ourselves that we banish into the glass coffin and view as a museum piece. This is narcissism instead of mature eros" (1986, p. 108).

Beverly, for example, groomed herself to be an *objet d'art*—a museum piece. She metaphorically put herself on the shelf, on view for others. As Madeleine Grumet (1988) observes, this objectified idea of the self is inscribed "in the visual images of women found in our great museums, tawdry porn theaters, and fashion magazines" (p. 113). But, for Beverly, even this effort to project the perfected image was not enough for her husband. She describes a night when this became clear:

> There was this very lovely restaurant that we used to go to and we sat in total silence for about thirty minutes, and then finally he looked at me and he said, "The problem is I feel you're aging before your time." And I said, "Excuse me?" And he said, "Well, when I walk into places I want heads to turn and I think of you as the Mona Lisa. And just as Mona Lisa is if it were taken out and put into the elements of rain and sun and so forth it would wither. And I feel that is what has happened to you."

Wife as Mona Lisa. Wife as museum piece. Wife on display for others. What a destiny for the real woman!

Jane, divorced after twenty-two years, describes herself as a floater, "free form," who, if she knew anything, knew only that she wanted to find someone "kind." Jane described no abuse in her background, only privilege and a "free-floating" upbringing. She sought a "kind" savior, found one, and married him. She married, she said, in order to become a cliché. But lo and behold!, her kind husband could not "pull sex" out of her. So Jane left him after twenty-two years, deciding she was "not an amoeba."

Jane, like myself, like Beverly, allowed herself to be molded. Our wife-vision was so high for our role-selves that we could not descend into our erotic depths. We yearned for someone else to tell us who we were. We yearned, it's so obvious, for a prince charming (a kind, noble man) who would lead us—not out of our depths, for we had not yet experienced our depths—but into our heights. We wanted display, social acceptance, the pedestal. We wanted to do more, be more. More, for us Snow Whites, meant more kindness. We were ready for the man who had not separated from his mother. We wanted only the kind man, who revered his mother almost as a saint and who would treat us in a saintly fashion. Jane's story is typical of the attraction we had to "kindness" (read order, read tell-me-who-to-be, read savior). We were gluttons for order. As Jane says of her background:

> We didn't have a lot of rules, we didn't have a lot of structure, but we had a lot of moralizing and fundamentally Christian values superimposed on a *nouveau riche* world.... We all ended up feeling like veritable orphans, spiritual orphans.... We all looked to something stable, something kind, something ... um, and definitely, people who really liked us.... There was this counselor at school who for some god unknown reason took an interest in me and of course I hated him because he singled me out; it made me feel self-conscious and I just wanted him to just die and go away, you know? And Mr. Adams, and I shall never forget him: he was this gray little man with rimless glasses and he drove me insane because he took an interest in me. He called my parents and he said, "Look, you've got a problem. You've got a massive underachiever, you've got to do something." And my parents said, "Okay what can we do?" and he said, "Boarding school."
>
> Mary: How did you feel about that?
>
> Jane: I was ... I wasn't really making my own decisions. I was going along with whatever happened. I was not making any decisions. I said, "Okay. This ought to be weird, I'll go."
>
> Mary: Unh unh. Um, you were happy enough to have someone ...
>
> Jane: Exactly. I didn't even ... I was no one. The big thing, the thing that I'll go to my grave wondering about is: How do you get to be so nonexistent?

Now, to look at Jane you would not think you were in the presence of a nonexistent person. As her voice reveals, Jane is vibrant. Her language reveals insight. One wonders how a person with a privileged background like hers and with intelligence like hers could have felt herself to be nobody! And yet we need more Janes to describe our experiences. There are a lot of smart nobodies out there.

Jane's situation, like mine, was cultural. We had a cultural construct of who we should be and who our mate should be. We were nobodies. And so, unconsciously we sought Snow White men who would treat us like their mothers. And they, unconsciously, played the role of our fathers. Such men "may be friendly and courteous, but they are not creative" (Seifert, 1986, p. 30). By "creative" Seifert means "erotic." The Snow White syndrome is dangerous for the psyche precisely because it selects public over private desire. It buries eros.

Some central questions the Snow White fairy tale poses, then, might be: How do we win back the life we thought we had lost? (Seifert, p. 14). What paralyzes us so that we cannot finally get going before it is too late? (Seifert, p. 106). How does the psyche reconnect with eros? The last question is especially important; for, as the myth of Psyche and Eros shows, there can be no birthing of the real woman until the psyche is aroused by erotic, not just social, desire.

RELEASE

At last a prince came and called at the dwarfs' house; and he saw Snow-drop, and read what was written in golden letters. Then he offered the dwarfs money, and earnestly prayed them to let him take her away. (Grimm & Grimm, 1823/1980, p. 236)

The third phase of women's entering-leaving sequence follows the fairy tale, as did the other phases. First there is the *vision*, then the *arrest*. Now the *release* from the buried life, which would not have occurred had it not been for a "prince." Having lived according to direction for two, sometimes three, decades, we found our existence not unlike that of being in a coma. The life we led regulated us and kept us on track but did not spur our creativity. It would take a "prince" to spring the trap for our release.

The outsider reveals meaning. The encounter with the outsider is an hermeneutic encounter, taking us back and down to secrets hidden, but there, nonetheless (Kermode, 1979). The buried treasure is none other than the real self. Without the outsider coming into our lives, unbidden, we would simply go along with the plot—or, as with Snow White and Sleeping Beauty, we would remain dormant. We would be projecting the false self with its false expectations and prepubertal behaviors.

The fairy tale depiction of the outsider is usually a prince or a king's son, "youths of royal blood, to whom the role of redeemer falls" (Seifert, p. 112). It would be a mistake to read this motif literally, so as to suggest that our fallen state can be redeemed by marriage only or by marriage only to a prince. The motif suggests, rather, that the prince represents the presence of an absolute opposite force in the unconscious. If we have been passive, we need an active figure to spur us into individuation. If we have been psychologically impoverished (without an abundance of inner images to guide us), we need a figure of privilege or wealth to counterbalance our inner poverty. If we have been immature, a wisdom figure in the form of an old man or woman will spark our creative fire. What is suggested here is a symbolic union within one person of these necessary opposite forces (what Jung refers to as the *coincidentia oppositorum*, or coincidence-bringing together, of opposites). In real life, as in existential novels, we find our "other" in the visitor, the stranger, the old friend, the unusual encounter, the unexpected question, the unfamiliar feeling, the disturbing dream, or the knock at the back door. The visitor awakens us and "marries" us to the creative wellspring lying inside.

Faith Ann's visitor was an old friend in another city who provoked her (Sister Antoinette) into her moment of truth. "Toni, you're not happy. When are we going to talk? About you? You're not yourself." With those words from an old friend living in another city, Faith Ann broke down. It was then she could begin to reflect on her unusual feelings during her past several years and she could begin to express buried anger. She realized:

> I hated everybody ... they had cheated me. I gave my whole life to what I thought was there and it wasn't and so I felt so angry. I was almost really a bitch to people, excuse me.

Faith Ann's dillusionment was the beginning of the removal of the veil. She was now, with the help of a far-away friend, able to get distance on herself. She was able to see more clearly. In doing so she related one of the incidents that brought back her feeling:

> And like I gave a talk one time to a group of men in Lafayette. And I didn't wear a habit because I had come to, at some earlier time in my life, I didn't want to be identified with me as a sister because people would be nice to me because they knew I was a sister. I wanted them to treat *women* right, not just the habit, like a sister.... But when I went to talk to these men and I didn't have the habit on they began hassling me.

> Mary: They didn't know you were a nun?

> Faith Ann: Yes they knew.... They began to say things. I barely began to get the introductory remarks out and they said, "Why don't you have the habit on? You're not a real sister, you don't even wear the garb of the sister".... Even lay men were heckling, you know, the whole idea of where I felt religious life was supposed to be and they were not there either, so I felt that the priests had let us down again because they hadn't even helped these men to get to the point they needed to be.

'The priests had let us down again.' That little phrase inside an otherwise public moment for an "unhabited" nun says a lot. Those of us on the outside do not know the politics of nuns and priests. But, to me, this comment suggests the extent to which nuns were dependent on priests to defend, counsel, and protect, not unlike the wife's dependency on the husband whom she should honor and obey.

Faith Ann's friend, to whom she had to travel a long distance (a key fairy tale motif), prodded Faith Ann into her deep psyche, so long covered over by "the habit." When Vatican II in the 1960s relinquished many of the strictures for people of the cloth, relinquishing the habit was one of them. What happened is that, uncostumed, many nuns began to feel closer to the bone.

Kathy had been a nun for five years when she was told she had a visitor. The visitor was the man she had left for the convent, her boyfriend in high school, the one to whom she had almost gotten engaged at the age of seventeen. There she was, five years later, in full habit: underskirt, tunic, body of the habit, pleated yoke, collar, scapular, belted rosary, pyrolin, linen cap, three layers of veil, black oxfords, white stockings. She had made her vows of poverty, chastity, and obedience and felt that any doubts about her commitment were mere temptations. So here was temptation. Is it by accident that she did something against rules? Instead of letting him in the front door of the receiving room, she let her visitor in the back door. They had a talk the content of which she has totally forgotten. That night she decided she had to leave. Jungians know that the "back door" is the entrance into the unconscious. Kathy termed her decision to leave a "call from God." Perhaps the call from the unconscious is the same thing.

Joanna, a nun for five years, was "visited" by the theologians she was studying in college. Through reading she had a crisis of faith. Although the community offered her what she thought would be a bigger world than she had ever known, Karl Rahner and C. G. Jung challenged the basis of her belief. "The structure fell apart," she said.

Sharon was not a nun but she was a member of a charismatic Christian community that demanded of Sharon total obedience. Her entire social structure was arranged: Outside relations were not encouraged, time was structured, and she was taught to set aside "natural" inclinations and affinities. Like a nun, Sharon willingly subjugated herself to this structure; she was committed to "forging" herself so as to be a good child, a sister in Christ.

Her visitor came in the form of expressed rage, long held victim by the pieties and abuses of her background and surroundings. She describes a particular moment when she knew the demands on her by the hierarchal, patriarchal organizational structure of her community were unreasonable. But when she tried to reason with her male chief coordinator, she got nowhere. Then, Sharon, a social worker for sexual abuse cases, attended, as required, a weekly Ladies meeting for the Outreach Ministry:

> I came into a Ladies Meeting with sweet, little, old nun-type ladies at one point. There had been another sexual abuse case where an eight-year-old had been raped by a boyfriend and, well, uh, my language was bad. And they were, 'Hunh, hunh, Sister, don't use that language, Sister.' 'What in the goddam hell is the matter with you!' I said. 'Don't you realize adjectives and expletives are not what is obscene in the world? It's eight-year-olds being fucked by their mothers' boyfriends that's obscene!'

Connie, married twenty-one years, was "visited" by a phone call from her daughter's school informing Connie that her daughter was being sexually molested by her husband (and had been for years). Intuitively, Connie had known that the marriage was not right, that the family was not together. But she felt she should "stick it out," even though she, a Ph.D., could not communicate with her husband. Connie made it clear that it took something catastrophic, the phone call with its message of terrible truth, for her to leave her marriage. Otherwise, she admits, she would have stayed.

These stories convey an Aha! moment when a *vision* is released from its arrested position. To achieve perspective on our visions, we need a visitor. My visitor has often been a night visitor, or a dream. A cycle of three dreams focused on the house I lived in with my father until I was eighteen. This dream cycle, dreamt as I was preparing to leave my marriage, was presenting me with the problems of my *arrest* and a solution for my *release*:

> My Chappaqua house is now owned by Bill. Lush greenery is outside and it is raining. A car circles in front, stirring up mud, and these strangers in the car seem lost.

My father's house owned by my husband? Of course. I had exchanged one father for another. I didn't own my own house. The greenery outside the house beckons with its lushness, as if fertility (it is raining) and the exotic lie elsewhere than the house. The vehicle in the dream muddies up the waters, circling with lost strangers. Two years later one can see that my "car," or my ego-driven self, which was stirring up the mud of my unconscious, had not made connection with "these strangers" of my unconscious. I was lost, at that time, a fully arrested bloom, you could say, in the lush greenery of my husband's house.

The second of the dream cycle is as follows:

> In the Chappaqua house again. From the second floor bathroom I look over into the Platt's yard to see, to my astonishment, a pool that fills their yard. It is shaped like a figure eight. Mrs. Platt calls me up to say, 'Mrs. Aswell, we so admire your husband.'

I am returning to my father's house again. I had not been getting the message. Now the question of identity is raised. I am being called by a name. But who am I? Am I Doll or am I Aswell? Is my neighbor calling me back to my birth name, back to my birthright? Something in my psyche was saying to me, "Look! Look! Your way to wholeness is through this house! Look! Look!" The dream points down to the "pool" of the unconscious in a neighboring yard. My ego was being drawn down and out in a near connection with my unconscious material shaped like a double four (four, the symbol of wholeness). As a grown woman I had not dealt sufficiently with the house of my childhood self and so I was not sufficiently whole. I had been allowing myself to be a child-woman, looking for daddies to take care of me. The fact that the pool of the unconscious is in the neighbor's yard, not my father's yard, suggests an urging to seek my roots in places other than the patriarchy, which had held me captive by the false pride I took in public acclaim ("we so admire your husband"). The ridiculous non sequitur from my neighbor, about her admiration for my husband, had nothing whatever to do with *my* selfhood or *my* authenticity. I needed to hear that. I needed to grow up.

On the eve of what would have been my twenty-ninth wedding anniversary (now having been divorced a year) I had a third house dream:

> I am in front of a large plot of green grass before the door to my house. Bill has plans for the land. Suddenly, I have a plan different from his: I want to make a vegetable garden. He says, 'I think we could arrange for that,' I say, 'Why *arrange*? Are you going to give me permission for what I want? That is no way to treat me.' I feel embarrassed by my outburst, because such frank talk is uncharacteristic of me. We then plan an eight-foot segment of land and I spend a very hot afternoon breaking ground.

Several motifs occur here, not the least of which is the door. Throughout this chapter I have commented on the door, or gate, as a significant symbol for women. A "door's" narrowness can open into the womb or down to the tomb; it is a portal, a transition point for death or rebirth. "Doors are sacred for women" Marge Piercy writes (1980). Reclaiming the door might be the beginning of re-claiming women's sacred, even more than political, right to full personhood in-side a culture that too often has closed our doors.[3]

This dream occurred a year after my leaving a twenty-eight year marriage. But even then I had neither completely "died" to my life as child-wife nor had I been fully "reborn" into new personhood. The fact that "my house" was the house I grew up in, my father's house, indicates that I was still attached to the patriarchy. It was the house of my childhood, the house where I learned throughout adulthood to remain a child. In the dream the door to this house of-fers some ambivalence, because "plot" suggests "grave" and "green grass" sug-gests rebirth, as does the double-four motif of the "eight foot segment of land."

The motif of "frank outburst" causes dreamer-me embarrassment. The dream forefronts my discomfort with argument (honest expressions of disagree-ment), even though the recognition that Bill was patronizing me was accurate: Nobody needs "permission" to pursue her "wants." Such a re-cognition is, of course, blasphemy to the patriarchy in general. But the dream was giving me words to release the hold patriarchal structures have had on my unconscious. The image of "vegetable garden" expresses this release, turning the word "plot" away from its death association with "grave": the "plot" of my life lived accord-ing to a patriarchal, dysfunctional narrative (Wear, 1999). Instead, there is a freeing association of cultivating, growing, and nutrition. And the image of spending a "very hot afternoon" suggests that in the afternoon of my life break-ing such "new ground" is fire work, arousing eros.

---

[3]The door of honor for an Islamic man is his wife's vagina. According to accounts emerging from the Kosovo war, women who were raped by Serbs do not dare tell of their defilement for fear of dishonoring their families and husbands (*The Times-Picayune*, 1999, June 21, p. A16). For the women, such disgrace is worse than death. For many men, such disgrace requires death.

To be released from the *vision* can feel like a death, is a death; for dy-ing-to-an-old-way is a necessary precondition for rebirth. So fairy tale teaches, so myth teaches, so the unconscious teaches. Visitors teach us this truth, too. I hope I will always listen to the knock at my back door.

One of my students received a knock to the door of her unconscious when she read Eudora Welty's (1941/1997) story "Death of a Traveling Salesman" and saw in the death figure, Mr. Bowman, a glimpse of herself. You would never know, to look at Lilly, that she had anything but a perfect life. She is perfection itself: expensive clothes, expensive perfume, well-wrought sentences, an Anne Bancroft look. But Lilly confided to me her inability to write a commentary on the Welty story, realizing that she was criticizing Mr. Bowman, adopting a critic's pose; when in actuality, she said, *she* was Mr. Bowman. Lilly's inability to write, and her confession of this problem, came at a moment I was dribbling at the chin eating a cucumber sandwich. At the moment I was thinking that Lilly was all perfection and I was the rather clumsy professor, nibbling. But when Lilly re-lated her dismay at the story, I realized as I sometimes do that the fiction I teach may really have a life's impact on my students. Subsequently, Lilly did write about Mr. Bowman, who is the death figure in the story because he has closed his heart off. But Lilly did not write "about" him; she wrote "to" him:

> Sometimes we choose to treat our hearts like the shoes you, Mr. Bowman, sold, which, enclosed in their boxes, never walked in the rain nor dried under the sun, nor saw the beauty of the world. The truth is, Mr. Bowman, some of us go through life building 'a wall, impenetrable, behind which people turned back after we had passed' (Welty, 1941/1997, p. 307). But who knows about the life circumstances that have contributed to our distant approach, Mr. Bowman?

Lilly's questions, together with her decision to engage the fictional character in dialogue, moves her into a place inside herself, closed off from inspection by the demands of the "wall" of the business, practical world—but opened, if only briefly, for another like myself and herself to glimpse and to tremble.

REVISION

> At the wedding-feast, when the queen's crime was exposed, slippers of iron were heated in a fire until red hot, and the queen was forced to put them on, and to dance until she dropped dead. (Grimm & Grimm, 1823/1980, p. 228)

We are used to having fairy tales begin "Once upon a time" and end "And they lived happily ever after." This tale ends instead with the macabre finale of the evil queen's death dance. One wonders, what does this have to do with Snow White?

Snow White's ever-after happiness depends on this image, I think. She who was easily fooled, did others' bidding, never thought twice, and always looked beautiful—*that* pure and innocent snow whiteness needs to be revisioned. Her too-perfect, eternally puerile child-self needs to be connected to what Freud calls the reality principle or what Jung terms the collective unconscious. In other words, Snow White, daughter of the patriarchy, will find happiness only when she witnesses the death of the stepmother (like her, a patriarchal daughter).

Like all tales, this incident should be read on a symbolic level. Just as Snow White's marriage to the prince is a metaphor for the union of opposites within the self, so too can the tortuous death of the stepmother be read symbolically. The evil woman, note, is not a mother; she is a stepmother. She does not represent the matriarchy, so she does not have any teachings to offer women. Her evil is that she perpetuates patriarchy's expectations of women. Because she is constantly checking her mirror, the stepmother is enslaved by the training of the kingdom. Her entire being pits woman against woman for the beauty title. Snow White must see the stepmother's hideous death in such red-hot detail that it will be seared into her unconscious. The image is palpable; thus it will not become invisible and capable of recurring. Snow White's happy marriage (to forces within herself), together with the stepmother's immolation, foretells the end of a false definition of womanhood.

In this fourth phase of the entering-leaving sequence, *revision*, the emphasis is on seeing. Snow White must "see" not the way the stepmother sees, not as reflection—a mirror image—of the patriarchy's view of women. No, she must see with insight, clarity, courage, and perception—a seeing that kills false modeling.

Gail Sheehy (1995) describes the second half of life, which all my interviewees are experiencing, as second adulthood. Whereas in the first half we were susceptible to stereotypes and patriarchal priorities, in the second half we are conscious now of where we need to go. There is, Sheehy writes, a "push toward authenticity," which for women often has been delayed, causing us not to master our situations but to merely survive them (p. 142). Now, in this revisioning of who we are, we might feel uncomfortable with this reinvented self. Adolf Guggenbuhl-Craig (1986), in his *Marriage Dead or Alive*, comments on the new person one feels one's self to be if one is truly "married" to one's inner opposites: "Individuation means an active, difficult, uncomfortable working through of one's own complex psyche towards a joining of its opposites" (p. 29). Instead of others forging identities for us, we begin to forge ourselves.

For some, like myself, having been "arrested" for half my life, we hardly know how to go about this task of forging the new identity. We need guidance. In my case a dream provided insight. The dream came on the night after I had been working on this chapter, filled with excitement about the new work I was doing. The dream had no plot, just three images: a baby, a tiger, and a large bathtub containing a naked man. The baby was strong and capable of unusual mental abilities such that it could understand computers better than I can. It was both mine and not mine. This combination suggests that the infant of my new self is born from the deep unconscious, and, as such, has something important and new to tell me. The dreamer-me feels that because this baby, not entirely mine, does not need to have its diapers changed it might be divine; it needs no mothering. The writer-me thinks that the baby is a side of myself "born" from a loving connection with symbols and truths that this other, less personal life reveals. The tiger in the dream is in a house, but not my house. Again, this image seems to be transpersonal. It is there, without context, to simply state the primal energy that is now appearing in the house of my self. The third symbol, the naked man in the tub, presents an image of maleness in a contained space. The male's penis is waving in the waters of the tub as if befriending me, saying in effect: "Come on in, the water's fine." These three images together present themselves to me as an invitation to transform myself from the passive person I was to the more creative person I can be if only I will connect with an energy drawn from primal, sexual powers offered to me from a divine source.

Because of the friendly phallus and its placement in an amniotic container, this dream would further seem to validate the language theory of Julia Kristeva (in Moi, 1986). In her rereading of the Oedipally-based language theory of Jacques Lacan (1968), Kristeva privileges the mother womb over against the father phallus as the source of an infant's perception of the world. Rather than seeing the infant self as submerged in an oceanic, illusory fusion with maternal life, Kristeva re-marks the authority of the mother's womb world, which connects the infant to its own image-making, life-affirming powers. Such an affirmation is, in Wendy Atwell-Vesey's (1998) words, the "maternal legacies" of body knowing, intersubjectivity, and attraction to the wider world (p. 55). My dream's limp penis waving in the water is like an infant male force beckoning me not, as in the tale of Snow White, from the father's palace (phallus) but from the mother's placenta.

For the women I interviewed, a newfound ability to offer up words immediately repositioned their vision and, for some, allowed them to reclaim their own bodies. Beverly used frank talk with her husband, the night he urged her to have a face lift and breast implants:

> And I just turned to him and smiled and said, "Well, now that I know what the problem is, the problem is not me: it's you. And you have an egotistical attitude plus an assininity about you. Your remark means something like me saying to you that I wanted a bigger penis to play with." Then he said, "That's different." And I said, "Why is it different? Your penis is as much a sexual organ to you as my breasts are to me." And he, um, he said, "Well, no, no, no." He just began kind of mumbling after that. And finally I just looked at him and I said, "Well, my hair is my hair, my voice, the way I speak, um, my actions, my whole being is me. And from this day forward I am going to be just that. Me. I don't care about you, I don't care about your home; your children are basically out of the picture, so you're on your own from here out." And I walked out and I left him.

Beverly's decision to leave did not involve another man at that point. But leave she knew she must, for the vision her husband was creating of her was one she knew she had to put to death. To revision herself, Beverly had to make her mark; she had to reclaim her bodied identity.

A necessary critical eye needs to be cast toward all those institutions that arrest female energy and define female being exclusively in terms of male authority, male objectivity, or male law. Rose, a former nun, is case in point. She was one of four siblings growing up in the Midwest in the 1940s and 1950s. All four of her siblings entered religious life. Her brother became a monk (and still is one—a Trappist, no less), and her two sisters, like Rose, joined a convent for multiple years. All the sisters have since left. When I saw Rose for our interview, we decided to visit a Catholic Church on a Native-American reservation near where Rose now lives in Albuquerque. I asked her, as part of my interview, if she would share her thoughts of that experience:

> What struck me immediately, of course, was here we were in a Native-American reservation in this incredibly beautiful (basically Hispanic chapel, however) … the one little sign of Native-American stuff was a tiny little mural of corn and then one bowl and one bird and the rest was all Spanish. I was immediately aware of the separation, really, between the reality of these people and what was being given them. And then, of course, this idiot walks up to the podium and in this monotone voice he talks about freedom as if he knew what he was talking about and he denies the fact that the basis of freedom … is personal choice. But he said you're only free to do whatever if it's good for the church—making everything all knotted up…. I looked at these people, how do they—I mean, I remember sitting through sermons like that, and my stomach would start to get … but it took a while. I used to just hear it just sort of waft over me.

> Mary: I didn't see one sign of rebellion, did you?

> Rose: I think they just put up with it…. What have we got? Our own spiritual lives have been stripped away from us, even our spiritual intuitions. We've all become liars. We've all become liars. We've all learned subterfuge to tolerate these jerks who run the organization.

Rose, once renamed Sister Thomas Aquinas, offers an insider's view of the Church that, for the women I interviewed, symbolized (to their great personal detriment) maleness. Rose re-cognized the sermon in the pueblo, seeing that not just the words from the pulpit but the very icons inside the church "spoke" of male authority demanding complete obedience. The language was all-surrounding, demanding all-surrendering. As the fairy tale ending of Snow White indicates, the time has come to stop stepmothering the patriarchy, lest women continue to walk in iron shoes and die in duty dance.

⚜7⚜

The P(r)ose of Clothes

If indeed clothes make the man—or the woman—are not sex roles as such, inherently, but travesties?

—Felman, 1981, p. 32

Do we truly need a true sex?

—Foucault, 1980, p. vii

I write this chapter shortly after the fall fashion collections shown during the week of Gianni Versace's murder. The death of the fashion designer dominated the news, one sideline being the lifestyle of style. Fashion, in all its manifold forms—from Versace's prostitute style made into high style on the runways; to the Versace, glitzy Miami Beach mansion; to the Versace funeral photos of Princess Di comforting Elton John—was on the air. Beyond the grizzly events of the murder, another material world was on show. This, the world of male cleavage, pneumatic shoulders, and black rubber cutaways was a spectacle: clothing laughing out loud.

Fashion is fun, political, and theatrical. Fashion is forensic. Fashion is travesty in all its forms: miscues, humor, and spectacle. Although words derived from the closet have entered our everyday speech—we skirt issues, apply coats of paint, enjoy fringe benefits and dress hamburgers, for example—these linguistic literalisms hardly cause a pause. But fashion, as writers and designers know, provides a language of its own, a language that can speak volumes if the gazer can but learn to read more "clothesly." Reading between the binary lines of sex loosens the ties of gender and shakes free the shackles of sartorial sexism. With help from literal writers of literal prose works, I suggest that a more metaphoric—indeed, a more playful—understanding of clothes can unzip possible selves.

It is in this spirit of the romp that I begin with Virginia Woolf's (1928/1956) *Orlando*. As she wrote in her diary, "*Orlando* was the outcome of a perfectly definite, indeed overmastering, impulse. I want fun. I want fantasy. I want (and this was serious) to give things their caricature value" (in Woolf, L., 1954, p. 134). And so, as a serious joke Woolf created a character liberated from the restraints of sex and time. First a he in the 16th century, Orlando changes into a she in the 17th century, flip-flopping sexes until the 20th century of Woolf's time. As the sex changes so do the costumes, causing Woolf to make trenchant remarks about the clothing code:

> there is much to support the view that it is clothes that wear us and not we them.... The man has his hand free to seize his sword; the woman must use hers to keep the satins from slipping from her shoulders. The man looks the world full in the face, as if it were made for his uses and fashioned to his liking. The woman takes a sidelong glance at it, full of subtlety, even of suspicion. Had they both worn the same clothes it is possible that their outlook might have been the same too. (p. 188)

Although the reader enjoys some swashbuckling, good humored adventures of the he-Orlando of the 16th century—*he* won the special affections of Queen Elizabeth, enjoyed the rank and privileges of the courtly life, dallied with writing poetry born of passion—we learn that as soon as this Elizabethan wizard has been made to don lace and paduasoy in the next century, *she* was immediately denied the privileges and rights of personhood—including even "knowledge of the alphabet" (p. 159). It is as if the stays and laces of the female costume—just those—hold the *she*-Orlando prisoner not only from social benefits and rights but also from the desires of the human heart.

Placing text on text, I digress to summon Woolf's feminist treatise "A Room of One's Own" (1929/1985), written a year after *Orlando*, possibly as commentary on the earlier work. In "Room" Woolf posits another what-if story for the enlightenment,[1] particularly, of young women. What if Shakespeare had had a sister? What if, indeed! Woolf has the reader imagine along with her how this gifted sister of the bard—for surely she, too, had inherited genius genes—had grown up in the same house. Although being as "agog to see the world as he was" (p. 1,380), she, because of her sex, would not have been allowed to learn, to read freely, to write, even to choose her partner; and so, having run away to be an actress in London, she would have been so ridiculed and thwarted that she would have had to kill herself rather than continue living. Here, too, Woolf "gives

---

[1]The word *enlightenment* for postmodern feminists is freighted with heterosexist assumptions; namely, that there is such a thing as the Law of Nature, used to control women's bodies. I use the term in the instance of Virginia Woolf's address to the young women scholars at Cambridge to suggest her purpose of shedding light on the inequalities of their physical surroundings as compared to the luxuries granted men scholars at the same institution.

things their caricature value." Although the description of Shakespeare's sister (like the she-Orlando) may seem overblown, loaded, fantastical, the caricature gives the sense of the straitjackets women wear.

Woolf's Orlando fantasy could, as Sandra Gilbert (1980) argues, be a feminist plea for a "third sex." But even the term "third sex" is too fixed, implying simply another solid identity: not that or that but this. To fix gender with a term is once again to play into a patriarchal "vested interest" (Garber, 1992) of naming male "stronger," female "weaker," third sex "other." Such terming limits, de-termines and marginalizes. If, as Woolf shows, it is clothes that "change the world's view of us" (1928/1956, p. 187), then it is style that Woolf says needs changing—not just fashion style, but writing style.

Writing for Woolf is political. It is highly subversive, totally ironic, maddeningly playful, seamingly fluid. "One reviewer says that I have come to a crisis in the matter of style," Woolf writes in her diary (p. 134); "it is now so fluent and fluid that it runs through the mind like water." Clearly, for Woolf, style is a travesty. According to Webster (1993), the first definition of "travesty" is "a literary or artistic burlesque of a serious work or subject, characterized by grotesque or ludicrous incongruity of style, treatment of subject matter, etc." Woolf shows that both gender and genre are travesties, constructed by the patriarchy so as to keep things straight.

It is thus that Woolf subtitles Orlando "A Biography," which purports to "write" a life. Although Orlando's transsexualism stretches the possibilities of sexual identity, Woolf's *writing* of that transsexualized life toys with objectivism, stretches the "truth" and adopts the pose of a narrator who can barely disguise a "libidinal partiality to and fondness for Orlando" (Hovey, 1997, p. 397), a character loosely based on and dedicated to Woolf's lesbian lover Vita Sackville-West. The result of this mix of facts and fantasies blurs the lines of opposites in a deliberately fluid style meant to stop fixities. The writing, for example, pretends to utter seriousness with the sort of puritanical remark one might associate with, as she puts it, "an elderly gentleman in a gray suit" (p. 280)—such as the line "Many people hold that (the change of sex) is against nature.... But let other pens treat of sex and sexuality; we quit such odious subjects as soon as we can" (p. 139). She sustains her biographical-biological joke further by the inclusion of photographs—"Orlando as a Boy," "Orlando as Ambassador," "Orlando on her return to England"—all of which lend verisimilitude to the classification "biography" or "sexed identity." But these photographs also draw attention to the category "gender," because when clothes change, so do the wearer's outlook and the reader's inlook. While the he-Orlando photos present postures of confidence in garments that portray worldliness, the she-Orlando's photograph reveals a blouse in need of adjustment at the shoulder and a sidelong glance away from the reader's gaze. "Gender," Woolf shows, can be as much the object of alteration as "biography"; each are but fashions, which change with the seasons.

That Woolf anticipates much of the now-current feminists' theorizing about the subversities of style seems, in retrospect, obvious. Woolf's writing is incontestably flowing. Luce Irigaray (1985), for example, claims that fluidity is a primary characteristic of female forms of expression as well as of female sexuality (pp. 110–111). Hélène Cixous (1981) expresses the ecofeminist idea that the female subject connects with sea, seaweed, tides, and waves (p. 260). Marjorie Garber (1992) argues that to change the signs by which gendered sexuality has traditionally been encoded (through language and clothing) is to articulate spaces for possibility (p. 11). And Gilbert (1980) suggests "we might all be transvestites of style" (p. 9). Less obvious and perhaps more surprising is to find these suggestions presented in a 13th-century French romance entitled *Silence* (1992), where the case is made in verse that the signs we see (or not see), or read (or misread) can be heard (or not heard) as well. The focus takes a Foucauldian turn from seeing to hearing. "There is not one but many silences," Foucault (1978) writes, "and they are an integral part of the strategies that underlie and permeate discourses" (p. 27).

Silence, absence, hiddenness, gap, the closet: These are the spaces into which the French romance *Silence* dives, with its magnificent ripple effect down to the present. The story involves the daughter of Cador and Eufemie, named Silence, who is raised as a boy because of primogeniture laws that grant inheritance privilege only to males. Silence is nature's mistresspiece—she is a blond beauty who plays the part of an epic hero doing battles "slicing off enemy legs and feet and fists" (lines 5,639–5,641) and winning women's hearts. The plot turns on a transvestite moment when the queen of the land falls in love with Silence who, because "he" does not return her favors, is set an impossible task to capture the magician Merlin. When Merlin unmasks "him" and grants her the right to inherit and to become the next queen, it is seen that Silence is then truly silenced by dwindling into wifedom.

The motifs of this medieval romance resonate with current gender issue debates: the question of inheritance, the privilege of speech as opposed to silence, the theme of nature or nurture. According to the text's Introduction, Nature appears frequently, in the genre of old French romance, whose function as procreatrix is to regulate the use of the organs of generation for species survival (p. xvii). As such, nature abhors the transvestite, seen as a perversion of the "natural" social order, which depends, for its continuity, on the heterosexual "silent" woman. Silence's "natural" punishment for cross dressing, then, is marriage—the only institution possible for maintaining phallocentric control.

The author of this text, Heldris, could be critiquing Lacan if the author weren't writing in the 13th century. The purpose of the writing seems clearly to offer a refutation of the definition of woman as a defective male lacking a visible—or in this case audible—sign. Accordingly, the author has fun writing with tongue in cheek, pulling the reader in on a "silent" joke made at the expense of the actors in the text. Like Woolf, Heldris plays with the reader: "Now wait till you hear what she had in mind!" (line 3,978). "Listen to how well she did it" (line 3,989). "Now you're going to hear something amazing!" (line 2,689). These supposedly incredulous remarks about the loudness of Silence's actions and thoughts, as well as the invitation to "hear" and "listen," signify the writer's intention to speak for Silence. There is in all of this a closet closeness between author, reader, and text that requires what Brent Davis (1996) refers to as "a sound alternative."

As an alternative, then, to the primacy of the eye, the ear in *Silence* is brought to the forefront. The mother of Silence is Eufemie (use of good speech, or euphemism) who is defined by convention and who sustains the linguistic and ideological code of courtly ideals. The queen who falls in love with the he-Silence is Eufeme (Alas! Woman) who represents the female as socially defined—without voice—and whose body ends a war. These two ladies, separated only by a letter, occupy the euphemistic world of wife or mother, whose speaking voice in marriage must be wadded by "pious obliviousness" (Sedgwick, 1990, p. 54). According to Webster (1993) "euphemism" means "the substitution of a mild, indirect, or vague expression for one thought to be offensively harsh or blunt." Euphemism thus gives birth to Silence, a live metaphor who almost opens up possibilities for the redefinition of gender but who, instead, must substitute mildness for direct speech and sophistry for bluntness when her sexed identity is revealed. Cross-dressing has the impact of what Garber in *Vested Interests* calls "a primal scene," such that what is witnessed cannot be uttered (p. 388). Silence's ruse, in other words, is considered taboo. It seems that Heldris, the author of this medieval tale, makes the case, however, that the primary opposition of speech and silence, women's voice and the master discourse, women's place or absence from the social contract—whether verbal, economic, or political—are all issues that clamor to be heard.

Mary Jacobus writes, in *Reading Woman* (1986), that the origin of gender identity is instituted by language with its "unitary schemes designed to repress the otherness of femininity" (p. 5). I have attempted to show that both Virginia Woolf and Heldris use language to undo unitary schemes and present gender-ambiguous subjects to juxtapose codes. Although the next part of my discussion does not concern the transvestite, it does concern women readers. Emma Bovary reads trashy romantic novels; Blanche DuBois teaches literature. Both characters are written by men who claim identity with their female tragic heroines: Gustave Flaubert reportedly said, "Madame Bovary c'est moi" (Flaubert, 1856/1992, p. 887); Tennessee Williams said, "I am Blanche DuBois" (in Londre, 1993, p. 21). Both Emma and Blanche "act" their femininity—one knowingly, one unknowingly—but both act with an understanding that being female, as Judith Butler (1990) observes, is "cultural performance" (p. viii). Who would know better about performance than two male writers longing to be female, writing about two females longing to be male?

Emma's flaw, in *Madame Bovary*, would seem to be her lack of imagination. "The words 'bliss' and 'passion' seemed so beautiful to her in books" Flaubert writes (1856/1992, p. 910). Reality, for Emma, is literal inscription: the books she reads in the convent; the metaphors she hears in sermons—"betrothed," "spouse," "heavenly lover," "mystical lover" (p. 912)—the stories told her by a spinster involving "skiffs in the moonlight," "nightingales in thickets," noble men beautifully dressed and white-plumed knights (p. 912); the painted pierrot figurines on lamp shades (p. 952); and even the captions on hotel supper plates praising the splendors of the court (p. 911). Had Emma followed the advice of Mary Wollstonecraft, author of "A Vindication of the Rights of Women" (1792/1985), she might have avoided her tragic fate and corrected the "barren blooming" of her early years that "enfeebled" her imagination:

> One cause of this barren blooming I attribute to a false system of education, gathered from the books written on this subject by men who, considering females rather as women than human creatures, have been more anxious to make them alluring mistresses than affectionate wives and rational mothers. (Wollstonecraft, p. 139)

But Emma does not follow Wollstonecraft's advice, although Flaubert, writing some sixty-four years after the publication of "Vindication," surely knew of its existence. In his essay "Narrative Strategies in Madame Bovary," Michael Peled Ginsberg (1988) identifies the novel's motifs of nested stories, mirrors, and repetition as literary devices that call attention to the fictiveness of fiction. Flaubert himself, despite his being a fiction writer, was writing about all the ways the world can be misread. Emma misreads because the fiction she reads is stupid. The result is a character created by imitation, which the reader sees because of the multiplication of symbols; the writer intends because of the insertion of expressions of disgust; but of which the character herself remains totally ignorant. She becomes precisely what Wollstonecraft warned against: a lady of fashion "puffed up with notions" and subject to "phosphoric bursts" (pp. 159, 160).

Flaubert, of course, was not what Wollstonecraft termed a "stupid novelist" (p. 157). Rather, he was writing a warning to women who read fictions like his that they should not be duped by the plot. Emma's desires, which so carried her away as a young girl reading, were shaped by the false sentiments of novels—not to mention supper plates and hurdy gurdies. Commenting on the poison of these fictions to Emma's mood swings and vapors, Flaubert writes, "So it was decided to prevent Emma from reading novels" (p. 970). She was becoming a mirror of their sentiments—what Ginsburg calls "a repetition without difference" (p. 139), doomed to repeat but not to reread. Several aspects of Flaubert's literary maneuvers interest me, which I will entertain as four comments, one corollary, one digression, and one dimension.[2]

My first comment has to do with Flaubert's lack of description of Emma's clothes (as opposed to the lavish attention he gives to the male characters' fashions). Once, she wears "a shawl-collared dressing gown, open very low over a pleated dicky with three gold buttons" (p. 927); once, she dresses in "a dressing gown with a fine scarf around her waist" (p. 969); once, she wears "a blue silk dress with four rows of flounces" (p. 1,033); once, her dress is described as having "trim folds" (p. 958); and once, her underclothes are seen through the eyes of the servant Justin, who "stares hungrily at all the feminine garments strewn about him—the dimity petticoats, the fichu, the collars, the drawstring pantaloons enormously wide at the waist and narrowing below" (p. 1,063). But these references, except for the last one with its unflatteringly unnecessary detail about the wide-waisted pantaloons, are sparse both in quantity and quality. It is as if Emma is somehow not fully bodied in the fashionable circles of 19th-century Rouen and Paris.

A corollary to this observation is the attention Flaubert gives to Emma's actions that, because they are so fleeting, lack agency. We see her constantly on the run: running to meet Rodolphe by their secret river cottage, grabbing kisses from her daughter, transacting hasty business, springing from chairs, bursting with laughter or rage, thronging with memories, and—"every Thursday" of her affair with Léon—riding in the Hirondelle ("lark") carriage, the galloping horses whisking her away from her marriage into the adulterous arms of Léon. Ultimately, these fleetings, like the tickings of the clock, run themselves down to her ill-fated end.

My second comment concerns Flaubert's lavish attention to the male characters' clothes—even the servants' often-mentioned wooden shoes. Emma seems to see herself glamorized by their finery—their swords, silks, and velvets—that lend luster to her otherwise dull life. Is Emma attracted to Léon or to the black velvet collar of Léon's frock coat? When she attends her first ball, she notices the men in the doorways:

> Their coats were better cut and seemed to be of finer cloth; their hair, brought forward in ringlets over the temples, seemed to glisten ... their long side whiskers drooped onto turned-down collars; they wiped their lips with handkerchiefs that were deliciously scented and monogrammed with huge initials. (p. 921)

Doesn't she glome in on hair and handkerchiefs! All this detail, seen through Emma's eyes, contrasts with the cursory mention of her "beautiful ball costume"

---

[2]By being overly clear about the arrangement of ideas in this Flaubert section, I am playing with Eve Sedgwick's (1990) over-dependence on logic to make her points, particularly in the "Introduction: Axiomatic" chapter of her *Epistemology of the Closet*, where she argues against the "axioms" of heterocentrism.

and "satin slippers." Flaubert is slyly indicating to the reader not just Emma's love of glamor but also her desire to be ... her own object of desire: a glamorous man!

Clothes are Emma Bovary's means of transcending her station in life as a bourgeois housewife married to a dullard. But it is the clothes of men that occupy Flaubert's paragraphs. This attention to the male closet is given even "clotheser" scrutiny when Rodolphe, Emma's first lover, enters the picture:

> His batiste shirt (it had pleated cuffs) puffed out from the opening of his gray twill vest at each gust of wind; and his broad-striped trousers ended at nankeen shoes trimmed with patent leather so shiny that the grass was reflected in it. (p. 978)

Rodolphe is presented as a fashion queen, whose clothes he knows have a seductive power: "Rodolphe had on a pair of high soft boots, telling himself that she had probably never seen anything like them" (p. 991).

Digressing, I offer Tom Stoppard's play *Travesties* (1975) as an Absurdist commentary on the sex role travesties found in Flaubert's text. The serious purpose of Stoppard's play is to call into question any "reals" usually taken for granted, like "nature," "truth," "patriotism,"or—in Flaubert's case—"gender." Stoppard plays with audience-viewer expectations that what we "see" is what we "get" (Doll, 1993). For him, lofty ideas, earnest words, and definite categories can be dressed up, or travestied. Through a sort of Dada logic, we are made to laugh, realizing that any so-called "original" is always derived.

Stoppard uses clothes as his major means of deconstructing the law of coherence, much as Judith Butler (1990) claims that drag subverts heterosexism (p. 139). One character, Henry Carr, recalls his wartime experiences chiefly through recollecting what he wore (war-wore):

> I had hardly set foot in France before I sank in up to the knees in a pair of twill jodhpurs with pigskin straps handstitched by Ramidge and Hawkes. And so it went on—the sixteen ounce serge, the heavy worsteds, the silk flannel mixture—until I was invalided out with a bullet through the calf of an irreplaceable lambswool dyed khaki in the yarn to my own specification. (p. 21)

Carr defended his country in battle chiefly because it was the fashionable thing to do. And he becomes interested in playing a part in the play-within-a-play (Oscar Wilde's *The Importance of Being Earnest*) because of the many changes of costume his part demands: "a bottle-green velvet smoking jacket with black frogging—hose white, cravat perfect, boots elastic-sided" (p. 36), and for act two "a debonair garden party outfit—beribboned boater, gaily striped blazer, parti-colored shoes" (p. 36). Fashion jokes continue in typically farcical Stoppardian style. When the Dadaist artist Tristan Tzara asks about the whereabouts of another character (James Joyce), Tzara describes him by his clothes:

often seen round about, in the library, in the cafés, wearing, for example, a black pinstripe jacket with gray herringbone trousers, or brown Donegal jacket with black pinstripe trousers, or gray herringbone jacket with brown Donegal trousers. (pp. 25–26)

Stoppard's point, with these hilariously overstated descriptions of clothes, is to make the serious comment on how fashion fashions meaning. As Stoppard's mouthpiece Tzara puts it, "In point of fact, everything is Chance, including design" (p. 37). Such playings as occur inside a Stoppard play are meant, through laughter, to shake us out of our comfortable false belief that fashion reveals the man or woman. The intention is what Virginia Woolf labeled a "serious joke," perhaps more appropriate to new science or queer theory than to the stage.

Criticism of Stoppard's work has tended toward belittlement of what critics like John Gardner (1978) calls Stoppard's "contrived" treatment of ideas "likely to be more fashionable than earnest-predictable talk" (p. 59). And yet, Stoppard's insistence on flux is serious. As quantum physics now shows, there can be no pinpointing of observable reality, because the observer is both "wave" and "particle" at the same time—both observed and observing, both center and margin. Writing on postmodern science, Steven Toulmin (1982) understands Tom Stoppard's intention to debunk modernist certainties like logic, causality, tradition, perception, and consequence: "Stoppard is right. The picture of 'pure spectator' is no longer open to us in natural science or philosophy, any more than it has ever been in social and political affairs" (p. 238).

This digression into the Absurd is meant to add a dimension to Flaubert's tragic novel about Emma Bovary, to suggest that perhaps Flaubert's interest to a deconstructionist like Harold Bloom implies that Flaubert was, himself, a deconstructionist before his time. Hazel Barnes (1988) makes a similar point, remarking on the "polyphonic voice" of Flaubert's text, which serves to distance the reader, possibly to warn the reader, from a too-close identity with Emma's dilemma. Flaubert's impersonal narrator demonstrates that gender is an absurd social construction formed by many social texts that we may not be aware of—from lamp shades and dinner plates to knee breeches and tool kits. Emma could not deconstruct the simpering fantasies of these texts any more than she could "read"—deconstruct—her childhood, trashy novels. She was therefore hopelessly at the mercy of her own humorless literalism, drawn ever deeper into a narcissistic urge to act out, be on display, perform. "She saw herself," Flaubert writes, "as one of those amoureuses whom she had so envied; she was becoming, in reality, one of that gallery of fictional figures" (p. 995). We are meant to see that the gender performances of the three main actors—Emma, Rodolphe, and Léon—are just that—performances—travesties of socially inscribed, gendered behaviors.

My third comment concerns performance. Flaubert's text seems to demonstrate that if one's imagination is uneducated or too literal, one is doomed to repeat the gender performances of dumb texts. This comment pertains not only to

Emma but also to Léon, Emma's second lover. That he, like Emma, is a senti-
mentalist can be seen by his naïve slippage into fantasy. He talks of the so-called
power of his reading: "I'm playing a role in the story I'm reading. I actually feel
I'm the characters—I live and breathe with them" (p. 942). Like Emma he
wants "to dream up ideals" and then "refashion" his life "to match them" (p.
1,042). It is Emma who literally refashions Léon, dressing him to look like the
portraits of Louis XlII: "She demanded that he dress entirely in black and grow a
little pointed beard" (p. 1,071). She wants to make him over into a king through
a new set of black clothes. She writes love letters to him as she wished him to be,
a phantom lover like the ones of her readings. He was, the author remarks, "becoming her mistress far more than she was his" (p. 1,071).

These playacting scenes of Emma and Léon in the amphitheater of Rouen
are persistently perverse because they are without self-conscious irony on the
part of the actors. Their impersonations are phantoms. Pirandello's actors, in
Six Characters in Search of an Author, come to mind in this regard: They are actors who only know how to act. There is no awareness; there is only acting. The
fictional actors in Flaubert mirror what so-called novels had concocted for
them in sugary, so-called styles. Their love affair is the froth of convention. But
Emma Bovary, who is Gustave Flaubert, seems to have the last laugh on the charade of her life in the final scenes of the novel.

My fourth comment concerns Emma's only original action. Before her death,
as we have seen, Emma had been unable to uncover an original way to be happy
or to escape sameness; she merely repeated what her books had shown her. She
was a repetition of a stereotype. And so repetition followed her every move. Her
first lover saw Emma as a copy, just like all his other mistresses. Their affair fiz-
zled when passion became a monotony, "which always assumes the same forms
and always speaks the same language" (p. 1,013). Her second lover she made
over into a copy of the stereotype of a lover. Her love letters to him were copies
of love letters. The mirrors that appeared on the walls of her rooms revealed
only likeness. When she became pregnant all she wanted was a boy who would
be "a promise of compensation for all her past frustrations" (p. 945). Instead, she
birthed a girl, her same sex. Even on her deathbed, the replications continued
when Charles dressed her in her bridal dress with her white shoes so as to be a
replica of the fairy tale princess with her three coffins—one oak, one mahogany,
one lead. After her death pathetic Charles buried his grief by copying, of all people, Emma. He copied her tastes and habits, buying himself patent leather
shoes, white cravats and signing—"just as she had"—promissory notes (p.
1,115); and, in meeting Rodolphe, he thought "he would have liked to be that
man" (p. 1,119). But although Charles seems not to have read the signs of corruption everywhere visible around him—doomed thereby, like Emma, to be a
social copy—Flaubert has Emma perform a gesture of complete originality by
one final, silent action of contempt on her deathbed. There, just after the finish-
ing touches had been made to her toilette and the still veil was drawn to cover

her down to her shoes—there, shrouded like a death bride—she poured black liquid poison out of her mouth "like a vomit" (p. 1108). This shows Flaubert's triumph of a woman who, at the last, sees all that copying, all that imitation, all that acting as vomit.

My last discussion of the travesties of clothes involves Tennessee Williams's Blanche DuBois, from *Streetcar Named Desire* (1947). Unlike Emma Bovary's, Blanche's sexuality is a conscious gender performance. Her behavior, speech, and particularly her dress are all masquerades of a femininity designed to entrap so as to replace the masculine world. Blanche knows how to read men and how to lure them; her purpose is ultimately to secure a place for herself in the public discourse of power by overthrowing the "father"—in this case her sister's husband, Stanley Kowalski.

My interpretation of a masculine Blanche comes from my reading of Judith Butler's *Gender Trouble* (1990) and Jennifer Blessing's comments in *Prose is a Prose is a Prose* (1997). From Butler I find useful the following observation: "Genders can be neither true nor false, neither real nor apparent, neither original nor derived"; instead, she continues, "genders can be rendered thoroughly and radically incredible" (p. 141). What could be more incredible than the contents of Blanche's wardrobe trunk that she brings to the Elysian Fields apartment, a trunk containing what Stanley describes as "worn out Mardi Gras outfits" (p. 127). Her opening appearance in white, with gloves and hat to match, shows her to be incredibly out of place—"a moth," the stage directions suggest, in what could otherwise be called a jungle.

Williams identifies Blanche with moth characteristics. She must avoid strong light, and she flits: "There is something about her uncertain manner ... that suggests a moth" (p. 5) he writes. Her frothy clothing also suits the moth motif. In his *Symbols of Transformation* Carl Jung (1911–1912/1952) comments on the intense psychic content of the figure of the moth, which expresses a passionate longing for the star (p. 84). Blanche's love for her sister Stella ("Stella for star," p. 18) may not be entirely sibling affection. It might be the longing of Blanche to repossess that which Stanley has taken from her. A Jungian reading of Blanche's mothlike attributes connects the moth with death, for it is a known fact that moths are fluttering paradoxes, attracted to that which kills them—light. The moth is thus a psychopomp, a leader of souls into darkness, into death. That Blanche is associated with death is another symbol of the play. After dealing with "the long parade" of her parents and cousins "to the graveyard" (p. 21), she takes a streetcar named Cemetaries to a place called Elysian Fields (which in myth is where the happy dead reside). These highly charged symbolic associations are woven into the fabric of Blanche's character so that we may see her in the most complex manner possible—as an incredibility. Here she is, all flitty and flighty, arriving into the jungle world where her sister's husband is king.

Blanche is an exaggerated woman who appears ultrafemme to mask her masculinity under a veil of decoration (Rivière, 1929). This masking is deliberate,
an attempt by the masquerader to appear to have what Lacan (1977) calls the
symbolic phallus. As such, she is a figure to contend with. That the dainty figure
in white (whose name "Blanche" means white) should become an antagonist of
manly Stanley charges the drama with a primal sexual energy. In a play where
the symbolic phallus, Blanche, meets the literal phallus, Stanley, the two characters are destined to fight. And their battleground revolves around the star,
Stella, whom both Blanche and Stanley desire to control.

Williams employs basic sounds and strong colors to bring out the primal elements of power and desire. The kitchen contains "lurid nocturnal brilliance,
the raw colors of childhood's spectrum" (p. 46), Williams writes. Street sounds
intrude upon the listener's ears at crucial points: Cats screech, trains roar,
streetcars rumble, and vendors cry. Jazz music from the blue piano down the
street and the "Varsouviana," a waltz tune, weave melodies in and around the
action, adding the feeling-tones of loneliness, rejection, and longing to the
characters' primal urgings. But for Blanche to attain her goal—repossession of a
lost past associated with Stella, repossession of Stella—she performs what had
always worked for her in the days when the family plantation (Belle Rêve) was a
beautiful dream: She performs the southern belle routine—an extraordinary
gender performance that hides latent lesbian intentions.

To make her performance seem real, Blanche must screen her desire to usurp
male privilege by flirting (flitting), by wearing costumes, and by keeping others
in the dark about her past or her motives. Mitch, the unattached momma's boy
bachelor, is the perfect foil for her intentions. In order to snare Mitch she must
pretend to obey the law of nature (gendered, behavioral, social definition).
"Which law is that?" Mitch asks, innocently. "The one that says the lady must
entertain the gentleman—or no dice!" she responds (p. 86). Blanche plays
Mitch for a fool. Mitch really believes such a thing as a world of ladies and gentlemen who obey the law of nature. Blanche's background training at Belle
Rêve has taught her that "a woman's charm is fifty percent illusion" (p. 41). Although she can't play Stanley for a fool, she can keep the illusion going for Mitch
by feinting fatigue, speaking French, and appearing both virginal and childish.

Blanche's costuming is another performance. "Clothes are my passion!" she
exclaims (p. 38). She stages her entrance to appear like a magnolia—white suit,
fluffy bodice, pearl necklace and earrings, white gloves and hat—whose steel interior is hidden. Her trunk contains fur pieces and costume jewelry, nice accents
for the Barnum and Bailey world she sings about, "just as phony as it can be" (p.
101). The gossamer scarf she removes from her trunk is used to lure the paper
boy into a kiss. Even in the final scene, when Blanche's game is up and she is being taken away to an institution, she wears a Della Robia blue jacket, explaining
it is "the blue of the robe in the old Madonna pictures" (p. 135).

Blanche's southern belle behavior changes around Stanley who, because he is no gentleman, is neither charmed nor fooled by her performance. While others remain in the dark about the lurid secrets of Blanche's past, Stanley unmasks the truth. Blanche has deprived him of what the Napoleonic Code laws claim are his by rights of marriage: the profit from the sale of Belle Rêve. Stanley is "on" to Blanche's game (the play was originally titled *The Poker Night*) and continues to expose her past. Her darkest secret is that she, like Stanley, has animal desires. Her past life as a schoolteacher provided a screen for luring adolescent boys into her hotel rooms. Stanley's tossing of clothes from out of her trunk can be seen as a metaphor for his "outing" her desire, deeply closeted, to be a male.

We could call this play a psychodrama, although that term is more closely associated with Harold Pinter.[3] Stanley and Blanche represent two sides of Williams's complex character—not just male and female sides, but opposite temperaments with frightening, dark depths (Williams, 1978). Blanche tries to hide her darkness from Stanley behind screens: the screen in the apartment, the door to the bathroom, the screen of language, and the screen of clothes. But all of these are flimsy separators, for Blanche and Stanley vie for the same territory: Stella. That a woman could have the same primal urges as a man is, I believe, the reason Stanley rapes Blanche—his punishment for her penetration into his male psychic space. Williams's poignant ending, when Blanche is led away to an asylum by strangers, seems to be a further acknowledgement by Williams that the phallocentric social order, where Stanley reigns, is intolerant of deviations from the norm.

What might be some implications that this tour of the literary wardrobe has provided? There are no simple conclusions. The way to transgress is not necessarily to transvest. The idea of a third sex does not necessarily offer an alternative to sexual binaries. Nor does transsexualism necessarily lead to a magical coming-out of one's self. Is there one self? Since the 13th century,[4] at the very least, authors have explored the difficulties with identifying gender according to fixed and recognizable codes, clothing being one such code. If, as Virginia Woolf travestied, "it is only clothes that keep the male or female likeness" (1928/1956, p. 189), then perhaps priests and bagpipers are in trouble.

As the authors presented here have demonstrated in one form or another, a gender-ambiguous subject is never invisible; "it announces the juxtaposition of

---

[3]The term *psychodrama* has most often been used to describe the plays of Harold Pinter's masterpieces *The Room* (1957), *The Caretaker* (1960), and *The Homecoming* (1966) which utilize silence and pause to give the sense of sexual menace.

[4]In many nonWestern preliterate societies ceremonial transvestism was regularly practiced. Strands of this tradition can be seen even today in Native-American tribal dances. The fixity of gender was, and also is, released during Carnival, the border time before Lent, when social controls are not only relaxed but mocked and excess is celebrated. For a psychosocial understanding of androgyny as an expression of the opposites within, see June Singer's (1989) work.

codes in one subject" (Blessing, 1997, p. 12). Hearing that announcement and seeing that juxtaposition, however, require a deconditioning of ears and eyes. This is an epistemological project that goes to the very heart of educational concerns. Eve Sedgwick (1990) argues that knowledge and ignorance are structural relations that emerge from the "closet," which is not a literal place but a metaphorical margin. The distinction "heterosexual-homosexual" has in modern Western culture become *the* basic binary that marginalizes the "other" and from which all other binaries logically follow. Sedgwick lists twenty-two of these, including growth-decadence, innocence-initiation, natural-artificial, art-kitch. As long as homosexual identity is the silent, divided, minoritized, other half of heterosexual identity, she argues, then the audible, visible, dominant, heterosexual culture acts without knowing its privileged status. To privilege not knowing (or not seeing or not hearing) is to privilege unknowing compulsions of hatred. Sedgwick's question of the closet seems to ask the question of the margin in the manner of Derrida (1982), who states, "beyond the ... text there is not a blank, virgin, empty margin, but another text, a weave of differences of forces without any present center of reference" (p. xxiii).

To render visible the largely invisible margins and contexts of the classroom is one of the educational issues raised by Dennis Sumara, notably in his *Private Readings in Public: Schooling the Literary Imagination*. What is at issue is the way role playing has defined classroom performance (much as clothes have defined gender). When teachers act like teachers, pointing out the hidden meaning of literary texts, students are encouraged to act like students; they respond to texts automatically, giving "correct" answers, instead of authentic thinking. Sumara argues for texts to become places—he calls them commonplaces—where roles are shed and writing in the margins is encouraged. Writing in the margins becomes a metaphorical as well as literal activity, accomplishing what Sedgwick urges: making the margins (of our thinking, our reading, our responding) visible to our selves. Had Emma Bovary written in the margins of her books, perhaps she would have been able to read through their romantic nonsense.

Indeed, to teach as Sumara suggests would go a long, long way in overturning automatic thinking and uncritical reading of whatever text is presented for inspection. Such teaching becomes a way "to learn about the complexity of ever-evolving curricular relations" (Pinar et al., 1995, p. 438). For another educational theorist, Maxine Greene (1995), the way to discover the margins of knowing is through releasing the imagination. For her, the imagination opens the metaphorical doors of the metaphorical closet by revealing what had previously been "unseen, unheard, unexpected" (p. 28). Imagination for Greene is most definitely not a static entity; it is a moving force, capable of awakening new connections and allowing that which had been hidden to emerge (Morris, 1998). One can only imagine how the teaching-learning relation could be transformed if students and teachers could read cultural and literary texts differently, more actively.

Finally, it is time to bring these remarks to a "clothes." I write this chapter out of years of dreams of clothes. There, in dream, either I wore second-hand clothes, sent my clothes to the cleaners, or had on layers upon layers of clothes. My greatest dream fear was to be naked in public. Clearly, my unconscious was trying to tell me something which, because I didn't seem to "get it," had to be repeated, dream after dream. I consider dreams the other side of the performance-acts we do consciously. Because dream performances come from the unconscious, they are like the day dramas we enact daily, but from a deeper, more knowing, more scary perspective. The following is one example from my dream book two years before I divorced:

> I am with a group on a cliff overlooking the ocean. We are playing a game: Each of us is given scraps of material from which we must make clothes. Janet manages to put together a very fine wardrobe. She makes a smart sailor suit dress and a shirt to wear over her bathing suit. I fumble and fiddle; then I fashion a skirt. Everyone agrees it is absolutely wrong for me. It is puffed and tucked around the waist and makes me look like a bell.

The dream presents to me an image of myself as a "fantasy of femininity" (Walkerdine, 1990, p. 144), which others know is "absolutely wrong" for me. The pun on the word "bell" is particularly witty, because unconsciously I was wanting to look (and act) like a belle. My Jungian analyst, so my notes report, made the observation based on my many similar belle dreams that those frilly cover-ups were not sufficiently valuing my inner masculine aggressiveness. One more dream from this notebook:

> I am on the phone to Marla, dressed in my nightgown, when the cleaners arrive, ringing the bell. At first I think I'll ignore them but then rush down in time to open the door. There are three men with hangers and hangers of clothes, including several dainty little baby dresses.

Here again is a bell, which the "cleaners" are ringing. The clothing-as-disguise motif reappears, this time in baby clothes. It is not uncommon for women to be treated like children, to act like children, even to think of themselves as childish. This dream image once again seemed to be showing me how readily I accepted my culture's infantilization of women.

Now, having left my marriage, I have discarded the fashion performances of myself as Snow White. In throwing out of my closet those white lace collar dresses, the pointed Dorothy shoes, all iridescent scarves, anything pink, I was also divesting, revamping. I don't want the unisex look, shan't go for the strong suit, am not ready for leather, won't return to ultrafemme frills, never have worn beaded camisoles. But sequins? Boas? Hats out to here? Perhaps I'll have to write another chapter someday on accessories.

Light Daughter/
Dark Goddess

Mrs. W: You yourself observed nothing ... strange? Amy: No, Mother, I myself did not, to put it mildly. Mrs. W: What do you mean, Amy, to put it mildly ...? Amy: I mean, Mother, that to say I observed nothing ... strange is indeed to put it mildly. For I observed nothing of any kind, strange or otherwise. I saw nothing, heard nothing, of any kind. I was not not there.

—Beckett (1977, p. 48)

Nothing so consoles that too inner pain/than pain from somewhere else.

—Rilke (1926/1986, p. 229)

I think I know why the tale of Demeter and Persephone resonates so strongly today. Not only is it about mothers and daughters (one of the few in our culture), but it is also about reunion coming from darkness. Figuratively, the reunion joins together what has been split apart in the psyche. On this deeper level the tale is about cultivating the symbolic dark that for a period of time has been made inaccessible to daytime knowing. Recall the story. While out playing in the field one day, Persephone is suddenly raped by the king of the Underworld, Hades. Her screams ring out for help. Demeter, grief stricken, searches for her daughter in vain for many days and vows to withdraw her grain bounty from earth. A deal is struck: Hades will return Persephone to her mother if Persephone does not eat any food in the Underworld. But before letting Persephone go, Hades slips her a pomegranate seed, thus ensuring her return to the dark realm every winter.

The tale offers a lesson our culture, mired in mimesis, needs to hear. It teaches of a need to honor the seasons of the soul. Valuing only upperworld consciousness, which stakes as real only those externals accessible by the senses, our culture has long held in suspicion the other mode of consciousness, calling it

131

primitive, lower, magical, or savage. And yet, this other mode is none other than the soul. The world of the imagination, which is the world of the soul, is just as real as physical reality; such is the wisdom of this female resurrection story that predates Christianity. In trying to validate only objective, upperworld reality, Gloria Anzaldúa observes, "Western culture has made 'objects' of things and people when it distanced itself from them, thereby losing 'touch' with them. This dichotomy is the root of all violence" (1989, p. 84).

What can Persephone's journey into darkness teach us about invisible strength? Our culture, even in a new millennium, is patriarchal, which means split off from things dark and deep. Governments, schools, churches, families are patriarchal, if not in structure then in attitude. Where is the lost power of the psyche, the power not of control or weaponry but of energy? Perhaps even more urgently, what can Persephone's time in the dark teach us about the interesting contours of the hidden interiors of men and women, young and old—contours that have nothing whatsoever to do with mimetic maneuvers, imitation assaults, or literalizing strategies?

I pose that question in the wake of a high school massacre masterminded by two male teenage students who killed fifteen people, including themselves, in Littleton, Colorado. It seems that darkness in our culture has been too absolutely split off, made to be evil. Sad young outsiders who saw themselves as the hidden "dark" ones sought revenge against the "bright" crowd. Their idea of the "dark" was guns, violence, revenge, and black dusters, an idea encouraged by a toxic culture. Choosing to identify themselves as outsiders, the teenagers were part of a gang that called itself the Trench Coat Mafia, whose reasoning was, "We want to be different, we want to be strange, and we don't want jocks or other people putting us down.... We're going to punish you" (Brooke, 1999, p. A18). Once upon a time, such writing may have been viewed as childish rambling; now it turns out to be the killing intention of two privileged White boys. Their plan, plotted over a year in a diary, was peppered with Nazi phrases. In fact, the massacre occurred on April 29 and was apparently meant to celebrate Hitler's birthday.

The boys who committed the crime in Colorado had already been in a detention center for another crime; they were released and supposedly rehabilitated. But like so many efforts to punish wrongdoing, the detention tactic only hardened the boys to further hatred against a group they perceived as putting them down. Newspapers and television commentators kept using the phrase "wake-up call" to alert the public to a slumbering menace among young people. "It could happen here" was a frequent refrain; and, indeed, in the wake of the massacre, many copycat school takeovers were attempted. Our outer culture lures lonely youths with Goth music, Doom games, and death films. The noise and glitz that come from these media, often manipulated in isolation, shout over the quieter speakings of the other self. Rather than attaching more metal detectors on school doors, gun locks on guns, or V-chips on television sets, what is needed is an awareness of the power of the psyche to erupt into violence when It is ignored. Because inner life tends to be pushed down in such an action culture, we need to find ways to wake up to Its call.

Persephone's wintertime in darkness is a metaphor for the necessary returns we all must make to revisit our inner kingdom. How necessary are such returns and times out! The wake-up call our culture does not seem to be heeding is the call to cultivate our own symbol-producing psyches, so as to balance the bombardments from without. I find it revealing that two of our culture's oldest storytellers, Ovid and Homer, omitted from their telling of the Demeter-Persephone myth any recounting of the daughter's time in the dark. The story of Persephone's other life has literally been buried beneath the story of Demeter and her upperground hysteria. Most commentators, then, tend to read the myth as simply a mother-daughter bond. "Both men and women alike find in the myth a compelling evocation of the archetypal Mother, the most numinous of all the archetypal figures," states Elizabeth Hayes in one typical response (1994, p. 2). But consider the archetypal Daughter! Persephone was ruler in the Underworld. She was not some Bluebeard's wife, strangled and hanging by her hair. She was queen, ruler, power. Nor was she merely the archetypal Mother's nymphet. It seems that the oldest myths of woman power in the Underworld, like that of Inanna, remain unsung. Their darks are misunderstood. But it is precisely the dark aspect of Persephone that interests me, because its potency can counter the sort of literal darknesses that child killers today are lured to mimic.

Speaking as a daughter, I have always been fascinated by the myth because of its portrayal of an hysterical mother. I saw myself as very much the Persephone whited out by my mother's huge emotions. My mother, suffering from an undiagnosed ailment that caused the outer layer of her skin to fall away in dust particles, was in a constant state of unrelieved itching that only self-hypnosis could ease. "You must enter a house of your past where you felt the most happiness," her doctor told her. "There, you can float among the rooms." The house my mother chose was The Folly Cove Inn where we had summered in the 1950s with several of my mother's colleagues on the editorial staff of *Harper's Bazaar*. It had been a glorious time of unending days in the salt water of the Atlantic and of long evenings playing parlor games in one of the several small, book-lined parlors of the inn. My mother knew exactly where she needed to go, but she could not find the front door. With the help of my memory, she was able to enter the front door and find her peace.

That was the only time my mother ever sought my help. Ours was an unusual mother-daughter relationship because I did not live with my mother. I grew up in my father's house and considered myself my father's daughter. My parents divorced when I was four. It was odd indeed that back then the mother would not receive custody of the children. But then, my mother was odd; she was a career woman who really did not want to raise children. She had plenty of daughters on the staff of *Harper's Bazaar*.

Visiting my mother on weekends in New York City and during summer vacations, I felt I was the guest in her special realm. She did not enter my world and never asked for my help in hers. But later in life, as a strange ailment overcame her, I traveled across the country to stay with her and, on that occasion, to keep her afloat. That I should have been the guide into my mother's rememory only confirms my understanding now that I was in some deep-blooded way the Persephone to her Demeter, able thereby to help her into her labyrinth. Rilke's (1926/1986) lines in "Interior Portrait" express this:

> You don't survive in me
> because of memories;
> nor are you mine because
> of a lovely longing's strength.
>
> What does make you present
> is the ardent detour
> that a slow tenderness
> traces in my blood ... (p. 175)

I see that moment at the end of my mother's life as the showing forth of our Persephone-Demeter relationship. Forgetting and remembering, losing and finding, being profoundly not there, psychosomatic illness, dark seasons: These are some motifs that entwine in the mother-daughter myth of Demeter and Persephone. Rather than exclusively focusing on the mother-daughter relationship, however, I will be tracing the "ardent detour" of the daughter as I envision it. For Persephone, this forms a pattern of what I call *invisibility*, *surrender*, and *recreating*. I present the tale as a drama between light and dark in three acts to suggest Persephone's dramatic, psychic movement from unconscious innocence, through unconscious awakening, to conscious awareness. I imagine Persephone in this scenario to be like those many blank, untutored, young psyches today—male and female—that are in such desperate need of deepening.

Act one concerns Persephone's surface relationship with her mother in a sunny setting of an exclusively matriarchal world. This is the act of *invisibility*, because, although the daughter is seen, she is yet invisible to herself. She is innocent and all-virginal, wreathed in flowers, bathed in the bright joy of an Edenic world without men. No shadows distinguish her apart from her mother or the other nymphs. She basks in summery happiness.

Many people experience this kind of unseasoned invisibility. There is a causal situation here: Because I am not recognized—seen—others cognate me. Others see me according to the identity fictions they read onto me. Who I am is not seen, because I am submerged by social constructs (Pinar, 1994). Even more deadly, I am not seen because I am invisible to myself. I am nobody. Not being there to oneself makes of one a ghostly presence (Doll, 1994). Demeter's loving protectiveness of her virginal daughter has, then, an omi-

nous side. The mother's dominating determination to keep her daughter exclusively to herself threatens Persephone's very selfhood (Goldenberg, 1993;
Downing, 1994b). That Demeter was herself a victim of rape, according to
variations on the tale, accounts for her fear of possible invasion to her daughter. Projecting aspects of herself onto her child, the Demeter-mother loves the
illusion that she has created. But somehow, in the midst of these projections,
the Persephone-child loses her soul to her Demeter mother (Bushe, 1994).
What does the daughter learn in such a fierce bonding? She learns that some
things go unsaid. She learns not to speak unspeakables. She learns that even
when she screams she cannot be heard. She learns in an unspoken way that
she is her mother's narcissistic mirror as well as her mother's shadow side. She
is what her mother cannot see.

In my own case, as long as I did not detour I was destined to follow the
straight social path that my mother had unsuccessfully maneuvered for herself,
first with her grandfather, then with her father, then with my father, then with
my stepfather. Not being able to please this long line of fathers, my mother har-
bored a fierce resentment against them and an unconscious idealization of me.
The very social plan she rejected for herself she activated for me, especially
when I reached age twenty-four and still was unmarried. We were traveling in
Mexico, I remember, when in joke one evening, strolling among the parading
couples serenaded by mariachi bands, my mother said in her stage voice, "Won't
one of you take my daughter!" We both laughed hysterically. It was our secret
hope that I would marry someone, anyone, soon. My nightmares during this period were about not being married. I was my dark mother's light side. I was like
so many students today, who, because no one is home inside, are easy targets for
toxic intrusion.

Act two I call the act of *surrender*, when Persephone must surrender to
Hades's rape. We know what Demeter is doing during this act: She is reacting.
She is sitting-staring, not washing, not eating, turning her emotions to stone.
Obsessively, she holds others accountable for what she herself did not do. But
what would the mirror opposite be to such reactive actions? What might
Persephone be doing down there in Hades? It is a sudden turning point for her
when the earth opens and she is pulled into the Underworld. Drawn into the
interior depths against her will, I imagine Persephone unlearning her mother's
social teachings. While being shown around the Elysian Fields, she is doing
several unthinkable things: meeting Pandora, opening Pandora's box, letting
all hell break loose, mating with Hades. She is also feasting as never before on
pig and pomegranate. Just as Demeter is negating the functions of her female
body in the upperworld, Persephone, I imagine, is affirming these in the Underworld, having been initiated into the mysteries of her body by the erotic
force of her king.

The rape is the central metaphor of the myth. Patricia Berry's (1975) insights
pave the way for my commentary when she writes:

It is not just any virgin who constellates or necessitates rape but primarily Persephone, whose devasting innocence and half-conscious teasing lead anyway into underworld realms, whatever they may be. (p. 193)

Equally insistent on an archetypal perspective to this mythic event is James Hillman (1975):

Hades's rape of the innocent soul is a central necessity for psychic change. We experience its shock and joy whenever an event is taken suddenly out of human life and its natural state and into a deeper and more imaginally 'unreal' reality. (p. 208)

The preceding remarks sound unacceptable if taken at face value. They sound as if rape is portrayed in art as an ennobling experience, when in fact it is literally a hideous violation (Monaghan, 1999). The mythic moment of Persephone's rape is different, however, because its form and intention are different. The reality that is being forced upon the innocent one can be read psychodynamically to suggest an urgency to make normalcy captive.

Today an ominous form of normalcy is called "virtual" reality, the world of cyberspace, the world young outsiders occupy. How really real those screen targets seem, how powerful the joystick. And, for innocent imaginations (those incapable of creating their own images), how seductive are the flashes, zaps, and buzzes that can lure a child away from her own more resourceful inner world. The rape metaphor in myth suggests that the journey into one's own space requires a forceful wrenching away from such screens of reality. Other interpreters of the rape, focusing on the narcissus flower the maiden was about to pick, see Persephone as "asking for it" (Bushe, 1994; Downing, 1994b; Goldenberg, 1994). The "it," in this instance, is not just asking to be raped but rather asking to be drawn forcibly into a deeper narcissism so as to be seen on a deeper level, separate from the mother's narcissistic projections. That such seeing requires penetration is a mythic way of saying that Persephone surrenders to erotic desire, which cannot be given her by her mother. Nor can erotic knowledge be acquired through a joystick. As Audre Lorde puts it, the erotic connection is an "open and fearless underlining of (the) capacity for joy" that, once experienced, steers one away from "the convenient, the shoddy, the conventionally expected (or) the merely safe" (1989, p. 211).

I teach mythically in an effort to encourage students to take the labyrinthian journey into their own darknesses—of dream, for example—so as to experience their Persephones. A Persephone pedagogy might construct assignments aimed at exploring what our culture denies, the inner depths. Persephone, because she is not the source of literal, physical life, has necessary gifts to offer a symbol-starved world.

Thus I offer dream assignments to my students, journal assignments, dialogue assignments to extend the depth dimension. Sometimes, like Carol

Christ's classes (1995) we journal together for ten minutes and share our mus-
ings. An assignment I thought of recently would be for students to look in their
closets and write an essay on what they find hanging on the racks. What tex-
tures, colors, patterns are there? Examine the shoes: Are they sturdy or, like so
many of mine during my phase of invisibility, flimsy? (I had Alice shoes, Dorothy
shoes, ballet slippers.)? What do shoes tell about one's grounding? Examine the
coats: Are they black trench coats? What do the coats tell about one's outer
persona and subsequent seduction by culture? The sort of textile introspection I
am urging seeks to critique the way the texts of culture have been inscribed too
insidiously into the closets of the psyche.

One of my students, Eric Durr, wrote in class last semester about the freeing
function of dream work: "Writing the dream made me feel like a writer. I was
writing from something that I could not control … My writing is improving simply because I have been observing the world around me and paying attention to
detail." And then he added, "I am learning that the best writing comes from
within. It comes from a deep desire to write about something significant to you.
The energy of emotion can drive one's writing into a whole new realm of possibility. Each passing day provides opportunities for achievement." Tim Breaux
also commented on writing from the dream: "Writing about this dream created
a burst of energy within me. I began to see the vivid images I haven't thought
about in years." Anyone who pays attention to dream images knows of their
qualitative difference from the images available to the sense organs. Dream images are adjusted to another stratum of consciousness altogether (Izutsu, 1981).
I wonder if Eric Harris and Dylan Klebold had ever discovered their own dream
energies? If so, could they have redirected their love of death into less literal
channels? I ask these questions because Persephone loved death (Hades). But
this is the love from the perspective of the soul that sees beyond and below life's
concerns. As Hillman puts it, "The richness of Hades-Pluto psychologically refers to the wealth that is discovered through recognizing the interior deeps of
the imagination" (1975, p. 207).

Perhaps one of my biggest dreams, in the Jungian sense that the big dream
connects with mythological archetypes, was a penetration dream at the time of
my mother's illness. I wrote about it in a work called Mother Matters (in Doll,
1995), all puns intended. I am in a boat rowed by an oarsman. We are surrounded by heavy fog. Suddenly the fog lifts and I see a fiord with a narrow entrance and thick fairyland cliffs going straight down. We make a difficult entry
and I find myself suspended, as in air, inside an empty structure. It is strikingly
serene with afternoon rays slanting through old panes. I see a quiet, perfectly
preserved, wondrously empty room, save for a rolltop desk. I know I am in a
world new found but long lost (Doll, 1995, p. 26). Could it be that what was familiar but strange was my own femaleness, which my mother and I had allowed
to atrophy? Here I was, penetrating the womb, which seemed to await my arrival via the oarsman, the womb waiting for me to unroll the desktop and get to

work, writing. The dream's curious spaciousness and wonder hold for me the magic of fairy tale kingdoms, both alluring and forbidding. The world seduces by its utter difference and—contrary to what one thinks of when one thinks of Hades—it is not terrible, only strange. It beckons.

That is how I view Persephone's surrender in act two. Released from her mother's fierce literalism, Persephone can explore the poetics of gender, her two-sided femaleness—what Genia Haddon (1987) calls "yang-femininity." Fairy tales lure virgins by revealing large, hidden castles inside deeply forested realms, underground spaces where little pieces of food and small mirrors tantalize the senses. In the deep womb, the fairy tale/Persephone figure (Little Red Riding Hood, Beauty, Snow White) sees a hairy other or a brown other or a negative mother. The princess encounters it with the eyes and mouth—not the sword and stratagems of male hero monomyths. Something other needs to be seen, needs to be touched, needs to be tasted. Myth strengthens the tale, for Persephone is no princess: She is queen. Eros is felt in the tactileness of Persephone's surrender, where she gives up defenses against Hades, sheds fear, and surrenders so as to "fall."

During the period of writing this chapter I had a strange dream about clothes. In this dream I am cleaning an outdoor toilet that is stuffed with heavy cottons and linens. I pull and pull and pull. Out come these clothes, filled with dung. The dream is warning me not to get too Snow Whitey about the underground experience; one meets shit down there.

Another series of dreams during this writing concerned food. As I got nearer and nearer to act two, the food was getting more outrageous. Last week it was only a tiny piece of cake that I was reaching out for in princess-fashion. Last night it was an entire banquet. I was attending a festive occasion where my dissertation advisor David Miller was to talk at my pastor's church (an event that actually happened). As I approached the table laden with food, I saw a cake placed way down among a thousand dishes of this and that. I wanted that cake. But to take a piece I had to disturb a precarious arrangement. I must have that cake! In reaching down for it I disturbed the pilings of meats and pastries. Food started spilling. I heard the pastor whisper in dismay, "Oh, Mary. No." Then the next thing I knew I was covered with gobs of cake. I found the experience so pleasurable that I spread the cake all over my body. As I reflect on this dream I recall David Miller's (1976) distinction between fairy tale and myth. It seems that my food orgy is a response to myth's refusal to be nice, like fairy tale. Fairy tales give a sense of comfort and conclusion; but myths, of which this dream partakes, unsettle and expand.

Carol Christ (1995) reminds us of the connection between food and mystery—something the Eucharist celebrates—in her discussion of Margaret Atwood's irreverently nonChristian novel *Surfacing* (1990). In my own work I have thought of the Eucharistic moment in similar terms, as a return to a pagan ritual (1995b). The preceding dream is replaying my "fall" from Christian piety into female eroticism with the minister's rebuke and my subsequent food orgy. The Persephone myth, with its narcissus and pomegranate motifs, connects food with ancient female vegetation rites and sexuality (Simeti, 1995). Persephone's abduction thus acts as an initiation into sexual experience both with the phallus narcissus flower and the seed-filled womb pomegranate (Downing, 1989). As the myth makes clear, the glistening flowers and red-juice dripping pomegranates are no Genesis apples; they are the lure into body.

In a workshop I gave on the myth of Demeter-Persephone, I presented a beautiful basket of pomegranates as centerpiece. When we came to the centerpiece of Persephone's journey (her surrender, act two), I wanted to "flesh out" the understandings of food as an erotic encounter. In a ritual of shared eating, we sliced into the incredible fruit, seeing and tasting for ourselves how this fruit, with its red pulp and deeply buried seeds, is sensuous through and through, unlike Snow White's crumbs or Sleeping Beauty's coma. As we ate the tangy meat it was impossible not to laugh. We gossiped, sputtered, and guffawed. Red juice spilled over our chins and blouses. For many of us, eating a pomegranate was a first. Perhaps for some of us the shared joy of raucous female laughter was a first. This ritual moment became, for me, a tangible expression of the myth's teachings. With its round shape, blood redness, and wine-sharp taste, the pomegranate allowed us to sense the generous fertility of femaleness. Someone at the end of the evening asked me what I thought the role of Hekate was, psychologically, for the mother-daughter relationship. I answered that the witch Hekate puts females in touch with the senses, something mothers seem afraid to do. Christine Downing's response is better. She writes, "Hekate represents the seriousness and precariousness of all transitions" (1994, p. 234).

The Sumerian myth of Inanna, precursor to the myth of Demeter-Persephone, also urges women to journey into the Great Below, and, once there, to feast. This is an amazing tale of feminine powers found in the sheepfold center of nature. As Diane Wolkstein writes, "In Sumerian, the word for sheep fold, womb, vulva, loins, and lap is the same.... They all relate to fertility" (In Wolksteing & Kramer, 1983, p. 146). In the middle of the tale, equivalent to what I have named act two of Persephone's myth, Inanna revels in the world of the senses—"drinking, eating, churning, dancing, singing, tasting, smelling. [She and her lover-brother] feed on and are nourished by one another's vital juices" (Wolkstein & Kramer, p. 152). The nourishment they share turns siblings into progenitors, each becoming parent and child. Incest, like rape, must be understood here from the logic of myth, not culture—as mythology's image, not pathology's disease.

We are meant to read all these mythic images not with our mind but with our ear. Mind, in Sumerian, means ear and wisdom (Wolkstein, p. xvii). We must read, therefore, with the mind of the ear, listening for "the meat of the tongue" (Warner, 1995, p. xv). The tale of Inanna is told in occasional repetitious lines of three, repetitious sections of three, as if hearing the words once is not enough.

The rhythms create a sense of mirroring back. Understanding comes through hearing. The speakings that the come from the Great Below resonate with something deep within the listener, like a gong—what Rilke calls "the strange harmony/of infinity's tide" (1926/1986, p. 59). In front of such ringing we must stand mute, for "what touches us /wants no more from our being than attention" (Rilke, p. 59). We are asked to remain silent in the soundings of images, so that a buried inner world may respond.

Myths, someone once said, awaken us from the unity of nature. They disillusion us about all unities: monotheism, the United States, the whole person, the tyranny of the I (eye). Demeter, in the wake of her daughter's abduction, embarks on a single-minded mission to find her lost one. Her dogmatic mission is but an outward manifestation of her inward insistence that she and her daughter are One, indivisible, with unity. Hers is an aggression of the mind, cut off from its metaphorical tongue or ear.

Before act three, two Demeter moments allow for Persephone's reappearance, as I see it. These moments are what I refer to as two interludes. One interlude moment is the stillness Demeter displays sitting by the well. Nine days of seeking have produced nothing. She sits. Later, she sits again, in silence, on a stool next to Iambe in the house of Keleos. Her silent sitting is accompanied by abstinence from food, drink, and bathing: the very opposite of what I imagine Persephone to be enjoying away from her mother. I think of this body denial of Demeter's as a need to see and feel everything in absolute terms. Her denial is the opposite of erotic generosity. But this sitting and silence is also, I think, a preparing. In her emptying out she can simply be. Such receptivity is like a bowl that will hold what will come forward from below.

A second interlude moment allows for Persephone's return when Iambe makes Demeter laugh. Iambe (called, variously, Baubo) does so by lifting her skirts and showing her genitals. What breaks the spell of Demeter's depression is not just the outrageous act but the laughter it evokes. This showing initiates Demeter into the joy of womanhood, delight of womanhood, and the secret of womanhood that lie buried within her own body. Laughter that turns toward the body abolishes hierarchy and cancels authority—two props to Demeter's aggressions against the gods. In the showing-laughing sequence, Demeter drops into her lower body, experiencing sexuality as the joy of the unexpected. Funny this is not; comical, in a deep sense, it is.

That Iambe is the spell breaker is also interesting, because we give the name iambic to a rhythm in poetic metrics. It is the unaccented syllable followed by the accented syllable, the most natural rhythm in language. My thought is that once again sound, not rational sense, is myth's intention, what Walter Ong terms the "presence" of the word (1967). The power of communication, Ong says, is felt more through speaking than through writing and situates a listener in the middle of actuality rather than in linear sequentiality. An iambic situation for Demeter would be honoring twoness within singleness—unaccented or weak with accented or strong. It would be incorporating "upper" into "lower" creative female functions.

By now my readers will be thoroughly exasperated with me. All this talk of rape and vulvas: Where am I going with this in the classroom, please! Why poeticize rape in a chapter that excoriates literalism? I do have a direction, but it is not the way of the literal, so rest assured I do not advocate body massage as part of the curriculum. I do, however, recommend developing the listening ear of student writers and dreamers. Teachers require so much reading; we depend almost exclusively on the print medium. But many students are functional nonreaders, meaning they do not have the reading habit and plainly resent the task. Recognizing this as a continual hurdle in my English classes, I have turned more to aural-oral approaches. Although, obviously, reading is a necessary component of my class, I try to bring the (for them) lonely and often frustrating experience into a more "tribal" ritual. Students write about self-selected passages from shared texts, then read their writings into a tape recorder in front of the class. These performances create drama and tension—everything one would want to enliven understanding (Doll, 1997). They also tend to bring students out of the solitary page into a shared space. By sharing reading responses, listeners both know and do not know that readers are also speaking aloud pieces of their own buried lives.

Finally, the third moment in the Demeter-Persephone myth is what I call *recreating*, when Persephone returns from the Underworld, for a while. The myth insists that this mother-daughter reunion be temporary. Like the female body's cycle, so is Persephone's journey a cycle—aboveground in society, belowground in psyche, each for a time only, each giving respite from the other. This return, or recreating from the shadows, brings back a new daughter—one no longer living in the literal shadow of the mother. This daughter has experienced the world not seen, a world over which she is now queen. She has a new power; her mother can see that. Persephone's is the power of the imagination.

For centuries, the return of Persephone has been celebrated by the Eleusinian Mysteries, when initiates, intending to understand their own grief patterns, imitate the wanderings of the mother's search. These mysteries are really offered to Demeter who awaits her daughter's long journey home (Downing, 1994). By walking and fasting for nine days, men and women recreate the feeling-tone of despair in their bodies, particularly as they perform circle dances to the left. By moving to the left, in the wrong direction—counter to Demeter's rightfootedness or groundedness in literalism—dancers move in the direction of death (Doll, 1994). Understood mythically, "death" is hidden wealth, such as that which resides in the soul. To dance in the direction of death is to join the physical body with the spiritual body.

If I were one of the dancers, I would imagine myself Demeter before the reunion with Persephone. My constant punishing pacing would have induced in me a stupor, and I would feel like a sleepwalker, there but not there. My resistances would be weakened, yet my body would press on. After nine days of walking and waiting, I would hear intonations, reverberations of great inexpressible meaning. Words would become fantasies in sound, landscapes would acquire faces (Kugler, 1978). I would forego the measured life in favor of lewdness and laughter from a different register. Such extra-ordinary measures are necessary for any Demeter's mothering. Demeter must die to literal (s)mothering. She must learn a different literalism by learning to read signs more imaginatively. She has caused herself and her world a terrible illness by projecting unconscious ideals and fears and hatreds onto others, most notably onto her daughter. These projections she must let go. Breaking psychic patterns is hard physical work; hardheadedness is not easily cracked. But Demeter performs this most difficult task and is ready to greet her daughter with flowers in her right hand and scissors in her left (Campbell, 1974).

The Eleusinian Mysteries, then, celebrate a poetics of death. In discussing the necessities of cutting the ties that bind us, Helen Luke (1985) writes of the magical change that can result:

> Once you begin to take projections back, this magical kind of tie changes. Once you begin to let go—and this takes a great deal of hard work and watching and attention and humility: when once you can ask what is it in me that must have this to depend on—the minute you begin to make that separation between yourself and that projection it may then become a sense of relationship.... The feeling of wishing to save the world comes very often out of a wish to escape from having compassion on your own darkness. (pp. 25, 27)

I imagine the compassion for one's own darkness to be an amazing grace. It is a grace that was denied to Eric Harris and Dylan Klybold and so many other young people who have engaged in literal acts of darkness. It is a grace that learns the hard task of letting go of projection, self-righteous fury, or too-fond parenting.

For Persephone, having just eaten the pomegranate seeds in Hades and re-emerging from the cleft in the ground, how does she greet her mother in this third act of her drama? When she left her dark king, did she "put on his knowledge with his power" (Yeats, 1924/1989, p. 215)? Her very return is, I believe, an incarnating of "his knowledge" that she now reveals to her mother. Hades knows invisibles, the wealth of emptiness. So does Persephone, now. Those who see her see silence, a vital part of seeing. This silent daughter is no longer invisible, as in act one. Her silence draws eyes. Myth tells us that Demeter gave obeisance to the silent power emanating from within Persephone by holding in her right hand flowers and in her left hand scissors. What could this greeting mean for us moderns?

In my workshop, I asked each participant to greet their own silent Persephone. We each held a flower in our right hand and a pair of scissors in our left hand. When it came our turn we were to say out loud what aspect of our shadow selves we were snipping, so as to cut loose a bit from our literal darknesses. Snap! I cut loose my perfectionism. Snap! I cut out my fear of risk-taking. Snap! I cut away my envy of blond hair. Snap! I release myself from my mother. Snap! Snap! Persephone, I imagine, listens, knowing she will return again, knowing that spring needs winter needs spring. With her is the sense that sadness and suffering will never go away. Persephone does not overcome. She endures.

▦ ▦ ▦

Assignment: Read the following poem and write a personal response to it based on your interactions with the Persephone myth:

Spring

O spring, you who aren't human, speak;
sing your cries, O spring!
Nothing so consoles that too inner pain
than pain from somewhere else.

Does your song come from pain? Oh
tell me, is it some unknown state?
Can we be moved by anything, except
by what helps and by what wounds us?
(Rilke, 1926/1986, p. 229)

Like Letters Written
in Running Water

FOUNTAINHEADS

The highest good is like water. Water gives life to the ten thousand things and does not strive. It flows in places men reject and so it is like the Tao.

—Lao Tzu (551–479 B.C.E./1975, p. 64)

Now on the last, the great day of the feast, Jesus stood and cried out, saying, "If anyone thirst, let him come to me and drink.... as the Scripture says, 'From within him there shall flow rivers of living water.'"

—John (7:37–38—New American Catholic Edition)

I have found that my real home is in the water, that the earth is only my stepmother. My old man, the Sun, sired me out of the sea

—Hurston (1942/1997, p. 170)

Words can be ritualized acts, if they are put in the river, in the stream of imagination.

—Moore (1983, p. 7)

How would it be to write letters in water or wind? What would it be to be "like" water or wind? The question makes no sense to Eurocentric ears. To a culture bred on demarcation, categorization, and method, the primacy of the eye is what takes effect. The effect it takes is to see only what is in front of face or scope. Scope as suffix is that which is at the end of an instrument for viewing, as in micro, tele, or periscope. Possibly soon there will be cyberscope. To scope out is to take a look-see for what is around the corner. I'll scope out the room, we say, looking for an empty table. There is a "but" lurking in this rhetorical set up. It is the exception this section will take to the predominance of virtual see-ing—what Beckett (1981a) calls "the filthy eye of flesh" (p. 30).

Virtual seeing uses the eye as instrument for observing only what something is out there, not what something might be "like" in here. Seeing out, aided by even the best of instrumentation, narrows sight and focuses gaze. I must squint when I look through my telescope. When scoping for that table I have some-thing specific in mind. To focus narrowly is to accept blindly a web of interlock-ing commonsense assumptions about things, bodies, communities, human nature, the world, relationships (Procter-Smith, 1995). To see into interiors takes a third eye or, as in the case of the writers in this section, it is to encourage "seeing" with the sensible ear (Davis, 1996).

The first two parts of this book have presented cases against literal seeing, that which blocks heads, freezes feeling, and turns ideas to stone. To be like let-ters carved in rock is be rigid in thought and action, accepting only what domi-nates the landscape. To be like letters written in sand is to give way a bit to the dichotomies of dominance but still to be dominated by the discourse of dualism as the measure of self. Sand, as the residue of rock, does not quickly disappear by the oncoming tide; its composition is rocky. These two ways of being, the Bud-dha has said, posit being as fixed, permanent, and intractable. I have been push-ing my argument toward a different way of being, the way of running water, which is a third way. If, as I propose, teaching is more than instructing, more than training, more than method and more, much more than instrumentation, then what is it? The "it" teaching is is the third thing, neither this nor that. It is to encourage being "like" letters in running water. It is, as Elizabeth Bishop writes, "what we imagine knowledge to be:/dark, salt, clear, moving, utterly free" (1955/1985, p. 1,748).

Fluid writing is that which can be found in the writers featured in this part. The works of Toni Morrison, Eudora Welty, and the network stories of Spider Woman represent three colors of the cultural rainbow: Black, White, and Red. Their writing is fluid, as is the writing of such others as Jamaica Kincaid, Virginia Woolf, Margaret Atwood, William Faulkner, and Samuel Beckett. That women writers are primarily focused here suggests my belief that the fluid third way of being is feminine, but not in a genital sense. Feminine writing is that which hon-ors absence, silence, the forbidden, and the ignored. But it also honors the triv-ial. In common parlance, "trivial" is that which is petty; not just unimportant, but very unimportant. But, recalling the origin of "trivial" as "tri" and "via," that which is trivial goes by way of the third way, three roads that meet in the delta. And Trivia in Roman religion, defines Webster (1993), was Hekate, so-called because she was the goddess of the crossroads (deriv. of *trivium* place where three roads meet). Language goes to roots, origins, primal meanings. Language is key to a discovery of the original self: that which we were before social micro-scopes flattened us. But not any language. A third, new language governed by the goddess Hekate, say, is what I invoke here.

Hekate's story (herstory) is entirely appropriate for a third, new language:

One of the oldest Greek versions of the trinitarian Goddess, Hekate was derived from the Egyptian midwife-goddess ... in command of all the *hekau* or "Mother's Words of Power." ... In Greece, Hekate was one of many names for the original feminine trinity, ruling heaven, earth, and the underworld. Hellenes tended to emphasize her Crone or underworld aspect, but continued to worship her at places where three roads met, especially in rites of magic, divination, or consultation with the dead. Her images guarded three-way crossroads for many centuries.... In the Middle Ages, Hekate become known as Queen of the Ghostworld, or Queen of Witches. (Walker, 1983, pp. 378–379)

What herstory lies here! Her story, however, has nothing to do with "his story"; Hekate's "history" has been depotentiated and reviled. Her original, manifold nature has been subtracted to a single diabolical connection with hell, especially by the church. Nevertheless, the church fathers appropriated the trinitarian aspect of Hekate for their own male deity, the three-in-one Father, Son, and Holy Ghost (Walker, 1983). Along with this takeover of the goddess of the three roads began a shrinking of language into literalisms and clichés—at least by the phallic imagination. It becomes, then, the province of the Mother writers to reappropriate that which once was theirs: the birthing of powerful words.

The writers I discuss in this last part write, I like to say, of trivialities. A new language is heard in these texts that speaks of the abundant generosity of littleness overlooked by scoping eyes. To articulate some of the territory, it is a language of birds, food, and color; the language of gossip and nonsense; the language of alluring alliterations and luscious images; even the language of meals and clothes. This new language is fluid and metaphorical, "like letters written in running water." It is the language of love and laughter.

The 13th-century Japanese Zen master Dōgen distinguishes between literal texts and these other, more cosmic, speakings—scapes rather than scopes:

What we mean by the sutras is the entire cosmos itself ... the words and letters of beasts ... or those of hundreds of grasses and thousands of trees.... The sutras are the entire universe, mountains and rivers and the great earth, plants and trees; they are the self and others, taking meals and wearing clothes, confusion and dignity. (In Parkes, 1997, p. 118)

I am thinking that older cultures and wilder terrains have a sense of this "speaking scape." On a recent trip I took to Sicily I felt the landscape speaking to me in a particular way. The land is rough, hilly, with steep rocky cliffs jutting from sea to sky. In a very short space one feels immediate contrasts harmonizing. I took a tourist's trip to one of the many grottoes that the coastline harbors. The approach to the grotto is made by a singing boat man, who delights tourists with falsetto versions of "O Solo Mio" or a Verdi aria while steering his small craft into the hollow. There, in darkness, boatloads are astonished by an amazing azure water, the color made, we are told, by the mineral substance of the rocks. Such beauty rests inside the grotto which, were it not for my operatic gondelier, I might never dare the venture to see for myself! From outside, the rock cave looks forbidding; inside supreme splendor resides. "Every showing," Julian of Norwich reminds us, "is full of secrets" (in Petroff, 1986, p. 309). The secret is caught inside the word "grotesque," which literally means "odd or unnatural in shape, appearance or character; fantastically ugly or absurd; bizarre" (Webster, 1993). But there is a grotto inside the grotesque. That which is deemed "unnatural" or "odd" contains an azure beauty shaped out of nature. Not simply grotesque, that which is odd is grotto-like. Language itself contains hidden delights, origins, secrets not released by defining Websters.

How can we unliteralize language? How can we rediscover the grotto-esque natures that hide within, below, underneath surfaces? How can we seek out the hidden secret of the caves that line our own rocky shores? There is language within words, worlds within words. But these must be de-centered because they are eccentric; they are the grottoes of the grotesque. My project is against the grain, excavatory. My project seeks to escape literalism by studying scapes—the running waters inside us, inside language, inside the cosmos.

When I teach Eudora Welty's stories, for example, my students often don't "get it." Her comedic vision seems childish to my young sophisticates, who come to English classes in search of the symbol they can put in their pockets. When I read out loud to my students, something I love to do, some of my students are really, deeply charmed, forgetting themselves as their mouths drop open in amazement at the spin of words. Others, the sophisticated, self-conscious ones, eye the door. My point is that we can teach the power of the mother language if we lower the voice and disappear into the grottoes of the text.

Finally, a word about wisdom. Ours is not a time that yearns for wisdom, alas; but, surely, it is wisdom not instruction that will help us find the way in the nuclear age. When Ron Padgham (1988) called for a revisioning of curriculum, he had in mind a curriculum that respected the inner resources and energies of human beings, a "vision quest" (p. 140)—coursings found in dream and story, for example. America is not an ancestor-worship or nature-worship culture, nor can it be expected to become what it has never been. Still, the America that will emerge in the 21st century will be different. The challenge, in part, for teachers is to prepare for that difference, to prepare for difference. The challenge is also to feel "the transmission of a living energy" (Dooling, 1979, p. 3) that human beings exchange, anyway, naturally, but too often not in the classroom. Few wisdom figures emerge in the flesh to show the way at this juncture. The Dalai Lama is one. Others, I submit, are prophets and mystics called writers who write in a third, new language. Listening to their language may not change minds, but it may soften the deeper mind of hearts, the better to course with life forms large and small, the better to be the currents beneath the mainstream (Moses, 1997, p. xxi).

✤ 9 ✤

The Suchness of Suffering

Because when a man is in turmoil how shall he find peace
Save by staying patient till the stream clears?
How can a man's life keep its course
If he will not let it flow?

—Lao Tzu (551–479 B.C.E./1975, p. 33)

O! that this too too solid flesh would melt,
Thaw and resolve itself into a dew.

—Shakespeare (1603/1988, p. 129)

Can we imagine ... that human experience breaks out beyond
the envelope of flesh?

—Jardine (1997, p. 18)

Our souls are where we play and of course also where we suffer,
where we fall down, where we fail.... How do we guide, that is educate,
the soul?

—Fox (in Fox & Sheldrake, 1997, p. 83)

The three universal qualities of human existence, according to Buddhist teaching, are impermanence, suffering, and the nonexistence of the self (Das, 1997). The base from which the four noble truths proceeds is the axiom we suffer, "Buddhism's fundamental principle" (Kohno, 1998, p. 45). Suffering is a given with a human condition if one sees oneself as the center of the universe, attributes all reality to the flesh, and yearns for fixity, fearing flux. Certainly, Western thinking, with its emphasis on externals, extroversions, and dualities, has difficulty accepting Eastern notions that require a profoundly different shift in attitude. Even though the prophet Isaiah of the Hebrew scriptures reminds us that all flesh is grass (40:6—New American Catholic Edition), Western thinking—so bold and bodied—does not easily dance with metaphor. From a Western perspective, grass is grass, flesh is flesh.

Carl Jung (1930/1973) spoke to the difficulty Westerners have in understanding the introverted attitude associated with Eastern thought. Westerners tend to consider Eastern quietism as withdrawn, archaic, ancestral, or mystical. Not practical. Not visible. Not scientistic. At the core of such Western disbelief is a defining attitude of mind that overvalues rationalism and knowledge at the expense of intuition and wisdom. Along with a Western prejudice to see flesh only as flesh is a predilection to ignore the promptings of the unconscious. "The assertion that the Mind 'has no existence,'" Jung writes, "obviously refers to the peculiar 'potentiality' of the unconscious.... When I tell a patient he is chock full of fantasies, he is often astonished beyond all measure, having been completely unaware of the fantasy-life he was leading" (1930/1973, p. 501). In other words, what is invisible or unconscious is potent because it contains potentiality. Emptiness is full.

In Part I, Faulkner, Morrison, Wright, and certain modernists write about characters who are blockheads to the degree that they are deeply repressed or entirely too egotistical. They are chock full of themselves. They suffer by being completely unaware. Out of their stubborn refusal to examine their thoughts and actions, they close themselves off from the world. Even the characters in Part II are not fully enough disengaged from the dominant discourse of patriarchy to be aware of the potentiality of their unconscious minds, although cracks to their mental shells enable some small filtering of otherness to shine through. They, too, suffer, although to a lesser degree. In Part III, I have selected writers who, in my judgment, demonstrate the middle way. This is the way that conquers not external events and people, but internal thoughts like craving and clinging. It is, after all, clinging that keeps the suffering alive as a stubborn indulgence for the ego. "Nirvana is always trying to seep through the small chinks in our ego's armor," writes Lama Das. "When we really do 'let go' and get used to letting go, that inner conflict, that irritation, that friction heat of dukkha actually does die down, and we can experience more and more of the inner peace that nirvana epitomizes" (1997, p. 88). This process, at its best, is transformative.

Perhaps it is surprising that I select Jamaica Kincaid as my first wisdom writer in an Eastern mode, because her work has been viewed as nihilistic, polemical, cryptic, and obsessive, and she is not Eastern. One reviewer of At the Bottom of the River (1992) called Kincaid's imagery "too personal and peculiar," lacking of any "sensible communication" (Milton, 1984, p. 22); another called it "insultingly obscure" (Tyler, 1983, p. 33); while Suzanne Freeman (1984) commented that Kincaid's writing challenges "our very definition" of the should be's of genre (pp. 15–16). There lurk too many secrets in the text, this reviewer felt, to appeal to a reading audience. These negative reviews by feminist writers indicate how strongly even they have been influenced by the requirements of the master discourse, which claims as "ours" correct definitions of genre or style. But who is "us?" Correct definition according to whom? Kincaid subverts the superiority of the imperialist "we" by writing in a style that is politically "incorrect." Growing up in British-controlled Antigua, she had read the works of the literary masters—Milton's *Paradise Lost*, Charlotte Brontë's *Jane Eyre*—and saw that their themes of cruel and unjust power related ironically to her own situation as the daughter of a slave. The madwoman in Edward Rochester's attic could as well be her mother as the much-maligned Bertha Mason. And yet, Kincaid's teachers insisted on perpetuating the "fairy tale" of an England all bright and only beautiful (Simmons, 1994). Kincaid sees through England's hypocrisy with the piercing eyes of a colonized, young woman slave. Her language speaks truth in the king's English:

Let me tell you something: This Master and friend business, it is not possible; a master is one thing and a friend is something else altogether.... For this man who says 'My Master and my Friend' builds a large house, warms the rooms, sits in a chair made from a fabric that is very valuable because its origins are distant, obscure, and involve again the forced labor, the crippling, the early death of the unnamed many. (1997, pp. 134–135)

In her autobiography, Kincaid recalls a further irony of having to sing "Rule, Britannia! Britannia, rule the waves; Britons never, never shall be slaves" (1990, p. 135).

Kincaid's work is woven around two mothers: the mother country of Antigua, controlled by slave-holding British colonists; and her own real mother, a slave holder of a different sort. Although Kincaid's feelings about these two mothers are those of hurt, humiliation, shame, anger, and hatred, she achieves a remarkable distance from their effect. She observes in the manner of a Buddhist's focused mind, being aware without condoning or condemning, repressing or emoting. Such awareness recognizes that "just as this hatred rises, so will it pass away" (Batchelor, 1997, p. 60).

But many in the West misread her observations and attitude, not understanding the purpose of her ironic position. Her essay *A Small Place* (1989), for example, was a study about the effects of colonialism on her native country. The controlling powers were so outraged by the book's wide awakeness to colonial abuse that she was banned for many years from returning to her land. No wonder that she identified with Milton's Satan who, like her, was thrown out of paradise! No wonder that the name "Lucy" in Kincaid's (1990) novel derives from Lucifer. Nor is it any wonder that, to draw attention to herself as a Jamaican woman, she changed her name in 1973 from Elaine Potter Richardson to Jamaica Kincaid (Simmons, 1994). About her own mother, Kincaid has said, "I've never really written about anyone except myself and my mother" (Kincaid, 1993, p. 2,367). These two mothers form the crucible of Kincaid's consciousness. Having been expelled from both their paradises, one by politics the other by birth, Kincaid writes as the ultimate outsider always seeking to birth herself from the womb of another vessel.

The search, despite its suffering sense of loss and betrayal, is remarkably detached. It is neither here nor there. It just is, like growing grass. Kincaid creates a landscape of the mind where things exist for their own sake, not for domination or power (Ferguson, 1994). Hers is the landscape of suchness, as in this Zen poem (cited in Ross, 1966, p. 158):

> Sitting quietly, doing nothing,
> Spring comes and the grass grows by itself.

In *The Autobiography of My Mother* (a title that destroys the Western sense of selves as separate beings), the mother (imagined by the writer/daughter) says, "Everything is my life, good or bad, to which I am inextricably bound is a source of pain" (1997, p. 7), but then later says, "The present is always perfect ... The present is always the moment for which I live" (p. 205). What Kincaid achieves is her own mother tongue: completely nonWestern, completely feminine, unsettlingly nondualistic. Her artistic achievement, in my eyes, is political without being strident and poetic without being nonrealistic. It also enacts through language an entirely different sense of the self that can, *ex nihilo*, birth itself. I find this achievement remarkably close to the nondual Dzogchen-Mahamudra teachings about emptiness, a concept that is not "nothing" or a nihilistic void but rather a "vividly dancing with sounds and colors ... (in) the fertile womb of emptiness" (Das, 1997, p. 122).

The blurring of boundaries between mother and daughter, which I will discuss in greater detail, is perhaps the central ambiguity of Kincaid's work that connects her thinking with Buddhist thought, in my view. Although on the one hand she refuses to be "colonized" by the power of her mother, on the other hand she suffers the loss of embryonic oneness once felt with the mother as two bodies, one skin. To achieve her own selfhood, however, Kincaid must birth herself through her imagination. She must unskin the union. As the snake sheds its skin and becomes born again, so must she. Kincaid's unusual style—more Eastern than Western—takes us into transformation processes where subject and object, inside and outside, upside and downside merge. It is as if the text becomes a vast alchemical vessel wherein this too too solid flesh can melt.

My emphasis on flesh and skin is deliberate. Jung (1976a) writes how alchemists, myths, and Mexican ancient religious practices all saw unskinning or peeling as a first step toward renewal and rebirth: "The prototype of this renewal is the snake casting its skin every year, a phenomenon round with primitive fan-

tasy has always played" (p. 228). Dennis Sumara (1996) writes about the need
to "unskin the curriculum" in an effort to transcend dualisms in the teaching
classroom. "Our skin is what separates our inside from our outside. Therefore,
more than any other organ," Sumara contends, "it is skin that reminds us that
all of our interactions in the world are embodied.... Once the skin is removed
the body dissipates into its surrounding. Unskinning repudiates the idea that
the human body is other to the world" (pp. 88, 90). As long as we remain in our
solid flesh, my skin a different color from yours, my skin not the skin of a tomato
or a grape or an onion or a blade of grass, the world is perceived as divided. The
Zen master Thich Nhat Hanh (1998) sees the trope of skin in a political sense
(as does Kincaid) to argue for a Buddhism that can engage people's needs in
Vietnam. He writes, "Casting off the old skin is not something a culture does
overnight or without resistance.... if there is subservience, culture is not true
culture" (p. 51). Casting off skin, or unskinning, begins a decomposing process
that transcends all opposites so as to achieve the "unity of all life, the Is-ness, or
Such-ness, or existence itself" (Ross, 1966, p. 155). This is in accord with the
idea in classical Buddhism that the body separate from other life forms is an illusion. According to the 9th-century philosopher Kūkai, all seemingly discrete
entities are interdependent forms of the one ultimate reality underlying the diversity of all natural phenomena: "Existence is my existence, the existences of
the Buddhas, and the existences of all sentient beings.... They are not identical
but are nevertheless identical; they are not different but are nevertheless different" (in Hakeda, 1972, p. 232). How completely foreign these ideas and expressions are to Western minds not attuned to paradox.

   The skin trope provides the background for my presentation of Kincaid's
work. Actually, I think it is amazing the editors of *The Harper American Literature* (1993) text, read in thousands of college classrooms, included Kincaid's
work, because her writing is as noncanonical as any I have come across; she is as
far away from Western thinking as any Western writer I have read. Perhaps, for
that reason, only two critics as of this writing have written entire books on her.
And of the articles written about her, most, like Giovanni Covi (1994) discuss
her in terms of French feminism or radical postmodernism. Even so, despite the
"obscurity" or possibly because of it, I come back time and time again in my
memory to the strange images Kincaid presents, because they share something
of my dream life and they speak from the inside out, as if emerging from the
grotto. They unskin boundaries. And so I will focus my discussion primarily on
the one anthologized section of her writing, "My Mother," in the preceding
Harper text. In style, trope, structure, and theme, "My Mother" gives rise to
what I refer to as the suchness of suffering.

   Kincaid's style has most often been compared to that of Toni Morrison and
Gabriel García Márquez, whose blend of fantasy and realism is called "magical
realism." For magic, one only has to recall Morrison's time blends of past and
present, sudden irruptions of images, the aliveness of the spirit world, and inex-

plicable actions for a reader to sense being in a different place inside her work. In *Sula* (1973/1996), anthologized in the second edition of *The Norton Anthology of Literature by Women* (with a more politically correct subtitle than the first edition, making plural the word "tradition"), the magic has a disturbing quality; as when, on a day when the wind was doing strange things and the heat was hotter than it had ever been, the elements in nature seem to conspire to bring about endings. Eva kills a son she loves, to save him, and then falls out of a window to save her daughter from burning in a yard fire. Extraordinary events occur both in nature and in social relations; these events, Morrison insists, have nothing whatsoever to do with ordinary (traditionally inherited) morality. They serve, rather, to thicken thinking about the concept "love." Morrison implies that morality, together with the notion of good and evil, is culturally determined, and so her political emphasis is always to redefine and reintroduce and complicate what the dominate culture dictates.

In "Love Constant Beyond Death" (1992) Márquez uses the trope of the circus to make a political point. Writing to draw attention to political corruption in Colombia, South America, Márquez juxtaposes cardboard figures with political hotshots come to a small town to promise amazing feats for the people. Fantasy functions as a reaction to the authorities' assumption that they can declare what is real and what is not. For Márquez, Colombian history is all too fantastic in a dreadful sense, violence being the norm. In "A Very Old Man with Enormous Wings: A Tale for Children" (1988), any traditional understanding of angels is overturned. Here the angel has buzzard wings and speaks with a sailor's voice. This disgusting creature, who comes out of the mud and lives with chickens, nevertheless performs miracles. By encouraging a belief in impossibles, as children do, Márquez celebrates the wonders of pure, unadulterated fantasy.

Many writers, of course, have turned to dreams and myths to explore the potentialities of fantasy. These are called visionaries because they beckon readers into the shadows, where an other world of sounds, colors, scents, images and movements converge (Highwater, 1994). Clearly, Kincaid's work resonates with this group of magical realists. All express a genuinely Third World consciousness wherein impossible things happen quite plausibly under the midday sun. But something else is happening in Kincaid's work that connects her even more closely with Buddhism's nondualities. Her surrealism plumbs the soul of being to its original self, and it is this sense of a fluid return to origination that I see as her impulse to awaken the other self within, the one she was before she was colonized.

To engage this project, Kincaid (1992) writes in a manner that emphasizes emptying out:

> I stood above the land and the sea, and I felt that I was not myself as I had once known myself to be: I was not made up of flesh and blood and muscles and bones and tissue and cells and vital organs but was made up of my will, and over my will I had complete dominion.... I felt myself swing my feet back and forth in a carefree

manner, as if I were a child . . . eyes darting here and there but resting on nothing in particular, a mind conscious of nothing—not happiness, not contentment, and not the memory of night, which soon would come. . . . I had no name for the thing I had become, so new was it to me, except that I did not exist in pain or pleasure, east or west or north or south, or up or down, or past or present or future, or real or not real. (pp. 79–80)

Kincaid plunges us down to the bottom of the river of life. As her title *At the Bottom of the River* indicates, she is reaching down into the rivers of memory and imagination; she is imagining being before doing defined her. This kind of imagining, I submit, is totally foreign to Western readers. The writing is more akin to Henri Rousseau's painting or Claude Debussy's music, which I think may be part of her intention. Certainly, the idea of the need for language to rid itself of words so as to acquire tonality and texture is not new. Jamake Highwater discusses a facility in the mentality of primal people that imparts a form of communication with an alternative objective. He calls this the effort "to get the 'language' out of literature" (p. 103). Samuel Beckett's plays, notably *Waiting for Godot*, consist of characters who do nothing, say nothing meaningful, and who have no quality other than to be present. What is surprising is the degree to which the emptiness nevertheless holds together. The experience is, to use Beckett's pun, "extra-audenary" (1938, p. 293). This move backward is part of what Beckett later referred to an "unveiling towards that which cannot be unveiled" (in Harvey, 1970, p. 426). These writers resonant with Kincaid; it is as if her entire writing project is a Zen koan: questions posed to defy the answer, words written to dislocate the mind.

Kincaid's words, emptied of traditional (read master) meaning, yet are not without meaning. The meaning is found in space and place, not time (Deloria, 1994). Her space is an entirely preliterate world that is fresh, a world that reviews the imagery of origins (Snyder, 1979). In this watery world, we are confronted with strangeness that is beautiful, weird, and terrifying. Kincaid accomplishes these sensations through such devices as parody, repetition, and inversion (what Henry Gates (1988) called signifying), looping, questioning, chanting, and juxtaposing. Instead of linearity she constructs synchronicity (in Campbell, 1971). Her lists are another feature of her style:

The deerflies, stinging and nesting in wet, matted hair; broken bottles at the bottom of the swimming hole; mosquitoes; a family of skunks eating the family garbage; a family of skunks spraying the family dog. (1992, p. 33)

These are not like the cataloging techniques of Walt Whitman or Richard Wright in that they are neither ecstatic nor despairing. They are just the way things are, together: without logic, without category, without label, without order. We must follow this path, suspending all beliefs (Batchelor, 1997). In following, we are just there. How strange this is: "The feeling at times of being below sea level" (Beckett, 1981a, p. 9). Yet it is no more strange than the suchness suggested by this Zen poem (cited in Ross, 1966, p. 158):

> In the landscape of spring …
> The flowering branches grow naturally
> Some long, some short.

At the Bottom of the River contains ten sections, none of them narrative in any traditional sense, of course. In an effort to reach bottom and recreate the self of the before-birthed One, the narrator is not at one with herself. This is Kincaid's intention: to elude definition by shifting, changing, fragmenting, breaking down and down, until the concept of identity as singular (a Western, phallic construction) is demolished (Covi, 1994). Because the ninth story of the collection, "My Mother," is anthologized for college students, I am considering it as my focus for discussion of Kincaid's suchness.

I must admit to my terror when I first chose to teach Kincaid. What is going on here?, I wondered aloud to my students. As with my confusion in teaching Morrison, I felt the text was beyond me; even so, I was pulled in. Something. In looking over my teaching notes for this story, I see these jottings: "imagistic, evocative prose; fantasy drawn from primal nature, dream vision and goddess wisdom; one does not find self by building a house to suit the mother; return to reptilian knowledge; mother always bigger, her accomplishments always better, more praiseworthy. Need for connection with and disconnection from mother love. Journey into selfhood." Notes aside, I couldn't seem to find any sense in them. It was a male student who made the first, simple breakthrough in class discussion. He remarked that the nine segments inside the piece were stages in the evolution of the daughter's consciousness together with but distinct from that of her mother. Yes, I had seemed to have noted that idea, but hearing it from the other side of the desk made the idea come alive for me. I heard the strangeness of it: together, not together. Once again, my failure to "conquer" a text for my students liberated them to liberate me from teaching a "master" class so as to "occupy" (Block, 1995) their reading.

The ninth story, with its nine segments, resonates with the idea of the nine months of birth. The story is indeed, as my student intuited, a separation story; as such it is a birth story. Nine, with its components of triple threes, resonates with very old creation mysteries. In explaining alchemical symbolism, Jung (1950/1976a) insisted that the process of changing base lead to gold was, for the alchemists, more a psychological transformation than a chemical one; it was a birthing of an original self. The outer shell of mortals contains an inner, eternal being, alchemists believed, which, when released or transformed from inside out, could cure the sickness in the human mind. Citing Gerald Dorn's 17th-century commentary, Jung quotes, "'For in the One … is the One and yet not the one'." … and concludes, "The One is the midpoint of the circle, the centre of the triad ... ; it is as the number nine" (pp. 150–151).[1] According to natural wisdom, a single "one" is never just itself any more than a single individual is a plugged unit. The center is everywhere. And it is the number three that resolves the dualism of the number two (with its either-or sense of split), three leading to the middle, which is the One. Plurality thus comes out of unity. These relations among three, two, and one as the perfect whole culminates the mystic art of the alchemists, as stated in the axiom of Maria the Prophetess: "One becomes Two, Two becomes Three, and out of the Third comes One as the Fourth" (p. 151).

So began, over a year ago, my ponderings on Kincaid's text that have nagged me to this writing. That I have turned to the East and Buddhism (via Western esotericism) to explore Kincaid's wisdom is the result of many of my own evolutions. But I find such "orientations" more persuasive of her intention than references to poststructuralist language theory, for example, or deconstruction, because I think the gestations in "My Mother" share a basic Buddhist understanding of "emptiness," a word that derives from the Sanskrit word meaning "to swell," which is connected to the idea of hollowness. Something swells in the hollow (Waldenfels, 1980, p. 19). For Professor Keiji Nishitani (1982), the middle is the place in which radical negation becomes radical affirmation, because everything that is, is what it is. The absolute uniqueness of things is that each and every thing becomes the midpoint, therefore the absolute center. Emptiness is full. In emptiness, everything comes to light "as it is" (Waldenfels, p. 102). Kincaid seems to be working with these ideas to birth herself away from the two mothers who have colonized her very being: her mother country and the mother who physically birthed her. Her images push toward a backward place, what Izutsu refers to as "the darkness of the sphere of No-Image" (1981, p. 4). By turning back, Kincaid attempts the discovery of an original self in the manner of the advice of the *Fukanzazengi*, a classic text of Japanese Buddhism: "You should therefore cease from practice based on intellectual understanding, pursuing words and following after speech, and learn the backward step that turns your light inwardly to illuminate your self. Body and mind of themselves will drop away, and your original face will be made manifest. If you want to at-

---

[1]Samuel Beckett uses the number nine in two works involving women quests. In *Footfalls* (1977) May is talking to her mother, who listens but is absently present. May seeks to make her mother present by narrating a story and creating a circular space. She seeks well inside the sequel she narrates (Beckett's pun is intended), walking and talking in a wheeling circle composed of nine revolving steps "a little off centre" (p. 42). The nine paces form a space into which May's story about the absence of her mother can be contained and possibly birthed. In *Rockaby* (1981b) a woman sits in a rocking chair facing a window, searching for another one like herself, "a little like" (p. 13). This sitting-search is punctuated by a phrase repeated nine times: "all eyes/all sides." It could be interpreted that the "little like" one she seeks is her daughter. But the ambiguity is such that it could be that both women in the two plays are incompletely born, seeking to find their truer inner selves in the magic circle of emptiness. For more on Beckett, see my "Walking and Rocking" (1988).

tain suchness (*tathata*), you should practice suchness without delay" (in Waldenfels, p. 179).

In the first of the nine moments, as I call the textual spacings in "My Mother," the narrator begins with a sentence that sets the scene as in a not-real place: "Immediately on wishing my mother dead and seeing the pain it caused her, I was sorry and cried so many tears that all the earth around me was drenched" (Kincaid, 1993, p. 2367). Sorrow creates the waters out of which the daughter will begin her long, backward-seeking journey. The water, which the daughter forms into a small pond, is "thick and black and poisonous" (p. 2,367), presumably because words cause poison. But even with the beginning moment of remorse and shame, the narrator attempts no analysis or cognitive discrimination. Her only uttered word is "So." It is this nonreaction that effectively weakens the narrator's intellect so that, according to the teachings of Buddhism, oppositions can be transcended and the original self can be born (Ross, 1966).

The second moment is unrelated to the first. Only the two characters are the same. The scene is a dark room with all the windows covered over and "all the crevices stuffed with black cloth " (p. 2,367). Out of this womb-like insulation, the mother and daughter are mesmerized by their large shadows, which make a place between themselves "as if they were making room for someone else" (p. 2368). The shadows are larger than either mother or daughter and express an eerie intentionality. In Jungian thought, one's unconscious, or the undiscovered self, is called the shadow:

> What our age thinks of as the "shadow" and inferior part of the psyche contains more than something merely negative. The very fact that through self-knowledge, i.e. by exploring our own souls, we come upon the instincts and their world of imagery should throw some light on the powers slumbering in the psyche. (Jung, 1958, p. 107)

The shadow powers of both mother and daughter are irrupting and dancing around. The shadow, as the other self within, prompts the narrator to get a good look at herself, to discover who she really is apart from her mothered self. That she tries to see this other face, and is unsuccessful, does not mean that there is no shadow self slumbering. It only means that everything is in process and the shadow is heeded.

The third moment begins the unskinning, first by the mother, then the daughter. The transformation that occurs is from human to reptile, a terrifying one as seen with the mother but not with the daughter. The mother grows metal plates on her back and long rows of teeth. "Taking her head into her large palms, she flattened it so that her eyes, which were by now ablaze, sat on top of her head and spun like two revolving balls" (p. 2368). The daughter, too, becomes a snake, but not a scary one. She merely travels on her underbelly and flickers her tongue. These remarkable transformations elicit one word, "Look," a word that expresses no opinion whatsoever. "Look" beckons the daughter to stay quietly attentive.

According to Jungian interpretation, the snake is a symbol of rebirth because of its shedding skin and thus it represents wisdom:

> The wisdom of the serpent, which is suggested by its watchful lidless eye, lies essentially in mankind's having projected into this lowly creature his own secret wish to obtain from the earth a knowledge he cannot find in waking daylight consciousness alone. This is the knowledge of death and rebirth forever withheld except at those times when some transcendent principle, emerging from the depths, makes it available to consciousness. (Henderson & Oakes, 1990, pp. 36–37)

This third moment for the daughter suggests that, in unskinning and traveling on her underbelly, she is going to acquire wisdom from close communion with the earth. She will have nothing to fear and may let go of all emotion so long as she feels earth's touch and remains grounded. That her tongue can no longer be used for words is significant, for language prevents the silence from being articulated.

The fourth moment contains different places and long intervals of time. At first the mother and daughter stand "on" the seabed, intertwined by arms and sighs. Not only are they in a watery underworld, they are at the bottom of the water on the seabed itself. It is here that another miracle of form-changing occurs. The narrator describes coming out of her skin in another image of transmutation, this time as a tortoise: "My skin had just blackened and cracked and fallen away and my new impregnable carapace had taken full hold" (p. 2,368). There is wordless communication and a sense of uneasy peace. When the two walk to the Garden of Fruits and feast, the reference to Genesis is evident; but then they leave by "the southwestly gate" (p. 2,368), implying that their Edenic existence as human bodies will end. The two are not Adam and Eve but prehistoric sea creatures exploring an uninhabited world. The fruit they eat is not from the tree of knowledge but from the tree of life.

In the fifth moment, womb images of a cave, a hole, and a floorless house are all depicted as places the daughter's emerging self might be contained for rebirth if she can but sever herself from the domineering mother. But no. The mother is one step ahead of her, always. The daughter builds the floorless house in colors that the mother favors and with windows the mother likes, so as to entice her to her death. The two exchange sentences, repeating each other's phrases. They seem as one. The house, designed to lure the mother, is the house of the old self, the one who is too attached and too full of ruse. Even the daughter's attempt to kill the mother does not work: When the mother enters the house, she does not drop through the floor; she does not "fall" for her daughter's trickery. Instead, she is ever the supernatural woman, who pounds her heel in the air and vanishes. The segment ends by the daughter's burning down the house. One cannot build the house of the self to suit or kill the mother. One must detach.

The sixth moment reveals to the daughter the fruitlessness of pleasing actions and unpleasing emotions. Her mother looms ever larger, with ever more amazing feats that prove her superiority and win her praises. The daughter is consumed with anger, an anger that is fed by more anger when her mother lives on the opposite side of a pond in a house of her own and refuses to acknowledge the daughter's presence. The water, as in the first moment, is not life-giving; it is a dead pond that separates the two, where "small invertebrates with poisonous lances" live (p. 2,369). As long as the daughter is filled with anger, the waters of rebirth will be poisoned.

As with the sixth moment, the seventh moment suggests that the daughter's journey into selfhood is a dream from which she is trying to awaken. She undertakes a journey across waters to a new island. Just as in real life, the real Jamaica Kincaid walked to the jetty and left her homeland for another place, a greater opportunity, and a chance to discover herself. This dream segment contains the same motif. But physical distance does not lessen the daughter's attachment. On the new island she meets another woman who takes the place of the mother, even more so. "I could not see where she left off and I began, or where I left off and she began" (p. 2,370). This identification is made complete by the way both women have identical feet, "especially around the arch of the instep" (p. 2,369). If they walk the same walk and talk the same talk, however, the return to origination will be stymied.

In the eighth moment, the image of a house reappears as the mother's "beautiful" house filled with shared memories. "The rooms are large and empty, opening on to each other, waiting for people and things to fill them up" (p. 2,370). The two walk through the rooms, merging and separating. The daughter's sense is that the final stage of her evolution is nearing: "Soon we shall enter the final stage of our evolution" (p. 2,370).

Finally, the ninth moment arrives. A paradise of oneness is pictured by lambs, lime trees, blossoms, perfume, small darts of light, and pink feet. The narrator-daughter's pink feet imply that she will at last be able to walk her own walk with fresh imprints. Having been born back, she sits in the lap of mother-comfort: "It is in this way my mother and I have lived for a long time now" (p. 2,370). Space and time collapse into an oceanic sense of oneness. As Lama Surya Das emphasizes, "Enlightenment is not about becoming divine. Instead, it's about becoming more fully human ... 'To be enlightened is to be one with all things'" (p. 14). It would appear that the conundrum of enlightenment is that to be at one requires an attitude free from thought but awake to awareness. To be awake is to sit in front of concrete particularity so as to affirm the continuity of all nature (Ingram, 1997).

Anyone who dreams will recognize in Kincaid's nine moments the fragmentary nonlogic of dream life that puts one in a continuous flow with all things.

This re-cognition is a remembering of what we have forgotten when we are too tied into the world of fixity. Kincaid unmoors us. Her writing is a form of meditation, wherein senses, not concepts, turn the tide. The fragments are fluid like dreams and continuous like the passing moments themselves; time assumes a spatial rather than a linear quality. We drift. All is impermanence; even the desire to get born again, backward, is incomplete. But, as Batchelor reminds us, the focus on momentary images is what constitutes awareness, that which draws attention to the suchness of each passing moment:

> One of the most difficult things to remember is to remember to remember. Awareness begins with remembering what we tend to forget.... To stop and pay attention to what is happening in the moment is one way of snapping out of ... fixations. It is also a reasonable definition of meditation. (pp. 58–59)

The impulse to return to origins is, indeed, a different kind of journey altogether from the sort of outward bounding of Western, heroic, male journey tales of adventure. It takes an extraordinary writer to attempt this recall to origins. In the Western tradition, few have attempted the backward plunge, considered negatively regressive except among the neo-Platonists, Romantic poets, Transcendentalists, and some stream-of-consciousness writers.

Samuel Taylor Coleridge, for example, distinguishes between primary and secondary imagination, privileging the primary over the secondary. He describes primary imagination as "the living power and prime agent of all human perception, and as a repetition in the finite mind of the eternal act of creation in the infinite I AM" (1815/1993, p. 387). Secondary imagination is only "an echo of the former" (p. 387) and only a matter of the conscious will. These definitions resonate with Eastern ideas like inner vision, Buddha nature, pure perception, or sacred outlook. The Dharma's view of the self is that the self is "no-self," meaning that "each of us is a process rather than a fixed, independent, eternal self or concrete entity" (Das, p. 119). To realize the no-self is to lose ego so as to awaken what Coleridge calls "the infinite I AM," what Carl Jung calls the archetype of the self, or what Buddhism calls Buddha nature. The Romantic poet William Wordsworth also "reverses" thought by writing, "Our birth is but a sleep and a forgetting" (1802–1804/1993, p. 190). Beckett, whom many might be surprised to be associated with a neo-Platonic tradition, writes on our "first nature" (1938, p. 11), which is awakened in suffering. "The suffering of being: that is, the free play of every faculty," he claims (p. 9), thereby insisting that suffering is "the main condition of the artistic experience" (p. 16).

Virginia Woolf, too, distinguishes between moments of being and nonbeing in her autobiographical account of first memory. She credits true aliveness with the freshness of impressions that came to her in the nursery:

> The buzz, the croon, the smell, all seemed to press voluptuously against some membrane; not to burst it; but to hum round one such a complete rapture of plea-

sure that I stopped, smelt, looked…. The strength of these pictures—but sight was always then so much mixed with sound that picture is not the right word—the strength anyhow of these impressions makes me again digress. Those moments—in the nursery, on the road to the beach—can still be more real than the present moment…. Later we add to feelings much that makes them more complex; and therefore less strong; or if not less strong, less isolated, less complete. (1939/1993, p. 1,992).

Woolf's comment about the complexity of later, added feelings helps explain a Buddhist understanding of how intellect interferes with awareness. By complicating the suchness of absolute experiencing, the analytical mind becomes distracted: less clear, less complete, less flowing. "All water has a perfect memory," as Toni Morrison put it (1987, p. 99). Consciousness is a stream when it goes with the flow of impressions trying to reach back to where memory began, not forward to where intellect strains.[2]

One does not "suffer" being to become more alive when one closes oneself off from the universe. Opening out is unskinning, and unskinning is experiencing an intrinsic interrelatedness, fusing, confusing. Call it "intercoursing." In her book on making soul, Gloria Anzaldúa remarks on the particular perspective of Third World women writers: "Our strength lies in shifting perspectives, in our capacity to shift, in our 'seeing through' the membrane of the past superimposed on the present, in looking at our shadows and dealing with them" (1990, p. xxvii). When Kincaid burns down the house of the mother, an ongoing attempt is made to deal with the shadow of an overarching presence: Even houses have the mother's skin. Anne Sexton writes: "Some women marry houses./It's another kind of skin" (1985, p.1,993). Ay, and there's the torment. When the "membrane" of the past imposes itself, present cannot be made present. It is no wonder that throughout *At the Bottom of the River*, Kincaid's skin is removed, left in the corner of the house, shed, and cracked. Her trope of skin portrays the idea of being inward and outward at the same time so that the process of multidimensionality and everchangingness can begin to be felt. This transformation shows the insignificance of form (Simmons, 1994). The skin is what separates by form, class, label, name. To shed skin is to be inside and outside at the same time; it is to reconcile oneself to all that exists. To unskin is to unchain humans from their lonely, lofty perch atop the Great Chain of Being. Skin, as

---

[2]This reaching-back memory as a stream is seen in Thomas Wolfe's *Good Child's River*, when Esther exults in her feeling of being in the middle of the cosmos:

Lily and I went in without anything on, and I turned over on my back and floated and, God! I seemed to be right in the very middle of the universe … and I looked up in the sky that was so deep and blue and it all seemed to be part of my body, it seemed to fill me and come from me and flow into me; I was the earth and the sea and the sky and all things were born in me and preceded from me, it was like something that had gone on forever, it was like music, it was like a star. (1991, p. 77)

Kincaid's major trope, is what connects her most directly to the Buddhist doctrine of interdependent co-arising:

> This experience (of awakening to one's true self) involves a revolution in one's way of seeing and relating to everything in the universe. One way to describe the experience is the arrival at what can be called a *zero-point*, wherein opposing concepts of being and nonbeing, doing and nondoing, having and nonhaving, plus and minus, and so on, converge and cancel each other out. This zero point, the separation between subject and object, between the 'I' and the world, is overcome, and the practitioner is opened to an entirely new way of seeing and way of being. (Habito, 1997, p. 168)

In *The Autobiography of my Mother*, Kincaid goes inside her mother's skin imaginatively. This sympathetic portrait is another attempt by the writer to free herself from her mother's spell. Or perhaps it is the daughter's way of trying to acquire the mother's unconsciousness so that she, too, can be codependent with the cosmos. The following passage of the imagined mother is of particular poetic significance:

> I could hear the clap of thunder, the roar of water falling from great heights into great pools and the great pool wending its way slowly toward the sea; I could hear clouds emptying themselves of their moisture as if by accident, as if someone had kicked over a goblet in the dark, and their contents landing on an indifferent earth; and I could hear the silence and I could hear the dark night gobbling it up, and it in turn being gobbled up by the light of yet another day. (pp. 94–95)

There are many such passages in the text, suggestive of the magical thinking of the imagined mother. What is remarkable is the degree to which Kincaid negotiates the two sides of her mother, the inside and the outside, together with the two faces of the mother, the kind one and the terrible one:

> I would never become a mother, but that would not be the same as never bearing children. I would bear children, but I would never be a mother to them.... I would bear children, they would hang from me like fruit from a vine, but I would destroy them with the carelessness of a god. I would bear children in the morning. I would bathe them at noon in water that came from myself, and I would eat them at night, swallowing them whole, all at once. (p. 97)

In this imaginative biography, Kincaid is portraying the miracles of strangeness that are available to us everyday, if we just look. Our days are as open to miracle as to horror. She shows, in this telling of the mother's story, the complicated manifestations of living fully alive to the inner dynamisms of the ordinary. Her achievement is that she captures, for me, the utter suchness of impermanence, constantly drifting in and out. The effect is both spiritual and political. She speaks as her mothers' outsider (the two mothers of country and birth), while yet going inside both. She is not skinned inside herself: not quite the same, not quite different. "The moment the insider steps out from the inside she is no longer a mere insider. She necessarily looks in from the outside while also looking out from the inside" (Minh-ha, 1990, p. 374).

How completely, utterly unique this threshold awareness is, how spiritual and ecological, is amusingly in contrast to the portraits Kincaid offers of characters she does not like. The mother's half-sister, for example, is not open. "The strangeness of life had not yet occurred to her, the short-livedness of each moment, each day, each existence itself, had not yet occurred to her; I do not now believe it ever has" (p. 122). And for her mother's husband, a special scorn is reserved. He loves money, would be undone by the uncertainties of truth, and is not at all a part of the breathing cosmos: "When he looked at the night sky, it was closed off; so too was the midday sky, closed off; the seas were closed off, the ground on which he walked was closed off. He did not have a future, he had only the past, he lived in that way" (p. 217).

How to live a life? How not to? To not live is to be tied up and boxed in. To live is to open out to each suffering moment without regret. That is, at least, one conclusion we could draw from the incredible writings of Kincaid. To suffer loss, craving, and yearning is to be alive as never before; it is to be alive in the empty now. It is to feel the shadows of the self. Kincaid ends the fragments that compose *At the Bottom of the River* with indications that her suffering is beyond definition or direction because it is simply what it is:

> I had no name for the thing I had become, so new was it to me, except that I did not exist in pain or pleasure, east or west or north or south, or up or down, or past or present or future, or real or not real.... And so, emerging from my pit ... I step into a room and I see that the lamp is lit. (pp. 80–82)

As I consider the educational implications of this chapter, I recall the saying of a wisdom figure of the West: "Let the little children come to me, and do not hinder them, for of such is the kingdom of God" (Mark: 10:14—New American Catholic Edition). In this instance, "suffer" means "to allow or permit" (Webster, 1993). But "suffer" also means "to be the object of some action," "to undergo, be subjected to." Subjects become objects, objects become subjected to—an interesting dynamic of inner and outer that suggests transformation. If our students, the little children, will suffer the kingdom, surely they will experience suchness, for such is the kingdom. Such word play is serious, if one will suffer such. Writings like Kincaid's and the sayings of sages take us back to places we need to go. For Rebecca Luce-Kapler, literature breaks through the cotton wool (what Virginia Woolf called nonbeing) and offers the reader "rooms to explore the shape" of one's living (in Pinar, 1998, p. 150). Dennis Sumara agrees, saying that we don't just read to add new knowledge but to find a location that will occasion "opportunities for re-viewing, re-interpreting, re-conceptualizing" (1996, p. 234). Terry Carlson (1998) distinguishes between identity politics (that which defines and limits) and the politics of the self (that which refuses defining labels): a distinction that resonates with Kincaid's decolonization project. Just the other day, an editorial ran in my paper, "Injustice for Jamaica" (1999). No, not the author: the place and its politics. It seems that children from Jamaica entering a national spelling bee might be banned from entering the contest because of some small legality. As the editorialist said, perhaps these children should learn how to spell "'exclusionary,' 'inequitable,' and maybe even 'obdurate'" (p. B6). One cannot have one's imagination released when one is boxed in and tied down by defining rules. One must cut loose back toward beginnings (Greene, 1998).

Surely, the project of trying to get oneself born (unboxed, untied, unskinned) is the great work of life. Kincaid goes back to the mother image for that reason. I believe she accomplishes in her texts what Bill Pinar (1998) means when he argues for the "de-oedipalization of the person and, with it, the de-oedipalization of the intellect " (p. 235). By imagining a differentiated relation to the mother, one captures the immediacy and complexity of experience that portray "the simultaneity of thought, feeling, and action" (Pinar, p. 236) without being subsumed. Reconstructed knowledge is, accordingly, Kincaidian. Through strange stories all givens are complexified. Tibetan lamas are fond of telling stories about supernatural events and mystical happenings, forcing one to pause between the sound bytes. These stories are not meant to be swallowed whole; they should be chewed slowly, for self-discovery (Das, 1997). The force behind awakening to the true, original self is imagination, as Marla Morris describes Maxine Greene's educational philosophy. It is imagination, Morris writes (1998), that "releases the doors of perception" and opens onto ambiguities (p. 133).

Finally, a word about the children we teach. They are not, alas, children. They perceive themselves as young adults with responsibilities and checkbooks, things to measure, fields of gravity to weigh. So when I ask what Wordsworth means by the line "The Child is father of the Man" (1802/1993, p. 187), they are confused. Let us keep introducing poetic confusions into our discourses! We must complicate so as to bring forth suchness. As Deborah Simmons said of Jamaica Kincaid: "In a world in which things are themselves, it suddenly becomes possible that one may be oneself, may see oneself in a way that cannot be changed by the view of another" (p. 99). Perhaps, with any luck, our adult students can become like children, who, seeing things in simple suchness, may then know themselves.

☙10☙

Circles, Loops, and the Wheel of Comedy

At last after many variations and unstable circlings and curvings we come to rest in the kingdom of life.

—Nicolas of Cusa (1401–1464, in Moore, 1983, p. 51)

This colorful, moving, active, disturbing universe opens to us as we open ourselves to it.

—Moon (n.d., p. 97)

They moved around and around the room and into the brightness of the open door.

—Welty (1979a, p. 170)

Let us space. The art of this text is the air it causes to circulate between its screens.

—Derrida (1986, p. 75)

Probably because Aristotle's treatise on comedy has been lost, the Western tradition has not afforded comedy the same dignity as that granted to the genre of tragedy. In his *The Name of the Rose*, however, Umberto Eco (1980) made the missing second book of Aristotle a key text within his text, found at last only to be devoured (literally eaten) by a monk. Eco suggests that Aristotle's treatise on comedy was too disruptive to the teachings of Christianity because comedy uses the word to tells things differently, as if lying. Seen in this light, comedy obliges us to examine how things are metaphorically rather than literally. Comedy instructs, but differently. Whereas tragedy uses fear to achieve catharsis, comedy uses laughter to distract fear. What is marginal thus leaps to the center. Margins, freedoms, pleasures, ridicules, riddles, puns, metaphors, vulgarities all spring forth as from the dung heap. Comedy is a celebration, a festival, a multitude, a generosity. Unlike tragedy, comedy bursts the seams of what straitjackets us, returning us not to our ego selves but to our relating selves. Comedy, thus, because it is about relationship and not imitation, is thereby a genre entirely suited for the postmodern classroom as well as for a postmodern spirituality.

There are, of course, many different types of spiritualities and comic books. Flannery O'Connor's comedy is hilarious, outrageous, religious. Pitching her stories around what she calls the "Christ-haunted South" (1980, p. 418), she introduces hardheaded egocentrics who undergo a conversion experience against their will. "I am just trying to isolate this kind of abandonment of self," she explains, "which is the result of sanctifying grace" (p. 455). O'Connor has a particular, Catholic notion of grace that infuses her work; interestingly, even though she insists on a difference between this notion and Eastern religions, similar ideas of emptying out can be seen in both.

Less Christian but equally, in my view, spiritual is Eudora Welty's comic writing. Each time I teach Eudora Welty I am more convinced of the brilliance of her work—brilliant less in the sense of a hard shining, more in the sense of an aura or a rainbow or a just-right simile. I am proud to connect Eudora with my mother, who was one of her first editors at *Harper's Bazaar* back in the 1940s and whom Eudora singled out for thanks for introducing many of her stories (1980, p. x). In "The Key," which my mother published, a line suggests a way into the mystery of comedy: "As he held the match close he gazed straight ahead, and in his eyes, all at once wild and searching, there was certainly, besides the simple compassion in his regard, a look both restless and weary, very much used to the comic" (1980, p. 37). Recently, I taught one of those early pieces, "Death of a Traveling Salesman," using it as a companion piece to the more well-known "A Worn Path." I teach both as examples of what I call the "wheel of comedy," the purpose of which is to gather multitudes into "the wide net" (title of another of her stories). Welty's vision is all-encompassing, connecting, and relational in the way that reflects what Charlene Spretnak describes as a Buddhist sensibility: "The fact that everything is relationships and interconnections: you get closer to seeing that what's interconnecting is vibrations and patterns of vibrations: that is very exciting because you're getting down to the 'isness' of what's happening" (in Boucher, 1993, p. 286). Welty places the reader directly inside 'isness,' perhaps accounting for the fact that students don't quite know what to do with her stories. Could this be that her notion of the livingness of life, a comedic notion, is too real? Too inexperienced by readers? Are student readers not used to being amazed or delighted by a text? By life? Do they think such emotions are not educational? In any case I urge in my classes, as I am urging in this chapter, the profundity of comedy, which should be taken "seriously" because it shows forth the marvel of life and opens the door of the heart. These marvels are similar to what the Buddha hoped to reveal in teachings that went against the mainstream because they are "deep, intimate, delicate and hidden" discoveries not to be reached by reason alone (Ross, 1966, p. 90).

I ask my students to consider this question: How do you know you are alive? Here is a basic list we compose while reading and discussing the work of Welty: I see colors, I hear sounds, I enjoy food that I share with others. I experience sorrow, I experience joy, seeing the one as part of the other. I cherish my treasures, I talk to the animals, I make up images in my head. I swap insults, I know myths, I engage in the immediacy of the moment. I see darkness, I see light, I see light inside the darkness. I feel rhythm, I toy with littleness, I remember the pleasure of being a child. As Doc, in "The Wide Net" (1979a), puts it, "the outside world is full of endurance" (p. 33), and "the excursion is the same when you go looking for your sorrow as when you go looking for your joy" (p. 31). Using these prompters, I ask my students to consider how Bowman, in "Death of a Traveling Salesman," is *not* a figure of comedy and how his traveling is *not* a journey, such as that undertaken by Phoenix, in "A Worn Path." Considering negation is another way of seeing affirmation.

In this regard of negation, Toni Morrison's work draws my attention. Hers is another form of the comedic vision, which, because it has been born out of sorrow, includes sorrow. Perhaps, like the Buddhist understanding, a first principle for Morrison is the nature of suffering in the face of which the African-American experience is seen as assertive, inventive, idiosyncratic, and circulatory. Like a fountain, the sorrows and losses of the text gush up and circle around and around in a style that is itself dynamic and flowing. As such, the reader does not get stuck on the sorrow but at the same time cannot forget the many experiences of dead loss. In this sense, Morrison writes letters in running water and engages the reader's gut, heart, brain, and compassion in a very full-bodied way.

I teach *The Bluest Eye* as the final project in my Women and Literature course. My text, as I have mentioned earlier, is *The Norton Anthology of Literature by Women*, with its subtitle, for the first edition, *The Tradition in English*. As chapter two argued, Morrison writes against "the tradition," and so it is with a bit of mind play that I attempt in this chapter to indicate some of the ways she accomplishes her deconstruction. As I see it, even in this, her first novel, the reader discovers a new kind of writing that, while raising basic, critical questions about American culture, does so in a nonconfrontative style. A paradox immediately is felt. On the one hand, Morrison's themes and situations are pessimistic and shocking, but on the other hand her presentation of the shocks is something else—not the opposite of pessimistic, not the opposite of shocking (not "optimistic" nor "soothing"). The "something else" is the third thing Morrison's style accomplishes, which is to fill in what White writing, with its tradition of oppositions, has largely left out: the Black (w)hole of language (Baker, 1984). As Philip Novak comments, "what Morrison gives us ... is a ceaseless celebration of African-American culture born of an acute sensitivity to the culture's continuity fragility" (1999, p. 192).

How is it possible for White, middle class students to apprehend Black language? One answer is by reading out loud. I teach Morrison largely as an oral experience, to awaken the reader's ear. As Morrison herself put it, "My writing expects, demands, participatory reading, and I think that is what literature is supposed to do" (in Tate, 1983, p. 125). Two scenes are wonderful for this exercise, the gargoyle scene in the beginning and Pecola's dialogue with Claudia at the end. In the first instance, I select five readers—the three gargoyles (whores), a narrator, and Pecola. The script, taken directly from the text, is four pages and takes no more than ten or fifteen minutes to perform. During that time, I contend that students are taken imaginatively into the upper room where Marie, China, and Poland live together over the Breedloves' apartment. Theirs is, indeed, a world apart from Pecola's confined world (Morrison's names here and elsewhere in the novel are symbolic); and that Marie (who occupies the "upper room" with its Christ overtones) is one of the three suggests that these three whores cannot be defined—which is to say, limited—by language, for they serve a holy function. They are what Nancy Qualls-Corbett (1988) calls sacred prostitutes, precisely because they expand Pecola's world, if only momentarily, by their refusal to accept damaging labels. Qualls-Corbett writes:

> It is this moving, changing, transformative aspect of the feminine that is associated with the goddess of love and with which the sacred prostitute is identified. When it is active, we view the world and ourselves in a different light. Creative juices are stimulated, and rational boundaries or limitations push into the realm of the unconventional and irrational. New attitudes usher in a certain excitement and life itself takes on new meaning. (p. 57)

Except for the word "irrational" I find this discussion of the sacred prostitutes' love function entirely appropriate for what I feel Morrison doing. This is one scene wherein we actually hear Pecola ask questions. She is able to do so because of the license and recognition given her. There, in the upper room, she is free. Too, the self-effacing humor of the three "merry gargoyles" (p. 2098) gives Pecola permission to laugh at her ugliness, just as the gargoyles laugh at theirs, living as they know they do outside the confines of accepted (White) decorum. Through laughter, a new morality emerges that is both subversive and liberatory (Kushel, 1994). This is indeed a divine comedy.

Besides exploding the stigma of the "loose" woman, this scene torpedoes the idea of beauty. The class can discuss what other ideas of "beauty" operate here; how, for example, we get a beautifully good feeling from hearing the women's conversational intercourse. Their easy laughter, their jokes about underwear and sex, enable class discussion that is freer of embarrassment and shame around such topics as the female body. Pecola's absolute conviction that her female body is ugly is a conviction that holds no weight with the three. To the whores she is "dumplin'" (p. 2,095), a loving nickname that washes away the sting of her earlier encounter with mean Mr. Yacobowski.

The other scene the students dramatize is the dialogue at the end, when Pecola, now completely split off from her core self, believes she has blue eyes.

Again, I situate two readers in the front of the room, one playing Pecola the other playing Claudia. They read eight pages right from the text, a performance that takes up almost the full period. The enactment of this mad scene complexifies the "fact" of Pecola's insanity. Clearly, what has happened to this child is tragic: Not only has she been raped by her father, but she is despised by the neighborhood store owner, taunted by her classmates, and tricked by Soaphead Church into thinking she really has, finally, the bluest eyes. Further, the only thing she might call her own, her baby, died when her mother knocked her down; no amount of seed planting or mythical, magical incantations by Claudia could bring back what was once "that living, breathing silk of black skin" (p. 2,173).

As chapter two discussed, the theme of a Black child overcome by the ideals of the White world makes this novel an inquiry into tragedy. But not in a classical sense. I find the experience of hearing this child's delusion more profound than hearing, say, Ophelia's pathetic mad song. And here is where Morrison plumbs a new depth in the genre of tragedy. I know of no tragedy in Eurocentric literature that projects a child as the tragic hero, much less a girl child, much less a Black girl child. But that is what Morrison does, at the end of the novel. For the bulk of the novel the reader hears Claudia's voice or an omniscient narrator telling in a most nonsequential, nonAristotelian "plot" the story of Pecola's down-spin. Only at the final dialogue does the reader hear Pecola speak extensively. The sounding of her voice is surprising, because she appears both charming in her point of pride and sassy in her delusion. For a tragic protagonist to be so named, Aristotle contends, the protagonist's action must be an imitation, an "imitation of people better than we are" (in Heath, 1996, p. 25). But what Pecola imitates is White people, who—far from being "better"—are in Morrison's view evil for perpetrating only one ideal of beauty. Additionally, Aristotle's classic definition of tragedy includes its cathartic impact on the audience. But in Morrison's novel the audience is only indirectly us. The one who acts as audience is Claudia, who makes the following knowing recognition into the causes of Pecola's insanity: "We substituted good grammar for intellect; we switched habits to simulate maturity; we rearranged lies and called it truth, seeing in the new pattern an old idea of the Revelation and the Word" (p. 2,183). Is this what Aristotle means by catharsis: the "purification," through pity and fear, of excessive emotions (in Heath, 1996, p. xxxvii)? If Claudia is "purified," if she achieves catharsis, it is at the expense of her core self. Her recognition only propels her into her own tragic, new pattern: an imitation of old White ideas. This is not knowledge of most worth for Black children.

The fact that Claudia knows what is happening to her, that she is being diminished, deepens what is commonly understood as "tragedy." In chapter two I argued that Claudia was an Absurd hero because she understood the limits of her condition as a minority. As she put it, "Our peripheral existence was something we had learned to deal with—probably because it was abstract" (p. 2,075).

In this last scene, however, the abstract becomes concrete: Her best friend has been driven mad. What I hear in reading Morrison out loud is a response to Aristotle's classic definition of tragedy, with its patriarchal denigration of women and slaves (in Heath, 1996, p. 24), its insistence on imitation and purification, and its limited understanding of character. Instead, Morrison's pen takes us into a deeper wellspring of the human character, one that includes Black children.

"Why is it," I wonder aloud with my students, "that it takes us humans so long to discover who we are? How many of us mold our entire lives around imitations and copies? What do we copy, whom imitate?" Recently, I watched an interview with June Allyson, one of my matinée idols when I was growing up. I remembered so well her voice, her hair, the pouty lower lip. And there it all was, forty years later: The hair, voice, and lip—nothing had changed. How uncomplicated were her memories, how nice her persona—just as in the movies. I wondered last night if June Allyson was an imitation of "June Allyson." Teaching Morrison is one way to complicate the idea of "character." It is at once difficult and stimulating for students to recognize complexity in character. It is especially stimulating when Morrison presents Black characters who are so completely nonstereotypical. That, of course, is Morrison's intention: to fret the cliché of Black stereotypes as found primarily in White texts.

To prepare my students for the final exam, I give them their Morrison question ahead of time, in part to have them track their reading, but also and always to nudge some connection between reading and understanding of the social-psychical self. The question is as follows: "Select one or two characters from Toni Morrison's *The Bluest Eye* and discuss the complexities of that character. Include in your discussion particular instances of both positive and negative aspects of character. In your discussion consider why Morrison chooses not to present her characters as clearly all good or all bad." Here is Christine's response:

> Cholly's drinking led to fighting with and abusing his wife. It also led to the rape of his daughter. Most people would think he was a terrible monster for committing such a crime. But even in this terrible act, Morrison tries to show the reader his good side. It is very subtle, yet present throughout the rape: "He wanted to break her neck—but tenderly" (p. 2,158). This was not his usual sexual desire. It had "a tenderness, a protectiveness." The two sides of Cholly mixed together confused him. So the reader sees both good and evil sides of Cholly in this novel.... He was never connected to anyone, having been left alone in the world at thirteen. There was not much hope for him. The reader sees him as human, having turned out as any human would under the circumstances. I have never really thought about what life would be like growing up in a poor Black family.... Pecola was ugly, Black, and had terrible parents. The boys teased her about these things, which she could not help, and made her feel terrible. This makes me think about my own life and my feelings towards others.

The student goes on to conclude that we are all human, we are all equal, there is no such thing as color—implying that we are all the same.

The more I read Morrison and study the "politics of knowledge" (Said, 1993), however, the more I know that that fair-sounding conclusion is too thin. Those of us engaged in the knowledge enterprise should disengage the notion of liberal humanism from its foundation in Eurocentric (White male) knowing. Liberal humanism is, at bottom, a marriage of sames. In its profession of color blindness ("we are all human"), the liberal humanist is blind to color. In today's paper, Clinton's race advisory president addresses the matter of color blindness, which is really an excuse to ignore race. "The idea that we should aspire to a 'color blind' society is an impediment to reducing racial stereotyping," John Hope Franklin writes (in Ross, 1998, p. A8). Morrison teaches us, rather, that seeing color makes all the difference in thickening imagination. Her writing is therefore an excellent introduction to an understanding of difference.

There are many other ways besides oral reading that allow appreciation of the meaning of difference. Take, for example, the cliché "at bottom," which I used in the above paragraph. One of the stereotypes I find Morrison deliberately fretting is the casting of Blacks to the bottom of the social hierarchy. In *Sula* (1987b), Bottom is the name of the Black community that is, wittily, located on top of a hill. The novel begins:

> In that place, where they tore the nightshade and blackberry patches from their roots to make room for the Medallion City Golf Course, there was once a neighborhood. It stood in the hills above the valley town of Medallion and spread all the way to the river. It is called the suburbs now, but when black people lived there it was called the Bottom. (p. 3)

Morrison's Bottom is "that place," which, because of specificity, defies the sort of generality into which stereotypes slide. It is a place with berry patches, not unlike the collard patches and briar patches found in folklore. Bottom rises up out of the stereotypes of those at the bottom, those whose roots had been torn from Africa and whose bodies were displaced on plantations. In Bottom the reader meets people who have formed their community with village values, which means different types commingle, different situations evolve, and difference is celebrated, not merely tolerated.

Morrison, then, re-races White stereotypes to build up the texture of the word Bottom, to give it face, form, and substance. Indeed, the entire novel conveys the texture of a village community which, in Morrison's view, is "a real place." For unlike the White suburb Medallion, the people of Bottom live intensely, having survived "floods, white people, tuberculosis, famine, and ignorance. They knew anger well but not despair, and they didn't stone sinners for the same reason they didn't commit suicide—it was beneath them" (p. 90). Those at the social bottom are, Morrison punningly shows, really at the ethical top: They know how to live nonjudgmentally with one another, without stoning sinners (a reference, I believe, to Shirley Jackson's "The Lottery," which I discussed in chapter two). Hearing the intersubtextuality of references, I feel the richness of Morrison's words, which in only a few opening sentences contain so much history. In such a way she deconstructs the narrow typecasting of a racial stereotype (what Claudia in *The Bluest Eye* calls "the Word"). As B. H. Rigney (1991) puts it, in such a way, Morrison breaks the back of words.

Another stereotype the "happy darky,"—on which the Uncle Remus stories are based, is overturned in all of Morrison's works, but particularly in *Tar Baby* (1987c). Just as Morrison used the Dick and Jane primer as the frame text of *The Bluest Eye*, so does she use the Uncle Remus "Tar Baby" story to frame her novel by that title. Joel Chandler Harris was as much an influence in shaping White attitudes in the early part of this century as were the Dick and Jane series; if both were not actually taught in schools, lessons were drawn from both—to the detriment of Blacks. Clearly, it was Harris's intention to portray the Southern plantation as a utopian paradise, where Blacks were contented with their lot. As Darwin T. Turner writes, "Harris's memorable Negroes, in general, fit comfortably into the familiar stereotypes of the plantation myth: the wise, venerable old-time Negro, the devoted slave, the mammy, the comic darky, and the pathetic freedman" (1981, p. 117). So Morrison responds to the politics of racist teachings that have been reflected in the language and thinking of White America.

The phrase "nigger in the woodpile," for example, occurs in the story "Uncle Remus's Political Theories" and in Morrison's *Tar Baby*. In the Harris story, Uncle Remus portrays an Uncle Tom attitude, protesting against any interest in Constitutional rights for Blacks, preferring to think, argue, and talk about food, like "Marse John's pot er greens an' Miss Sally's biled ham" (1918, p.169). To show his disapproval of Blacks being in political office instead of working in the fields alongside their neighbors, Uncle Remus uses the metaphor of "the nigger in the woodpile":

> De nigger in de wood-pile—dey put 'im in dar, an' now dey dunno how ter git 'im out. Dey fling de wood fus' on one side de fence an' den on de udder, an' den dey hove it 'round de yard, but de nigger he in dar, an' dar he gwineter stay. Hit's my idee dat he ain't playin' no fav'rites dis season. (p. 167)

The metaphor seems to suggest that Blacks during Reconstruction are stuck up with their new freedom and don't know how to be citizens, much less officials. They should return to the simpler life before Reconstruction (the life of the genteel plantation days), when slaves understood their "place."

Morrison reappropriates the phrase "nigger in the woodpile" with its condescending nastiness. She does this by situating *Tar Baby* in the part of the part of the world (West Indies) that provided source material for Harris's folklore. In the West Indies there were Brer Spider, Brer Hawk, Sis Ground Dove, and many other animal characters who employed wit to "outfox" their enemies. The fables, like the Remus stories, contained a Mammie figure of the West Indian bush and the old Gagool of the African West Coast (Anonymous, 1905, 1981). Morrison rewrites Harris by emphasizing the wisdom of Black lore on the one hand and the evils of modern day slavery, called colonialism, on the other hand. In the novel Margaret Lenore, a White colonist in the Caribbean, uses the phrase "nigger in the woodpile" (p. 83) to refer to the presence in her dark closet of a Black man, Son, who is hiding. Suddenly, out of the White woman's closet, or woodpile, appears the Black man—surely a sexual metaphor of the overly civilized (overly repressed) Margaret Lenore's desires. Son is a runaway Haitian, very, very Black, whose difference is everything the White colonists are not.

> A man without human rites: unbaptized, uncircumcised, minus puberty rites or the formal rites of manhood. Unmarried and undivorced. He had attended no funeral, married in no church, raised no child. Propertyless, homeless, sought for but not after. (pp. 165–166)

To further his difference—his presence as the "other"—Morrison emphasizes his dreadlocks, his hunger, his smell, his sex, and his dream magic.

A counterpart to this scene of Son in the closet looking at Margaret is a flashback to Margaret in the nursery looking at her son. In one of the more bizarre confessions in literature, the scene describes Margaret's loathing of her son sleeping in "stupid trust" (p. 236). Outraged at her baby's needfulness, she had developed the habit of marking his "sweet creamy flesh" with "a delicious pin-stab" (p. 231). Marking, during slavery, was the sign that indicated White ownership of Black flesh. In this bizarre confession of Margaret's marking of her son's White flesh, the horror of marking, once considered acceptable, takes on new register. What is indicated is how far removed from humanity is this White mother: "No world in the world would be imagined ... that would permit such a thing to happen" (p. 234). In these counterpart scenes Morrison turns stereotypes inside out and upside down, shaking them loose from their literal stigma against Blacks and turning them into White stigmas (stigmatas, even).

The flashback scene serves several purposes. It serves, for one, as another instance of the text-on-text approach I see operating in Morrison's writing. Besides the Harris stories, another text on which the counterpart scene comments is Jonathan Swift's satiric "A Modest Proposal" (1742/1988), in which it is suggested that to solve the Irish famine young children should be fattened for slaughter. "A young healthy child well nursed is at a year old a most delicious, nourishing, and wholesome food, whether stewed, roasted, baked, or broiled" (p. 34). Morrison's descriptors of her White baby's skin as "sweet creamy flesh" and the use of the food word "delicious" to describe Margaret's masochism provide clues into Swift's text.

Besides contextualizing stereotypes and traditional assumptions, Morrison draws attention to the uses and abuses of food. Food as a literal nourisher is featured prominently in all of Morrison's novels; every novel has at least one major food scene. In *The Bluest Eye* food is most associated with the least admirable character, Cholly. Cholly remembers watermelon on the Fourth of July in a scene that starts in stereotype and then dashes it to the ground. He watches through boyish eyes as a nice old man named Blue Jack holds a watermelon above his head:

> Watching the figure etched against the bright blue sky, Cholly felt goose pimples popping along his arms and neck. He wondered if God looked like that. No. God was a nice old white man, with long, white hair, flowing white beard, and little blue eyes.... It must be the devil who looks like that—holding the world in his hands, ready to dash it to the ground and spill the red guts so niggers could eat the sweet, warm insides. (pp. 2,141–2,142)

Cholly and his father then eat "the heart" of the watermelon, "the nasty-sweet guts of the earth" (p. 2,142).

What I find remarkable in this passage is the absolute lack of stereotype (while yet employing it on the surface) and the uncanny mix of opposites. Those kitsch pictures of happy Black children smiling over the wide pink watermelon mouth are brought to mind only to be smashed. The watermelon becomes a significant food, not just a pink pleasure; it is associated with the body and the body is associated with food (the melon has guts and a heart; watching the melon gives the boy goose bumps). The moment is at once orgasmic and primal for the boy, as he shares an eating moment with his father. But an undercurrent of violence is also felt, as if this food is truly awful. Like a primal eating ritual, the scene partakes of something sacred, like a communion, which symbolizes eating the body of Christ. Symbols, Morrison shows, are not "nice" and "neat." If symbols are to convey meaning, they must be awe-full. Eating is a symbolic act that brings together opposites: sacred and profane, old and young, father and son, red and black, sweet and mean, guts and heart, devil and God.

To understand the symbolic significance of food, its role not just in digesting and nourishing but in transforming, I turn to older texts. Carl Jung (1950/1976a) based his theory of the transformation of matter into spirit on the writings of the Greek alchemists of the first to sixth centuries, like Zosimos of Panopolis. In one of his visions, Zosimos saw a priest, called the sacrificer, tear off pieces of his own flesh and eat them (in Harding, 1947/1963, p. 397). Through the sacrifice of the fleshly body, one is symbolically transformed into a state that releases one from the conflict of opposites, called the "non-two" state in Tibetan initiation (Harding, p. 401). The idea of eating the flesh survives in today's priestly incantation at the moment of the Eucharist. Holding a wafer above his head, the priest recites the words of Christ at the Last Supper: "Take and eat; this is my body" (Matthew 26:26, New American Catholic Edition). Catholics, without blinking, chew.

Now, this digression is not meant to suggest that Morrison's food scene with Cholly transforms him. It does not. But I do mean to suggest that Morrison's emphasis on food is ritualistic and primal in the manner of the old texts. As such, her emphasis introduces for the reader another consciousness "as wide as the world and open to all the world" (Jung, 1959/1977, p. 22). Just so is my under-standing of Morrison's theme of love, which, if real must always be a complex of opposites. In *Sula*, for example, a mother's love for her constipated child leads her "to shove the last bit of food she had in the world (besides three beets) up his ass" (p. 34) to free his bowels. This is a mother's love for her child. Food and love and body. In *Tar Baby* personhood is defined by food. "I may be a cook," the Black Ondine says to her White colonist employer, "but I'm a person, too" (p. 207). She goes on to contrast herself to Margaret Lenore. "She's no cook and she's no mother." The two go together: motherhood and cooking, personhood and food.

Throughout *Tar Baby* food operates as a political metaphor. I believe this is Morrison's deliberate correction of the Uncle Remus stories, where Uncle's food obsessions seem simpleminded and naïve. Here, it is the White colonists whose food obsessions seem mindlessly automatic. Their food is cooked and served by the "help." It is White, upper class eating, immaculately prepared and presented by the Black, lower class. White food is elegant, expensive, exotic. It is sanitized. It is the expected "due" of privilege. Breakfast could be croissant and mangoes, lunch could be bisque or soufflé; dinner: lobster, corn on the cob, amaretti cake, and cognac. For the colonists, wine is a theology. Dinner conver-sation, when it is not bickering, consists of speech in food measurements and calorie counts. Morrison's attention to classed detail is both humorous and sub-tle. She spends paragraphs, for example, describing the butler's impeccable, quiet serving:

> Each plate he handled with a spotlessly white napkin and was careful, as he slipped it from the blue quilted warmer, not to make a sound. When the plates were in position, he disappeared for a few seconds and returned with a smoking soufflé. He held it near Valerian a moment for inspection, and then proceeded to the sideboard to slice it into flawless, frothy wedges. (p. 71)

This is a subtly political description of the invisibility of service: unbidden but prompt; eyes shielded; "steps as felt as blackboard erasers" (p. 62). Were her point not otherwise, one might be tempted to think this house were a charming plantation with quaint servants, food as White "right."

With a rush I am remembering the house of my stepgrandmother with its live-in "help." Like the colonists' house, my stepgrandmother's house was a well-run establishment, like a hotel, with cook, gardener, and Mrs. Wheatley. I grew up with Mrs. Wheatley. My visits during holidays took me into the life of these very wealthy relatives, my mother's father and stepmother. Mrs. Wheatley was the consummate butler, whose uniform was expertly pressed and whose demeanor was perfectly masked. I never heard her laugh. She wore yel-low, which offset her red hair and indicated, even to my young eyes, a step above the cook, who wore white and never left the kitchen. For all her rank in service, Mrs. Wheatley, like her name, seemed only like bleached wheat: a yellow blur moving around the table. I don't think I thought Mrs. Wheatley was a person, really. My remembrance is of Mrs. Wheatley appearing seemingly unbidden to pass us our dishes. It wasn't until I saw Aunt Dorothy moving her foot, stamping at the carpet in awkward impatience, that I found the secret of Mrs. Wheatley's mysterious entrances. There was a bell under the carpet, which occasionally my stepgrandmother lost when summoning service.

"Knappy," on the other hand, had presence, even though she was the invisible one in our dining room. Miss Knapp, the German cook, made such lunches: salads, together with something we called goldenrod (an egg affair, light and fluffy) served over toast points; and, thinking that my brother liked angel food cake (which he didn't), always angel food cake for dessert. Her Sunday dinners were roast beef roasts with Yorkshire pudding. Always there were perfect round balls of butter, punctuated with little spikes. Morrison captures the politics of fine dining so well that I now think of what I never thought about: how classed my background was.

Morrison does not become overtly political in *Tar Baby* until she takes us into the White woman's kitchen to meet the Black "help" and into the washerwoman's cottage to meet the natives. The food Ondine and Sydney, the "help," eat is completely different from what gets served to the dining room. It is as if the two rooms of the house are two worlds. We watch Ondine prepare her husband's breakfast. We are there as she wire whisks the eggs, then stirs them in the fry pan with a wooden spoon, then adds them to a fry pan of chicken livers. We are there when Jadine, their niece, joins them, not quite used to the earthiness of this food. "The chicken's eggs and its liver?" she asks. "Is there anything inside a chicken we don't eat?" (p. 37). The question reminds us that food comes from somewhere; it is not processed; it is not fake—like White food, in Ondine's view. When hens get delivered to the kitchen, their heads must be wrung, their feathers plucked, their joints broken, their wings and little elbows removed. Similarly, the natives eat and drink hearty fare: goat meat, onions, smoked fish, pepper-hot gravy, rice, rum. They, the poor, eat "splendidly from their gardens, from the sea, and from the avocado trees that grew by the side of the road" (p. 109). They don't eat mangoes (imported) or carrots, beans, or lettuce (also imported); they eat only what they themselves grow, catch, or slaughter.

Having established two quite different food politics of Blacks and Whites, Morrison turns her attention to the focal interest of the novel, the high-yellow girl Jadine, whose patrons are the wealthy White colonists and whose aunt is Ondine, the cook. Jadine is between the Black world of the kitchen and the White world of the dining room. She is the focus of the story because she has rejected her roots, having been brought up to believe White stereotypes. Because she chooses White dining, this means she chooses White, upper class rituals. Money bleaches. Morrison implies that Jadine needs tar in her life. Another way to say this is as the washerwoman Marie Thérèse put it: "She has forgotten her ancient properties" (p. 305).

Morrison indicates this loss of deep connection to a people and a culture by the food Jadine eats. She seems not to appreciate the breakfast her uncle eats—eggs and chicken livers—wondering what "else" can be eaten out of a chicken; and she prefers what her aunt says no one (except the upper class) eats for breakfast: mangoes. She has a yen for whipped cream. By such frothy indications she sets herself apart from Ondine and Sydney's hearty tastes and habits. Later, Morrison shows just how gentrified Jadine's food tastes are when her shopping list in Paris is described: "Major Grey's chutney, real brown rice, fresh pimento, tamarind rinds, coconut and the split breasts of two young lambs.... Chinese mushrooms and arugula; palm hearts and Bertolli's Tuscany olive oil" (p. 44). Educated, elite, and photographed, she is a model who dreams of White beauties like Norma Shearer, Mae West, and Jeanette MacDonald. She is everything the little Black child Pecola in *The Bluest Eye* is not; although, like the Black child, Jadine thinks beauty can only be White. It is my understanding that Jadine is Morrison's idea of the problem for liberated Black women who, fleeing Black stereotypes, run away from their souls. They need to see beauty in the tar.

One of the most controversial Black stereotypes Morrison raises is that of Mammy. Even today, Black feminists like bell hooks want nothing to do with the "all nourishing breast" idea implanted in Mammy. The rereleasing of *Gone With the Wind*, with Hattie McDaniel's nostalgic portrayal of Mammy, is obscene in this regard when one considers that McDaniel, who won an Academy Award for her role, could not attend the segregated movie house for the Atlanta premiere (Winbush, 1998). One wonders if the return to nostalgia for the past that never was will bring with it a new epic of stereotypes. But perhaps it is time to rethink the problem feminists have with body imagery. Perhaps, as Denise Taliaferro (1999) proposes, the Mammy idea of woman as nourisher serves to correct an overemphasis on woman as intellectual. That, in any case, is how I read Morrison's emphasis on breasts in *Tar Baby*, particularly the nightmare breasts that torture Jadine.

It is a recurring nightmare. Jadine's room fills with women. The dreamer knows they want something with her; their night visits are meant to remind her of something she has been denying or has forgotten: her connection to her own mother (not her patron mother Margaret Lenore) and to Ondine. They come to accuse her of assimilation. As dreams do, they speak in images. "They stood around in the room, jostling each other gently, gently—there wasn't much room—revealing one breast and then two" (p. 258). When Jadine protests that she has breasts too, the dream women don't believe her. And then her dream features the figure of a woman she had met in Paris, tar black and sassy, who had spat at Jadine. At the time, the incident in real life was upsetting, but not life-changing. In the nightmare, the tar woman reappears holding three eggs. It is clear to the reader that Jadine's confrontation with the tar black woman had been the sort of encounter that happens rarely but that offers opportunity to change a life's course. The nightmare, with its accusatory women, bodies forth breasts and eggs, the very symbols of female creativity. And because the women in the dream are of her race they demand recognition. Their representations are meant to reveal to her the "monstrosities" of her assimilation into the racist methods of liberal humanism (Sartre, in Fanon, 1963, p. 8). Her unconscious warns her. The question is: Is she too colonized to read the dream?

Morrison's use of dreams as the language of the unconscious is so important for modern readers. Too many students tell me they either don't dream or don't believe in dreams. Like Jadine, they are too busy in their day world to pay attention to their night world. But as this episode indicates, to ignore these speakings and visitations is to risk one's soul. In the novel, Jadine returns to Paris to resume her life as a model, leaving behind her adoptive mother and her native people who are like the mud mothers, connected to the soil and to their own sources of power. But because she follows the caprices and habits of the colonists, Jadine loses her real identity. As Franz Fanon (1963) analyzes the problem, she cuts her "moorings" and "breaks adrift" from her people (p. 217).

Jadine had several opportunities to make the connections that would root her inside her exceptional "Mammy" femaleness. Her dreams were telling her to identify with her natural body. Her aunt advised her that being a woman involves learning how to be a daughter first; that is, to remember that she had a Black mother. But the most prolonged symbolic passage occurs when Jadine becomes literally stuck in the mud. The experience, a sort of mud baptism, could have rebirthed her consciousness, for Morrison's descriptions imply that nature was trying to woo her back: "She ... grabbed the waist of a tree which shivered in her arms and swayed as though it wished to dance with her" (p. 182). Made immobile by the mud, Jadine thinks of the life-saving tree as her lover:

> Don't sweat or you'll lose your partner, the tree. Cleave together like lovers. Press together like man and wife. Cling to your partner, hang on to him and never let him go. Creep up on him a millimeter at a time, slower than the slime and cover him like the moss. Caress his bark and finger his ridges. Sway when he sways and shiver with him too. Whisper your numbers from one to fifty into the parts that have been lifted away and left tender skin behind. Love him and trust him with your life because you are up to your kneecaps in rot. (pp. 182–183)

The immersion scene loses its significance for Jadine, however. She only wishes to be free of swamp rot. Morrison has her play out Fanon's scenario of the estranged native: "because he feels that he is the living haunt of contradictions which run the risk of becoming insurmountable, the native tears himself away from the swamp that may suck him down" (Fanon, p. 218). And so Jadine, having lost her soul, becomes enslaved by arrogance.

Who is free? Who slave? These questions hover over the surface of every Morrison text. In the "Wonderful Tar Baby Story," Joel Chandler Harris' (1918) message is the "master" text that Morrison submerges in *Tar Baby* in order to subvert. I read the buried text as impetus to her comment on existential freedom and identity politics. Recall: Brer Fox (White master), for once, catches Brer Rabbit (Black slave)—an unusual feat since the rabbit usually eludes capture. The rabbit is outfoxed by a Tar-Baby (female lure); she just sits there in her hat (Jadine) not responding to his greetings or questions. Furious, Brer Rabbit hauls off and hits her, only to get stuck in tar. How does Morrison use this frame text? On a superficial level, Son (the trickster rabbit figure) is "stuck" on Jadine (whose hat nightmares connect her to the tar baby figure); but he escapes from her hold on him when he returns "lickety split" to the land where he had been bred and born. With this interpretation, I see Morrison calling for a symbolic return to native values so as to escape being "stuck" by stereotyping.

More. I am struck by the similarity I suspect Morrison was contextualizing between White and Black texts with the story of Son. The opening description of *Tar Baby* is of Son, a stowaway aboard a ship, seeking return to his native Haiti. At first I intuit White texts hovering. Son's return is the *Return of the Native*; it is Adam, the first son of man, returning to paradise at the end of the world, a world of daisy trees, parrots, "the sea-green green of the sea and the sky-blue sky of the sky" (p. 9). Son looks out from the deck of the ship. Morrison writes, "There he saw the stars and exchanged stares with the moon, but he could see very little of the land, which was just as well because he was gazing at the shore of an island that, three hundred years ago, had struck slaves blind the moment they saw it" (p. 8). But a Black text hovers, too, calling forth an irony between Son's return in full freedom to his native land versus African slaves' arrival in full servitude to their prison land. Compare, for example, "The Interesting Narrative of the life of Olaudah Equiano, or Gustavus Vassa, the African" (Equiano, 1789/1997):

> The first object which saluted my eyes when I arrived on the coast, was the sea, and a slave ship, which was then riding at anchor, and waiting for its cargo. These filled me with astonishment, which was soon converted into terror, when I was carried on board. I was immediately handled, and tossed up to see if I were sound, by some of the crew; and I was now persuaded that I had gotten into a world of bad spirits, and that they were going to kill me.... At last, we came in sight of the island of Barbados, at which the whites on board gave a great shout, and made many signs of joy to us.... They told us we were not to be eaten, but to work, and we were soon to go on land, where we should see many of our country people. This report eased us much. And sure enough, soon after we were landed, there came to us Africans of all languages.... O, ye nominal Christians! might not an African ask you—Learned you this from your God, who says unto you, Do unto all men as you would men should do unto you? Is it not enough that we are torn from our country and friends, to toil for your luxury and lust of gain? (pp. 9, 11–12)

I claim no one-on-one correspondence between these two passages; but, knowing Morrison's use of history in her fiction, I cite the slave narrative as a likely kind of text she may have had in mind while composing her novel. The juxtaposition of situations—both Black men aboard ships facing land in the West Indies—is an overpowering reminder, at the very least, of how the past cannot be forgotten, even in fiction. "Apparently," Faulkner writes, "there is a wisdom beyond that even learned in suffering necessary for a man to distinguish between liberty and license" (1942/1961, p. 278). To recall the slaves' arrival centuries earlier in the West Indies at the moment of Son's return is Morrison's brilliant way of pointing out that colonization is just a milder form of slavery. And that, oddly, sometimes benign tyranny poses the greater threat precisely because it is less obvious.

One of the effects of juxtaposing texts in Morrison's work is that it opens every situation. One of the effects, too, of showing characters in opposite pairs, as is so often the structuring device of her work, is to suggest that personhood is more than one, more than the ego self. In *Tar Baby*, Jadine's opposite is the tar woman in yellow who, because she troubles Jadine, functions as Jadine's shadow—a very tall (over six feet) shadow. The unnamed woman is the one Morrison describes as being tar black; it is she who haunts Jadine's dreams and lends another meaning to the title, *Tar Baby*. To see the tar baby as Jadine's "other" is to imply that one cannot simply move to Paris to escape one's roots or essence. No matter how far she travels, Jadine will be haunted by her shadow until, and only until, she acknowledges her Blackness and refuses to pass. This lesson is profound; it is a life lesson that Morrison's fiction teaches; it is a lesson on how to recover the true self from the artificial self and to know the difference between the two. As Morrison said, "If there is any consistent theme in my fiction, I guess that is it—how and why we learn to live this life intensely and well" (1972, p. 50).

Another of Morrison's oppositely paired characters are Nell and Sula in *Sula*. Like their personalities, the houses they grew up in were complete opposites. Nell's was oppressively neat and Sula's was "woolly": where "all sorts of people dropped in; newspapers were stacked in the hallway, and dirty dishes left for hours at a time in the sink, and where a one-legged grandmother named Eva handed you goobers from deep inside her pockets or read you a dream" (p. 29). Despite the differences, the girls were "two throats and one eye" (p. 147). Nell, simply put, loved Sula. And Sula, even though she stole Nell's husband and became the town's pariah, taught Nell about the vastness of love. In a speech I could call The Sermon on the Bottom, Sula knows that the village will love even her because of the impossibility of their ceasing to love one another:

> Oh, they'll love me all right. It will take time, but they'll love me.... After all the old women have lain with the teenagers; when all the young girls have slept with their old drunken uncles; after all the black men fuck all the white ones; when all the white women kiss all the black ones; when the guards have raped all the jail-birds and after all the whores make love to their grannies ... then there'll be a little love left over for me. And I know just what it will feel like. (pp. 145–146)

Once again, Morrison startles us with the fierceness of a love so strong that it can survive all improbabilities. She shows us, with these images, that being different—as Sula is to her community—is not cause enough to stop the loving. What an addition to the concept "love" that would be!

And, of course, that is Morrison's project: to turn assumed concepts into felt truths. She does this transformative magic by employing three distinct languages of comedy: the language of opposites that refuse opposition, the language of enchantment that insists on surprise, and the language of knowing that is not mentation. That each of these subsets of Black language is modified by negatives is, I believe, essential to Morrison's writing. She insists on "images of the zero, the absence, the silence that is both chosen and enforced" (Rigney, 1991, p. 25). A reader has to read through her litany of negatives in the beginnings of her novels in order for her to clear the path for a different kind of understanding—a third thing. In *Tar Baby*, for example, we meet an unnamed man in "a bracelet of water" that yanks him into "a wide, empty tunnel," described as "a wet throat" ready to swallow him. "He went down, down and found himself not at the bottom of the sea, as he expected, but whirling in a vortex" (1987c, p. 4). Into these deep waters this reader, too, is plunged, forced to wash away many traditional ideas about love. For Morrison, love is neither task nor splendor. It cannot be counted, any more than it can be counted on. It is not belief nor hope nor charity. It is not soft, but sharp. It is not possession—(most assuredly, it is not possession: that which capitalism praises and slavery entitles). All of those nice ideas have occupied the center places, "places in which we resist knowing and effectively will our own ignorance" (Edgerton, 1993, p. 233). Rather, Morrison describes what Susan Edgerton calls "love in the margins."

Morrison helps us chart the waters of these "othered" places primarily through depictions of her female characters or those who connect with their feminine side, like Son in *Tar Baby* or Milkman Dead in *Song of Solomon* (1987a). Her female characters are most often paired as necessary opposites: Claudia and Pecola, Jadine and the woman in yellow, Beloved and Denver, Nell and Sula, and the whole group of waifs and strays that occupy the convent, in *Paradise* (1998b). Most notable of these pairings are Pilate and Ruth Dead, sisters-in-law, in *Song of Solomon*:

> They were so different, these two women. One black, the other lemony. One corseted, the other buck naked under her dress. One well read but ill traveled. The other had read only a geography book, but had been from one end of the country to another. One wholly dependent on money for life, the other indifferent to it. But those were the meaningless things. Their similarities were profound. (p. 139)

Now, canonical tradition has prominently featured male pairings of opposite-likes. It is refreshing to find a writer who privileges the female double. Her purpose, I suggest, is to show for women, as has been shown for men, that energy and creativity can be activated when female opposites come together. The double in literature can be seen as a structure of consciousness. It not only broadens the notion of the singular ego-self, it also challenges the inertia of dualities. By seeing opposites together, especially female opposites, Morrison endows her female characters with the same kind of dynamic potential that male characters have traditionally enjoyed.

This is a consistent emphasis in her work. Polarities of all sorts combine, join, entangle, enmesh, and interact. By her so doing, Morrison puts together what Descartes split asunder, creating not a fusion or a melting pot, but a new, other, third thing; call it a perfect egg:

> Now, the water and the egg have to meet each other on a kind of equal standing. One can't get the upper hand over the other.... When the tiny bubbles come to the surface, when they as big as peas and just before they get big as marbles. Well, right then you take the pot off the fire. You don't just put the fire out; you take the pot off. Then you put a folded newspaper over the pot and do one small obligation. Like answering the door or emptying the bucket and bringing it in off the front porch. I generally go to the toilet. Not for a long stay, mind you. Just a short one. If you do all that, you got yourself a perfect soft-boiled egg. (1987a, pp. 39–40)

I don't believe Morrison is just talking about food here, although she is talking about food, too. She is having the earth mother Pilate teach an approach to cooking, living life, and bringing forth newness. That the egg, in the preceding passage, is a female symbol of birth is, in my view, deliberate. Pilate (traditionally assumed to be Christ-killer) becomes here a sort of pagan-female-Christ teacher. As Wendy Atwell-Vasey might put it, she is teacher as "agent of love and enterprise" (1998, p. 107). As such Morrison's women extend possibilities, explore affinities and celebrate ambivalence in ways that expand life's virtualities. She insists that identity be re-cognized in the double, one's own "other" (Harding & Martin, 1994).

Consistent with her presentation of twinned characters, Morrison occasionally has a solo figure, usually male, who undergoes a quest for wholeness. Even that quest, however, is different from the traditional male, heroic quest pattern described by Joseph Campbell as a monolithic journey, always the same, of departure-encounter-return (1949). Shadrack, the mad fringe character in *Sula*, opens and closes the novel, serving effectively as a marginal trickster figure. Made mad by his war experience, Shadrack returns home to the Bottom, where he initiates his own ritual, called Suicide Day, at the beginning of every new year. He is tolerated the way medieval societies tolerated madmen with their rope, bell, and childish dirges. Clearly, Shadrack is neither hero nor antihero, for he encounters no beasts and slays no dragons. He importantly reenacts a fool's role and inaugurates a ritual, strange as it was, for the community: "Easily, quietly, Suicide Day became a part of the fabric of life up in the Bottom of Medallion, Ohio" (p. 16). It is the creating power of Shadrack's frenzied ritual that paradoxically holds Bottom together, a holding that can only be described as "love." For, as Crazy Jane put it on the Day of Judgment, in Yeats's song poem, "'Love is all/ Unsatisfied/ That cannot take the whole/ body and soul'" (1933/ 1959, p. 252).

Similarly, *Song of Solomon* is a love song of one man's rediscovery of his roots. Milkman Dead, like Shadrack, is associated with female symbols—his are milk and moon, Shadrack's is moon—and so the quest pattern of these males partakes of a feminine heroism, which is noncombattive and relational. But Milkman's quest does not start out that way. At first he is his father's son, intent upon acquiring literal gold, property, and possession. But as he gets lost in the wilderness, on his quest for gold, he has troublesome thoughts. "Under the moon, on the ground, alone, with not even the sound of baying dogs to remind him that he was with other people, his self—the cocoon that was personality—gave way" (p. 277). Milkman's disintegration of "personality," like Shadrack's madness, puts him inside another mind place altogether, where he recovers an undiscovered self. Morrison ends her fable with a response to the opening scene of a man's plunge to his death. At the end, Milkman's reconnection with his roots is symbolized by a fantasy of flight: "If you surrendered to the air, you could *ride* it" (p. 337). Without ever leaving the ground, he flies. His newfound "lightness of being" (Kundera, 1988) is, well, the miracle of rootedness.

Morrison shows that love, besides speaking the language of connected opposites, speaks the language of enchantment. This language embraces the miracles that occur, unbidden, to those who cherish the metaphorical gold in their souls—dreamers, imaginers, and fantasy seekers. Little visits with and reminders of the dead, for example, occur with regularity to these people; the dead are not separated from the living. These visitations provide a sense of continuity to the characters, for whom the "real" world of commerce is unsustainable. Ruth, Milkman's mother, exists inside a loveless marriage to a man who seeks only the literal gold that he collects from renters. His wife disgusts him. Ruth is able to bear her existence because of her "posthumous communication" (p. 139) with her father, whose grave she visits for solace. She feels his presence, too, in the watermark on her dining room table. The mark had been made when she lived with her father and adorned the center of his table with flowers. The mark was her mooring, "a checkpoint, some stable visible object that assured her that the world was still there; that this was life and not a dream. That she was alive somewhere, inside, which she acknowledged to be true only because a thing she knew intimately was out there, outside herself" (p. 11).

It should not be difficult to understand the mooring of an object's hold on a person. Think back into childhood and any of us might recall the magic of an alabaster lamb or the enchantment of a first ring. It is an old idea that has long attracted writers and philosophers of art. Samuel Beckett (1931) called the experience of encountering objects "mystical" and "extra temporal," partaking of "sacred action" (p. 56). Borrowing from Marcel Proust, Beckett wrote that objects trigger "involuntary" memory because they "hoist" (p. 19) the deep source—an other world, a visionary experience—one not subject to the laws of will, conscious voluntarism, or reality. Its otherness takes one "out" of the sealed jar of literalism. Suzanne Langer (1953), in a phrase that unhappily recalls cyberspace, wrote of art's "virtual" reality, which reveals the character of subjectivity while being objective, "its purpose to objectify the life of feeling" (p. 374). T. S. Eliot's (1932) theory is that poetry offers an "objective correlative." The shift from subject to object enables what Owen Barfield (1960) called "double vision" or what Philip Wheelwright (1968) termed "hovering presence." All of these observations and experiences are no more superstitious than is kissing the cross. Rather, they are endowed with meaning because they "rend the curtain that veils the cosmos" (Jung, 1930/1950, p. 90).

Magic and mystery, accordingly, are not given special places *out there* or *back then* but in here, *as well as* out there, back then, and down always. The enchantment objects bring to the senses and to memory is the enchantment that comes from the nonhuman realm, like objects, dreams, or ghosts. As Morrison herself put it: "My own use of enchantment simply comes because that's the way the world was for me and for the black people I knew.... It functioned as a raiment—the body that was in the middle was something quite different—and also it was part and parcel of this extraordinary language" (in Taylor-Guthrie, 1994, p. 226). I suppose New Agers would call this concept "aura"; but Morrison's word is more specific. According to Webster (1993), raiment means "clothing; apparel; attire. See array." Under array: "2) to clothe with garments, esp. of an ornamental kind; dress up; deck out." Emphasis here is on decorative layering. The body, material being, is less attracting than what is draped around it. Morrison is careful to distinguish what she means by enchantment or raiment from the evasive label "magic realism," because for her there is "this other knowledge or perception" (in Taylor-Guthrie, p. 226) that is both informing and clarifying; important in a way that the label "magic realism" dismisses. That so many of her characters have the ability to perceive raiment is not just wonderful, it is salvivic and psychologically necessary. One of the most striking instances might be the memory of Beloved's raiment. The raiment is of the white stairs the baby loved to climb. The whiteness seems to encase Beloved the baby in a cocoon of love that is, however, unreal. The baby, after all, was murdered by her mother. She hates being dead. The white stairs image reappears mysteriously in the text, such that the reader feels haunted by the "scariness of things with no name" (in Leonard, 1998, p. 29). When the murdered baby reappears as a ghost, she becomes what Yeats called "love's skein" (1933/1959, p. 253), the intertwining connection of the ordinary with enchantments.

Indeed, Morrison's extraordinary writings deliteralize a reader's expectations. This is her language of love. Isn't that what we should be doing more of in the classroom: speaking scary love-language so as to nudge ourselves and our students' selves off the rock of literalism? David Jardine (1994) comments that his teaching of mathematical language through story (of all modes!) was painful for some students in his Early Childhood Education class. He counters, "The work they did in this class was not meant to make their lives *easier*, but to begin to free them for the real difficulty, the real claim that language makes on us" (p. 227). Yes. To be rocked off the rock of the literal letter is to plunge into the running water. According to Lao Tzu, the course of life is letting the waters flow: "How can a man's life keep its course if he will not let it flow?" he asks (in Bynner, 1944/1980, p. 15). Morrison continually demonstrates that enchantment occurs naturally, in nature, in our surroundings, in other speakings through other tongues. Like dreams. Listen to Sethe, mother-murderer of Beloved, responding to her dreams:

> When her dreams roamed outside 124, anywhere they wished, she saw them sometimes in beautiful trees, their little legs barely visible in the leaves. Sometimes they ran along the railroad track laughing, too loud, apparently, to hear her because they never did turn around. (1988, p. 39)

Like nature. Listen to Paul D. talking as a slave in the corn field about the corn stalks: "How loose the silk. How jailed down the juice" (p. 27). Nothing to the eyes of these beholders is just as it is; the thing is more, always more. Never one solitary isolation.

And listen, too, to the way nature became a text for illiterate slaves, like Paul D. He read his way to freedom by watching the blossoms take bloom from South to North:

> So he raced from dogwood to blossoming peach. When they thinned out he headed for the cherry blossoms, then magnolia, chinaberry, pecan, walnut and prickly pear. At last he reached a field of apple trees whose flowers were just becoming tiny knots of fruit. Spring sauntered north, but he had to run like hell to keep it as his traveling companion. (p. 112)

Nature for fugitive slaves became a salvivic Book of Knowledge. It presented a marvelous, living energy, expressed in many blossoming forms, readable by those used to the chain of signifiers known as "the talking book." This "talking book" signified "upon another chain, the metaphorical Great Chain of Being" (Gates, 1988, p. 167). And so to achieve selfhood a slave had to "master" not only the text of nature but also the talk of the master culture. The way to freedom was by reading these various literacies. To think that knowledge systems of contemporary Eurocentric knowledge communities have monologolized the tongues is to regret the loss of the marvelous.

Morrison addresses this pedagogical question about how different "languages" can teach modes of knowing and how these modes are spokes on the wheel of comedy. These differences may have more to do with real knowing than what customarily passes as "the real" in academies. Certainly, as the previous paragraph indicated, what could have been more real than reading one's way to freedom by interpreting blossoms? It is curious that at the end of the 20th century our reading skills have not improved. Where once all of nature could be read, metals read, and stars read for wisdom, now all the rage is for "improving" reading skills by ever more testing. But the knowledge of most worth cannot be found in test scores or easy-to-read primers. Isn't that obvious? How many times have I misread a facial expression or kept my head buried in the sand lest I hear the unsaid thing that disrupts my complacency? How many gestures have I ignored because they did not fit into my picture (text) of my understanding of a person? How many repetitions of the same act must I undergo in my repressed ignorance until I learn to understand my obsession? When will I listen to my itch? These are merely some of the other speakings that Morrison's people continually hear. Understanding, for them, is always a coursing: "Sweet, crazy conversations full of half sentences, daydreams, and misunderstandings more thrilling than understanding could ever be" (1988, p. 67).

And, finally, love is con-fusing, Morrison's work shows us. Morrison would be the first not to reduce love to its most common denominator. Friendliness is not the same as love. When Black love is equated with wholesome environments, apology, forgiveness, and hope, something too simple is being advocated. The Essence message calling for a revolution of love is entirely too essentialist (Coleman, 1988, p. A15). Similarly, classrooms that promote a feel-good environment are not doing the difficult work of teaching understanding. Although joking, storytelling, music, orality, and laughter are all ways to diffuse literalism, and although they are enjoyable activities, these methods are not sufficient to produce the knowledge of most worth.

In another of Morrison's signature woman-monologues, she has Baby Suggs, the earthmother-priestess-Jesus figure in *Beloved*, give her Sermon in the Clearing. As you read it, listen for the texture and the song in the words. Listen for its edgy truth, what Milan Kundera calls the "revenge against the impersonality of the history of humanity" (1996, p. 16). Feel, too, its fierce lion's tooth bite. Then tell me if this is not what love can be:

> "Here," she said, "in this place, we flesh; flesh that weeps, laughs; flesh that dances on bare feet in grass. Love it. Love it hard. Yonder they do not love your flesh. They despise it. They don't love your eyes; they'd just as soon pick em out.... And all your inside parts that they'd just as soon slop for hogs, you got to love them. The dark, dark liver—love it, love it, and the beat and beating heart, love that too ... " Saying no more, she stood up then and danced with her twisted hip the rest of what her heart had to say while the others opened their mouths and gave her the music. (pp. 88–89)

❦11❧

Spider Woman

Thought-Woman, the spider,
named things and
as she named them
they appeared.

She is sitting in her room
thinking of a story now ...

—Silko (1986, p. 1)

I am sitting in my room, thinking about the way Native-American women have been taught from their mothers to think about themselves, based on the legend of Spider Woman. I draw on several resources to tell this story, which is not my story but which has much to teach me. I think of my hard chair as a rock at the outermost point of my house; of the gray computer screen as the void about to be filled; of the stirrings of uneasy agitation in my gut as the thread waits to spin out. As I imagine these four things—rock, void, gut, thread—perhaps I can articulate this story, which is not my story, but about which I am drawn to speak-write. Spider Woman's legend offers much to women brought up in a culture that has been formed by classical Western (not Native-American) myths, legends, and Bibles. Spider Woman teaches women many things, not the least of which is a different meaning of beauty and power. Spider Woman is as much a figure for woman power as Zeus or Jehovah is for male power; the difference, however, is absolute.

In Eastern-European culture, the closest representation of Spider Woman would seem to be Shakti or Kali; Western European's similitude would be Medusa or Hekate. These are destroyer goddesses, multi-armed and rapacious. Hekate, like Medusa, has a necklace of testicles and hair of writhing snakes (Leeming & Page, 1994). A frequent pattern in their myths is that of the god-

189

dess as serpent. Once, however, the serpent was a symbol of inner knowledge, wisdom, and fertility. Medusa, accordingly, was long ago a serpent goddess who ruled Africa and who was beautiful. Eve's serpent can also be read more primally, not as a tempter but as a connector to earth's knowledge:

> The snake as a symbol of rebirth following death is an ancient, yet ever-present conception which can be traced through endless patterns of sculpture, painting, verse, and the *myths of gods, demigods or heroic mortals.* This is so because during its yearly period of hibernation the snake sheds its skin and reappears as if renewed. The wisdom of the serpent, which is suggested by its watchful lidless eye, lies essentially in *mankind's* having projected into this lowly creature *his own secret wish to obtain from the earth a knowledge* he cannot find in waking daylight consciousness alone. (Henderson & Oakes, 1990, pp. 36–37, italics added)

The book from which the preceding quote is taken is dedicated "To the Memory of Professor C. G. Jung." The quote, although useful, bears out a prejudice in Jungian circles toward an exclusive use of masculine references. The urge to know, seen as a godly heroic quest, is male, heroic, rational, and driven. A far more believable association of snake with female knowing is its cyclical shedding, which relates to a woman's menstrual pattern. Seen thus, females do not need to "obtain from the earth a knowledge" because such knowledge lies hidden within the female body.

The hideousness of the serpent goddess can clearly be seen in the myth of Medusa, one of the three sister Gorgons who turned men to stone. I find it telling that Campbell's (1974) compendium *The Mythic Image* does not mention the Gorgons and gives only one phrase to Medusa (p. 121). Could this be that the hairy one is too much a fearsome crone? Barbara Walker (1985) speculates that the crone's wisdom and power, located in the birth-giving womb, was a source of male envy: "The whole premise of Christianity was, like ascetic Buddhism, that to achieve a rejection of death, man must reject the Mother manifested in all women" (p. 82). More to the point is Christine Downing's (1989) treatment of mythological images, wherein Medusa receives four entries that explore the treatment of her frightening image by such scholars as Jane Harrison and Sigmund Freud. The latter, of course, saw Medusa's head as representing the terrifying genitals of the Great Mother; but Downing argues, convincingly I think, that Medusa represents simply another side of Athene's heady, rational character:

> There is a powerful instinctual feminine side of Athene which she does not really hide at all. When she wears the Gorgon-head, it conveys the dark sources of her power but it does not destroy or petrify. Once again we are in the realm of reversal: the dark side is what redeems.... The Gorgon which originally was conceived as an ugly demon becomes, in later sculptural representations, a beautiful angel; thus, there develops a new myth: it was because of Athene's envy of her beauty that Medusa was killed. (pp. 124–125)

This discussion may sound a bit like he-said, she-said, but it is necessary so as to provide alternative readings, not just of the bad girl, but of the terrible woman. Something there is in the visage of Medusa and other goddesses, like Kali or Spider Woman, that has been transcribed (largely by male scholars) as horrible and death-dealing—but attracting, nonetheless. Perhaps, as Patricia Berry (1981) muses, this terrible beauty "is one way of stating the deepest mysteries of the earth.... We approach (Medusa) as a stopping, static threat" (pp. 83, 85). Women poets have been fascinated by this "still" power of Medusa. Louise Bogan (1923/1985), in "Medusa," places her in a "dead scene" "forever now" (p. 1,611), and pictures her standing still with "eyes on the yellow dust, that was lifting in the wind, And does not drift away" (p. 1,611). The poet captures in her oxymoron "still" an aliveness within nonmoving dust. Differently, Sylvia Plath (1962/1985) draws a connection between the negative power of Medusa and that of her own mother on the other end of a tentacled telephone cable, "old barnacled umbilicus" (p. 2,209). The mother's punishing reach is inescapable, unbeckoned, an "eely tentacle" (p. 2,210). More positively, May Sarton (1974) sees in Medusa's frozen rage a gift offered for her contemplation of another face of herself (p. 332).

I, too, have been drawn into Medusa's power, figuring myself as Medusa's daughter:

> I sit on your bed
> you amidst your bed sheets drinking
> coffee I cannot drink hair
> wild, not from the toss of nights
> but from the cortisone.
>
> Your gaze turns my heart to stone.
> I fasten my eyes on you
> and look and look. Better
> than Perseus, this meeting
> of the mother and the daughter, better
> because sadder.
>
> You tell me your scaly skin is cancer.
> 'It will be my last Christmas,' you say.
> I question you about this. My breath
> fills the room with a rush
> of wind and my eye
> stutters.
>
> Here, Mother, take my eye.
> Let us be Gray Women. We will
> sit in moonless caves and
> twist snakes from our hair.
> We will wait with our bones
> on the cliff to feel the wings

flap at our backs, and we will
look deep
into the eye that passes
back
and forth
between us. Let us feel
what our hearts cannot feel and see
what our eyes cannot see as we
shroud our selves
in twilight. (Doll, 1995, p. 57)

And in another poem, written decades earlier, I share a sense of sisterhood with witches, the folk equivalent of Medusa:

Witching Hour

Day takes back its hour for-
giving the sun's strength in summer
when no growth takes place
no root seeks soil bursting into
new soil.

This hour ours: the hour
between appointments.

We share it with the worm
with rain the color of dust
with chalk-white palms
pressed against the panes, fore-
telling our need to pluck thunder
from the tree, to whip it,
to give sky another stillness (forgetting that without the thunderclap
our sky is not cleared).

If, as Esther in *The Good Child's River* asks, "Do you think a woman who could act like this was a monster?" (Wolfe, 1991, p. 273), then it is up to poet-witches, spider-writers, and indecorous teachers to recover the monsters.

And so I put on my spider pin, with its lapis lazuli body and shapely silver legs. I wait atop my chair and look out into the green fronds that beckon the birds and my gaze. I have returned from inspecting my garden that shimmers from the morning dew, and I prepare to think my story back from the litter. The thread I shall be weaving is not common. It will join inners to outers, human to nonhuman, woman to bird to tree to worm to man to place. The thoughts I spin shall join what is known by the five senses to what will be known anew by the sixth sense. It is the shape that counts.

What is known about literal spiders is that they occupy web sites, arrange their attachment points for silk above the litter layer, avoid competition, and have poor eyesight. Despite their inability to see well, spiders maneuver nimbly on their webs (Wise, 1993). Freud was said to have observed a remarkable biological fact of female spiders' superiority in copulation (Weigle, 1982). And anthropologists have described the spindle whorls of webs as almond shaped, like the vulva (in Weigle). That the spinning activity of spiders has been negatively associated with spinsters—unmarried crones—is discounted by Mary Daly and others who associate spinning with a primal, even a ludic, occupation (in Weigle). "The spider persona," scientists tell us, "is a multi-faceted creature, with roles that differ markedly, either on the same stage or between different dramas.... web-spinning spiders of the forest understorey may have little in common with cursorial spiders that range across vegetation ... (and) even less with that of cursorial spiders in the leaf litter" (Wise, 1993, p. 280). Part of the lore of the literal spider is the drama and mystery of its multiple personae.

Further, it would seem that web spinning begins in unknowing. There are no preconceived goals, no predetermined objectives for the web spinner, because the point of attachment cannot be seen. Senses must be re-sensed, re-visioned, con-fused. Surely, this process of web spinning is like art in the making, where nothing is ever known in advance. And when we gaze at a work of art there is no certainty, no thesis, no message. Emily Dickinson imagines the spider "plying" its web "from Nought to Nought/ In unsubstantial Trade" (in Oates, 1996) or, in another poem, sewing "at Night/ Without a Light" (1891/1985, p. 863). What this bad eyesight does is transform the singleness of any one sense out of its literalness, turning mere sight into insight (Hillman, 1979b). Spider-seeing is prepositional, involving overtone, undertone, undersense. What is sensed is emergent, sense emerging throughout the making, not just at the end.

Implications of such redirecting of the literal gaze and reimagining of the production of labor are profound for an understanding of the Spider Woman myth. "Profound," not "seminal," because the possibilities for future development here do not come from semen. Spider Woman's female aesthetics come from another reality principle altogether, which seeks to deliteralize dependence on seeing so as to bring back the listening ear. Such a "sound alternative" (Davis, 1996) is what Derrida (in Kamuf, 1991) calls a "sterophany" (p. 572), each utterance echoing another layer. Spider Woman stories mesh meaning with telling; they are oralities with many, many variants. Preliterate, they share the quality of a postmodern film's soundtrack: "voices, noises, atmospheres, music—and above all the possibility of acting on two senses at once, the eye and the ear" (Robbe-Grillet, in Hoder-Salmon, 1992, p. 144). "My grandmother was a storyteller," N. Scott Momaday (1968/1993) writes "And the simple act of listening is crucial to the concept of language, more crucial even than reading and writing, and language in turn is crucial to human society" (p. 1,871). And so, because the Spider Woman stories derive from an oral tradition, each storyteller's version tells us something of the storyteller's imagination as well as of the kernel of the tale. With as many as 500 original cultures in North America, with 500 distinct languages (Lincoln, 1983), the task of a nonIndian like myself to sort out meaning is confusing, to say the least. But with my sequins to inspire and my rock-hard chair to steady, allow me to dream the dream of Spider Woman onward.

Last night my dead mother, who has visited me often during the writing of this piece, came to me again. She was in the audience of a play I was performing. Others had memorized their lines, but I was still dependent on the script. I read my one line, which apparently I had not been able to memorize, and then was whirled into performance, aware always of my mother in the audience. Afterwards, she gave me a heavy necklace with shiny, black coral rings. I told her I preferred chokers, but she insisted that I wear the heavy necklace. The language of this dream urges me ever deeper into the telling of Spider Woman, which, in accordance with tradition, I shall recreate rather than recite (Kroeber, 1983).

Spider Woman has many names: Grandmother Spider, Sky Woman, Yellow Woman, Spider Old Woman, The She Sacred Woman, Serpent Woman, Corn Woman, Earth Woman, Hard Beings Woman, Changing Woman, Thought Woman. She is Grandmother of the Light, Grandmother of the Sun. She is She Who Dreams. How can I possibly find the right one? I asked myself, when beginning this project. Wrong question. The one line I could not memorize in my dream comes out of an unease in the face of such abundance. Just as there could be many ways to say my one dream line, correctly rendering it is not the issue. The issue is intent. This Changing Woman Grandmother Spider Woman will not bite as long as I can convey something of her teaching, something about recovering the feminine (Allen, 1992).

Although she is a fertility goddess, similar to those of Egypt and Greece, Spider Woman is not limited to a female role, because roles, like labels, are straight jackets. She is, rather, a Creatrix, whose creating power comes from blood, vulva, web, and thought. She is supreme spirit, both Mother and Father, parthenogenetic, born of herself, embodied. "It's so simple," Allen (1992) writes. "The stories are told over and over. There were some women—sometimes two, sometimes three, sometimes more—and they did it" (p. 57). Reproduction in the beginning was not sexual, but magical, a falling out of the sky and a spinning out of thought, which weaves implications, extrapolations, and "a few elegant day-dreams into a satisfying pattern" (p. 120). The stories about Spider Woman are like the Creation, any word leading to its particular string, one word possibly containing "scores of stories" (p. 38). Myth, the mother of life, is a noun, ritual a verb; myth is weft, ritual is woof: twin beings, like storytelling and ceremony. Spider Woman's web is a metaphor both for the process and product of this primal pedagogy.

Unlike the creation story of Genesis, Spider Woman's creation stories have a gynosophic understanding of aesthetics and power. More, Spider Woman can be considered First Pedagogue because her stories all contain a teaching element. That which is beautiful, she instructs, makes a satisfying, harmonious pattern of connection. Opposites are not seen as opposites but as completions or responses. Power is maintaining right relation, which is dyadic and dialogic—a balance between internal and external—imaged by her offspring, either War Twins or Twin Sisters. Spider Woman's power is in woman's biological function of blood to make and to destroy and to vitalize with singing and shaking. Power is beauty; beauty is harmony, not cosmetics. Spider Woman creates, destroys, hexes, mends, bends, breaks; she is of the earth but also of the moon and stars. She sits on the shoulder to advise. She is heart (vulva) and thought, with a wide latitude given for personal style and easy sexuality. She has colors like the rainbow and lives under the world in the second world, lower world, or under world. It is from the center (of the world, of her body) that she creates; therefore she sees what is inside the center rather better than what is outside it. She is the eye of shadow consciousness. From her depth perception she sings, shows, tells, and teaches human beings how to care for the cosmos. She is all that courses and intercourses.

Spider Woman's teachings are still the subject of stories and songs in modernized versions. Many versions contain some sense of the auditory or olfactory importance of learning, as if wisdom is an impregnation of the ear or nose. In "Tiyo meets Spider Woman" (Mullet, 1993) a young Hopi hero cannot make his journey to the land of snakes until he has paid obeisance to the great Spider Woman. His lessons begin when he enters her special place, an underground kiva. The difficulty of this first step toward their meeting is like a downward birthing process:

> "Alas, how can I come to you," cried the perplexed Tiyo. "I have looked on every side and see only this tiny hole through which your voice comes, and it will scarce admit the point of my great toe." "Come," was the abrupt command. So Tiyo, without further question, placed his foot upon the hole; then, as if stirred to life, the tiny particles of sand began to whirl about and in a marvelous way the opening widened until it allowed the admission of his body as he was drawn gently downwards. (pp. 15–16)

Once there, the writer describes Spider Woman with all the composite of opposites necessary for divinity. She is as old as time but as young as eternity; she speaks in hisses but she gives forceful commands; she stays in one place but travels in a whisper at an ear. Tiyo remembers his lessons by attending to whispers.

In "As it was in the beginning," E. Pauline Johnson (1989) gives autobiographical account of her knowing she is Indian, not White, by smell:

I was in Hudson's Bay store when an Indian came in from the north with a large pack of buckskin. As they unrolled it a dash of its insinuating odor filled the store. I went over and leaned above the skins a second, then buried my face in them, swallowing, drinking the fragrance of them, that went to my head like wine. Oh, the wild wonder of that wood-smoked tan, the subtlety of it, the untamed smell of it! I drank it into my lungs, my innermost being was saturated with it, till my mind reeled and my heart seemed twisted with a physical agony. (p. 72)

In *SpiderWoman's Dream*, Alicia Otis (1987) spins a children's tale of Spider Woman, describing her as "the vixen lighting fires in your heart. She's Hide-Of-Deer thrown lightly on the wagon-chair.... See her love the devil's dust, beat clouds to fluff. Her song creeps through the morning" (pp. 16–17).

Besides the nonliteral, nonvisual aspect of Spider Woman stories is often the motif of a bundle or basket. It is from the bundle that a lesson in the proper care of the cosmos ensues. Spider Woman teaches the twin sisters how to sing everything in their baskets: heaves, waters, mountains, earth, spirit messengers, creatures, metal, cattle, pigs, sheep, highways and engines, plants (Allen, 1992). Here is a pedagogy of right relation, whereby it is taught that power can be dangerous if not translated properly—if not sung well or spoken well; if not planted well; if not dumped, if not usurped. From these teachings a pedagogy of respect emerges, which permeates all life forms and expressions of Indian art and culture. Commenting on a key difference between this and modern consumptive societies, Karl Kroeber remarks, "It is not easy to find any Western art that does not serve as a locus for collecting power to itself, rather than passing it on into socially productive activity" (1983, p. 332). It would seem that we at the end of the 20th-century are reaping what our technocracies have sown: a veritable Pandora's box of natural disasters.

Although the stories of Spider Woman in the North American continent are reverential and respectful, Indians of South America tend to emphasize her destructive powers. Mexicans, for example, see her as the great hole in the west, called by the Aztecs "The Place of the Woman," sucking into death all who have been born (Morton, 1989). The identification of woman with hole has given rise to fear of the vagina, often pictured as a mouth with teeth (*Vagina Dentata*). This hole is voracious, eager to devour whatever enters its realm. Hunger and appetite for sex are other negative attributes, which portray woman in her spider web as a luring predator. She waits with baited breath. She entraps. The motif of the toothed vagina, associated with early earth mother figures, clearly suggests a deep fear of female power found most particularly in Mexican machismo legends and songs (Carr & Gingerich, 1983).

Consistent with this background of the destroying mother goddess, but offering a significant modern variation, is *Kiss of the Spider Woman* (Puig, 1979), adapted in 1985 to the screen. Molina, a homosexual window dresser, is imprisoned in a cell in Latin America with Valentin, a revolutionary who hates "faggots." It is the warden's intention to plant Molina as a spy who will relay information concerning Valentin's Marxist comrades. It appears that Molina at first goes along with the entrapment plot. He brings food from his mother into the cell—two roast chickens, four baked apples, one pint egg salad, one loaf of rye bread sliced (the list goes on)—intended as bait to soften Valentin's tongue. As they spend time together in the small prison cell, Molina helps pass time and salve wounds by telling film stories. He doesn't just tell, he narrates. The stories contain good plots but it is the telling of them that is spellbinding. Gradually, Molina softens Valentin's Marxist heart by sharing food, telling stories, even washing filth from Valentin's body. Here the supposedly despised homosexual becomes a Christ figure. But will he, like Judas, offer the kiss of betrayal? Puig's interplay of Christian and mythic themes resonate. In a scene fraught with metaphor, Molina narrates yet another of his film stories to Valentin, this time a story of a fictional Spider Woman whom the audience recognizes as Molina, caught in a web of intrigue:

> she's wearing a mask, it's also silver, but … poor creature … she can't move, there in the deepest part of the jungle she's trapped in a spider's web, or no, the spider web is growing out of her own body, the threads are coming out of her waist and her hips, they're part of her body, so many threads that look hairy like ropes and disgust me, even though if I were to touch them they might feel as smooth as who knows what … (p. 280)

Ultimately, Puig portrays this homosexual as an androgynous Spider Woman: a creator, a storyteller, and a defier of death-dealing politics; for Molina does not betray Valentin's Marxist secrets. In fact, he dies a sacrificial death and becomes a savior. What he saves by dying is the harmony of a friendship and love born impossibly in a prison cell.

The magic of naming, of thinking of a story, of telling stories! Word-saying comprises the heart of the drama of *Kiss of the Spider Woman*. Words, images, metaphors, the sound of the human voice incantating—all are magic ingredients of the ritual ceremony "faggot" and Marxist undertake in their narrow prison cell. No props but the human imagination. No scenery but the images that form in the listener's imagination. Language passes into presence (Wheelwright, 1968) and what had been profane becomes transformed into what is sacred (Eliade, 1968). These are the resonances of an encounter between two men not meant to like each other but who come to let loose the labels that privilege hatred. Spider Woman has taught her lesson well.

Schools, of course, are not (meant to be) prisons, but there are similarities. Classrooms are like holding areas where (often) people do time. Teachers are guards of the canon. Verbs and nouns are given air time. There is a passivity that is pervasive. I was reminded of some of these uncanny resemblances while watching CNN outside The Wall, where Karla Faye Tucker was executed. Just the physicality of the building looked schoolish to me: that red brick, those steps leading up to a huge front door, staring windows. Wasn't the whole death ordeal meant to teach a lesson? Commentators underscored the lesson of the killing by boasting "ours is the best judicial system on earth" with its appeal process. Witnesses to Karla's dying relayed factual accounts: She smiled, she kept her eyes open, she asked for forgiveness, her hair hung down the gurney. Objectives were clearly met. Task on time. I for an I. In such a death culture, only a few voices, later in the evening, talked about the inequities of justice—a point made by Louise Erdrich's Indian in her story "Scales" (1993). When some have more power (influence, money) than others, the scales of justice do not balance.

Today, it seems, the powers that be balance federal budgets but ignore ethical bankruptcy. Stories handed down by the American-Indian tradition teach, among many other lessons, that ours should be an ecosystem (not a judicial system) that is a web of differences (not a web of intrigues) with power defined as relationship (not domination). But as Judith Plant reminds, "it would be very typical of the 'taking' attitude of Western society to think that Indian ways, traditions and rituals could simply be transferred to nonnative people. This would be stealing once again" (1989, p. 245). How do I learn how to teach radically different ideas of power and aesthetics without plagiarizing? Are there models of Spider Woman hidden in old texts in my own tradition that I can return to, teach differently?

I browse back over my *Norton Anthology of Literature by Women: The Tradition in English* to discover one (among many) surprising example of Spider Woman's aesthetics and power: Charlotte Brontë's *Jane Eyre* (1847/1985). Jane falls outside the good-bad split by being orphaned (and thereby not a member of the family romance), unattractive (and thereby needing to recover for herself and her readers a differing notion of beauty), and—most importantly—by being, even as a young girl, a power figure. She instills anger from her "superiors" by her constant refusals to go along with the unitary discourse of her culture. This Spider Woman trait of Jane Eyre is early demonstrated when she confronts the minister Mr. Brocklehurst and insists that her favorite Biblical readings are not the Psalms with their didacticisms, but Revelation and the book of Daniel because of their visionary quality. Jane Eyre is a different kind of heroine, neither good nor bad because she insistently defies labeling. More important, she draws her power from a spirituality that is other than canonical. Her sources for empowering herself come from nature, in a pagan awareness of her world that constantly "speaks," and from her artwork and her dreams, which "tell" of her inner turmoil. Another Spider Women writer, from another culture, is Jamaica Kincaid, who challenges Eurocentric ideas of piety in her wittily titled *The Autobiography of My Mother* (1997). Xuela, like Jane, is motherless in search of her imaginary mother. She, like Jane, is an outsider, because she comes from mixed stock—half-Scot, half-African. Her source of power comes from her sense that she is an outsider: She is a woman in a highly patriarchal society. Like Jane, Xuela refuses to be submissive or pious. Standing outside a church that she knows was built by slaves, she hears the congregation singing a hymn and reflects:

The words were: "O, Jesus, I have promised / To serve Thee to the end: / Be Thou for ever near me, / My Master and my friend." I wanted to knock on the church door then. I wanted to say, Let me in, let me in. I wanted to say, Let me tell you something: This Master and friend business, it is not possible; a master is one thing and a friend is something else altogether, something completely different; a master cannot be a friend. And who would want such a thing, master and friend at once? A man would want that. It is a man who would ask, what makes the world turn, and then would find in his own reply fields of gravity, imaginary lines, tilts and axes, reason and logic, and, quite brazenly, a theory of justice. (p. 134)

The word "master" labels. The gender "woman" separates. And so on. Spider Women know that labels split the self away from an energizing ambivalence that gives them power and beauty. "You say my name is ambivalence?" Gloria Anzaldúa (1983) asks. "Think of me," she responds, "as a sort of spider woman hanging by one thin strand of web. Who me, confused? Ambivalent? Not so. Only your labels split me" (in Anzaldúa & Moraga, p. 205).

Recognizing these splittings within our culture, the postmodern teacher has a special obligation in the widened gap. Perhaps "opportunity" rather than "obligation" is the more correct word, because, following Wolfgang Iser (1974), a "gap" allows for fluidity of movement and perspective, and even playfulness. The cultural "gap" offers several pregnant negatives for the postmodern teacher (a) not to romanticize (b) not to patronize and (c) not to literalize.

By not romanticizing, postmodern teaching does not look over its shoulder at the wistful wonders of an earlier, simpler time. Gynocracies were mother-right societies, which patriarchal, cybertechnical societies cannot, because of their peculiar history, imitate. Nevertheless, as current ecofeminist movements urge, earth teaches values that touch all life forms (Berry & Swimme, 1992). Recent blizzards and hurricanes manifest the destroying powers of an earth mother who has not been seen but will be heard. Nature worship need not be a romantic ideal. Second, by not patronizing, postmodern teaching proposes different models for the distribution of power based on equivalence and radical difference, what Elizabeth Johnson (1992) calls "radical equality." Chaos theorists have been telling us what traditional societies also teach: Order comes from chaos. But for order to emerge, matter should be understood to contain an emergent property, energy, yeast. Not patronizing means talking about power not as a top-down affair (Father knows best) but more as an out-thrusting. Some call this "yang power" (Haddon, 1987). I call it spider work.

Finally, a word about not literalizing. For so long Western-European cultures have acquired their knowledge base from the invention of the media—black and white. Perhaps we need to learn to see red. Perhaps, as Inés Hernández-Ávila argues, "it is humans who must be reinvented" (1995, p. 403). Red seeing is not literal seeing but seeing with the inner eye, the eye from the margin, the eye from the under earth, the eye that the gray women pass among them. It is metaphorical seeing. This reddening of vision owes its particular insights to the nuances of Native-American orality. Intoning, chanting, sequential repeating, drumming, singing are all aspects of this orality. The horizon of perception lowers. Time alters and opens. Red seeing also acknowledges anger when earth's discipline, taught by a strict Grandmother Spider, is not revered. "The earth purifies herself, either harmoniously or by blows," Hernández-Ávila remarks (p. 404), and surely El Nino's temper is case in point.

Although the postmodern teacher cannot literalize traditional Native-American ceremonial practices, she can alter classroom procedure so as to delve deeper into the knowledge that lies within. Where, for instance, does memory play? Why is memory an important aspect of learning? Can memory play? In my schoolgirl days we had to memorize lines from Coleridge, Shakespeare—the canon. I am not now talking about memorizing, however, nor about the canon. I am talking about the play of memory that can occur by simple exercises. Students should be able to hear a "clacking and whirring" (Levertov, 1990/1996, p. 228) inside the berry bushes of their imaginations, by the memory tasks we set before them. Consider this. Assign several pages of Emily Dickinson poems with the instruction to prepare two poems for class discussion. In class allow for memory work by asking students to write down phrases or words they remember from their assigned reading. Done often enough, students will remember more. Here is a verbatim list from one such exercise, in which certain Dickinson turns of phrase will be recognizable:

> no rack can torture me
> who are you
> are you nobody too
> like a frog
> I felt a funeral in my brain
> and I dropped down and down
> wild nights
> I heard them lift the box
> you cannot prick with saw
> don't tell
> to an admiring bog
> captivity is consciousness
> purple well
> and I sneered—softly

Each student wrote down the class list as well as their own list—a remarkable collection of words. "Purple well," for instance, put me in mind of Virginia Woolf's *To the Lighthouse*. I uncovered for myself a fresh understanding of the relationship between Mrs. Ramsay and Lily, as well as of the erotic quality of Mrs. Ramsay's melancholy described as "a wedge-shaped core of darkness" (1927/1981, p. 62). This association for me would never have happened had the class not offered their Dickinson memories. And, strangely, the list's earthiness—bog, frog, down and down—releases reading and literality from its de-pendence on eye mastery. It was as if the class and I could borrow the poet's consciousness together. In the naming was the appearing. The class was not a group of singulars in this exercise. We became a tribe.

I end this chapter as I began, sitting in my hard chair. Now many dots have been made on the computer screen. Perhaps they will form threads. Perhaps the webs will mandalas make.

ᎶᏣ12ᏣᏧ

Vegetative Fantasy and the Greening of Imagination

I dwell in dew and in the air and in all greenness.

—Hildegard of Bingen (1158–1163/1992, p. 85)

Such, such were the joys/ When we all, girls and boys,/ In our youth time were seen/ On the ecchoing green.

—Blake (1789/1993, p. 29)

The green garden has its place, so that renewal, creativity, childhood, and closeness with both divinity and animal life need not be taken literally.

—Moore (1983, p. 47)

"What is a man," said Athos, "who has no landscape?"

—Michaels (1997, p. 86)

In Samuel Taylor Coleridge's fragmentary dream vision "Kubla Khan," a picture is painted of an emperor who erects a "pleasure dome" among "enfolding spots of greenery" through which runs a "sacred river" down to underground caverns (1816/1993, p. 615). The place would be a paradise garden were it not for an eruption, which causes the sacred river to sink "in tumult to a lifeless ocean" (line 29). As my student Michelle Burus wrote, Kubla Khan believes that by building a walled-in garden he can master his emotions. "However," she continues, "the emperor cannot prevent the sacred river from turning tumultuous, just as humans cannot prevent their emotions from turning tumultuous." When that happens, "unrest begins to invade the human spirit." In other words, read psychologically, when the river of life within us becomes too controlled or repressed, our connection to the greater ocean of cosmic consciousness turns against us and our spirit becomes, in Coleridge's image, a cave of ice.

In this final chapter, I consider how writers show ways of keeping the inner stream flowing and connected to the larger ocean. I call this way "the greening of imagination" to suggest an ecological relationship between human and other myriad life forms in the cosmos. To sustain that relationship requires an imagination that reorients us toward the sources and resources of life; an imagination that, if not released (Greene, 1995), will keep us locked forever behind walls of egocentricism. This locked-in ego will kill the paradise that once was the world garden. To green the imagination is to turn it in new directions that reconceptualize the damaging ideals of progress and humanism. I propose several ways of greening that take us back and forth among ancient myth, Buddhist meditation, Romantic poetry, psychology, modern myth, and modern fiction. The metaphors encountered there provide a wide field for re-educating the imagination.

One way into this project is through myth. The Epic of Gilgamesh, a Sumerian hero during the third millennium B.C.E., is one of the earliest stories recorded in Western civilization to tell the tale of egotism restrained through loss, and spirituality restored though the power of a green plant. The story concerns Gilgamesh, a king, who thought of himself as autonomous, which means unconnected, chilly, and aloof—able to ride herd without recrimination. He is rescued from his barren egoistic life by his opposite, a forest god-youth who comes from nowhere, "eating the food of grass, drinking from the watery holes of herds and racing swift as wind or silent water" (1992, p. 4). The two meet at a watering hole and are fated to join forces. That the two are same-sex opposites is myth's way of reminding us that we are never solitary heroes, no matter how imperial our status, and our significant other need not be sexed differently. In Jungian psychology, drawing inspiration from myth, the figure of the double is an archetypal structure that "can provide an image of the self to grow into" (Walker, 1976, p. 169), expanding the one into a wider, deeper self that is twinned. The double, a constant configuration in myth and fiction, urges twice seeing, two pairs of eyes that can redirect single vision, blinkered and blinded, into deeper awareness. Think of such pairs as David and Jonathan, Castor and Pollux, Achilles and Patroclus, Huck Finn and Jim, Crusoe and Friday. In popular culture, too, the double is figured as Batman and Robin, even Beavis and Butthead. Something in the portrayal of the male hero requires a de-emphasis of ego. Interestingly, few female doubles occur in story or myth, with a notable exception of the myth of Demeter and Persephone.

Before he meets Enkidu, Gilgamesh dreams. Remembering his dreams and attending to their importance opens his channel. Gilgamesh thus appears an unusual hero for Western imaginative writings, for not only is his ego accepting of hidden sources of information but also his significant other is a beloved male. The union of the two is described as a marriage, Enkidu seeming to Gilgamesh "wholesome, young and ready as a woman" (p. 15). When the two pair, they blend as a mystical union of two-in-one: king with nature boy, court with forest, old with young. The point of the story is the narratation of an entirely different type of adventure, where the journey leads down into the depths of feeling and out into the cosmic stream. Unlike Hercules's battles with lions or Odyssey's sojourns with sirens, this hero travels inward.

Both Gilgamesh and his soul mate Enkidu look into water. They are not just looking; they are seeking, or perhaps apprehending. Enkidu first meets Gilgamesh at a watery hole. "Then Enkidu met a hunter at the watery hole on three consecutive days. And each time the face of the hunter signaled recognition of Enkidu" (p. 4). Later, in grief, Gilgamesh achieves equanimity by composing his face in the face of the river: "After learning how to pause his heart, Gilgamesh created just the same image in the face of a river" (p. 52). What is received in these watery mirrors is not just an absolute likeness of a literal face but an "ecchoing," to use Blake's word. A paused heart is mirrored back. The seeing pauses. The pause offers a moment of deep reflection and wide connection. Such is how Herman Hesse (1951) describes Siddhartha (the Buddha) rowing a boat and consumed by longing. But upon getting out of the boat, Siddhartha pauses and bends over the water "in order to hear better" (p. 133). In looking into water, one hears better! These connections among reflection, pause, and hearing are profoundly resonant in story making, suggesting that he who looks downward into the waters will hear the river's laugh. To "see" nature's echo is to apprehend a different, more "virtuous," reality:

> Open your eyes. Look at the water. Let all thoughts fall into the water and dissolve into the lake of your mind, like snowflakes settling and dissolving in the ocean.... The ocean's waves come and go; watch them until you forget yourself and become one with the waves. (Das, 1997, p. 387)

Gilgamesh, however, weeps by the river to glut his grief when Enkidu dies. He asks his spirit if grief will become its food (p. 55). Lapsing into a literalization of loss, Gilgamesh walks, weeps, and wails. "I can't stop pacing. I can't stop crying. My friend has died and half my heart is torn from me," he says (p. 66). What seems to be a climactic moment is Gilgamesh's dangerous journey into the nether world to secure reunion with his beloved Gilgamesh. His journey intends to discover the secret of eternal life so as to join his soul mate and "steer the craft that gods and goddesses use" (p. 69); he seeks, in other words, to become his own god—a self-enclosed narcissist. But at the point when Gilgamesh is to be rewarded with the green plant of eternal life—just then!—the plant is snatched away from him by a snake, whose literal skin-shedding is symbolic of emptying out into the cosmos.

I read the denial of the green plant to Gilgamesh as the wisdom of this myth. A doubled consciousness must not walk and pace endlessly but must pause in motionlessness to feel the thistle of temporality. To feel *that* thistle is to experience the fragmentary place of the self in the cosmic order of life so as to blend and fade and forget and let be. The denial of the plant to the ego desire of Gilgamesh thus allows for a renewal of the sacred psyche. As Thomas Moore (1983) remarks, "The psyche, too, is green in that it is alien, not human, resisting control by human will and designs" (p. 41). In other words, the green thistle plant reminds us of the inaccessibility of the cosmos to bend to human will. Similarly, the myth of Narcissus introduces Echo as the necessary pause for opening the ego out. For although Narcissus seems to fall in love with himself, he also longs to deepen the beauty of self-reflection. And even though Echo can only echo back the words of her beloved, there is an erotic value to de-emphasizing the literal nature of words. As Patricia Berry puts it, "Nothing in the myth of Echo and Narcissus gets fulfilled—there's no happy ending—at least not in any ordinary sense. The focus of the myth is on unfulfilled passion: Echo for Narcissus and Narcissus for his reflection" (1980, p. 58).

These ideas resonate with the writing of psychoanalyst Christopher Bollas (1997) on the dissolution of the ego, a notion which, when he first encountered it in Zen Buddhism, he dismissed as mere nonsense. "Nowadays," he writes, "I understand a little bit more about the idea; that is, that a form of consciousness must dissolve in order for a type of freedom to occur within the subject" (p. 31). The process involves a deepening of experience, a radiating out, and a dissolving of intensity: very much the description of Gilgamesh's journey in and through grief, loss, and denial of the sacred plant. Consistent with the myth and psychic exploration is the notion of an underlying current—call it the collective unconscious, call it a stream, call it by the Tibetan word *alia* (McDougall, 1997, p. 80)—with which all life forms are connected and can tap by "dying" in ego. It would seem that Gilgamesh teaches a most nonWestern lesson: Forfeiting ownership of the sacred plant is synonymous with giving up ego control. Egoistic "dying" is a divine act of renunciation that rejoins humans with all other life forms in the cosmos.

Coleridge's fascination with ice is another metaphor for the blocked ego that prevents passage into cosmic connection. When in "The Rime of the Ancient Mariner" (1798/1993) the mariner journeys to the South Pole, metaphorically he is journeying into the ice cave of the blocked ego. There, for no reason, he kills an albatross. Coleridge spends no poetic lines on the killing to make the point that it is an act of gratuitous violence that, precisely because it is without cause or reason, arises from a heart of indifference, an "ice cave" that causes the reason of the heart to freeze. The mariner's ship and all its occupants are cursed, the wind drops down, and "the very deep did rot" (p. 333). Nature's retribution indicates that the bird was humanity's only connection with forces beyond ego control. A lesson in the Arctic about the fragility of the cosmos is learned when, again without reason or cause, the Mariner blesses the slimy water snakes: "a spring of love gushed from my heart" (p. 339). A reasonless act of love is enough to melt the icy heart and cause a cosmic response. For, at the very moment of the Mariner's unconscious blessing, the spell is snapped and he is set free to tell his tale; that is, to bear witness. A blocked ego, for Coleridge, occurs in one without conscience or consciousness, in one whose heart is indifferent, in one whose inner springs have turned to ice, and in one without the eye of imagination that sees the invisible bond among human and bird and beast.

It is significant that writers of the West's earliest myth and of the Romantic period have predicted the dilemma of ecological unconsciousness. The issue has been a concern of Western writers since civilization began. I say "civilization" because it is humanity's "grown up" distance from nature that is the poets' concern. The Greeks' cult of Hestia warned of the danger of growing up and away from the sense that the planet is our home. As Ginette Paris puts it, "choices of civilization, as well as scientific knowledge, have all contributed to our loss of feeling for the earth as the center of the universe" (1986, p. 176). Appreciating earth-centeredness is not a backlash to pre-Ptolemaic beliefs but rather a bonding with planet earth.

Joseph Campbell (in Campbell & Moyers, 1988) urges the importance of myths for an identification of human life not with any local group but with the planet. The source of awe and mystery for primitive cultures was first the animal world and then the vegetable world (Campbell, 1972). Around these two worlds two distinct mythologies developed, each with a sense that the physical world is sacred; eating the fruits of the land was once a prayerful ritual that sustained and fulfilled connection between the human and the cosmic spheres. Artists and writers, as inhabitants of what Campbell calls the "night mind" (in Campbell & Moyers, 1988, p. 162), can guide our thinking about the larger connection by way of the imagination. William Faulkner's "The Bear" (1942/1966), for example, tells the story of a young hunter who, in learning how to hunt, learns the real meaning of awe and humility. The education of Ike McCaslin is a modern American initiation myth, taught to a ten-year-old Mississippi boy over a six-year period in the postslavery years of his shamans: Sam Fathers, son of an original Native-American and an African slave; Boon, a White primitive; and by his animal shamans, Old Ben, the bear; and the fierce little dog, Lion.

Another link in Faulkner's epic is the short story "Race at Morning" (1970), which, because it concerns Ike's nephew many years later, continues the same mythic intention of teaching generations of hunters the mysteries of the wilderness. The plot is the same, only the characters are different: the unnamed boy narrator; Mister Ernest, his surrogate father and wilderness teacher; Dan, the horse; old Eagle, the dog; and instead of a hunted bear, a hunted big buck deer. That Faulkner endows the buck with majesty and mystery becomes apparent with the boy's descriptions of him as various as any mystical shape changer. His antlers are like a "rocking chair" (p. 285); he is a "big old son of a gun" (p. 287, p. 289, p. 290, p. 291, p. 293); "a hant" (p. 291); "an elephant, with a rack on his head you could cradle a yellin' calf in" (p. 291); "a statue and red as gold in the sun" with "twelve lighted candles branched around his head" (p. 299). As a student reminded me, the twelve candles metaphorically represent the twelve sons of Jacob and the twelve disciples, from both the Hebrew and Christian scriptures, both written so as to be about the Father's business. This mix of colloquial and Biblical imagery in the boy's observations suggests the boy's readiness to be initiated into the mysteries of life; as well, it suggests the buck's two-in-one quality as a sacred animal who never appears but as a silent illumination. Even though the hunt is a literal failure, it is far more than that: It is a cosmic triumph. Because the hunters do not kill when given the chance, they form a bond between themselves and all of nature.

The high seriousness of the bonding moment is undercut in typical Faulkner fashion by a sort of Zen humor. A mistake occurs. There they are, riding hard through the brush on the trail of the buck, Mister Ernest in front and the boy in back of the saddle; when suddenly they are cut loose from the horse by a grapevine that catches the horn of the saddle. Faulkner returns imagination to its roots. The grapevine snaps the forward rush of the hunt and, like a divine vegetal symbol, joins the men, the horse, the dog onto the vine as branches of the vine. This sudden action provides a living reminder of all relations bound together: earth with air with fire with water with space with animal with plant with humankind. Rather than embellish the high seriousness of this idea, Faulkner presents it as matter of fact: utterly happenstance, a "hap" (Weinsheimer, 1987, pp. 7–8) that hovers at the heart of the world. Equally simple is Faulkner's profound idea of education. One must learn the rites that teach how "to come back into the big woods and hunt" (p. 304)—how to find proper place and right action. Or, if the boy must do the business of mankind by attending formal schooling, it should be the Father's business that is attended.

If Faulkner's work re-stories hunter mythologies, Margaret Atwood's might be to re-story planter mythologies. Planter religions centered downward (not outward, as in hunter religions), tending soil in such ways as watering, cutting, pruning, pinching, digging, sniffing, and watching. This downward shift expresses a primordial truth: What the earth gives forth in the branch form of food—banana, coconut, breadfruit-yam—is the flesh of earth blooming in the vine substance, of which we all partake. As Campbell explains, "What roots the self in selfhood is not at all a sense of action … rather a sense of passion, suffering, surrender, and willing sacrifice" (1959, p. 186). Planter rites thus consisted of the life cycle itself: generation and death and regeneration; sowing/generating/; planting/harvesting. Life lives in order to die in order to give new life, a paradox captured in the maxim of Jesus: "Amen, amen, I say to you, unless the grain of wheat falls into the ground and dies, it remains alone. But if it dies, it brings forth much fruit" (John 12:24, New American Catholic Edition). What these myths and sayings teach is the necessity to lose ego, to prepare for the empty, pathless area of the wilderness, to be amazed. For, just as the wanderer through a labyrinth feels lost and bewildered, the planter initiate loses ego stability so as to be launched into a wider terrain. Death in planter religions serves a primary, imaginary function of losing ego attachment.

Margaret Atwood, modern Canadian fabulist, focuses on the female body as terra-tory. For Atwood, one of the last natural wilderness areas on the planet is female flesh, too often owned, controlled, or harmed by some external system—politics, materialism, false fairy tales. Women no longer perceive themselves as natural extensions of the environment, connected to the land, presiding over the preparation of earth's food, nourishing their own bodies properly. Ironic food feasts thus play a significant role in the Atwood canon, turning eating into neurosis: Marion's anorexia in *The Edible Woman* (1984); Joan's obesity in *Lady Oracle* (1996). Such problems with eating and the body reflect Atwood's critique of "civilized" notions of beauty.

In *Surfacing* (1990) the unnamed female protagonist is a modern everywoman whose quest is quintessentially nonheroic and, because undertaken by a female, suggests that the way to green the imagination is to plunge beneath surfaces. Hers is a quest to recover a portion of her past that has been buried within her unconscious by an act she cannot bear to remember: an abortion forced on her by her then-husband. The character's journey takes her to her parental home in the newly poisoned Canadian wilderness. The poisoned wilderness is both literal and figurative; for just as pollutants spoil the virgin forests of Canada, so too has the narrator's purer, wilder soul been poisoned by the memory of the abortion. She must take back the night. She must enter her night mind, the depths of unconscious memory, if she is to reclaim what James Hillman calls the "imaginal ego," which exists to prepare "for old age, death, and fate by soaking it through and through in *memoria*" (1972, p. 187).

The journey takes the narrator into breakdown. She exists between two worlds (one visionary, one physical) and experiences a full range of emotions long denied her—fear, anger, mourning—all the while performing obsessive acts designed to obey the "rules" of the universe she obviously thinks she has betrayed. She acts like one on the run, wanting to appease the hidden powers but terrified lest they overpower her: "The fear arrives like waves, like footfalls, it has no center; it encloses me like armor, it's my skin that is afraid, rigid" (p. 208). Because Atwood writes in prose and follows novelistic conventions, I interpret these scenes at the end in much the manner of Doris Lessing's (1973) *The Golden Notebook*: as a writerly account of a psychological breakdown. Temporary madness is seen as the path into wisdom and humility because of a visit to the other side. I could take the same approach to Jamaica Kincaid's fragment entitled "My Mother," but I feel something else is going on in the Kincaid piece that is more poetry than prose, more strictly imaginary and primary—not an account. I read Kincaid as I do Coleridge, whose vision tales and fantastic adventures are written to reveal a dark poetry of the soul, but not necessarily a breakdown.

In the end, Atwood's narrator chooses her own destiny, to live by her own wits among the gardens and trees and birds of her parents' house. She has let go of her rage, she has dived beneath the surface of her consciousness in order to recover an original self, and she has returned, forever changed. She is not like the mythical heroes who return from their dangerous adventures able, now, to save humankind with strengthened egos. Rather, she returns to something deep within herself that requires a total renunciation of both civilization and of strengthened ego. She is letting go of her attachment to her body and all that surrounds her:

> I haven't had time to be hungry and even now the hunger is detached from me, it does not insist; I must be getting used to it, soon I will be able to go without food altogether.... I'm not frightened, it's too dangerous for me to be frightened [of a wolf]. It gazes at me for a time with its yellow eyes, wolf's eyes, depthless but lambent as the eyes of animals seen at night in the car headlights. Reflectors. It does not approve of me or disapprove of me, it tells me it has nothing to tell me, only the fact of itself.... I do not interest it, I am a part of the landscape, I could be anything, a tree, a deer, skeleton, a rock. (pp. 222–224)

The wolf seems from another time and place and contains a gift to rescue her with its wise wolf eyes. It is like the story "The Wolf's Eyelash," which teaches the right question: not where is the next food, the next fight, the next dance, but "where is the soul?" (Estés, 1997, p. 368). The answer: out in the woods. What would a pedagogy of the woods entail, I wonder? Getting lost.

I find most trenchant the analysis a student gave of *Surfacing*, which encourages me to continue teaching myth with literature whenever I teach. Nicole writes:

> In *Surfacing* I liked the narrator's competentness, that she was an expert fisher, that she knew about the land. I want to say that I liked how masculine she was but what I mean is that she was so strong, she really was powerful, and it's sad that I relate that to being male. But so often women's strengths are attributed to masculinity. It is when she is newly empowered that she becomes most like the goddesses. Like Diana and Medusa, she can now take control of her fertility, menstruation, pregnancy: it is her body now. She is also like Artimus [*sic*], shy and most comfortable with the animals. She is wild. She is strong. She can refuse sex. She can initiate sex. She is like Venus, full of love. She is aware that her connection with the earth had been severed. She is now reconnected, more alive than she ever was. She is not a pastel-colored princess. She is on her hands and knees, naked in the dirt, baying at the moon, full of life, literally, unafraid and unapologetic.

What Nicole shows me here is more of my own intuition that the goddess religions teach us the joys of female inner maleness, without which women's eroticism cannot flourish.

Atwood's fictional journey into the unconscious has parallels in Zen Buddhist experience. Zen, a product of the combination of Mahayana Buddhism with Chinese Taoism, was later transported to and refined in Japan. Its introduction into China was attributed to the semilegendary Indian monk Bodhidharma, credited with a short verse summary of Zen doctrine (cited in Avens, 1980, pp. 77–78), which reads:

> A special tradition outside the scriptures,
> No dependence upon words and letters,
> Direct pointing at the soul of man,
> Seeing into one's own nature and the attainment of
> buddhahood.

With the preceding verse as my guide, I interpret Atwood's narrator's experience as a breakdown that was necessary to see the source of her suffering: civilization's deluded (poisoned) belief that she could separate herself from her griefs, her others, and nature. In recovering the wilderness within, she affirms the total interrelatedness of herself with all things "just so." Hers has been a journey into the unconscious. An eighth century Chinese Zen master, Shen-hui, describes the unconscious in an Eastern way:

> What is the unconscious? It is not to think of being and non-being; it is not to think of good and bad; it is not to think of having limits; it is not to think of measurements (or of non-measurements). It is not to think of enlightenment, nor is it to think of being enlightened; it is not to think of Nirvana, nor is it to think of attaining Nirvana: this is the Unconscious. (in Suzuki, 1977, p. 61)

I taught this novel in my Myth and Literature class, during which we had debates about the nature of the narrator's breakdown and whether at the end she was crazy in a narrow sense. I found myself defending craziness, arguing against the straight "civilized" idea of sanity that purges the soul of depth. Apparently, although not all my students were convinced, one student in particular wrote me a letter in which she described her own diving into the depths and surfacing. Part of what she wrote follows:

> Thank you for taking me on a mythical journey this semester. I have gained so much insight, yet felt so much in my heart.... I had put off taking my literature electives for fear of what I would encounter: a lot of 'out there' information. You made literature so real, so close to real life. I enjoyed the novel immensely. I could relate to the narrator to such an extent that it often became frightening ... I need knowledge/wisdom to help keep me on the searching path.

I teach Leslie Marmon Silko's *Ceremony* (1986) in much the manner that I teach Atwood's *Surfacing*. Both are wisdom texts. Both concern initiation rites presented from a matriarchal point of view. Interestingly, the journey in *Ceremony* is undertaken by a male character, whose contrast with his male friends sharpens Silko's intention to critique Western hero tales. For, in the manner of Campbell's thousand heroes (1949), Tayo journeys through a departure, an encounter, and a return. But unlike the journey of his veteran friends Rocky, Leroy, Harley and Robert, Tayo returns to what is really the beginning of his next, real journey, which I describe as *initiation, ceremony, and renewal*. This three-stage adventure re-educates Tayo to the way of his Laguna tribe with its commitments to memory, story, and respect for all living forms. "Stories," as Clarissa Pinkola Estes (1995) states boldly, "are medicine.... They do not require that we do, be, act anything—we need only listen. The remedies for repair or reclamation of any lost psychic drive are contained in stories" (p. 15). And so, Tayo, returning from his hero journey must journey into the stories of his tribe to recover his soul.

In the first outward bound journey, the Indian boys leave their pueblo culture to fight the White man's big war, World War II. To the people of the Laguna tribe, the boys are looked up to as heroes: good guys going to win the world against bad guys. Ironically, the Japanese are like the Indians by the fact of their being nonWhite; the White world sends nonWhites to kill nonWhites. Tayo returns from his encounter with death in the jungles, sickened: "He didn't know how to explain what had happened. He did not know how to tell [his grandfather] that he had not killed any enemy or that he did not think that he had. But that he had done things far worse, and the effects were everywhere in the cloudless sky, on the dry brown hills, shrinking skin and hide taut over sharp bone" (p. 37). Were it not for Tayo's psychic sickness, he would not be Silko's chosen hero, whose next three journey stages take him back into the culture he had left and down into psychic renewal.

Tayo begins his *initiation*, before he departs. Silko describes a moment in the summer before the war, when a drought was plaguing the people. Tayo decided to do what the holy men did during dry spells. He rode into the canyon, studied the night skies, listened to the wind, watched a spider, remembered the Spider Woman stories his grandmother used to tell him, and observed the frogs. These are the ancient actions that place one in a waiting position, less actor than observer. Silko writes:

> Shadows were gone, the cliff rocks began to get warm, the frogs came out from their sleeping places, swam across the pool to the sunny edge and sat there looking at him, snapping at the tiny insects that swarmed in the shade and grass around the pool. He smiled. They were the rain's children. He had seen it many times after a rainstorm. In dried up ponds and in the dry arroyo sands, even as the rain was still falling, they came popping up through the ground, with wet sand still on their backs. (p. 95)

Louis Haulard, a student, makes the following observations about this scene:

> The shadows are the way the frogs experience the world without the rain. It is dark and cold and they remain buried in the dry sand until the rains come and disperse the shadows. The frogs are children of the rain. They know the rain is a signal for them to emerge from their sleeping places. It is knowledge that has been passed from one generation to the next, from the time of the first frog. It is the time to be reborn. They cleanse themselves of the sand by diving into the pool. They emerge on the other side to bask in the warmth of the sunlight and to feed on the insects nature has provided for them. Silko uses Tayo's fascination with the frogs as a way of foreshadowing what will be Tayo's rebirth. Just as the rain is a catalyst for the frogs, his grandmother's stories are a catalyst for him to begin his journey of understanding. The old ways, the way things were done when the animals talked to humans, are his salvation. For Tayo, the shadows are the lies, deceits, and false promises of the white man. Before he can bask in the warmth of the sun, he must immerse himself in the ancient stories and legends and cleanse himself with the knowledge they hold. We as readers are able to make connections and see where Silko is taking Tayo, but for him it is only the beginning of his understanding of who and what he is. Just as he had felt the presence of the deer after the hunt, he senses here that he is somehow connected to the frogs.

To awaken from his long psychic sleep of forgetting because of contamination with White ways, Tayo must re-remember the ancient ways. He must undergo a *ceremony*. He does this with the help of a medicine man, Betonie, who lives on the north side of Gallup next to the river and the White man's dump. To the young, sickened, returned soldier, the old man is beyond understanding: He seems (and is) nonjudgmental. The old man knows he lives where the White men dump, but he is comfortable with his sense of "belonging with the land and the peace of the hills" (p. 117). More disturbing to Tayo is the fact that the old man laughs. Even as he faces what Tayo sees only as cardboard houses, tin cans, and broken glass, the old man laughs; even as he dresses in what Tayo sees only as greased-stained trousers and a baggy, worn sweater, the old man laughs. He smiles as he sees through the eyes of Tayo, who sees his medicine man's paraphernalia inside the hogan as only so much rubbish. It is the laughter of the archetypal Old Man who laughs for the pleasure of life, a theme in myth. The rain god must be made to laugh so that he lets fall his water. In Eastern cultic drama, when the bringer of salvation laughs, the earth begins to blossom. As Karl-Joseph Kuschel puts it, "Laughter at the fullness of life can at the same time be understood as laughter against all that is contrary to life" (1994, p. 72).

This laughter comes out of a wisdom that is utterly human, which is to say, connected. In his journal entitled *Fragrant Palm Leaves* (1998), Thich Nhat Hanh addresses the sort of one-sided perception that Tayo at this moment is experiencing, by saying, simply, "Reality is neither pleasant nor unpleasant in and of itself. It is only pleasant or unpleasant as experienced by us, through our perceptions" (p. 108). He goes on to say, "No one sees the existence of suffering more deeply than a bodhisattva (an enlightened being), yet no one maintains as refreshing and unwavering a smile" (p. 111). It is the laughter of the old man Betonie that initiates Tayo into a shiver of remembering and a feeling of strange inner power, "but there was no way to be sure what it was" (p. 124).

Indian ceremonies, for Tayo, are suspect. "I wonder what good Indian ceremonies can do against the sickness which comes from their wars, their bombs, their lies?" he asks Betonie about the White man (p. 132). The answer Betonie gives is not as important as the ceremonial sand painting he draws, placing Tayo in the center of a space around which he draws rainbows, hoops, a mountain range of blue, yellow, and white colors, and bear footprints. As easily as the old man had laughed, as quickly the old man cut Tayo across the top of his head, until blood oozed down his scalp and into his hair. The old man then lifted Tayo, walked him in the footprints of the bear, then led him through the doorway and into the night, where Tayo was told to sleep. When he awoke, Tayo was in a different psychic space:

> He remembered the black of the sand painting on the floor of the hogan; the hills and mountains were the mountains and hills they had painted in sand. He took a deep breath of cold mountain air: there were no boundaries: the world below and the sand paintings inside became the same that night. The mountains from all directions had been gathered there that night. (p. 145)

If you have ever seen a sand painting or a chalk sidewalk painting, you will recall your own amazement. Here was a beautiful picture, drawn with great care and precision, meant to be seen but briefly. For when the elements come to wash away or blow away the drawing, then all is invisible and the beauty is as if it had never been. Such "illustrates" the Buddhist teaching of impermanence. To have Tayo experience actually being in the center of an impermanent but beautifully crafted sand painting would be medicine indeed for a soul sick of the world's witchery. For there, in the center, Tayo's suffering disappeared, and with the sense of boundarilessness, of merging, and of gathering, Tayo was, in Buddhist terms, experiencing the nonexistence of the self. As Sandy Boucher explains, "in experiencing oneness with all phenomena, one taps into an unshakable strength far deeper than the capacities of personality" (1993, p. 16).

What is the magic of sacred space? It can be the shrine, the temple, the church that pilgrims seek; the quiet corner, the forest bower, the time out that others seek. There, set off, the seeker finds an age-long memoried self, that buried self, brought forward from its sleeping state by the power of imagination. "Far from being a kind of surrogate of our natural material pragmatic world," writes Philip Sherrard about the imagination:

> it is a world in its own right, on its own level.... The Imagination has, therefore, a magical creative potency which, through giving birth to the sensible world, re-

veals the ultimate world of Mystery in physical modes, in sounds, forms, colors, and scents. It is because of this that all creation is essentially an epiphany ... everything that exists has a sacred character. (1981, p. 3)

Writing from a Native-American perspective, Jamake Highwater (1981) devotes an entire section of his book *The Primal Mind* to the notion of place, which is synonymous with the idea of space. "Our sense of place—of space—is largely determined by the manner in which we see ourselves in relation to nature," he asserts (p. 119). "Essential to such a definition of space is the ritualized means by which to fix the centers of sacredness. A ritually defined center ... is taken to be the actual center of the world" (p. 122). Similarly, when Tayo undergoes a ceremony that places him in the center of a created space called a sand painting, his off-balance is being rebalanced. What was off-balance was Tayo's disastrous assimilation into White ways. He must be reinvented. He must be recreated. He must recover the sense that the earth is a complex, exact, and intentional manifestation of the Creative Spirit. He must shed such "civilized" (Western-European) intellectualization of terms like "landscape," "wilderness," or "nature" (Hernández-Ávila, 1995, p. 403) that permits hatchetting and fire balling in the name of "progress." He must find the story in the problem, to bring reality to the phrase "ecological sustainability."

The end of the novel is Tayo's reckoning with his misplaced identity, his correction of that misplacement, and his *renewal* back into his tribal self. He now sees that he had allowed himself to be a part of the White man's death culture:

> There was no end to it; it knew no boundaries; and he had arrived at the point of convergence where the fate of all living things, and even the earth, had been laid.... From that time on, human beings were one clan again, united by the fate the destroyers planned for all of them, for all living things; united by a circle of death that devoured people in cities twelve thousand miles away, victims who had never known these mesas, who had never seen the delicate colors of the rocks which boiled up their slaughter. (p. 246)

Tayo refers to the Los Alamos laboratory and the Trinity Site at White Sands, where the atomic bomb was first launched, territories that the American government had taken from Cochiti Pueblo so as to destroy the earth and its people halfway around the world. The death culture has also infiltrated his friends' behaviors, leaving them defenseless against their newly acquired death rituals involving alcohol and scapegoating. Tayo must complete the ceremony that will save his Indian soul from the White man's laboratories: "The transition was completed. In the west and in the south too, the clouds with round heavy bellies had gathered for the dawn.... The ear for the story and the eye for the patterns were theirs; the feeling was theirs: we came out of the land and we are hers" (p.

255). With the promise of rain, the story of Tayo ends with the clear implication that he, like the frogs, has been reborn.

The last way I propose to suggest a greening of imagination is with Virginia Woolf's transitional section in *To the Lighthouse* (1927/1981) entitled "Time Passes." Here, as in her "Death of a Moth" (1942/1988), for example, the sense of nature's absolute otherness is felt. Indeed, what we romantically call "nature" is seen as alien, utterly indifferent to the machinations of civilized folk.

Coming from her own experience, Woolf sees the natural world as on a more perfect plane than the human world. Nature is the essence, of which humans are the appearance. Perhaps this insistence on nature's indifference is Woolf's way of explaining away what had happened to her in her own childhood, so she can achieve distance from memory's insults. For Woolf to urge an indifferent viewpoint might be a way for her to objectify her own personal feelings so that she can create fiction coldly. "Cast a cold eye/ On life, on death./ Horseman, pass by" (Yeats, 1939/1993, p. 1,897).

The "Time Passes" section of the novel is a short interlude of only twenty pages between the two longer sections, "The Window" (one hundred twenty-two pages) and "The Lighthouse" (sixty-four pages). It seems so unrelated to the story line that I, for years, did not teach it, skipping over to the rest of the "story" as told in the last section, "The Lighthouse." Imagine! My students, however, corrected this oversight in my Curriculum and Fiction class, noting how extraordinary are the nature descriptions in the section—nature that busts rocks and swirls feathers, together and separately, willy-nilly, over time. What Woolf focuses on is the house, emptied of the Ramsays and their guests, left to the elements that "met nothing in bedroom or drawing room that wholly resisted them" (p. 129). With no humans, the house is unassailed: "Here one might say to those sliding lights, those fumbling airs that breathe and bend over the bed itself, here you can neither touch nor destroy" (p. 126). The references to sexual night attack operate on one level, but are canceled out on another level of action. For it is the air, the lighthouse light, the wind that take on action—action that is not treacherous; action, simply, that advances time and, left to its devices, breaks down the accouterments of "civilization." Interspersed between passages of nature's actions, Woolf tells of the fate of the Ramsays in purely parenthetical terms. It is not important that Prue died in childhood, that Andrew was killed by a mine bomb, or that Mr. Carmichael had success with his volume of poetry. Nor is it in the least important that Mrs. Ramsay, the main character of the first section, has died. This de-emphasis on character serves Woolf's function of re-emphasizing her metaphysical concerns.

Without the people with their noisy daytime activities and their furtive nighttime forays, without the brooms of the Scottish maids, the house becomes redecorated by the work of the elements. Strangely, all is commingled: carnation with cabbage, thistle with tile, butterfly on chintz, broken china on the lawn, lawn tangled with grass and berries. The careful decorum and hierarchy of the Ramsay household of earlier times is, now in this passage, "tangled." Classism is gone, tyranny is gone; divisions, preferences, hidings are gone. "What power could now prevent the fertility, the insensibility of nature?" Woolf asks. Nature's power looks with disinterested eye upon all things scattered and lets all things be. The "fertility" is the blooming of a new order born of nature's chaos. When the lighthouse light shines through the window it "looked with equanimity at the thistle and the swallow, the rat and the straw" (p. 138). What is presented here, in the middle of a novel about painterly projects, is Woolf's idea about another sort of art that can be found in the commingled forms of objects and animals and humans and elements.

Nature's equanimity and indifference to human activity is expressed, also, in Wolfe's meditational piece, "The Death of the Moth." Observing the frantic efforts of a dying moth not to die, Woolf contrasts its energy, "a tiny bead of pure life" (1942/1988, p. 47), with another sort of energy she feels outside the window, where all is seemingly still. "Yet the power was there all the same, massed outside, indifferent, impersonal, not attending to anything in particular" (p. 48). Because it is invisible, this elemental earth power does not partake of appearances; nevertheless, it exists on a realm entirely indifferent to ego's eye. I call her thinking about nature a "fantasy in green," to suggest the idea that creative energy is not the province only of the human mind. The creativity that Woolf observes going on in the cosmos has an archetypal, timeless sense. That nature's creativity is quirky and alien suggests its resistance to control by human will and design and, thereby in Woolf's view, its absolute authority.

Do not these ideas resonate with Buddhist and ecological thought? Zen Master Dōgen, in asserting the basic doctrines of Buddhism in the 13th century, remarked that most people see only the superficial aspects of sound and color; they are unable to experience "Buddha's shape, form, and voice in the landscape" (in Parkes, 1997, p. 117). Seeing only appearances is not seeing deeply enough. What is needed is a more radical revisioning of the human relation to the natural world, so as to see it not only as a source of wisdom and revival but also as divine art.

These remarks about the greening of imagination urge a greening of the psyche, too. We can think of the psyche as green (Moore, 1983) in that it is not ego, it cannot be developed, it must remain alien, and it will not be walled. Perhaps that is what Maxine Greene (1995) means when she calls for a "release" of the imagination. Imagination has, for too long, been tamed by ego needs and thereby has been held prisoner to merely private concerns. Greene writes: "Now and then when I am in the presence of work from the border, let us say, from a place outside the reach of my experience until I came in contact with the work, I am plunged into all kinds of reconceiving and revisualizing" (p. 3). There is the sense of surrender in these words, whereby ego lets go its "chill structures of autonomy" (Jacobs, M.-E., 1998, p. 85). Before civilization erected its time lines, borders, and walls, there was a belief in experience as truth

(Deloria, 1994). Reconceiving and revisualizing just might be ways to shed the artifices of civilized constructs the better to experience art in "the variety of beings about us" (Berry, 1988, p. 11).

So many *re's*, so many agains: releasing, reimagining, revisioning, reconceptualizing, reconceiving, reconstructing, relating, revealing. The list goes on. There is the urging to do again, see again, acquire double vision, listen. There is the sense things haven't gone right the first time, so we need the wisdom figures to tell us, again, what we are missing, what we are resisting. Ah, there's the rub. Recall (re call) that Freud once said that ignorance is a desire, a dynamic state of determined resistance (Salvio, 1998a). What a retort that is to not knowing. No, we cannot afford to resist our ignorances; we cannot afford not to know. We cannot, because not to know about our own resistances is to renege our responsibility to be human in an awakened way.

To be human. David Jardine (1992) reminds us that to be human is to be full of *humus*; "The whole Earth is our "kind," our kin" (p. 47). Similarly, David Smith (1997) remarks that *humus* means being grounded, that which the human species requires so as to give the sense of humility. What this book has attempted is a call back to such grounded basics, to *residua*. "Residue: that which remains after a part is taken, disposed of, or gone; remainder, rest" (Webster, 1993). Ashes to ashes, dust to dust, the church reminds Catholics at Lenten: Humans, remember that we shall return from whence we came, our bones as ashes to earth, to *humus*. Religion links back, *re-ligio*, linking humans back to whatever remains after all the hurrahs (may the earth rest in peace). The call is to turn back so as to concentrate utterly, to focus attention in a process of "off-consciousness" (Rugg, 1963, p. 295). We are linked, we need to re-member, our members joined with all multivariagated life forms around us that call to us, if we care to hear the voices that are not our own. To know is to acquire the humility that wisdom teaches. To know is to venture where we do not will to go. To know is to feel the coursing inside our living stream that flows into the wider cosmic ocean. To run the course of the inner coursing is curriculum's most urgent call. Then perhaps we can respond to the sights, sounds, tastes, touches, smells, spaces, and consciousnesses that surround us. What joy lies there, in the "ecchoing green"!

REFERENCES

Allen, P. G. (1990). *Spider Woman's granddaughters: Traditional tales and contemporary writing by Native American writers*. New York: Fawcett Columbine.

Allen, P. G. (1992). *The sacred hoop: Recovering the feminine in American Indian traditions*. Boston: Beacon.

Anonymous. (1981). Uncle Remus again. In R. B. Bickley, Jr. (Ed.), *Critical essays on Joel Chandler Harris* (pp. 43–44). Boston: G. K. Hall. (Original work published 1905)

Anzaldúa, G. (1987). *Borderlands: La frontera*. San Francisco: aunt lute books.

Anzaldúa, G. (1989). Entering into the serpent. In J. Plaskow & C. P. Christ (Eds.), *Weaving the visions: New patterns in feminist spirituality* (pp. 77–86). San Francisco: HarperSanFrancisco.

Anzaldúa, G. (Ed.). (1990). *Making face, making soul (Caciendo caras): Creative and critical perspectives by women of color*. San Francisco: an aunt lute book foundation.

Anzaldúa, G., & Moraga, C. (Eds.). (1983). *This bridge called my back: Radical writings by women of color*. New York: Kitchen Table Women of Color Press.

Aristotle: Poetics (M. Heath, Ed. & Trans.). (1996). New York: Penguin.

Armstrong, K. (1987). *Through the narrow gate*. New York: St. Martin's Press.

Aswell, D. (1984). The puzzling design of *Absalom, Absalom!* In E. Muhlenfeld (Ed.), *William Faulkner's Absalom, Absalom!: A critical casebook* (pp. 93–107). New York: Garland.

Aswell, M. L. (Ed.). (1947). *The world within: Fiction illuminating the neuroses of our time*. New York: Whittlesey House/McGraw-Hill.

Atwell-Vasey, W. (1998). *Nourishing words: Bridging private reading and public teaching*. Albany: State University of New York Press.

Atwood, M. (1984). *The edible woman*. New York: Bantam.

Atwood, M. (1990). *Surfacing*. New York: Fawcett Crest.

Atwood, M. (1996). *Lady Oracle*. New York: Bantam.

Auerbach, E. (1971). The brown stocking. In C. Sprague (Ed.), *Virginia Woolf: A collection of critical essays* (pp. 70–89). Englewood Cliffs, NJ: Prentice-Hall.

Avant, J. A. (1979). Review of *Hungry ghosts*. In L. W. Wagner (Ed.), *Critical essays on Joyce Carol Oates* (pp. 36–37). Boston: G. K. Hall.

Avens, R. (1980). *Imagination is reality: Western nirvana in Jung, Hillman, Barfield & Cassirer.* Irving, TX: Spring Publications.

Avens, R. (1984). *The new gnosis: Heidegger, Hillman and the angels.* Dallas, TX: Spring Publications.

Bachelard, G. (1971). *On poetic imagination and reverie* (C. Gaudin, Trans.). Dallas, TX: Spring Publications.

Baker, H. A., Jr. (1984). *Blues, ideology and Afro American literature: A vernacular theory.* Chicago: University of Chicago Press.

Bakhtin, M. (1981). *The dialogic imagination: Four essays by M. M. Bakhtin* (M. Holquist, Ed.). Austin, TX: University of Texas Press.

Baldwin, J. (1990). *Notes of a native son.* Boston: Beacon. (Original work published 1955)

Baldwin, J. (1993). *The fire next time.* New York: Random House. (Original work published 1963)

Ball, E. (1998). *Slaves in the family.* New York: Farrar, Straus & Giroux.

Barfield, O. (1960). The meaning of the word "literal." In L.C. Knights & B. Cottle (Eds.), *Metaphor and symbol* (pp. 50–72). London: Butterworth.

Barnes, D. (1995). *Ladies almanack.* Normal, IL: Dalkey Archive. (Original work published 1928)

Barnes, H. (1988). The biographer as literary critic: Sartre's Flaubert. In H. Bloom (Ed.), *Gustave Flaubert's Madame Bovary* (pp. 83–109). New York: Chelsea.

Barthes, R. (1974). *S/Z.* New York: Hill & Wang.

Batchelor, S. (1997). *Buddhism without beliefs: A contemporary guide to awakening.* New York: Riverhead.

Beal, A. (Ed.). (1956). *D. H. Lawrence: Selected literary criticism.* New York: Viking.

Beckett, S. (1931). *Proust.* New York: Grove Press.

Beckett, S. (1938). A review of "Intercessions" by Dennis Devlin. *transition: Tenth anniversary, 289–294.*

Beckett, S. (1954). *Waiting for Godot.* New York: Grove Press.

Beckett, S. (1958a). *Endgame: A play in one act.* New York: Grove Press.

Beckett, S. (1958b/1965). The unnamable. In *Three Novels by Samuel Beckett* (pp. 291–414). New York: Grove Press.

Beckett, S. (1977). Footfalls. In *Ends and odds: Eight new dramatic pieces by Samuel Beckett* (pp. 39–50). New York: Grove Press.

Beckett, S. (1980). *Company.* New York: Grove Press.

Beckett, S. (1981a). *ill seen ill said.* New York: Grove Press.

Beckett, S. (1981b). Rockaby. In *Rockaby and other short pieces by Samuel Beckett* (pp. 7–24). New York: Grove Press.

Bell, A. O. (Ed.). (1984). *The diary of Virginia Woolf: Volume five (1936–1941).* New York: Harcourt Brace. (Original work published 1941)

Benfey, C. (1999). The mystery of Emily Dickinson. *The New York Times Book Review, 39–44.*

Bent. (1997). S. Mathias, screen version. [Play by M. Sherman].

Bergman, I. (Director). (1961). *Winter Light* [Film]. (Available from AB Svensk Film- industri.)

Bergman, I. (Director). (1966). *Persona* [Film]. (Available from AB Svensk Filmindustri.)

Bergman, I. (Director). (1973). *Scenes from a marriage* [Film]. (Available from AB Svensk Filmindustri.)

Berry, P. (1975). The rape of Demeter/Persephone and neurosis. *Spring, 186–198.*

Berry, P. (1980). Echo and beauty. *Spring: An Annual of Archetypal Psychology and Jungian Thought, 49–60.*

Berry, P. (1981). Stopping: A mode of animation. *Spring, 77–88.*

Berry, T. (1988). *The dream of the earth.* San Francisco: Sierra Club.

Berry, T., & Swimme, B. (1992). *The universe story.* San Francisco, CA: HarperCollins.

Bishop, E. (1985). At the fishhouses. In S. M. Gilbert & S. Gubar (Eds.), *The Norton anthology of literature by women: The tradition in English* (pp. 1746–1748). New York: Norton. (Original work published 1955)

Black, M. F. (1992). The quintessence of Chopinism. In L.S. Boren & S. dS. Davis (Eds.), *Kate Chopin reconsidered: Beyond the bayou* (pp. 80–94). Baton Rouge, LA: Louisiana State University Press.

Blake, W. (1993). The ecchoing green. In M. H. Abrams, E.T. Donaldson, A. David, H. Smith, B. K. Lewalski, R. M. Adams, G. M. Logan, S. H. Monk, L. Lipking, J. Stillinger, G. H. Ford, C. T. Christ, D. Daiches, & J. Stallworthy (Eds.), *The Norton anthology of English literature* (Vol. 2, pp. 28–29). New York: Norton. (Original work published 1789)

Blessing, J. (1997). *Prose is a prose is a prose: Gender performance in photography.* New York: Guggenheim Museum.

Block, A. (1995). *Occupied reading: Critical foundations for an ecological theory.* New York: Garland.

Block, A. (1998). Curriculum as *affichisste:* Popular culture and identity. In W. F. Pinar (Ed.), *Curriculum: Toward new identities* (pp. 325–342). New York: Garland.

Bly, R. (1990). The road to Mecca. In K. Barnaby (Ed.), *C. G. Jung and the humanities* (pp. 144–149). Princeton, NJ: Princeton University Press.

Bogan, L. (1985). Medusa. In S. M. Gilbert & S. Gubar (Eds.), *The Norton anthology of literature by women* (p. 1,611). New York: Norton. (Original work published 1923)

Bolen, J. S. (1992). *Ring of power: A Jungian understanding of Wagner's ring cycle.* New York: HarperCollins.

Bollas, C. (1987). *The shadow of the object: Psychoanalysis of the unthought known.* New York: Columbia University Press.

Bollas, C. (1995). *Cracking up: The work of the unconscious experience.* New York: Farrar, Straus & Giroux.

Bollas, C. (1997). An interview. In A. Molino (Ed.), *Freely associated: Encounters in psychoanalysis* (pp. 5–52). New York: Free Association.

Bontemps, A. (Ed.). (1974). *American Negro poetry.* New York: Hill & Wang.

Boucher, S. (1993). *Turning the wheel: American women creating the new Buddhism.* Boston: Beacon.

Brenneman, W. L., Jr. (1978). *Spirals: A study of symbol, myth and ritual.* Washington, DC: University Press of America.

Britzman, D. P. (1998a). Is there a queer pedagogy? Or, stop reading straight. In W. F. Pinar (Ed.), *Curriculum: Toward new identities* (pp. 211–232). New York: Garland.

Britzman, D. P. (1998b). *Lost subjects, contested objects: Toward a psychoanalytic inquiry into learning.* Albany, NY: State University of New York Press.

Brontë, C. (1985). Jane Eyre. In S. M. Gilbert & S. Gubar (Eds.), *The Norton anthology of literature by women* (pp. 351–735). New York: Norton. (Original work published 1847)

Brooke, J. (1999, April 29). Diary reveals assault in works for year. *The Times-Picayune,* pp. A1, A18.

Brown, M. (1997). *Le style est l'homme meme:* The action of literature. *College English, 59*(7), 801–819.

Bruner, J. (1986). *Acts of meaning.* Cambridge, MA: Harvard University Press.

Bushe, V. (1994). Cycles of becoming. In C. Downing (Ed.), *The long journey home: Re-visioning the myth of Demeter and Persephone for our time* (pp. 173–185). Boston: Shambhala.

Butler, J. (1990). *Gender trouble: Feminism and the subversion of identity.* New York: Routledge.

Butler, R. J. (1995). The invisible woman in Wright's *Rite of passage.* In R. J. Butler (Ed.), *The critical response to Richard Wright* (pp. 185–189). Westport, CT: Greenwood.

Bynner, W. (1980). *The way of life according to Laotzu: An American version.* New York: Perigee. (Original work published 1944)

Campbell, J. (1949). *The hero with a thousand faces.* New York: Pantheon.

Campbell, J. (1959). *The masks of god: Primitive mythology.* New York: Viking.

Campbell, J. (Ed.). (1971). *The portable Jung* (R. F. C. Hull, Trans.). New York: Penguin.

Campbell, J. (1972). *Myths to live by.* New York: Viking.

Campbell, J. (1974). *The mythic image.* Princeton, NJ: Princeton University Press.

Campbell, J., & Moyers, B. (1988). *The power of myth.* New York: Doubleday.

Camus, A. (1955). *The myth of Sisyphus and other essays.* (J. O'Brien, Trans.). New York: Vintage. (Original work published 1942)

Carlson, T. (1998). Who am I? Gay identity and a democratic politics of the self. In W. F. Pinar (Ed.), *Queer theory in education* (pp. 107–120). Mahwah, NJ: Lawrence Erlbaum Associates.

Carr, P., & Gingerich, W. (1983). The *vagina dentata* motif in Hahuatl and pueblo mythic narratives: A comparative study. In B. Swann (Ed.), *Smoothing the ground: Essays on Native American oral literature* (pp. 187–203). Berkeley, CA: University of California Press.

Chopin, K. (1985). The awakening. In S. M. Gilbert & S. Gubar (Eds.), *The Norton anthology of literature by women* (pp. 991–1,102). New York: Norton. (Original work published 1899)

Chopin, K. (1988). The story of an hour. In S. Barnet, M. Berman, & W. Burto (Eds.), *Literature for composition* (pp. 63–64). New York: Scott, Foresman. (Original work published 1900)

Christ, C. P. (1995). *Diving deep and surfacing: Women writers on spiritual quest.* Boston: Beacon.

Christ, C. P. (1999, March 7). *Trusting the dark.* Lecture given at the Unitarian Universalist Church of New Orleans.

Cixous, H. (1981). The laugh of the Medusa. In E. Marks & I. de Courtium (Eds.), *New French feminisms* (pp. 245–264). New York: Schocken.

Coleman, K. (1998, July 6). Black people urged to heal. *The Times-Picayune,* p. A15.

Coleridge, S. T. (1993). Biographia literaria. In M. H. Abrams, E. T. Donaldson, A. David, H. Smith, B. K. Lewalski, R. M. Adams, G. M. Logan, S. H. Monk, L. Lipking, J. Stillinger, G. H. Ford, C. T. Christ, D. Daiches, & J. Stallworthy (Eds.), *The Norton anthology of English literature* (Vol. 2, pp. 377–392). New York: Norton. (Original work published 1815)

Coleridge, S. T. (1993a). The rime of the ancient mariner. In M. H. Abrams, E. T. Donaldson, A. David, H. Smith, B. K. Lewalski, R. M. Adams, G. M. Logan, S. H. Monk, L. Lipking, J. Stillinger, G. H. Ford, C. T. Christ, D. Daiches, & J. Stallworthy (Eds.), *The Norton anthology of English literature* (Vol. 2, pp. 330–346). New York: Norton. (Original work published 1798)

Coleridge, S. T. (1993b). Kubla Khan. Or, a vision in a dream: a fragment. In M. Mack, B. M. W. Knox, J. C. McGalliard, P. M. Pasinetti, H. E. Hugo, P. M. Spacks, R. Wellek, K. Douglas, & S. Lawall (Eds.), *The Norton anthology of world masterpieces* (Vol. 2, pp. 614–616). New York: Norton. (Original work published 1816)

Comandini, D. L. F. (1988). The octopus: Metamorphoses of an imaginal animal. *Spring: A Journal of Archetypal Psychology and Jungian Thought,* 91–107.

Connelly, M., & Clandinin, J. (1991). Narrative inquiry: Storied experience. In E. Short (Ed.), *Forms of curriculum inquiry* (pp. 121–154). Albany, NY: State University of New York Press.

Conrad, J. (1993). Heart of darkness. In M. H. Abrams, E. T. Donaldson, A. David, H. Smith, B. K. Lewalski, R. M. Adams, G. M. Logan, S. H. Monk, L. Lipking, J. Stillinger, G. H. Ford, C. T. Christ, D. Daiches, & J. Stallworthy (Eds.), *The Norton anthology of English literature* (Vol. 2, pp. 1,758–1,817). New York: Norton. (Original work published 1902)

Covi, G. (1994). Jamaica Kincaid and the resistance to canons. In C. B. Davies & E. S. Fido (Eds.), *Out of the Kumbla: Caribbean women and literature* (pp. 345–354). Trenton, NJ: Africa World.

Creighton, J. V. (1979). Unliberated women in Joyce Carol Oates's fiction. In L. W. Wagner (Ed.), *Critical essays on Joyce Carol Oates* (pp. 148–156). Boston: G. K. Hall. (Original work published 1978)

Cutler, W. E. (n.d.). *Into thin air.* Unpublished manuscript.

Das, L. S. (1997). *Awakening the Buddha within: Tibetan wisdom for the Western world.* New York: Broadway.

Davies, C. B. (1994). *Black women, writing, and identity: Migrations of the subject.* New York: Routledge.

Davis, B. (1996). *Teaching mathematics: Toward a sound alternative.* New York: Garland.

Dean, A. V., & Kolitch, E. (1998). Unmasking good girlism: Reinventing ourselves through mathematics and writing. *Journal of Curriculum Theorizing, 13*(4), 13–19.

deCastell, S., & Bryson, M. (1998). Don't ask; don't tell: "Sniffing out queers" in education. In W. F. Pinar (Ed.), *Curriculum: Toward new identities* (pp. 233–252). New York: Garland.

Deloria, V., Jr. (1994). *God is red: A native view of religion.* Golden, CO: Fulcrum.

Denzin, N. K. (1997). Performance texts. In W. G. Tierney & Y. S. Lincoln (Eds.), *Representation and the text: Re-framing the narrative voice* (pp. 179–217). Albany, NY: State University of New York Press.

Derrida, J. (1973). *Speech and phenomena* (D. B. Allison, Trans.). Evanston, IL: Northwestern University Press.

Derrida, J. (1982). *Margins of philosophy* (A. Bass, Trans.). Chicago: University of Chicago Press.

Derrida, J. (1986). *Glas* (J. P. Leavey, Jr. & R. R. Rand, Trans.). Lincoln, NE: University of Nebraska Press.

Derrida, J. (1991). Ulysses gramophone: Hear say yes in Joyce (T. Kendall & S. Benstock, Trans.). In P. Kamuf (Ed.), *A Derrida reader: Between the blinds* (pp. 571–597). New York: Columbia University Press.

Derrida, J. (1992). *Acts of literature.* New York: Routledge.

DeSalvo, L. (1989). *Virginia Woolf: The impact of childhood sexual abuse on her life and work.* New York: Ballantine.

Dewey, J. (1934). *Art as experience.* New York: Minton Balch.

Dickinson, E. (1960). *The complete poems of Emily Dickinson* (T. H. Johnson, Ed.).. Boston: Little, Brown. (Original work published 1862)

Dickinson, E. (1985). In S. Gilbert & S. Gubar (Eds.), *The Norton anthology of literature by women* (pp. 839–873). New York: Norton. (Original work published 1891)

Doll, M. A. (1988). Walking and rocking: Ritual acts in *Footfalls* and *Rockaby.* In R. J. Davis & L. St. J. Butler (Eds.), *Make sense who may: Essays on Samuel Beckett's later works* (pp. 46–55). Gerrards Cross, England: Colin Smyth.

Doll, M. A. (1993). Stoppard's theatre of unknowing. In J. Acheson (Ed.), *British and Irish drama since 1960* (pp. 117–129). New York: St. Martin's Press.

Doll, M. A. (1994). Ghosts of themselves: The Demeter women in Beckett. In E. Hayes (Ed.), *Images of Persephone: Feminist readings in Western literature* (pp. 121–135). Miami, FL: University Press of Florida.

Doll, M. A. (1995a). Medusa's daughter. In *To the lighthouse and back: Writings on teaching and living* (p. 57). New York: Peter Lang.

Doll, M. A. (1995b). *To the lighthouse and back: Writings on teaching and living.* New York: Peter Lang.

Doll, M. A. (1997). Winging it. In T. R. Carlson & D. Sumara (Eds.), *Action research as a living practice* (pp. 1–10). New York: Peter Lang.

Donaldson, L. E. (1987). The perpetual conversation: The process of traditioning in *Absalom, Absalom! Modernist Studies: Literature and Culture, 4,* 176–194.

Dooling, D. M. (1979). Focus. *Parabola: Myth and the Quest for Meaning: Storytelling and Education, IV*(4), 3.

Douglass, F. (1994). Learning to read and write. In N. R. Comley, D. Hamilton, C. H. Klaus, R. Scholes, & N. Sommers (Eds.), *Fields of writing: Readings across the disciplines* (pp. 62–67). New York: St. Martin's Press. (Original work published 1841)

Downing, C. (1989). *The goddess: Mythological images of the feminine*. New York: Crossroad.

Downing, C. (1994a). Hekate, Rhea, and Baubo: Perspectives on menopause. In C. Downing (Ed.), *The long journey home: Re-visioning the myth of Demeter and Persephone for our time* (pp. 233–242). Boston: Shambhala.

Downing, C. (1994b). Persephone in Hades. In C. Downing (Ed.), *The long journey home* (pp. 219–232). Boston: Shambhala.

Dufrechou, J. P. (1998). Raw astonishment. *Calliope: Leap of Faith, 39*.

Dunmore, H. (1996). *Talking to the dead*. New York: Little, Brown.

Eco, U. (1980). *The name of the rose*. (W. Weaver, Trans.). New York: Warner Books.

Edgerton, S. H. (1993). Toni Morrison teaching the interminable. In C. McCarthy & W. Crichlow (Eds.), *Race, identity, and representation in education* (pp. 220–235). New York: Routledge.

Edgerton, S. H. (1996). *Translating the curriculum: Multiculturalism into cultural studies*. New York: Routledge.

Eliade, M. (1968). *The sacred and the profane: The nature of religion* (W. Trask, Trans.). New York: Harcourt Brace.

Eliot, T. S. (1932). *Hamlet. Selected essays, 1917–1932* (pp. 121–126). New York: Harcourt Brace.

Ellsworth, E. (1989). Why doesn't this feel empowering? Working through the repressive myths of critical pedagogy. *Harvard Educational Review, 59*(3), 297–324.

The epic of Gilgamesh. (D.P. Jackson, verse rendition & R.D. Biggs, Introduction). (1992). Wauconda, IL: Bolchazy-Carducci.

Equiano, O. (1997). The interesting narrative of the life of Olaudah Equiano, or Gustavus Vassa, the African. In E. L. Ayers & B.C. Mittendorf (Eds.), *The Oxford book of the American South: Testimony, memory, and fiction* (pp. 8–12). New York: Oxford University Press. (Original work published 1789)

Erdrich, L. (1993). Scales. In D. McQuade, R. Atwan, M. Banta, J. Kaplan, D. Minter, R. Stepto, C. Tichi, & H. Vendler (Eds.), *The Harper American literature* (Vol. 2, pp. 2370–2379). New York: HarperCollins.

Ernest, J. (1998). The reconstruction of whiteness: William Wells Brown's *The Escape; or A Leap for Freedom*. *Publication of the Modern Language Association, 113*, 1108–1121.

Estés, C. P. (1995). *Women who run with the wolves*. New York: Ballantine.

Estés, C. P. (1997). The wolf's eyelash. In M. M. Hall (Ed.), *Wild women* (pp. 365–370). New York: Carroll & Graf.

Estess, T. (1974). The inennarable contraption: Reflections on the metaphor of story. *Journal of the American Academy of Religion, 42*(3), 415–434.

Fanon, F. (1963). *The wretched of the earth*. New York: Grove.

Faulkner, W. (1962). Impressions of Japan. In R.A. Jelliffe (Ed.), *Faulkner at Nagano* (pp. 178–184). Tokyo: Kenkyusha Press. (Original work published 1956)

Faulkner, W. (1966). *Three famous short novels by William Faulkner*. New York: Vintage. (Original work published 1942)

Faulkner, W. (1970). *Selected short stories of William Faulkner*. New York: The Modern Library.

Faulkner, W. (1987). *Absalom, Absalom!* New York: Vintage. (Original work published 1936)

Faulkner, W. (1992). *The sound and the fury*. New York: Random. (Original work published 1929)

Felman, S. (1981). Rereading femininity. *Yale French Studies, 62*, 19–44.

Ferguson, M. (1994). *Jamaica Kincaid: Where the land meets the body.* Charlottesville, VA: University Press of Virginia.

Flaubert, G. (1992). Madame Bovary (F. Steegmuller, Trans.). In M. Mack et al. (Eds.), *The Norton anthology of world masterpieces* (Vol. 2, pp. 884–1119). New York: Norton. (Original work published 1856)

Forster, E. M. (1989). *A room with a view.* New York: Vintage. (Original work published 1923)

Foucault, M. (1978). *The history of sexuality* (Vol. 1, R. Hurley, Trans.). New York: Pantheon.

Foucault, M. (1980). Introduction. In R. McDougall (Trans.), *Herculine Barbin: Being the recently discovered memoirs of a Nineteenth-Century French hermaphrodite* (pp. vii–xvii). New York: Pantheon.

Fox, M., & Sheldrake, R. (1997). *Natural grace: Dialogues on creation, darkness, and the soul in spirituality and science.* New York: Doubleday.

Franklin, V. P. (1995). *Living our stories, telling our truths: Autobiography and the making of the African American intellectual tradition.* New York: Scribner's.

Freeman, S. (1984). Three short story collections with a difference. *Ms, 12*, 15–16.

Freud, S. (1961). *Civilization and its discontents* (J. Strachey, Trans.). New York: Norton. (Original work published 1930)

Frost, R. (1993). Mending walls. In D. McQuade, R. Atwan, M. Banta, J. Kaplan, D. Minter. R. Stepto, C. Tichi, & H. Vendler (Eds.), *The Harper American literature* (Vol. 2, p. 1,247). New York: HarperCollins. (Original work published 1914)

Fujita, M. (1985). Modes of waiting. *Phenomenology + Pedagogy, 3*(2), 107–115.

Garber, M. (1992). *Vested interests: Cross-dressing and cultural anxiety.* New York: Routledge.

Gardner, J. (1978). *On moral fiction.* New York: Basic.

Gates, H. L., Jr. (1989) The blackness of blackness: A critique of the sign and the signifying monkey. *Black Literature and Literary Theory,* 285–321.

Gates, H. L., Jr. (1988). *The signifying monkey: A theory of Afro-American literary criticism.* New York: Oxford University Press.

Gates, H. L., Jr., & Appiah, K. A. (Eds.). (1993). *Toni Morrison: Critical perspectives past and present.* New York: Amistad.

Genesis 2:9. Genesis. *New American Catholic edition of the holy bible* (pp. 1–51) New York: Benziger Brothers.

Gilbert, S. (1980). Costumes of the mind: Transvestism as metaphor in modern literature. *Critical Inquiry, 7*(2), 391–417.

Gilliam, D. (1974, March 6). *The black book:* How it was. *The Washington Post,* pp. B1–B5.

Gilman, C. P. (1985). The yellow wallpaper. In S. M. Gilbert & S. Gubar (Eds.), *The Norton anthology of literature by women* (pp. 1148–1161). New York: Norton. (Original work published 1892)

Ginsberg, M. P. (1988). Narrative strategies in *Madame Bovary.* In H. Bloom (Ed.), *Gustave Flaubert's Madame Bovary* (pp. 131–152). New York: Chelsea.

Golden, A. (1997). *Memoirs of a geisha.* New York: Vintage.

Goldenberg, N. R. (1993). *Resurrecting the body: Feminism, religion, and psychoanalysis.* New York: Crossroad.

Goldenberg, N. R. (1994). Sightings of maternal rage and paternal love in the *Homeric Hymn to Demeter.* In C. Downing (Ed.), *The long journey home* (pp. 248–253). Boston: Shambhala.

Goodson, I. (1998). Storytelling the self: Life politics and the study of the teacher's life and work. In W. F. Pinar (Ed.), *Curriculum: Toward new identities* (pp. 3–21). New York: Garland.

Gordon, B. (1993). Toward emancipation in citizenship education: The case for African American cultural knowledge. In L. Castenell & W. F. Pinar (Eds.), *Understanding curriculum as racial text* (pp. 263–284). Albany: State University of New York Press.

Gotz, I. (1987). Camus and the art of teaching. *Educational Theory, 33*(1), 1–9.

Graczyk, M. (1998, June 11). Dragging death shocks town: But region has history of lynchings. *The Times-Picayune*, p. A20.

Gray, P. (1998). Paradise found. *Time, 151*, 62–68.

Greene, M. (1965). Real toads and imaginary gardens. *Teachers College Record, 66*, 416–424.

Greene, M. (1971). Curriculum and consciousness. *Teachers College Record, 73*(2), 253–270.

Greene, M. (1973). *Teacher as stranger*. Belmont, CA: Wadsworth.

Greene, M. (1978). *Landscapes of learning*. New York: Teachers College Press.

Greene, M. (1988). *The dialectic of freedom*. New York: Teachers College Press.

Greene, M. (1995). *Releasing the imagination: Essays on education, the arts, and social change*. San Francisco: Jossey-Bass.

Greene, M. (1998). Towards beginnings. In W. F. Pinar (Ed.), *The passionate mind of Maxine Greene: "I am ... not yet"* (pp. 256–257). London: Falmer Press.

Grimm, J., & Grimm, W. (1980). Snow-Drop. In I. Opie & P. Opie (Eds.), *The classic fairy tales* (pp. 230–238). New York: Oxford University Press. (Original work published 1823)

Grumet, M. (1988). *Bitter milk: Women and teaching*. Amherst: University of Massachusetts Press.

Grumet, M. (1989). Word worlds: The literary reference of curriculum criticism. *Journal of Curriculum Theorizing, 9*(1), 7–23

Grumet, M. (1995). The curriculum: What are the basics and are we teaching them? In J. L. Kincheloe & S. R. Steinberg (Eds.), *Thirteen questions: Reframing education's conversation* (pp. 15–22). New York: Peter Lang.

Guggenbuhl-Craig, A. (1986). *Marriage dead or alive* (M. Stein, Trans.). Dallas, TX: Spring Publications.

Gunn, J. (1982). *Autobiography: Toward a poetics of experience*. Philadelphia: University of Pennsylvania Press.

Habito, R. L. F. (1997). Mountains and rivers and the great earth: Zen and ecology. In M. E. Tucker & D. R. Williams (Eds.), *Buddhism and ecology: The interconnection of dharma and deeds* (pp. 165–175). Cambridge, MA: Harvard University Press.

Haddon, G. P. (1987). Delivering yang-femininity. *Spring: An Annual of Archetypal Psychology and Jungian Thought, 133*–142.

Haggerson, N. (1986). Curriculum as figurative language: Exalting teaching and learning through poetry. *Illinois School Research and Development, 22*(1), 10–17.

Haiken, E. (1997). *Venus envy: A history of cosmetic surgery*. Baltimore: The Johns Hopkins University Press.

Hakeda, Y. S. (Trans.). (1972). *Kukai: Major works*. New York: Columbia University Press.

Hakutani, Y. (1996). *Richard Wright and racial discourse*. Columbia: University of Missouri Press.

Hanh, T. N. (1987). *The miracle of mindfulness: A manual on meditation* (M. Ho, Trans.). Boston: Beacon.

Hanh, T. N. (1998). *Fragrant palm leaves: Journals 1962–1966* (M. Warren, Trans.). Berkeley, CA: Parallax.

Harding, M. E. (1963). *Psychic energy: Its source and its transformation*. Princeton, NJ: Princeton University Press. (Original work published 1947)

Harding, W., & Martin, J. (1994). *A world of difference: An inter-cultural study of Toni Morrison's novels*. Westport, CT: Greenwood.

Harris, J. C. (1994). *Uncle Remus: His songs and sayings*. Gatlinburg, TN: Historic Press/South. (Original work published 1901)

Harris, J. C. (1918). *Uncle Remus returns*. New York: McKinlay, Stone & Mackenzie.

Harvey, L. E. (1970). *Samuel Beckett: Poet and critic*. Princeton, NJ: Princeton University Press.

Hasselriis, M. (1990). Artists' roundtable: Jung's influence. In K. Barnaby & P. D'Acierno (Eds.), *C. G. Jung and the humanities: Toward a hermeneutics of culture* (pp. 206–216). Princeton, NJ: Princeton University Press.

Hayes, E. T. (1994). The Persephone myth in Western literature. In E. T. Hayes (Ed.), *Images of Persephone: Feminist readings in Western literature* (pp. 1–20). Miami: University Press of Florida.

Haymes, S. N. (1995). *Race, culture and the city: A pedagogy for black urban struggle.* Albany: State University of New York Press.

Heath, S. (1983). *Ways with words: Language, life, and work in community and classrooms.* Cambridge, England: Cambridge University Press.

Heinz, D. (1993). *The dilemma of double-consciousness: Toni Morrison's novels.* Athens: University of Georgia Press.

Heldris. (1992). *Silence: A 13th century French romance* (S. Roche-Mahdi, Trans.). East Lansing, MI: Colleagues Press.

Henderson, J. L., & Oakes, M. (1990). *The wisdom of the serpent: The myths of death, rebirth, and resurrection.* Princeton, NJ: Princeton University Press.

Hernández-Ávila, I. (1995). Seeing red: American Indian women speaking about their religious and political perspectives. In R. Reuther & R. S. Keller (Eds.), *In our own voices: Four centuries of American women's religious writing* (pp. 401–424). New York: HarperCollins.

Hesse, H. (1957). *Siddhartha* (H. Rosner, Trans.). New York: New Directions.

Highwater, J. (1981). *The primal mind: Vision and reality in Indian America.* New York: New American Library.

Highwater, J. (1994). *The language of vision: Meditations on myth and metaphor.* New York: Grove Press.

Hildegard of Bingen. (1158–1163/1992). The book of life's merits. In F. Bowie & O. Davies (Eds.), *Hildegard of Bingen: Mystical writings* (pp. 85–89). New York: Crossroad.

Hillman, J. (1972). *The myth of analysis: Three essays in archetypal psychology.* New York: Harper & Row.

Hillman, J. (1975). *Re-visioning psychology.* New York: Harper & Row.

Hillman, J. (1979a). *Dream and the underworld.* New York: Harper & Row.

Hillman, J. (1979b). Image-sense. *Spring: An Annual of Archetypal Psychology and Jungian Thought,* 130–143.

Hillman, J. (1996a). Marriage, intimacy, and freedom. *Spring: A Journal of Archetype and Culture,* 1–11.

Hillman, J. (1996b). *The soul's code: In search of character and calling.* New York: Random House.

Hillman, J. (1997). Culture of the animal soul. *Spring 62 (American Soul): A Journal of Archetype and Culture,* 10–37.

Hoder-Salmon, M. (1992). *Kate Chopin's The awakening: Screenplay as interpretation.* Gainesville: University Press of Florida.

hooks, b. (1996). Black women intellectuals. In C. Sotello, V. Turner, M. Garcia, A. Nora & L. Rendon (Eds.), *Racial and ethnic diversity in higher education* (pp. 360–369). Needham Heights, MA: South End.

Horowitz, S. (1994). Voices from the killing ground. In G. Hartman (Ed.), *Holocaust remembrance: The shapes of memory* (pp. 42–58). Oxford, England: Blackwell.

Hovey, J. (1997). "Kissing a Negress in the dark": Englishness as a masquerade in Woolf's *Orlando. Publication of the Modern Language Association, 113*(3), 393–404.

Howe, S. (1985). *My Emily Dickinson.* Berkeley, CA: North Atlantic Books.

Humphries, J. (1996). The discourse of Southernness: Or how can we can know there will still be such a thing as a South and Southern literary culture in the Twenty-First Century? In J. Humphries & J. Lowe (Eds.), *The future of Southern letters* (pp. 119–133). New York: Oxford University Press.

Hurston, Z. N. (1997). Looking things over. In W. B. Horner (Ed.), *Life writing* (pp. 167–171). Upper Saddle River, NJ: Prentice-Hall. (Original work published 1942)

Hwu, W-S. (1998). Curriculum, transcendence, and Zen/Taoism: Critical ontology of the self. In W. F. Pinar (Ed.), *Curriculum: Toward new identities* (pp. 21–40). New York: Garland.

Ingram, P. (1997). The jeweled net of nature. In M. E. Tucker & D. R. Williams (Eds.), *Buddhism and ecology* (pp. 71–85). Cambridge, MA: Harvard University Press.

Injustice for Jamaica. (1999, January 16). [Editorial]. *The Times-Picayune*, p. B6.

Irigaray, L. (1981). "And the one doesn't stir without the other" (H. V. Wenzel, Trans.). *Signs*, 7(1), 60–61.

Irigaray, L. (1985). *This sex which is not one* (C. Porter with C. Burke, Trans.). Ithaca, NY: Cornell University Press.

Isaias 40:6. The prophecy of Isaias. *New American Catholic edition of the holy bible* (pp. 761–724). New York: Benziger Brothers.

Iser, W. (1989). *Prospecting: From reader response to literary anthropology*. Baltimore: Johns Hopkins University Press.

Izutsu, T. (1981). Between image and no-image. *On images: Far Eastern ways of thinking* (pp. 3–37). Dallas, TX: Spring Publications.

Jackson, S. (1988). The lottery. In S. Barnet, M. Berman, & W. Burto (Eds.), *Literature for composition: Essays, fiction, poetry, and drama* (pp. 463–469). Boston: Scott, Foresman/Little, Brown. (Original work published 1948)

Jacobs, H. (1997). Incidents in the life of a slave girl. In E. L. Ayers & B. C. Mittendorf (Eds.), *The Oxford book of the American South* (pp. 50–64). New York: Oxford University Press. (Original work published 1861)

Jacobs, M-E. (1998). Confinement, connection and women who dare: Maxine Greene's shifting landscapes of teaching. In W. F. Pinar (Ed.), *The passionate mind of Maxine Greene* (pp. 81–89). London: Falmer Press.

Jacobus, M. (1986). *Reading woman: Essays in feminist criticism*. New York: Columbia University Press.

Jameson, F. (1981). *The political unconscious: Narrative as a socially symbolic act*. Ithaca, NY: Cornell University Press.

Jardine, D. (1992). Reflections on education, hermeneutics, and ambiguity: Hermeneutics as a restoring of life to its original difficulty. In W. F. Pinar & W. M. Reynolds (Eds.), *Understanding curriculum as phenomenological and deconstructed text* (pp. 116–127). New York: Teachers College Press.

Jardine, D. (1994). *Speaking with a boneless tongue*. Bragg Creek, Alberta: Makyo Press.

Jardine, D. (1997). The surroundings. *Journal of Curriculum Theorizing, 33*(3), 18–21.

Jenkins, L. (1981). *Absalom, Absalom!: Faulkner and black–white relations: A psychoanalytic approach*. New York: Columbia University Press.

John 7:37–38. The holy gospel of Jesus Christ according to St. John. *New American Catholic edition of the holy bible* (pp. 94–122). New York: Benziger Brothers.

John 12:12. The holy gospel of Jesus Christ according to St. John. *New American Catholic edition of the holy bible* (pp. 94–122). New York: Benziger Brothers.

Johnson, E. A. (1992). *She who is: The mystery of God in feminist theological discourse*. New York: Crossroad.

Johnson, E. P. (1989). As it was in the beginning. In P. G. Allen (Ed.), *Spider Woman's granddaughters: Traditional tales and contemporary writing by Native American women* (pp. 69–78). New York: Fawcett Columbine.

Johnson, M. (1973). *Virginia Woolf*. New York: Frederick Unger.

Jones, S. W. (1985). *Absalom, Absalom!* and the Southern custom of storytelling. *Southern Studies, 24*, 82–112.

Joyce, J. (1966). *A portrait of the artist as a young man*. New York: Viking.

Joyce, J. (1954). *The Dubliners.* New York: The Modern Library. (Original work published 1926)

Joyce, J. (1993). Finnegan's wake. In M. H. Abrams, E. T. Donaldson, A. David, H. Smith, B. K. Lewalski, R. M. Adams, G. M. Logan, S. H. Monk, L. Lipking, J. Stillinger, G. H. Ford, C. T. Christ, D. Daiches, & J. Stallworthy (Eds.), *The Norton anthology of English literature, Vol. 2* (pp. 2,076–2,079). New York: Norton. (Original work published 1939)

Jung, C. G. (1950). Psychology and literature. In H. Read, M. Fordham, & G. Adler (Eds., R. F. C. Hull, Trans.), *The spirit in man, art, and literature: CW 15* (pp. 84–108). Princeton, NJ: Princeton University Press. (Original work published 1930)

Jung, C. G. (1952). *Symbols of transformation: Collected Works* (Vol. 5, R. F. C. Hull, Ed. & Trans.). Princeton, NJ: Princeton University Press. (Original work published 1911–1912)

Jung, C. G. (1958). *The undiscovered self* (R. F. C. Hull, Trans.). Boston: Little, Brown.

Jung, C G. (1971). The spiritual problem for modern man. In J. Campbell (Ed.), *The portable Jung* (pp. 456–479). New York: Viking. (Original work published 1933)

Jung, C. G. (1973).The difference between Eastern and Western thinking. In H. Read, M. Fordham, G. Adler, & W. McGuire (Eds., R. F. C. Hull, Trans.), *Psychology and religion: CW 11* (pp. 475–508). Princeton, NJ: Princeton University Press. (Original work published 1930)

Jung, C. G. (1973). Transformation symbolism in the mass. In H. Read, M. Fordham, G. Adler, & W. McGuire (Eds. & R.F. C. Hull, Trans.), *Psychology and religion: CW 11* (pp. 201–298). Princeton, NJ: Princeton University Press. (Original work published 1942)

Jung, C. G. (1973). Answer to Job. In H. Read, M. Fordham, G. Adler, & W. McGuire (Eds., R. F. C. Hull, Trans.), *Psychology and religion: CW 11* (pp. 355–474). Princeton, NJ: Princeton University Press. (Original work published 1952)

Jung, C. G. (1976). H. Read, M. Fordham, G. Adler, & W. McGuire (Eds., R.F.C. Hull, Trans.). *Alchemical studies: CW 13.* Princeton, NJ: Princeton University Press. (Original work published 1950)

Jung, C. G. (1977). Conscious, unconscious, and individuation. In H. Read, M. Fordham, G. Adler, & W. McGuire (Eds., R. F. C. Hull, Trans.), *The archetypes and the collective unconscious: CW 9,1* (pp. 275–289). Princeton, NJ: Princeton University Press. (Original work published 1940)

Jung, C. G. (1977). Archetypes of the collective unconscious. In H. Read, M. Fordham, G. Adler, & W. McGuire (Eds., R. F. C. Hull, Trans.), *The archetypes and the collective unconscious: CW 9,1* (pp. 3–41). Princeton, NJ: Princeton University Press. (Original work published 1959)

Kafka, F. (1992). The metamorphosis. In M. Mack, B. M. W. Knox, J. C. McGalliard, P. M. Pasinetti, H. E. Hugo, P. M. Spacks, R. Wellek, K. Douglas, & S. Lawall (Eds.), *The Norton anthology of world masterpieces* (Vol. 2, pp. 1686–1725). New York: Norton. (Original work published 1915)

Kazin, A. (1998, April 9). God's own terrorist. [Review of *Cloudsplitter,* by R. Banks]. *New York Review of Books,* 8–9.

Kent, G. E. (1984). Richard Wright: Blackness and the adventure of Western culture. In R. Macksey & F. E. Moorer (Eds.), *Richard Wright: A collection of critical essays* (pp. 37–54). Englewood Cliffs, NJ: Prentice-Hall.

Kermode, F. (1979). *The genesis of secrecy: On the interpretation of narrative.* Cambridge, MA: Harvard University Press.

Kincaid, J. (1989). *A small place.* New York: New American Library/Dutton.

Kincaid, J. (1990). *Lucy.* New York: Plume.

Kincaid, J. (1992). *At the bottom of the river.* New York: Plume.

Kincaid, J. (1993). My mother. In D. McQuade, R. Atwan, M. Banta, J. K. Kaplan, D. Minter, R. Stepto, C. Tichi, & H. Vendler (Eds.), *The Harper American literature* (Vol. 2, pp. 2,367–2,370). New York: HarperCollins.

Kincaid, J. (1997). *The autobiography of my mother.* New York: Plume.

Kincheloe, J. (1993). The politics of race, history, and curriculum. In L. A. Castenell, Jr. & W. F. Pinar (Eds.), *Understanding curriculum as racial text* (pp. 249–262). Albany, NY: State University of New York Press.

King, J. E. (1991). Dysconscious racism: Ideology, identity, and the miseducation of teachers. *Journal of Negro Education, 60*(2), 133–116.

Kohno, J. (1998). *Right way, right life: Insights of a woman Buddhist priest* (J. M. Vardaman, Trans.). Tokyo: Kosei.

Krakauer, J. (1996). *Into thin air.* New York: Anchor Books.

Krall, F. (1979). Living metaphors: The real curriculum in environmental education. *Journal of Curriculum Theorizing, 1*(1), 180–185.

Kroeber, K. (1983). Poem, dream, and the consuming of culture. In B. Swann (Ed.), *Smoothing the ground: Essays on Native American oral literature* (pp. 323–333). Berkeley, CA: University of California Press.

Kübler-Ross, E. (1991). *On death and dying.* New York: Macmillan. (Original work published 1969)

Kugler, P. (1978). Image and sound: An archetypal approach to language. *Spring: An Annual of Archetypal Psychology and Jungian Thought, 136–151.*

Kumin, M. (Ed.). (1981). *Anne Sexton: The complete poems.* Boston: Houghton Mifflin.

Kundera, M. (1988). *The unbearable lightness of being* (P. Kussi, Trans.). New York: HarperCollins.

Kundera, M. (1996). *Testaments betrayed: An essay in nine parts* (L. Asher, Trans.). New York: HarperPerennial.

Kushel, K-J. (1994). *Laughter: A theological essay.* New York: Continuum.

Lacan, J. (1968). *The language of the self* (A. Wilden, Trans.). New York: Dell.

Lacan, J. (1977). *Écrits: A selection* (A. Sheridan, Trans.). New York: Norton.

Langer, S. (1953). *Feeling and form: A theory of art.* New York: Scribner's.

Lao Tzu. (551–479 B.C.E. /1975). *Tao te ching* (D.C. Lau, Trans.). New York: Pengun.

Lauter, A. (1979). Anne Sexton's "Radical discontent with the awful order of things." *Spring: An Annual of Archetypal Psychology and Jungian Thought,* 77–92.

Lawrence, D. H. (1965a). The fox. *Four short novels* (pp. 111–180). New York: Viking. (Original work published 1923)

Lawrence, D. H. (1965b). The ladybird. *Four short novels* (pp. 41–110). New York: Viking. (Original work published 1923)

Leeming, D., & Page, J. (1994). *Goddess: Myths of the female divine.* New York: Oxford University Press.

Leonard, J. (1983). Mystery and myth: Curriculum as the illumination of lived experience. *Journal of Curriculum Theorizing, 5*(1), 17–25.

Leonard, J. (1998, January 26). Review of the book *Paradise* [Review] *The New York Times Book Review,* 25–29.

Lessing, D. (1973). *The golden notebook.* New York: Bantam.

Lessing, D. (1995). *Love, again.* New York: HarperCollins.

Levertov, D. (1996). Work that enfaiths. In S. Cahill (Ed.), *Wise woman: Over 2000 years of spiritual writing by women* (pp. 223–231). New York: Norton. (Original work published 1990)

Lincoln, K. (1983). Native American literatures. In B. Swann (Ed.), *Smoothing the ground* (pp. 3–38). Berkeley, CA: University of California Press.

Little miss muffet. (1990). In Z. Sutherland (Ed.), *The orchard book of nursery rhymes* (p. 31). New York: Orchard. (Original work published 1765)

Londre, F. H. (1993). *Tennessee Williams*. New York: Frederick Ungar.

Long, R. E. (1994). *Ingmar Bergman: Film and stage*. New York: Harry N. Abrams.

Lorando, M. (1997, May 16). No contest. *The Times-Picayune*, pp. D1–2.

Lorde, A. (1989). Uses of the erotic. In J. Plaskow & C. P. Christ (Eds.), *Weaving the visions* (pp. 208–213). San Francisco: HarperSanFrancisco.

Luce-Kapler, R. (1998). The slow fuse of aesthetic practice. In W. F. Pinar (Ed.), *The passionate mind of Maxine Greene* (pp. 148–159). London: Falmer Press.

Luke, H. (1985). Letting go. *Parabola: Myth and the Quest for Meaning*, x (1), 20–27.

Macdonald, J., & Leeper, R. (Eds.). (1966). *Language and meaning*. Washington, DC: ASCD.

Macdonald, J. B. (1995). *Theory as a prayerful act: The collected essays of James B. MacDonald* (B. J. MacDonald, Ed.). New York: Peter Lang.

Maher, F. A., & Tetreault, M. K. J. (1997). Learning dark: How assumptions of whiteness shape classroom knowledge. *Harvard Education Review, 67*(2), 321–349.

Mark 10:14. The holy gospel of Jesus Christ according to St. Mark. *New American Catholic edition of the holy bible* (pp. 35–37). New York: Benziger Brothers.

Márquez, G. G. (1988). A very old man with enormous wings. In S. Barnet, M. Berman, & W. Burto (Eds.), *Literature for composition* (pp. 138–142). Boston: Scott, Foresman.

Márquez, G. G. (1992). Love constant beyond death. In M. Mack, B. M. W Knox, J. C. McGalliard, P. M. Pasinetti, H. E. Hugo, P. M. Spacks, R. Welleck, K. Douglas, & S. Lawall (Eds.), *The Norton anthology of world masterpieces* (Vol. 2, pp. 2,082–2,091). New York: Norton.

Martin, B. (1997). Teaching literature, changing cultures. *Publication of the Modern Language Association, 112*(1), 7–25.

Matthew 26:26. The holy gospel of Jesus Christ according to St. Matthew. *New American Catholic edition of the holy bible* (pp. 1–35). New York: Benziger Brothers.

McCall, D. (1988). The bad nigger. In H. Bloom (Ed.), *Richard Wright's Native Son* (pp. 5–22). New York: Chelsea.

McCullers, C. (1988). *The heart is a lonely hunter*. New York: Bantam. (Original work published 1940)

McDermott, T. (1991, June 6). Cross burnings, racism strike "nice little town." *The Times-Picayune*, p. A18.

McDougall, J. (1997). In A. Molina (Ed.), *Freely associated: Encounters in psychoanalysis* (pp. 53–93). New York: Free Association.

McGee, P. (1993). Decolonization and the curriculum of English. In C. McCarthy & W. Crichlow (Eds.), *Race, identity, and representation in education* (pp. 280–288). New York: Routledge.

McIntosh, P. (1992). White privilege and male privilege: A personal account of coming to see correspondences through work in women's studies. In M. Andersen & P. H. Collins (Eds.), *Race, class, and gender: An anthology*. Belmont, CA: Wadsworth.

Meyers, J. (1990). *D. H. Lawrence: A biography*. New York: Knopf.

Michaels, A. (1997). *Fugitive pieces*. New York: Knopf.

Micklem, N. (1979). The intolerable image. *Spring: An Annual of Archetypal Psychology and Jungian Thought*, 1–18.

Miller, D. L. (1976). Fairy tale or myth? *Spring: An Annual of Archetypal Psychology and Jungian Thought*, 157–164.

Miller, D. L. (1989). *Hells and holy ghosts: A theopoetics of Christian belief*. Nashville, TN: Abingdon.

Miller, D. L. (1990). An other Jung and an other.... In K. Barnaby & P. D'Acierno (Eds.), C. G. Jung and the humanities (pp. 325–330). Princeton, NJ: Princeton University Press.

Miller, D. L. (1995). The death of the clown: A loss of wits in the post modern movement. Spring 58: Disillusionment: A Journal of Archetype and Culture, 69–82.

Miller, E. E. (1990). Voice of a native son: The poetics of Richard Wright. Jackson, MS: University Press of Mississippi.

Miller, J. L. (1990). Creating spaces and finding voices: Teachers collaborating for empowerment. Albany, NY: State University of New York Press.

Milton, C. (1904). Making a virtue out of diversity. New York Times Book Review, 89, 22.

Milton, J. (1983). Paradise lost. New York: Buccaneer. (Original work published 1667)

Minh-ha, T. T. (1990). Not you/like you: Post-colonial women and the interlocking questions of identity and difference. In G. Anzaldúa (Ed.), Making face, making soul (pp. 371–375). San Francisco: an aunt lute foundation book.

Mobley, M. S. (1993). A different remembering: Memory, history, and meaning in Beloved. In H. L. Gates, Jr. & K. A. Appiah (Eds.), Toni Morrison: Critical perspectives past and present (pp. 356–365). New York: Amistad.

Moi, T. (Ed.). (1986). The Kristeva reader. New York: Columbia University Press.

Momaday, N. S. (1993). House made of dawn. In McQuade, D., Atwan, R., Banta, M., Kaplan, J., Minter, D., Stepto, R., Tichi, C., & Vendler, H. (Eds.), The Harper American Literature (Vol. 2, pp. 1,869–1,877). New York: HarperCollins. (Original work published 1968)

Monaghan, P. (1999, January 11). Casting a critical eye on canonized works, a scholar reinterprets images of rape in art. The Chronicle of Higher Education, pp. A13–14.

Moon, S. (n.d.). Out of darkness. Centerpoint: A new modality for experiencing analytical psychology. Unpublished pamphlet from the Guild for Psychological Studies.

Moore, T. (1983). Rituals of the imagination. Dallas, TX: The Pegasus Foundation.

Moore, T. (1992). Care of the soul: A guide for cultivating depth and sacredness in everyday life. New York: HarperCollins.

Moore, T. (1994). Meditations: On the monk who dwells in daily life. New York: HarperCollins.

Morris, M. (1998). Existential and phenomenological influences on Maxine Greene. In W. F. Pinar (Ed.), The passionate mind of Maxine Greene (pp. 124–136). London: Falmer Press.

Morris, M. (1999). Curriculum as musical text. In M. Morris, M. A. Doll, & W. F. Pinar (Eds.), How we work (pp. 11–18). New York: Peter Lang.

Morris, M. (in press). Curriculum and the Holocaust: Competing sites of memory and representation. Mahwah, NJ: Lawrence Erlbaum Associates.

Morrison, T. (1972, September 11). Talk with Toni Morrison. New York Times Book Review, 48, 50.

Morrison, T. (1974). (Ed.). The black book. New York: Random House.

Morrison, T. (1984). Rootedness: the ancestor as foundation. In M. Evans (Ed.), Black women writers (1950–1980): A critical evaluation (pp. 339–345). New York: Anchor.

Morrison, T. (1985). The bluest eye. In S. M. Gilbert & S. Gubar (Eds.), The Norton anthology of literature by women (pp. 2,067–2,183). New York: Norton.

Morrison, T. (1987a). Song of Solomon. New York: Plume.

Morrison, T. (1987b). Sula. New York: Plume.

Morrison, T. (1987c). Tar baby. New York: Plume.

Morrison, T. (1988). Beloved. New York: Penguin.

Morrison, T. (1989). Unspeakable things unspoken: The African-American presence in American literature. Michigan Quarterly Review, 28, 1–34.

Morrison, T. (1992). Playing in the dark: Whiteness and the literary imagination. Cambridge, MA: Harvard University Press.

Morrison, T. (1993). Song of Solomon. In D. McQuade, R. Atwan, M. Banta, J. Kaplan, D. Minter, R. Stepto, C. Tichi, & H. Vendler (Eds.), *The Harper American literature* (Vol. 2, pp. 2188–2199). New York: HarperCollins.

Morrison, T. (1995). The site of memory. In W. Zinsser (Ed.), *Inventing the truth: The art and craft of memoir* (pp. 83–102). Boston: Houghton Mifflin.

Morrison, T. (1996). Sula. In S. M. Gilbert & S. Gubar (Eds.), *The Norton anthology of literature by women: The traditions in English* (2nd ed., pp. 1993–2072). New York: Norton. (Original work published 1973)

Morrison, T. (1997). *The dancing mind.* New York: Knopf.

Morrison, T. (1998a, January 8). Interview. *New York Review of Books,* 8–11.

Morrison, T. (1998b). *Paradise.* New York: Knopf.

Morton, N. (1989). The goddess as metaphoric image. In J. Plaskow & C. P. Christ (Eds.), *Weaving the visions* (pp. 111–118). New York: HarperCollins.

Moses, D. D. (1997). Preface. In D. D. Moses & T. Goldie (Eds.), *An anthology of Canadian Native literature in English* (pp. ix–xxix). New York: Oxford University Press.

Mullet, G. M. (Ed.). (1993). Tiyo meets Spider Woman. In *Spider Woman stories: Legends of the Hopi Indians* (pp. 15–20). Tucson, AZ: The University of Arizona Press.

Murfin, R. C. (1983). *The poetry of D. H. Lawrence: Texts and contexts.* Lincoln, NE: University of Nebraska Press.

Musil, R. (1994). *Precision and the soul: Essays and addresses* (B. Pike & D. S. Luft, Eds. & Trans.). Chicago: The University of Chicago Press.

Nietzsche. F. W. (1996). *Human, all too human: A book for free spirits* (M. Faber & S. Lehmann, Trans.). Lincoln, NE: University of Nebraska Press. (Original work published 1878)

Nishitani, K. (1982). *Religion and nothingness.* Berkeley, CA: University of California Press.

Novak, P. (1999). "Circles and circles of sorrow": In the wake of Morrison's *Sula. Publication of the Modern Language Association, 114,* 184–193.

Oates, J. C. (1974). The goddess. *The goddess and other women* (pp. 402–424). New York: Vanguard.

Oates, J. C. (1975). In the region of ice. In S. Cahill (Ed.), *Women and fiction: Short stories by and about women* (pp. 314–332). New York: New American Library.

Oates, J. C. (1978). Ice age. *Women whose lives are food, men whose lives are money: Poems.* Baton Rouge, LA: Louisiana State University Press.

Oates, J. C. (1985). Where are you going, where have you been? In S. M. Gilbert & S. Gubar (Eds.), *The Norton anthology of literature by women* (pp. 2276–2290). New York: Norton.

Oates, J. C. (1994). The nature of short fiction; or, the nature of my short fiction. In G. Johnson (Ed.), *Joyce Carol Oates: A study of the short fiction* (pp. 122–128). New York: Twayne.

Oates, J. C. (Ed.). (1996). *The essential Dickinson.* Hopewell, NJ: The Ecco Press.

O'Connor, F. (1969). *Mystery and manners* (S. Fitzgerald & R. Fitzgerald, Eds.). New York: Farrar, Straus & Giroux.

O'Connor, F. (1980). *The habit of being* (S. Fitzgerald, Ed.). New York: Vintage.

O'Connor, F. (1983). Everything that rises must converge. In *Three by Flannery O'Connor* (pp. 271–285). New York: Signet.

Olney, J. (1972). *Metaphors of self: The meaning of autobiography.* Princeton, NJ: Princeton University Press.

Ondaatje, M. (1992). *The English patient.* Toronto, Canada: McClelland & Stewart.

Ong, W. (1967). *The presence of the word: Some prolegomena for cultural and religious history.* New Haven, CT: Yale University Press.

Ong, W. (1982). *Orality and literacy: The technologizing of the word.* New York: Metheun.

Otis, A. (1987). *Spider Woman's dream.* Santa Fe, NM: Sunstone.

Otten, T. (1989). *The crime of innocence in the fiction of Toni Morrison*. Columbia, MO: University of Missouri Press.

Otto, R. (1958). *The idea of the holy: An inquiry into the nonrational factor in the idea of the divine and its relation to the rational* (J. W. Harvey, Trans.). New York: Oxford University Press.

Padgham, R. E. (1988). Thoughts about the implications of archetypal psychology for curriculum theory. *Journal of Curriculum Theorizing*, 8(3), 123–146.

Paris, G. (1986). *Pagan meditations: The worlds of Aphrodite, Artemis, and Hestia* (G. Moore, Trans.). Dallas, TX: Spring Publications.

Parker, R. D. (1990). *Absalom, Absalom! The questioning of fictions*. Boston: Twayne.

Parkes, G. (1997). Voices of mountains, trees, and rivers: Kukai, Dogen, and a deeper ecology. In M. E. Tucker & D. R. Williams (Eds.), *Buddhism and ecology: The interconnection of dharma and deeds* (pp. 111–130). Cambridge, MA: Harvard University Press.

Patmore, C. (1993). The angel in the house. In M. H. Abrams, E. T. Donaldson, A. David, H. Smith, B. K. Lewalski, R. M. Adams, G. M. Logan, S. H. Monk, L. Lipking, J. Stillinger, G. H. Ford, C. T. Christ, D. Daiches, & J. Stallworthy (Eds.), *The Norton anthology of English literature* (Vol. 2, pp. 1599–1601). New York: Norton.

Perera, S. B. (1990). Descent to the dark goddess. In C. Zweig (Ed.), *To be a woman: The birth of the conscious feminine* (pp. 234–244). Los Angeles: Jeremy P. Tarcher.

Petroff, E. A. (Ed.). (1986). Julian of Norwich, From "Showings: Long text" (E. Colledge & J. Walsh, Trans.), In E. A. Petroff (Ed.), *Medieval women's visionary literature* (pp. 306–314). New York: Oxford University Press.

Phillips, A. (1993). *On kissing, tickling, and being bored: Psychoanalytic essays on the unexamined life*. Cambridge, MA: Harvard University Press.

Piercy, M. (1980). *The moon is always female*. New York: Knopf.

Pinar, W. F. (1988). Time, place, and voice: Curriculum theory and the historical moment. In W. F. Pinar (Ed.), *Contemporary curriculum discourses* (pp. 264–278). Scottsdale, AZ: Gorsuch Scarisbrick.

Pinar, W. F. (1991). Curriculum as social psychoanalysis: On the significance of place. In J. Kincheloe & W. F. Pinar (Eds.), *Curriculum as social psychoanalysis: Essays on the significance of place* (pp. 167–186). Albany, NY: State University of New York Press.

Pinar, W. F. (1993). Notes on understanding curriculum as a racial text. In C. McCarthy & W. Crichlow (Eds.), *Race, identity, and representation in education* (pp. 60–70). New York: Routledge.

Pinar, W. F. (1994). *Autobiography, politics, and sexuality: Essays in curriculum theory, 1972–1992*. New York: Peter Lang.

Pinar, W. F. (1995). The curriculum: What are the basics and are we teaching them? In J. L. Kincheloe & S. R. Steinberg (Eds.), *Thirteen questions: Reframing education's conversation* (pp. 23–30). New York: Peter Lang.

Pinar, W. F. (1998). Understanding curriculum as gender text: Notes on reproduction, resistance, and male–male relations. In W. F. Pinar (Ed.), *Queer theory in education* (pp. 221–244). Mahwah, NJ: Lawrence Erlbaum Associates.

Pinar, W. F., & Grumet, M. (1976). *Toward a poor curriculum*. Dubuque, IA: Kendall/Hunt.

Pinar, W. F., Reynolds, W. M., Slattery, P., & Taubman, P. M. (1995). *Understanding curriculum: An introduction to the study of historical and contemporary curriculum discourses*. New York: Peter Lang.

Pinter, H. (1957). *The room*. New York: Grove Press.

Pinter, H. (1960). *The caretaker*. New York: Grove Press.

Pinter, H. (1966). *The homecoming*. New York: Grove Press.

Pinter, H. (1968). *The birthday party and The room: Two plays by Harold Pinter*. New York: Grove Press.

Pirandello, L. (1992). Six characters in search of an author. In M. Mack, B. M. W. Knox, J. C. McGalliard, P. M. Pasinetti, H. E. Hugo, P. M. Spacks, R. Welleck, K. Douglas, & S. Lawall (Eds.), *The Norton anthology of world masterpieces* (Vol. 2, pp. 1,467–1,511). New York: Norton. (Original work published 1924)

Plant, J. (1989). The circle is gathering ... In J. Plant (Ed.), *Healing the wounds: The promise of ecofeminism* (pp. 242–253). Philadelphia: New Society.

Plath, S. (1985). Medusa. In S. M. Gilbert & S. Gubar (Eds.), *The Norton anthology of literature by women* (pp. 2,209–2,210). New York: Norton. (Original work published 1962)

Plotinus. (205–270/1967). *Enneads* (Vol. 3, A. H. Armstrong, Trans.). Cambridge, MA: Harvard University Press.

Poirier, R. (1971). "Strange gods" in Jefferson, Mississippi: An analysis of *Absalom, Absalom!* In A. Goldman (Ed.), *Twentieth Century interpretations of Absalom, Absalom!* (pp. 12–31). Englewood Cliffs, NJ: Prentice-Hall.

Porter, H. (1984). The horror and the glory: Richard Wright's portrait of the artist in *Black Boy* and *American Hunger*. In R. Macksey & F. E. Moorer (Eds.), *Richard Wright: A collection of critical essays* (pp. 55–67). Englewood Cliffs, NJ: Prentice-Hall.

Procter-Smith, M. (1995). *Praying with our eyes open: Engendering feminist liturgical prayer.* Nashville, TN: Abingdon.

Proulx, A. A. (1993). *The shipping news.* New York: Scribner's.

Puig, M. (1979). *Kiss of the spider woman* (T. Colchie, Trans.). New York: Vintage.

Qualls-Corbett, N. (1988). *The sacred prostitute.* Toronto, Canada: Inner City Books.

Rains, F. V. (1996). Holding up a mirror to white privilege: Deconstructing the maintenance of the status quo. *Taboo: The Journal of Culture and Education, 1,* 75–92.

Randolph, D. (1997). Pastel color dreams. *Calliope,* 45.

Randolph, D. (1998). Nothing goes right for me. *Calliope,* 31.

Reed, D. (1999, May 8). Jefferson relatives reject slave family inclusion. *The Times-Picayune,* p. A3.

Rigney, B. H. (1991). *The voices of Toni Morrison.* Columbus, OH: Ohio State University Press.

Rilke, R. M. (1986). *The complete French poems of Rainer Marie Rilke* (A. Poulin, Jr., Trans.). Saint Paul, MN: Graywolf. (Original work published 1926)

Rivière, J. (1929). Womanliness as a masquerade. *International Journal of Psychoanalysis, 10,* 303–313.

Rorty, R. (1989). *Contingency, irony, and solidarity.* Cambridge, MA: Harvard University Press.

Rosenblatt, L. (1938). *Literature as exploration.* New York: Appleton-Century.

Rosenblatt, R. (1988). Bigger's infernal assumption. In H. Bloom (Ed.), *Richard Wright's Native Son* (pp. 23–37). New York: Chelsea.

Ross, N. W. (1966). *Three ways of Asian wisdom: Hinduism, Buddhism, Zen and their significance for the West.* New York: Simon & Schuster.

Ross, S. (1998, June 13). President's advisor on race urges aggressive U.S. action. *The Times-Picayune,* pp. A1, A7.

Ross, S. (1998, July 8). Clinton waved off colorblind strategy. *The Times-Picayune,* pp. A1, A8.

Roszak, T. (1970). Educating contra naturam. In R. Leeper (Ed.), *A man for tomorrow's world* (pp. 12–27). Washington, DC: ASCD.

Rugg, H. (1963). *Imagination.* New York: Harper & Row.

Rushdy, H. A. (1997). "Rememory": Primal scenes and construction in Toni Morrison's novels. In D. L. Middleton (Ed.), *Toni Morrison's fiction: Contemporary criticism* (pp. 135–161). New York: Garland.

Said, E. (1993). The politics of knowledge. In C. McCarthy & W. Crichlow (Eds.), *Race, identity, and representation in education* (pp. 306–314). New York: Routledge.

Salvio, P. M. (1997). *The scholar/teacher as melancholic: Excavating scholarly and pedagogic (s)crypts in Anne Michaels's Fugitive Pieces.* Paper presented at the Journal of Curriculum Theorizing Conference, Bloomington, IN.

Salvio, P. M. (1998). On using the literacy portfolio to prepare teachers for "willful world traveling." In W. F. Pinar (Ed.), *Curriculum: Toward new identities* (pp. 41–74). New York: Garland.

Salvio, P. M. (n. d.). *Risk and excess: Portraits of the pedagogical performances of Anne Sexton.* Manuscript submitted for review.

Samuels, W. D., & Hudson-Weems, C. (1990). *Toni Morrison.* Boston: Twayne.

Sarton, M. (1974). *Collected poems.* New York: Norton.

Sartre, J. P. (1963). Preface. *The wretched of the earth by F. Fanon* (pp. 7–31). New York: Grove Press.

Schubert, W. H., & Willis, G. (Eds.). (1991). *Reflections from the heart of educational inquiry: Understanding curriculum and teaching through the arts.* Albany, NY: State University of New York Press.

Schwab, G. (1996). *The mirror and the killer-queen: Otherness in literary language.* Bloomington, IN: Indiana University Press.

Sedgwick, E. K. (1990). *Epistemology of the closet.* Los Angeles: University of California Press.

Seifert, T. (1986). *Snow White: Life almost over* (B. Matthews, Trans.). Wilmette, IL: Chiron Publications.

Serres, M. (1982). *Hermes: Literature, science, philosophy* (J. V. Havari & D. F. Bell, Eds. & Trans.). Baltimore: Johns Hopkins University Press.

Sexton, A. (1985). In celebration of my uterus. In S. M. Gilbert & S. Gubar (Eds.), *The Norton anthology of literature by women* (pp. 1,991–2,001). New York: Norton. (Original work published 1969)

Sexton, A. (1978). Radical discontent with the awful order of things. In L. G. Sexton (Ed.), *Words for Dr. Y.* Boston: Houghton Mifflin.

Sexton, A. (1985). Housewife. In S. M. Gilbert & S. Gubar (Eds.), *The Norton anthology of literature by women* (pp. 1,993–1,994). New York: Norton.

Shakespeare, W. (1988). The tragedy of Hamlet: Prince of Denmark. In S. Barnet, M. Berman, & W. Burto (Eds.), *Literature for composition: Essays, fiction, poetry, and drama* (pp. 229–301). Boston: Scott, Foresman. (Original work published 1603)

Sheehy, G. (1995). *New passages: Mapping your life across time.* New York: Random House.

Sherrard, P. (1981). Editorial: The arts and the imagination. *Temenos: A Review Devoted to the Arts of the Imagination,* 1–7.

Shields, C. (1995). *The stone diaries.* New York: Penguin.

Showalter, E. (1994). Joyce Carol Oates's "The dead" and feminist criticism. In G. Johnson (Ed.), *Joyce Carol Oates: A study of the short fiction* (pp. 167–170). New York: Twayne.

Silko, L. M. (1986). *Ceremony.* New York: Viking/Penguin.

Simeti, M. T. (1995). *On Persephone's island: A Sicilian journal.* New York: Vintage.

Simmons, D. (1994). *Jamaica Kincaid.* New York: Twayne.

Singer, J. (1989). *Androgyny: The opposites within.* New York: Sigo.

Smith, D. (1991). Hermeneutic inquiry: The hermeneutic imagination and the pedagogic text. In E. Short (Ed.), *Forms of curriculum inquiry* (pp. 187–209). Albany, NY: State University of New York Press.

Smith, D. (1997). The geography of theory and the pedagogy of place. *Journal of Curriculum Theorizing, 13*(3), 2–4.

Smith, J. (1992). Mythic images. *Calliope,* 36–38.

Snyder, G. (1979). Hear/say. *Parabola: Myth and the Quest for Meaning, IV,* 58.

Spender, S. (Ed.). (1973). *D. H. Lawrence: Novelist, poet, prophet.* New York: Harper.

Spoto, D. (1985). *The kindness of strangers: The life of Tennessee Williams*. Boston: Little, Brown.

Steinbergh, J. (1991). To arrive in another world: Poetry, language development, and culture. *Harvard Educational Review, 61*(1), 51–70.

Stevens, W. (1993). Thirteen ways of looking at a blackbird. In D. McQuade, R. Atwan, M. Banta, J. Kaplan, D. Minter, R. Stepto, C. Tichi, & H. Vendler (Eds.), *The Harper American literature* (Vol. 2, pp. 1276–1278). New York: HarperCollins. (Original work published 1923)

Stoppard, T. (1975). *Travesties*. New York: Grove Press.

Storace, P. (1998, January 11). The scripture of Utopia. *The New York Review of Books*, 64–69.

Sumara, D. (1996). *Private readings in public: Schooling the literary imagination*. New York: Peter Lang.

Suzuki, D. T. (1977). *The Zen doctrine of No-Mind*. New York: Samuel Weiser.

Swift, J. (1988). A modest proposal. In S. Barnet, M. Berman, & W. Burto (Eds.), *Literature for composition: Essays, fiction, poetry, and drama* (pp. 32–37). Boston: Scott, Foresman. (Original work published 1742)

Taliaferro, D. (1999). Writing my love child. In M. Morris, M. A. Doll, & W. F. Pinar (Eds.), *How we work* (pp. 41–54). New York: Peter Lang.

Tate, C. (Ed.). (1983). Interview with Toni Morrison. *Black women writers at work* (pp. 117–131). New York: Continuum.

Taylor, C. (1991). The re-birth of the aesthetic in cinema. *Wide Angle, 13*, 3,4.

Taylor-Guthrie, D. (Ed.). (1994). *Conversations with Toni Morrison*. Jackson: University Press of Mississippi.

The teaching of Buddha. (1990). Tokyo: Kosaido Printing.

The Times-Picayune Headlines. (1997, October 3), p. A1.

The Times-Picayune. (1999, June 21). n.t., p. A16.

Tilove, J. (1998, June 28). America's white majority likely to end. *The Times-Picayune*, p. A14.

Toulmin, S. (1982). *The return to cosmology: Postmodern science and the theory of nature*. Berkeley, CA: University of California Press.

Trible, P. (1996). Eve and Adam: Genesis 2–3 reread. In S. Cahill (Ed.), *Wise women: Over 2000 years of spiritual writing by women* (pp. 359–366). New York: Norton.

Turner, D. T. (1981). Daddy Joel Harris and his old-time darkies. In R. B. Bickley, Jr. (Ed.), *Critical essays on Joel Chandler Harris* (pp. 113–129). Boston: G. K. Hall.

Tuso, F. (1968). Faulkner's "Wash." *Supplicator, 27*, 17.

Tyler, A. (1983). Mothers and mysteries. *New Republic, 189*, 32–33.

van Manen, M. (1991). *The tact of teaching: The meaning of pedagogical thoughtfulness*. Albany, NY: State University of New York Press.

Von Franz, M-L. (1972). *Patterns of creativity mirrored in creation myths*. Dallas, TX: Spring Publications.

Waldenfels, H. (1980). *Absolute nothingness: Foundations for a Buddhist–Christian dialogue* (J. W. Heisig, Trans.). New York: Paulist.

Walker, B. G. (1983). *The woman's encyclopedia of myths and secrets*. New York: Harper & Row.

Walker, B. G. (1985). *The crone: Woman of age, wisdom, and power*. New York: Harper.

Walker, M. (1976). The double, an archetypal configuration. *Spring: An Annual Publication of Jungian Thought*, 165–175.

Walkerdine, V. (1990). *School girl fictions*. New York: Verso.

Warner, M. (1995). *Six myths of our time*. New York: Random House.

Watkins, F. (1984). What happens in *Absalom, Absalom!* In E. Muhlenfeld (Ed.), *William Faulkner's Absalom, Absalom! A critical casebook* (pp. 55–64). New York: Garland. (Original work published 1967)

Wear, D., & Castellani, B. (1999). Conflicting plots and narrative dysfunction in health care. *Perspectives in Biology and Medicine, 42*(4), 544–558.

Weaver, G. (1994). *Joyce Carol Oates: A study in short fiction.* New York: Twayne.

Webster's encyclopedic unabridged dictionary of the English language (1993). New York: Gramercy.

Webster's third international dictionary. (1981). Springfield, MA: G & C. Merriam.

Weigle, M. (1982). *Spiders and spinsters: Women and mythology.* Albuquerque, NM: University of New Mexico Press.

Weinsheimer, J. (1987). *Gadamer's hermeneutics.* New Haven, CT: Yale University Press.

Welty, E. (1997). Death of a traveling salesman. In E. L. Ayers & B. C. Mittendorf (Eds.), *The Oxford book of the American South: Testimony, memory, and fiction* (pp. 306–317). New York: Oxford University Press. (Original work published 1941)

Welty, E. (1979a). *Thirteen stories* (R. M. V. Kieft, Ed.). New York: Harcourt Brace.

Welty, E. (1979b). The little store. *The eye of the story: Selected essays and reviews* (pp. 326–336). New York: Vintage.

Welty, E. (1980). *The collected stories of Eudora Welty.* New York: Harcourt Brace.

Wertham, F. (1947). The dreams that heal. In M. L. Aswell (Ed.), *The world within: Fiction illuminating neuroses of our time* (pp. xi–xxxiv). New York: Whittlesey House/McGraw-Hill.

West, C. (1989). Black culture and postmodernism. In B. Kruger & P. Mariani (Eds.), *Remaking history.* Seattle, WA: Bay Press.

West, C. (1994). *Race matters.* New York: Vintage.

Wheelwright, P. (1968). *Metaphor and reality.* Bloomington, IN: Indiana University Press.

Wilde, O. (1993). The importance of being Earnest. In M. H. Abrams, E. T. Donaldson, A. David, H. Smith, B. K. Lewalski, R. M. Adams, G. M. Logan, S. H. Monk, L. Lipking, J. Stillinger, G. H. Ford, C. T. Christ, D. Daiches, & J. Stallworthy (Eds.), *The Norton anthology of English literature* (Vol. 2, pp. 1,628–1,667). New York: Norton. (Original work published 1895)

Wilde, O. (1994). De profundis. In *The complete works of Oscar Wilde* (pp. 873–957). New York: Barnes & Noble.

Wilder, T. (1985). *Our town: A play in three acts.* New York: HarperCollins.

Wise, D. H. (1993). *Spiders in ecological webs.* New York: Cambridge University Press.

Williams, T. (1947). *A streetcar named desire.* New York: Signet.

Williams, T. (1978). On a streetcar named success. In C. R. Day & B. Woods (Eds.), *Where I live: Selected essays* (pp. 15–22). New York: New Directions.

Winbush, R. (1998, July 5). Anger, controversy haven't gone with the wind. *The Times-Picayune,* p. A21.

Wolfe, T. (1991). *The good child's river* (S. Stutman, Ed.). Chapel Hill, NC: The University of North Carolina Press.

Wolkstein, D., & Kramer, S. N. (1983). *Inanna queen of heaven and earth: Her stories and hymns from Sumer.* New York: Harper & Row.

Wollstonecraft, M. (1985). A vindication of the rights of women. In S. M. Gilbert & S. Gubar (Eds.), *The Norton anthology of literature by women* (pp. 138–160). New York: Norton. (Original work published 1792)

Woolf, L. (Ed.). (1954). *A writer's diary: Being extracts from the diary of Virginia Woolf.* New York: Harcourt Brace.

Woolf, V. (1955). *To the lighthouse.* New York: Harcourt Brace. (Original work published 1927)

Woolf, V. (1956). *Orlando: A biography.* New York: Harcourt Brace. (Original work published 1928)

Woolf, V. (1957). *A room of one's own.* New York: Harcourt Brace. (Original work published 1929)

Woolf, V. (1976). *Moments of being: Unpublished autobiographical writings.* J. Schulkind (Ed.). Orlando, FL: Harcourt Brace. (Original work published 1928)

Woolf, V. (1981). *To the lighthouse* (Eudora Welty, Introduction). New York: Harcourt Brace. (Original work published 1927)

Woolf, V. (1985). A room of one's own. In S. M. Gilbert & S. Gubar (Eds.), *The Norton anthology of literature by women* (pp. 1,376–1,383). New York: Norton. (Original work published 1929)

Woolf, V. (1988). The death of a moth. In S. Barnet, M. Berman, & W. Burto (Eds.), *Literature for composition: Essays, fiction, poetry, and drama* (pp. 47–48). New York: Scott, Foresman. (Original work published 1942)

Woolf, V. (1993). Moments of being and non-being. In M. H. Abrams, E. T. Donaldson, A. David, H. Smith, B. K. Lewalski, R. M. Adams, G. M. Logan, S. H. Monk, L. Lipking, J. Stillinger, G. H. Ford, C. T. Christ, D. Daiches, & J. Stallworthy (Eds.), *The Norton anthology of English literature* (Vol. 2, pp. 1,990–1,997). New York: Norton. (Original work published 1939)

Wordsworth, W. (1993). My heart leaps up. In M. H. Abrams, E. T. Donaldson, A. David, H. Smith, B. K. Lewalski, R. M. Adams, G. M. Logan, S. H. Monk, L. Lipking, J. Stillinger, G. H. Ford, C. T. Christ, D. Daiches, & J. Stallworthy (Eds.), *The Norton anthology of English literature* (Vol. 2, p. 187). New York: Norton. (Original work published 1802)

Wordsworth, W. (1993). Ode: Intimations of immortality. In M. H. Abrams, E. T. Donaldson, A. David, H. Smith, B. K. Lewalski, R. M. Adams, G. M. Logan, S. H. Monk, L. Lipking, J. Stillinger, G. H. Ford, C. T. Christ, D. Daiches, & J. Stallworthy (Eds.), *The Norton anthology of English literature* (Vol. 2, pp. 189–193). New York: Norton. (Original work published 1802–1804)

Wright, R. (1954). *Black power: A record of reactions in a land of pathos.* New York: Harper.

Wright, R. (1966). *Black boy.* New York: Harper & Row. (Original work published 1937)

Wright, R. (1991). *Early works: Lawd today!, Uncle Tom's children, Native son.* New York: The Library of America. (Original work published 1938–1945)

Wright, R. (1993a). *Black boy (American hunger): A record of childhood and youth.* New York: HarperPerennial. (Original work published 1945)

Wright, R. (1993b). *The outsider.* New York: HarperPerennial. (Original work published 1953)

Yeats, W. B. (1959). *The collected poems of W. B. Yeats.* New York: Macmillan. (Original work published 1933)

Yeats, W. B. (1989). Leda and the swan. In R. J. Finneran (Ed.), *The collected poems of W. B. Yeats* (pp. 214–215). New York: Collier. (Original work published 1924)

Yeats, W. B. (1993). Under Ben Bulben. In M. H. Abrams, E. T. Donaldson, A. David, H. Smith, B. K. Lewalski, R. M. Adams, G. M. Logan, S. H. Monk, L. Lipking, J. Stillinger, G. H. Ford, C. T. Christ, D. Daiches, & J. Stallworthy (Eds.), *The Norton anthology of English literature* (Vol. 2, pp. 1,894–1,897). New York: Norton. (Original work published 1939)

Author Index

Subject Index

SUBJECT INDEX

Barbie, 89
Barn Burning, 17
Basics, the, viii, 59
Bear, The, 206
Beauty, 31-33, 88-89, 96, 148, 171, 179, 189,
        191, 195, 208, 213
Belief, 86
    suspension of, 155
Belle, 130
Beloved, 28, 33-40, 188
Bent, xvii
Bible, The, vii, 6, 40, 90, 198, 207
Birth (Birthing), 66, 85, 120, 147, 152-161, 184,
        195
Black Boy, 45, 48-51, 56-59
*Black Power: A Record of Ractions in a Land of
        Pathos,* 63
Blockhead (Blockheadedness), 1-7, 146, 150
Blood, 9, 11, 42, 134, 139, 154, 194, 213
"Bluebeard," 45-47, 50-53, 63, 66, 133
Bluest Eye,The, 24-33, 169-173, 179
Body, 140-141, 170, 176, 185-186, 190, 197, 209
Boundary, 213-214
Bovary, Emma, 120, 126, 129
Breakdown, 2, 56, 208, 210
Breast(s), 38, 89, 95, 114, 179-180
Bride, 100
Buddha, the, vii-viii, xviii, 82, 86, 146, 168, 204
    Buddahood, 210
    Buddha-nature, 161
    Buddhism, 149, 153-154, 157-158, 161,190,
        205, 216
    Buddhist, 53, 151, 157, 162, 163, 168, 169,
        203, 213, 216

C

Cake, 138
Canon, the, 200
Caretaker, The, 128
Cellar, 45-47, 53, 65-66
Center, 34, 167, 195, 208, 213
    eccentric, 148
    sacred, 214
Ceremony, 210-214
Ceremony, 194, 197, 213
Ceremony, 211-214
Charge of the Light Brigade, The, 74
Child, 4, 127,155, 164, 169, 185
Christ, *see also* Jesus, 68, 95, 100, 109, 170, 176
Christ figure, 184
Christ-haunted, 168
Christian, 109, 138,181, 207
Christianity, 167, 190
Church, 3, 68,73, 99, 115, 138, 147, 198, 213,
        217

Cinderella, 89
Circle, viii, 9, 56, 104, 141, 156, 167
Civilization, 7, 68, 70, 75, 88, 175, 208-210
        214-217
Civilization and its Discontents, 68
Classism, x, xvi, 13, 177-178, 215
Classroom, ix, xiv-xviii, 38, 77, 153, 168, 188,
        197, 200
Cliché, 35-36, 105, 147, 172
Closet, 116, 119, 128-129
Clothes, 116-130, 138, 147, 186
Code, 7, 12, 16, 24, 68-69, 72, 80, 83, 91,
        117-120, 128-129
    of civilization, 7
    of class, 16
    of clothing, 17
    of gender, 22
    of gentility, 7
    of patriarchy, 13
    of privilege, 7
    of silence, 13
    of The White Man, 50
    of tradition, 14
Codependence, 163
Coffin, 98
Collective unconscious, *see also* Unconscious,
        27, 205
Colonialism, 177, 180, 182
Coma, 139
Comedy, 148, 167-188
Commonplace, 76, 129
Communion, 72
Connection, *see also* Relation, 212
Consciousness, 20, 49, 52, 62, 73, 75, 86,
        131-134, 156, 159, 184, 195,
        201-205, 217
    doubled, 204
    female, 87
    lack of, 70
    stream of, 161-162
Convent, 41, 104, 109, 115, 183
Convention, 67-68, 80, 91-92, 125, 136
Cosmos, 72, 94, 147, 148, 163, 186, 196-206,
        216-217
    balance of, 42
Coursing, x-xiv, 77, 148, 188, 195, 217
Creation, 55, 63, 66, 156, 161, 194-195, 214
    Creative Spirit, 214
    creativity, 69, 180, 184, 216
Creole, 1-2, 72, 90
Crone, 91, 147, 190, 193
Cronus, 4-5
Culture, 136-139, 145, 169, 187, 198-199,
        211-214
Currere, xi-xiv
Curriculum, viii-xii, 129, 141,148, 153, 217